COMPUTERS AND THE INFORMATION SOCIETY

COMPUTERS AND THE INFORMATION SOCIETY

RICHARD S. ROSENBERG
Dalhousie University

JOHN WILEY & SONS
NEW YORK   CHICHESTER   BRISBANE   TORONTO   SINGAPORE

Cover and text design: *Karin Gerdes Kincheloe*

Library of Congress Cataloging in Publication Data:

Rosenberg, Richard S.
  Computers and the information society.

  Includes bibliographies and index.
  1. Computers.   2. Computers and civilization.
I. Title.

QA76.5.R58   1986   004   85-24680
ISBN 0-471-82639-1

Printed in the United States of America

10 9 8 7 6 5 4 3 2

In memory of my parents, Louis and Molly, who planted the seed of concern, helped it grow, but could not see it flower.

. . . But not because I am out of sympathy with their feelings about technology. I just think that their flight from and hatred of technology is self-defeating. The Buddha, the Godhead, resides quite as comfortably in the circuits of a digital computer or the gears of a cycle transmission as he does at the top of a mountain or in the petals of a flower.

◇ *Robert M. Pirsig*, Zen and the Art of Motorcycle Maintenance ◇

PREFACE

*I do not believe that the kind of society I describe
necessarily will arrive, but I believe . . . that
something resembling it could arrive.*

◇ *George Orwell, author of* 1984, *in a letter to his publisher,
Fredric Warburg.* ◇

*The Third Wave brings with it a genuinely new way of
life based on diversified, renewable energy resources,
on methods of production that make most factory assembly
lines obsolete; on new non-nuclear families; on a novel institution that might be called the "electronic cottage."*

◇ *Alvin Toffler,* The Third Wave, *1979* ◇

These two quotations delimit the futures that a rapidly evolving technology makes possible.
Will we move towards a society in which government is all-powerful and, by virtue of
its mandate to protect the country, assumes extraordinary powers to monitor the daily
behavior of its citizens? Will technology free the members of advanced industrial (or post-
industrial) societies from a scarcity of goods and pave the way for a new age of enlight-
enment?

No definitive answers to such questions will be provided here. Rather, this book should
be viewed as a guide to current and future applications of computers and their associated
benefits and problems. Among the basic themes presented are the following:

- The increasing importance of information as a commodity in its own right.
- The emergence and influence of Artificial Intelligence (AI).
- The changing nature of work in response to technological innovation.
- The relation between people and computers, at work and play.

- The relationship of advances in computer technology and the possibility of increased centralization of authority.
- Personal freedom in the machine age with respect to privacy, work, and play.
- Computers as a dominant force in society.

More specifically, this book discusses a number of issues that have either not been examined or have not been treated in sufficient depth in one source. These include the following:

- Computers and the human imagination, including computers in the arts and popular attitudes toward computers.
- Robotics and industrial automation.
- Military applications of computers.
- Computers and the home.
- The emerging information society.
- Office automation.
- Videotex systems.
- Computers and telecommunications.
- Job safety: the controversy over video display terminals.
- Patent and copyright issues with respect to computer hardware and software.
- The use of information technology in the political process.
- Government regulation of the telecommunications and computer industries.
- Japan and fifth-generation computers.
- The impact on women.
- Ethics and professionalism in data processing.

No field that is growing and changing as rapidly as computers and microelectronics can be easily captured within the confines of one book. Inevitably there are many topics, some quite important, which have been mentioned here only in passing, or not at all—the most noteworthy omission being the application of computers in both the natural and social sciences.

People are becoming increasingly familiar with computers through exposure at home, schools, and work. To spark attention and interest in the effects of computers on society, this book begins with several speculations before proceeding to the real world. A variety of current computer applications, along with the social problems that sometimes result, are examined. The new technology, in many of its manifestations, will present an image of a rapidly changing world full of promise and hope; the associated difficulties and problems can be overcome only by an informed and concerned populace.

The fourteen chapters in this book can be grouped under four major headings:

Chapters 1–3 present background information that is vital for any understanding of the present effects of computers on society. Chapters 4–7 discuss some major applications of computers, and Chapters 8–10 explore social issues relevant to its development. Finally, Chapters 11–14 discuss the new computer technology currently being spawned throughout the world.

Some major topics—such as privacy, videotex, Artificial Intelligence, electronic funds-transfer systems, home and personal computers, and the impact of computers on work—are discussed in more than one place. Because several social issues are associated with each application, a certain measure of redundancy is inevitable. Thus, each major application is treated in depth in one place but referred to whenever relevant social issues are examined.

To make full use of the material presented here, the Notes and Additional Readings given at the end of every chapter should be consulted. In such a rapidly changing field, it is necessary to refer on a regular basis to relevant journals, magazines, and books. A list of these, as well as of professional societies, is given in Appendix B.

The material in this book should be accessible to most university students who have had an introductory course in computer science. Self-taught or sufficiently motivated individuals who have gained an understanding of how computers operate and how they are programmed should also profit from this book. Especially useful are backgrounds in sociology, economics, history, or political science. Although many topics will be covered, nothing will be said about the details of programming or computer hardware. Such information is available in abundance elsewhere.

ACKNOWLEDGMENTS

Many people have helped in the writing of this book, either directly or indirectly; I therefore apologize in advance to anyone I may have left out. Let me mention, in no particular order, Kelly Gotlieb, David Flaherty, Abbe Mowshowitz, Andrew Clement, Ray Reiter, Bernie Mohan, Marilyn Mohan, Robert Franson, David Brown, Alan Mackworth, Harriet Rosenberg, Richard Lee, Susan Hurlich, Robert Goldstein, Paul Gilmore, Kevin Moriarty, Al Folwer, Colin Archibald, Carol Whitehead, Teresa Fong, Lindsay Wey, Julie O'Grady, Laura Smith, Gretchen Smith, Paula Flemming, the Vancouver local of the Telecommunications Workers Union, Olwen Sutton, Timothy Bult, Wendy Moore, Rob Puchyr, Stanton LeFort, Reg Hody, Michael Thompson, Graeme Hirst, Joyce Frazee, and Gerry Weinberg. I also acknowledge the many students at the University of Toronto, the University of British Columbia, and Dalhousie University—who have asked all the right questions—and anonymous reviewers who offered helpful advice. I appreciate the important assistance of my editors Richard Bonacci, Nina R. Lewis, Martha Cooley, and especially, Martha Ramsey.

Of course, I take sole responsibility for the final version of this book. Nothing would have been possible without the constant support of my wife, Sheryl, and my children, Aryeh and Rebecca.

CONTENTS

CHAPTER THREE
CRITICISM AND HISTORY

CHAPTER SEVEN
GOVERNMENT AND COMPUTERS

CHAPTER NINE
PRIVACY AND FREEDOM OF INFORMATION

CHAPTER TEN
EMPLOYMENT AND UNEMPLOYMENT

CHAPTER ELEVEN
BUSINESS AND GOVERNMENT

CHAPTER TWELVE
ROBOTICS AND INDUSTRIAL AUTOMATION

COMPUTERS AND THE INFORMATION SOCIETY

1
COMPUTERS ARE EVERYWHERE

*"**P**lastics," a well-meaning elder whispered to
young Benjamin in* The Graduate. *It was sound
financial advice, but "silicon" would have been closer
to the mark.*

◇ *Dirk Hanson,* The New Alchemists, *1982* ◇

INTRODUCTION

You are about to begin the study of both computers themselves and how they have affected
and will continue to affect society. In the long history of technological innovation, the
computer in some sense is no more notable than such major inventions as the steam engine,
the train, electricity and electronics, the telegraph and telephone, the automobile, the
airplane, radio, motion pictures, and television. Yet there is something special about the
computer that makes it more than just another machine. Its ability to be programmed to
perform an incredible variety of tasks distinguishes it from all others.

The first electronic computers filled large rooms, weighed many tons, and generated
vast quantities of heat. Now computers of equal or greater power sit comfortably on the
tops of desks. Within the last few years, electronics engineers, physicists, and computer
specialists have produced a powerful microprocessor that can slide easily through a paper
clip. Such microprocessors are used in watches, cameras, microwave ovens, portable
computers, automobiles, and assembly line robots. Other applications are sure to follow.
Computers are now commonplace in schools, offices, and (more recently) the home. They
generate our checks, our bills, and our receipts. They are used to store and retrieve
enormous quantities of information for an incredible variety of purposes. Work and play
are equally affected, as the following examples show.

- A recent advertisement shows pictures of a number of geniuses (unidentified)
  including Leonardo da Vinci, Shakespeare, Isaac Newton, Thomas Jeffer-

son, Charles Darwin, Madame Curie, and Albert Einstein. Below these
pictures appears the question: "Of all the world's thinkers which is the
greatest?" The answer begins, "A single chip can already remember over
256,000 pieces of information. And come up with answers in milliseconds."

- On October of 1981, the *New York Times* reported that the Universal Life
  Church had used an Apple Computer to perform several marriage cere-
  monies. Couples are required to respond to questions typed by the computer
  with "yes," rather than "I do."
- From a newspaper report in late 1982:

  *Erroneous information supplied by a police computer prompted a Vancouver po-
  lice patrol to begin a high-speed car chase that ended in death for 18-year-old
  Orville Andrew McAuley, a coroner's jury in New Westminster was told Tuesday.*
  (Vancouver Sun, *Dec. 15, 1982, p. H5.*)

- In early 1983, the *Toronto Globe and Mail* reported that bill collectors were
  using computer-stored voice messages to remind delinquent customers that
  they were overdue and to ask them whether payment would be made in the
  near future. Upon recording the answer the voice responds with: "Did you
  really mean to say this?" One system can make 450 calls per hour with
  about 200 obtaining a response.
- Oxford University Press has launched a three-year project to put the Oxford
  English Dictionary (OED) on-line. The OED will be implemented as an
  information retrieval system to enable users to access words and quotations.
  Subsequent updating will be made much easier as will the printing of hard
  copies. IBM (in the U.K.) is contributing to the project a 4300 system worth
  about $1.25 million. (John Lamb, *Datamation,* February 1984, pp. 88, 91.)
- Apple ran a four-page color advertisement answering the question, "Will
  someone please tell me exactly what a personal computer can do?" Among
  the 100 answers given are the following: FBI offices are using Apples for
  detective work; Bendo Kogowa, a Zen priest in Japan, uses his Apple to
  help people meditate; an Apple tests new recipes; the Grateful Dead uses
  Apples for accounting and scheduling; a sweater company uses Apples to
  design patterns.
- The Connetquot Public Library in Bohemia, New York, announced that it
  would soon make three personal computers available for home loan. Almost
  immediately there were 150 reservations. (*The New York Times,* May 9,
  1983, p. 1)
- Neal Patrick, 17, one of the "Milwaukee 414," testified in September 1983
  before a hearing of the House Committee on Science and Technology's
  subcommittee on Transportation, Aviation and Materials. He was one of a
  group of teenagers who broke into several computer systems across the
  United States. He defended his actions on the basis of curiosity but warned

that security measures must be improved or others without scruples would wreak havoc.

- Also in September 1983, the United States Court of Appeals for the Third Circuit upheld an appeal by Apple Computers against Franklin Computers. Apple claimed that Franklin had copied the Apple II. This ruling means that computer software can be copyrighted even when it exists in the ROM (read only memory) of a computer.
- A headline in *The New York Times* of November 17, 1983 reported, "Computer Input Error Suspected in South Korean Airliner's Wrong Course." The airplane, shot down by a Soviet fighter plane on September 1, had violated Russian air space. It may have been off course because of a simple error made when the takeoff location was entered on the onboard computer.
- Control Data is marketing the CSD Home Escort system, a leg-banded transmitter with embedded wires that sends a signal, with a range of 175 feet, to a receiver plugged into a home telephone. Worn by work-release or parole-probation prisoners, the transmitter produces a signal that is monitored by a central computer to make sure that, except for legitimate absences, the person remains close to his home. (*Electronics Week,* March 4, 1985, p. 30.)

The range of concerns in this limited group of selections is indicative of the degree to which computers have made a major inroad into the national consciousness. It is difficult to avoid either reading about computers, encountering them directly, or having someone tell you about his or her most recent experience with them. Furthermore, it is possible to appreciate their impact without knowing how they work or how to program them, just as one may be able to appreciate the effects of traffic jams or automobile pollution without understanding the principles of the internal combustion engine or even how to operate a motor vehicle.

A VARIETY OF APPLICATIONS

The new information technologies—telecommunications and computers—may
change our lives more than any other fields of technological development.[1]

The number of applications reveals how pervasive computers have become. Many of these applications incorporate microprocessors, tiny computing elements that perform a decision-making function when supplied with information from a variety of sensors. As such, much computer-governed behavior is hidden from view, and thus the true extent of computer penetration into contemporary technology is probably unappreciated. It is important to recognize that while computers have opened up many new possibilities, society for the most part functioned in a quite similar manner prior to the onset of the "computer age." Checks were processed, taxes collected, students educated, products manufactured, airplanes flown, medicine practiced, people entertained, and wars fought all without the benefit of computers. Not to deny the many advantages that have accrued from the introduction of computers into all areas of life, some balanced perspective should be maintained. Computers are indeed marvelous inventions that are transforming the workings of society, but their diffusion brings a variety of real and potential problems.

The following applications, chosen from disparate areas, illustrate the flexibility and versatility of computer-mediated equipment. In some instances computers improve the efficiency of existing processes; in others, they make possible new and innovative ones. New industries have been created—home computers, for example—and others have disappeared—for example, slide rules.

Smart Automobiles

A major effort is underway to increase automobile performance in the areas of handling, fuel efficiency, riding comfort, informational aids, and entertainment. Microprocessors have been used for several years to control engine functions in order to improve fuel economy. For example, the 1985 Oldsmobile has a control system that receives input from the following sources:

Injection-pump metering valve potentiometer (engine load).

Alternator (engine rotations per minute).

Engine coolant sensor.

Absolute pressure sensor: altitude and vacuum signal for control of exhaust gas recirculation (EGR).

Transmission gear state.

The system prevents engine overheating and compensates for altitude and cold by automatically adjusting the EGR, the timing, and the torque-converter-clutch calibration.

This is just one area in which microprocessors have begun to play an ever-increasing role in automobile operation. Consider the following applications:

An Integrated Systems Approach.   Ford Motor Company's experimental Mark VII Continental will have a cathode ray terminal (CRT) on its dashboard to display such information and control functions as temperature, fuel levels, trip parameters, time and calendar functions, service record, and diagnostic reports.

Travel Information.   A variety of travel computers are available in several models with such features as conversion from kilometers to miles, expected range given current fuel quantity and rate of consumption, and average vehicle speed.

Diagnostics and Servicing.   The 1985 Cadillac will be able to display up to 43 different system malfunctions. A technician, at a service center, will be able to monitor these reports to guide the repair process. A side effect of such systems may be the disappearance of neighborhood stations unable to afford the specialized, expensive diagnostic equipment.

Automatic Vehicle Ride Adjustment. An optional feature of 1985 Ford automobiles is an automatic, rear-leveling suspension system that depends on inflatable rear shock absorbers, sensors, and a microcomputer.

Anti-skidding Control. Speed sensors send information continuously to the microcomputer, which compares the speed of all four wheels. If there is a substantial imbalance during braking, an appropriate braking system is activated to control the skid.

On the horizon is a navigational system that includes an on-board computer and CRT together with a receiver for satellite signals. The computer stores detailed road maps that can be obtained on disks. The currently relevant map can then be displayed on the CRT. A system of satellites will be available in the late 1980s to provide instantaneous information about the car's location which can be shown on a local map. The car's position is updated automatically and new maps are slected when necessary.

Electronic Libraries

Space and time are two problems of prime importance facing today's libraries. The capital costs necessary to provide buildings to store ever-increasing numbers of books, journals, newspapers, and reports are soaring. The burden on librarians to help people find what they are looking for is increasing, and thus there are longer delays. Both problems are being addressed by developments in computer hardware and software. Computers are faster and cheaper than catalogs and make larger amounts of memory available. Database management systems have been developed to deal with the storage of large amounts of data in a structured fashion. Advances in information retrieval have resulted in methods for selecting specific information from the enormous amounts stored in the database.

For the present, libraries are committed to books, because the costs of converting existing libraries to electronic storage are enormous. Developments in publishing, by which books are entered into a computer for editing and formatting purposes prior to printing, may provide an answer. The electronic version could be available in libraries for computer retrieval purposes. Most useful currently is a method for determining what information is available that has led to the development of bibliographic databases. The user formulates a query that attempts to characterize the domain of interest as clearly as possible by incorporating a number of keywords. Upon execution by an information retrieval system, a list of references are returned to the user on a video display terminal or in a more permanent form. Some databases actually allow full text retrieval. The *New York Times* maintains a database of all its news stories. For retrieval either of bibliographic references, with or without abstracts, or full text articles, they must first be indexed with descriptive keywords. For the most part this task must still be done by people.

Other databases are available in such areas as patents, medical and chemical information, and legal issues. Professionals need to obtain up-to-date information rapidly and are willing to pay for the convenience. The *Academic American* is an electronic encyclopedia carried by the Dow Jones/Retrieval Service and Bibliographic Retrieval Services. In 1982 the service had nearly 100,000 subscribers, including 200 public and university libraries in three states. It costs about 60 cents per minute using a personal computer and $22 per month over cable. The system is quite easy to use and supplies short articles as well as bibliographic references that can be printed if a printer is connected to the computer terminal. Students find the computer system easier to use than a traditional library. One other important aspect: the encyclopedia can be updated much more easliy than a printed version and at a lower cost. Furthermore, this process can be done continuously, ensuring that the information is up-to-date. One cautionary note: the quality of these systems depends on the experience and knowledge of the people who actually characterize the stored information.

In July 1985, Grolier Electronic Publishing announced that the entire 21-volume *Academic American* was now available on a compact disk at a suggested retail price of $199. Its use requires a computer-controlled disk drive, a personal computer, and a monitor.

One other development will have an impact on libraries. The possibility of storing large amounts of information, both text and pictures, with rapid access has been realized in the form of the optical videodisk. Such disks have enormous capacity, about one and one-quarter billion characters. For example, a 12-inch disk can store the text equivalent of approximately 1500 books, of average length, per side. Information is stored by using a laser beam to burn tiny pits in the disk; as such, current versions cannot be erased and rerecorded, although recordable versions should be available soon. Therefore optical disks are currently very much the equivalent of books, phonograph records, or films—that is, a permanent information medium. Another way of looking at the vast amounts of information that can be stored on a disk is that each side can hold 54,000 single TV frames, enough for a half-hour show. Under control of a computer, arbitrary individual frames can be accessed in about five seconds, not particularly fast but quite adequate for the purposes of human browsing. Optical videodisk-microprocessor systems are currently in use in education, technical training, and for sales and marketing information. Their major use down the road will probably be as permanent cheap mass storage devices, ideal for libraries and home use alike.

Air Traffic Control

The current U.S. system of controlling air traffic is based on computer technology of the 1960s. It is inadequate for current needs and is becoming unsafe as air traffic increases. The Federal Aviation Administration has a plan to build a $15 billion system over the next 20 years. Components of the new system are more powerful regional computers, automated ground-air communication, and microwave landing systems. One result will be a reduction in the number of air traffic controllers because of the introduction of automated air traffic control (ATC) functions. There is general agreement that major technological steps must be taken. Currently the ATC system does not usually supervise small, private airplanes. Air traffic controllers must manually determine the spacing of planes to avoid collisions during take-offs and landings. The thrust of many of the improvements is to transfer part of the responsibility of humans to computers.

The current computer systems, based on IBM equipment of the early 1960s, must be replaced by either modern IBM or IBM-compatible machines. The newer equipment will be faster, of course, will have larger memories, and will make much more useful information readily available on graphic displays. Air traffic controllers will have minicomputer-controlled terminals with three display screens for (a) aircraft position, (b) flight data (currently flight data information is printed out on strips of paper placed next to the console), and (c) planning aircraft paths. The distributed computer system that is envisioned will be more resistant to failure because local failures will not bring the whole facility down. The current voice communications system between air and ground will be augmented by a digital data link as well as a link among aircraft. Another important step is the introduction of a system for allocating the spacing between planes to improve safety and efficiency.

Computing the Weather

Weather data is collected by thousands of ground stations all over the world and by orbiting satellites. This data, carried by an international telecommunications system to computerized weather centers, is used in weather models for predicting local conditions. At present, short-term forecasts 12 hours ahead are not very accurate. The basic limitations reside in inadequate data, imperfect models, and insufficiently fast computers. In the United States, weather information is gathered and checked at the National Meteorological Center and then used in a new cycle of the North American model and the world-wide model. Predictions made by these models from the previous cycle are compared with the current data and appropriate adjustments are made. The models produce predictions for 12-hour intervals 48 hours ahead—96 hours ahead for the global model. Maps are then sent to regional stations for use by local weather forecasters.

One of the problems with data is the accurate determination of wind speed. A standard method is to observe the positions of the same cloud pattern on successive scans of the monitoring system to compute the speed. Currently, interactive computer systems permit skilled operators to select which cloud patterns to follow. A computer system to perform this task automatically is under development. A massive amount of computation is necessary to run the computer models, and there is a possibility of speed-up by parallel computation. Weather models are typically based on updating the crucial variables, temperature, wind speed, pressure, and so forth at large numbers of points on a grid-like pattern. The form of the computations is similar at every point, suggesting a need for computers that can process many grid points simultaneously or in parallel. The national center will be acquiring computers 10 times faster than the current ones. Called vector-processing computers, they will perform an increased number of computations in parallel. The result will be 36-hour forecasts with accuracy approximating current 24-hour forecasts.

Longer-range forecasts—of the order of 6 to 10 days—also present computational problems at present and, in fact, are usually carried out by humans. Only the fastest computers available are adequate for the necessary computations. The importance of this problem has motivated research in what are now called supercomputers (see Chapter 14). These are also necessary to perform simulations of very complex computer models of the world's climate. Such experimental models, which must take into account components such as atmospheric and ocean systems, are too complex for even the fastest computers available. Nevertheless, certain simplifying aasumptions permit some predictions to be made—for example, the famous "greenhouse effect:" increased quantities of carbon dioxide in the atmosphere may lead to higher temperatures around the world, causing increased melting of the polar caps, a rise in the sea level, and the flooding of many coastal cities. Such predictions require much more analysis and refinement of the models before any action would be considered.

Video Games

There is certainly little need to describe video games to anyone who has been alive in the 1980s, when they suddenly captured a large share of the entertainment market. Teenagers were the prime group to whom advertisers devoted their attention. A number of companies—Atari, Mattel, Coleco—suddenly achieved national prominence, attracting considerable attention on the stock market as well. As their popularity mounted, so did public criticism. Children seemed to be so mesmerized that they would use their food allowance on video games and even steal money to play. Video game arcades sprang up everywhere, especially in downtown commercial areas, shopping malls, and near schools. Individual machines appeared in many stores. Their appearance in the home has accompanied the popularity of home computers. In fact, many would suggest that the reason most families have purchased home computers is to play video games, other more frequent explanations such as financial management and education notwithstanding.[2]

As video games gained in popularity, voices were raised in concern, arguing that children were becoming "hooked," to the detriment of other responsibilities such as school. Furthermore, the games existed in an essentially dehumanizing environment that emphasized human-machine interaction at the expense of interpersonal relations. Supporters argued that the games were educational and improved hand-eye coordination. They were criticized for excluding girls by reinforcing the male-oriented nature of both the games themselves and the arcades. Occasionally even bounds on ordinary decency were exceeded as games appeared in which success involved inflicting punishment on women. Competition became heated both in the arcades and in the sale of game cartridges. Increasing pressure to produce new and better games shortened the life cycle of the games and severely lowered the profit margins of some of the leading companies. Atari, a division of Warner Communications, suffered considerable losses in 1983 and 1984 and was sold. In any case, by 1982 the bloom had worn off. From average weekly earnings for an arcade video game of $102 (1980) to a high of $140 (1981), there was a fall to $109 (1982) and $93 (1983).

Manufacturers are looking to new technological developments to rekindle the flame in the arcade market. The home market for video game cartridges and players continues to boom. Sales in 1983 were estimated at \$6.5 billion, up 58 percent from the previous year's. The future for video games holds such promising developments as 3-D effects on high resolution screens, a wider range of brighter colors, intelligent adaptation to an individual player's skills, the use of speech recognition as an additional communication channel, more powerful graphics, and the use of videodisks to supply large amounts of memory storage. These improvements will result from improved microprocessors as well as sophisticated software. From their primitive beginnings as variations of the game Pong to their current level, video games have depended on developments in microelectronics. The games can be seen as a logical outgrowth of pinball machines and simultaneously as an introduction to a new age of sophisticated computers, graphics, and software.

Although the video game arcade has begun to lose its hold on the nation's youth, video games have had an impact beyond their initial use. For example, they have been integrated into educational programs to attract students and keep their attention. Some argue that an interest in video games will lead to an interest in computers and programming. Perhaps this is true, but on the other hand remember that personal computers have been mainly used for game playing, not for programming. Other uses for video games are in job training and to improve the hand-eye coordination of stroke victims and other disabled people.

SOCIETAL ISSUES

> *While bringing many benefits to society, the revolution [computers and electronics] will also bring problems, tension, and disbenefits.*[3]

Discussions about technological change and society generally take a form similar to the above quotation. That is, technology brings many important benefits—better communication, less dangerous work, faster transportation, and reduction in home labor, among others—but there are drawbacks. At one level, somewhat abstract, are the fears that we will become slaves to our own machines (this topic will be explored at some length in Chapter 3). An extreme form of this position is that in the long run machines will actually be able to solve problems and replace people in most of their jobs. The evolution of machine intelligence will be steady and inexorable until gradually people will literally serve machines. Although this theme is usually one for science fiction, recent work in Artificial Intelligence has suggested to some that with the arrival of the computer, especially in its current form, a serious beginning has been made on the road to producing intelligent robots.

Recent publicity about the Fifth Generation project in Japan has stimulated public and private support in the United States for a major research investment in a race with the Japanese to develop practical intelligent machines that can understand spoken language and the world around them (see Chapter 14). None can doubt that such machines will have a profound impact on society in more ways than can be imagined, but it is not necessary to wait for them—if indeed they ever arrive—to be concerned about how computers have already affected our lives. If we agree with the accepted view that the benefits of computers far outweigh any associated detrimental effects, it is still necessary to delineate these effects and to gauge their significance.

Issues and Problems

There are several ways to present and discuss social issues arising from the increasing use of computers. One method is by category; that is, each major area of application is studied and the particular problems recognized. Another method is to propose a list of areas of concern, or possible problems, and then study each application to see if it illustrates any of these problems. Both approaches can be combined by first listing and describing a number of application areas and a number of social issues and then constructing a diagram that depicts which social issues are relevant to which applications. The simple metaphor is to view society as a fabric woven with warp and woof threads. The *warp* consists of the lengthwise threads of a woven cloth through which *woof* threads are woven, and the *woof* consists of the crosswise threads carried back and forth by the shuttle and interwoven with the lengthwise threads of the *warp*. These definitions are interdependent just as the issues and applications are. For the purposes of this metaphor, societal issues are the warp, and computers, technology, and applications are the woof. The dividing lines are not always sharp, however,

Application areas and technological developments include the following:

> *Robotics and Industrial Automation.* The integration of computers and movable electromechanical arms—to perform such tasks as assembling parts, welding, and spray painting—define industrial automation. Robots may also be used for jobs dangerous to humans in hazardous environments such as under the sea, mines, space, and nuclear reactors. Flexible manufacturing systems represent a new way of organizing production.

> *Office Automation.* The integration of computers, mainframes and personal, local and long-distance communication networks, facsimile machines, and printers will transform the office. Word-processing, electronic filing and retrieving, electronic mail, automatic scheduling of meetings, management information systems, and remote data entry and programming are among the new possibilities.

> *Telecommunications.* The interconnection of computers with communciation networks opens up a wide range of possibilities for distributed computing, distributed work, and worldwide information networks for business and government use.

> *Electronic Money Systems.* The use of automatic teller machines (ATMs), point-of-sale terminals (POSs), and computer communication systems results in electronic fund, transfer systems, the so-called "cashless" society. A vast network linking financial institutions, retailers, wholesalers, and the public will change shopping and banking habits.

Personal Computers. The explosion of microcomputers available for use in the office, school, and home has brought computers out of the private preserve of data processing professionals into the hands of the general public. Marketed as just another consumer item, they may have been oversold but do provide an ever-expanding range of possibilities for the family, including games, financial programs, educational programs, and access to information systems.

Microprocessors. The miniaturization of computing power in the form of microprocessors has enabled the computer to be incorporated in an ever-increasing variety of consumer products. Among these are cameras, automobiles, television receivers, and microwave ovens. Improvements in efficiency and repair will change production practices and servicing procedures. Consumer products can be more energy-efficient and more flexible.

Service Professions. These include medicine, education, and law, among others. Computer-based devices will improve medical record keeping, diagnosis programs, medical imaging systems such as CAT scanners and, of course, billing systems. The computer in the school is being hailed as a major aid to education both in traditional instruction and as an exciting new subject in its own right. Legal information retrieval systems will help case preparation.

Home Information Systems. Teletext or videotex systems, which provide communication via television broadcast systems, cable, or telephone lines, are on the verge of reaching many Americans and Europeans. Services available over specially adapted television sets or personal computers include banking, shopping, reservations, educational material, electronic polling and opinion surveys, and solicitation of donations.

Electronic Mail and Teleconferencing. The use of computer terminals and communication networks will permit messages to be sent across the country and stored in computers or printed and delivered locally as ordinary mail. New networks will encourage a novel form of information sharing.

Government Regulation. The role of government in regulating communication systems is undergoing a change in emphasis. AT&T has separated from its regional companies, and more competition in the long-distance and data transmission market is being encouraged. Less concern with antitrust regulations is also apparent. The government suit against IBM was dropped, and a more aggressive posture resulted, evidenced by IBM's enormous success in the personal computer market. Other issues for government concern are its support of high technology developments, its control of high technology exports (technology transfer), and the free flow of research results.

The Arts. Artists are making use of computers in movies, graphics, and music. Digital computer-controlled synthesizers provide enormous possibilities for technically minded composers. High resolution graphics systems and recent developments in software permit the generation of sophisticated images.

Artificial Intelligence. From the halls of academia and private research laboratories to the market place, developments in Artificial Intelligence (AI) are achieving national importance. Whether in the design of expert sytems, vision systems for robots, intelligent English interfaces for databases, or diagnosis system for doctors, AI has come to the fore.

Computers and the Law. Computers, because they are so necessary and are used for so many purposes, can be used for illegal activities such as, for example, embezzling money, accessing information without permission, and using computer time without payment. How to legally safeguard software and hardware under patent, copyright, or trade secrets regulations is also a problem.

This list provides a sense of how important computers have become to the functioning of a modern society. It now remains to outline an accompanying list of social issues. For some of these, computers are only the next stage in technological development, and so the problems are only existing ones exacerbated. Others are unique to the computer and must be treated as directly associated phenomena. Among the social issues are the following:

Work. How do all these computer-related developments affect the employment of people? Will the number of available jobs increase or decrease? Will the skill requirements change? How will people accommodate to the increased use of computers on the job? What will happen to the traditional social organization of the office under office automation, sometimes called the "office of the future"?

Health. Is sitting in front of a video display terminal (VDT) dangerous to your health, both physically and psychologically? Are other computer-related activities problematic? For example, there is increased incidence of individuals becoming so infatuated with computers that they withdraw from human contact.

Privacy and Personal Freedom. Computers permit enormous amounts of information to be gathered, stored, processed, and linked. There is a concern about how these records are used, incorrect information, and the right to inspect one's own file. Can the collection of information inhibit individual action? Who has access to personal information? Under what conditions must the government reveal what it has collected (the freedom of information issue).

Centralization of Control. Will computers be used to extend the power of management over workers? Is it inevitable that increased amounts of more accurate information will shift power to the top, or will distributed computing lead to distributed responsibility and control? Will governments become more powerful and centralized as in Orwell's *1984*?

Responsibility. Will the widespread use of computers and communication systems fragment society? Will families cluster around their home information systems for entertainment, shopping, education, and even jobs, forsaking outside contacts? Will fewer and fewer people actually produce things and more and more people engage in service activities and information processing? How will this change society?

Human Self-Image. How does the computer affect our self-image? Is there a threat to human dignity as machines continue to perform more activities formerly the sole province of people? Is technology an irresistible force with its own imperative? Can one maintain human(e) qualities in a computer age?

Ethics and Professionalism. How responsible are computer professionals for their actions? Should they adopt codes of behavior similar to doctors and lawyers? Do computer-mediated situations present new problems for ethical behavior?

National Interests. Does the future economic well-being of a society depend on its achievements in high technology? Will success for some countries mean failure for others?

Meritocracy. Will the use of computers accentuate the tensions between the educated and the untrained? Will the work of society be divided between challenging and interesting jobs and routine and boring jobs? Will the poor and uneducated view computers as yet another powerful tool in the hands of the rich, and will they be right?

Which issues apply to which technological areas? Figure 1-1 is not a precise formulation, because the definitions themselves are not precise. It should suggest the general patterns of interaction of social issues and technological innovations. As times goes on, the number of rows and columns will vary as new concerns emerge in response to new applications. It is important to be aware of the possible consequences of technological developments, but this awareness requires a familiarity with the technology itself as well as with the economic, political, social, and legal structures of society. Only a beginning is attempted here, but an old Chinese saying is appropriate: ''A journey of a thousand miles begins with one step.''

Public Opinion

We have articulated a selection of possible problems associated with computer use in today's society. Their severity is a matter of debate among computer specialists and social scientists—but how do nonexperts, ordinary people, feel about computers? It was not until the late 1950s that the computer emerged as an object of praise and fear. Cartoonists of the period depicted computers or robots as challenging the ability of humans at work and at play. Operators at consoles in front of floor-to-ceiling computers typed in queries that elicited humorous responses. The cartoons reflected such concerns as possible loss of jobs, threats to human problem-solving skills, personal liberty, and an increasing intrusion into all aspects of human life. Did the cartoonists and editorial writers truly capture the hopes and fears of the general population?

From a survey of public opinion conducted in 1963, the following results emerged:[4]

While very few people had direct, personal contact with computers, most described them with such words as ''amazing'' and ''astounding'' and appreciated the fact that only educated people could really understand them.

FIGURE 1-1 Social Issues and Computers.

	Work	Health	Privacy & personal freedom	Centralization of control	Responsibility	The information society	Human self-image	Ethics & professionalism	National interests	Meritocracy
Robotics and industrial automation	X	X					X		X	X
Office automation	X	X		X	X		X	X		X
Telecommunications			X	X		X		X		
Electronic money systems	X		X	X	X			X		
Personal computers		X				X				X
Microprocessors	X		X			X				X
Service professions	X			X	X	X		X		X
Home information systems	X		X		X	X		X		X
Electronic mail and teleconferencing	X		X			X				
Government regulation		X	X	X					X	
The arts						X	X			
Artificial Intelligence	X					X	X		X	
Computers and the law			X		X					

People thought of computers as general-purpose devices that solve numerical problems in such business applications as payroll and accounting as well as in space, scienific research, and defense matters.

They tended to believe that computers were all-powerful, always produced correct results, and were some kind of powerful electronic brain. They did not seem to be aware that computers had to be programmed and monitored by humans.

> They did perceive a threat to human dignity arising from a view of computers as all-powerful but did not associate this threat with potential loss of jobs.

The challenge to human dignity presented by computers is one more link in a historic chain of scientific challenges to assumptions about human dignity. The chain stretches from Copernicus (the earth is not the center of the universe) to Darwin (humans are not uniquely created but are part of the evolutionary process) to Freud (there is a major part of our internal world—the unconscious—over which we have little control).

In 1971 *Time* magazine and the American Federation of Information Processing Societies, Inc. (AFIPS) conducted a major survey to determine the public's attitudes towards computers.[5] Over 1000 adults from a representative sample of the U.S. population were interviewed on a wide range of topics. The survey results are extensive and lengthy, but a few observations are revealing.

> Almost half of the working public has some contact with computers.
>
> About 90 percent felt that computers will provide much useful information and many kinds of services.
>
> Thirty-six percent felt computers actually create more jobs than they eliminate; 51 percent believed the opposite.
>
> Eighty-four percent wanted the government to regulate the use of computers.
>
> With respect to privacy, 58 percent were concerned that computers will be used in the future for surveillance and 38 percent believed that they were a threat to privacy (but 54 percent disagreed).
>
> Only 12 percent believed that computers could think for themselves but 23 percent expected that they might disobey their programmers in the future.
>
> Fifty-four percent thought that computers were dehumanizing people and 33 percent believed that they were decreasing freedom; 59 percent disagreed.

On the whole, the general public displayed a reasonable attitude to the current ability of computers and the potential threats they posed. (Chapter 9 presents more detailed results about concerns with privacy.)

Some twelve years later (September 1983) Lou Harris and Associates, Inc. conducted a study for Southern New England Telephone entitled *The Road After 1984: The Impact of Technology on Society.*[6] Conducted well into the age of the home computer, this survey should reveal a more sophisticated public awareness. Some highlights follow:

> Some 67 percent of the general public believes that personal information is being kept in files, somewhere, for purposes unknown to them.
>
> Forty-five percent acknowledges that they know how to use a computer, most of the beginner level.
>
> Eighty-eight percent believes that the computer will make the quality of life somewhat or a lot better.
>
> Eighty-five percent agrees that computers can free up time for individuals to do creative and highly productive work.

Fifty-five percent feels that computers can make human robots out of workers by controlling every minute of their day.

One might have expected a drastic reduction over the years in the uncritical respect awarded to computers if for no other reason than that a wider segment of the general population have had dirct exposure to home computers. Surely this experience should temper the conception of the computer as all-powerful. Perhaps a distinction is being made between the small, limited home computer and the large, mysterious computers maintained by government and business. The latter are probably viewed as almost a different species of machine. Be that as it may, the fact remains that after thirty years of use computers have managed to retain a somewhat amazing image. The public media are partially responsible, in that they have eagerly exploited the glamorous and powerful impression of the computer. It is much less interesting (and less profitable) to characterize the computer in a more realistic way. One of the purposes of this book is to attempt to do so.

SUMMARY

Computers have become pervasive in contemporary society. They have been used to perform marriages, steal information, monitor prisoners on parole, and provide a variety of on-line services. Other applications include improved automobile performance, modernization of libraries, air traffic control, weather forecasting, and the entertainment of youth.

Associated with the benefits of computers are a number of real and potential problems. The many and varied applications of computers, including robotics, office automation, electronic money systems, personal computers, home information systems, and Artificial Intelligence, have given rise to social problems. Relevant issues include work, health, privacy, responsibility, self-image, and national interests.

From their earliest appearance computers have aroused feelings of fear, awe, and concern, as has been revealed in public opinion surveys. Despite increased familiarity, the general public's perception of computers seems still to be conditioned more by media exaggerations than by reality.

NOTES

1. Edward Cornish, ''The Coming of an Information Society,'' *The Futurist,* April 1981, p. 14.
2. ''How Our Readers Are Using Computers,'' *Consumer Report,* September 1983, pp.

470–471. This report states that 69 percent of the respondents actually used their home computers for games, compared to 63 percent for learning about computers, 61 percent for learning to program, and 59 percent for word processing. The readership of *Consumer Report* is particularly well motivated, it should be noted.

3. Philip H. Abelson, "The Revolution in Computers and Electronics," *Science,* February 12, 1982, p. 753.

4. Robert S. Lee, "The Computer's Public Image," *Datamation,* December 1966, pp. 33–34, 39.

5. *A National Survey of the Public's Attitudes Towards Computers* (New York: Time, 1971).

6. Louis Harris and Associates, *The Road After 1984: The Impact of Technology on Society* (for Southern New England Telephone, 1983). The complete results are particularly interesting because in them the opinions of the general public are compared to those of congressmen and aides, corporate executives, science editors, and superintendents of schools.

ADDITIONAL READINGS

A Variety of Applications

Brody, Herb. "Video Games Enter Technology Time Warp." *High Technology,* June 1983, pp. 36–9, 42–6.

Douglas, John. "Micro Memories," *Science 82,* July/August 1982, pp. 40–5.

Jurgen, Ronald K. "More Electronics in Detroit's 1985 Models." *IEEE Spectrum,* October 1984, pp. 54–60.

Keller, Erik L. "Automotive Electronics Shifts into Overdrive." *Electronics,* January 26, 1984, pp. 101–112.

Lerner, Eric J. "Automating U.S. Air Lines: A Review." *IEEE Spectrum,* November 1982, pp. 46–51.

Lerner, Eric J. "The Great Weather Network." *IEEE Spectrum,* February 1982, pp. 50–57.

Olson, Steve. "Computing Climate." *Science 82,* May 1982, pp. 54–60.

Perry, Tekla S., and Paul Wallich. "Design Case History: The Atari Video Computer System." *IEEE Spectrum,* March 1983, pp. 45–51.

Siegel, Efrem, Mark Schubin, and Paul F. Merrill. *Video Discs.* White Plains: Knowledge Industry Publications, 1980.

Siwolop, Sana. "Touching All the Data Bases." *Discover,* March 1983, pp. 68, 70–71.

Toong, Hoo-min D., and Amar Gupta. "Automating Air-Traffic Control." *Technology Review,* April 1982, pp. 40–49, 54.

Societal Issues

Anderson, Ronald E. ''Sociological Analysis of Public Attitudes Towards Computers and Information Files.'' *Spring Joint Computer Conference Proceedings,* The American Federation of Information Processing Societies, Inc., 1972, pp. 649–657.

Florman, Samuel C. *Blaming Technology: The Irrational Search for Scapegoats.* New York: St. Martin's, 1981.

Gotlieb, C. C., and A. Borodin. *Social Issues in Computing.* New York: Academic, 1973.

Lee, Robert S. ''Social Attitudes and the Computer Revolution.'' *The Public Opinion Quarterly,* Spring 1970, pp. 53–59.

Mowshowitz, Abbe. ''Afterthoughts and Reflections.'' In Abbe Mowshowitz, ed., *Human Choice and Computers 2.* Amsterdam: North Holland, 1980, pp. 291–299.

Mowshowitz, Abbe. *The Conquest of Will: Information Processing in Human Affairs.* Reading: Addison-Wesley, 1976.

''A Problem-List of Issues Concerning Computers and Public Policy.'' *Communications of the Association for Computing Machinery,* September 1974, pp. 495–503.

Taviss, Irene. ''A Survey of Popular Attitudes Towards Technology.'' *Technology and Culture,* vol. 13, no. 4, 1972, pp. 606–21.

Weizenbaum, Joseph. *Computer Power and Human Reason.* San Francisco: W. H. Freeman, 1976.

2

COMPUTERS AND THE HUMAN IMAGINATION

A *yet more complex form of interaction can be found in the processes of interaction that constitute a partnership of computer and artist, bent upon making art jointly.*

◇ *Nicholas P. Negroponte, in* The Computer Age: A Twenty-Year View, *1980.* ◇

INTRODUCTION

Machines that can move, talk, play games, or mimic human behavior in some other way have held a considerable fascination for people in every era. It is not surprising these days to encounter at the newsstand one or more magazines that report yet another human ability recently achieved by a computer. The mechanisms used to produce such interesting behavior have ranged from steam, clockwork devices, and electromechanical systems to today's mainframes and micros.

Contemporary depiction of robots is generally favorable—witness the lovable robots of the *Star Wars* movies and their part in the series' phenomenal success. Only a few years earlier, however, one of the main protagonists in *2001: A space odyssey* was a malevolent computer called HAL. As robotic machines, computers have had an unusual relationship with the imagination. They have been perceived as threats both to society in general and humans in particular and as tools or even partners in the process of civilization.

Contemporary artists in many fields have been eager to use computers as partners in the process of creating imaginative works. Music and the visual arts have been the primary beneficiaries (perhaps too strong a term in the opinion of many) of the advances in computer technology. Recently, computers and sophisticated graphics terminals have been used in movie animation to produce extraordinarily complex images. This development will permit directors to combine humans and computer-generated images without recourse to the construction of physical sets. Less interesting results have been achieved in the application of computers to the written or spoken arts. Except perhaps for free verse, where much of the art is in the ear and mind of the beholder, computers and language have not meshed successfully.

There has always been (or so it seems) a curious attraction to artifacts that resemble humans. In our own time, the digital computer has become the test bed for exploring the possibility of Artificial Intelligence (AI), that branch of computer science concerned with the attempt to develop programs that exhibit intelligent behavior. Indeed, AI has become not only a major branch of computer science but also a growing presence in the market-place. AI is also an important factor in many of the computer applications discussed in this book.

THE INTELLIGENT MACHINE IN FACT AND FICTION

Charlie had his way, and I was soon on the show. Charlie was right: Abdullah [a mechanical figure controlled internally by a hidden person] pulled them in because people cannot resist automata. There is something in humanity that is repelled and entranced by a machine that seems to have more than human powers. People love to frighten themselves. Look at the fuss nowadays about computers; however deft they may be they can't do anything a man isn't doing, through them; but you hear people giving themselves delicious shivers about a computer-dominated world. I've often thought of working up an illusion, using a computer, but it would be prohibitively expensive, and I can do anything the public would find amusing better and cheaper with clockwork and bits of string. But if I invented a computer-illusion I would take care to dress the computer up to look like a living creature of some sort—a Moon Man or a Venusian—because the public cannot resist clever dollies. Abdullah was a clever dolly of a simple kind and the Rubes couldn't get enough of him.[1]

Automata and Androids

In his interesting and informative book *Human Robots in Myth and Science,* John Cohen has traced the human fascination with the possibility of living and thinking artifacts.[2] He describes a variety of instances in antiquity of statues that were supposed to speak and offer advice and prophecies. Hephaestus, also known as Vulcan, god of fire, was accompanied by two female statues of pure gold that assisted him in his activities. In the fifteenth century B.C., the statue of King Memnon near Thebes, supposedly emitted a variety of sounds depending on the time of day. Hero of Alexandria (285–222 B.C.) built mechanical birds that apparently flew and sang.

There are many stories of devices originating in the East that moved and talked. Consider this tale of a robot of the third century B.C. in China.

> *King Mu of Chou made a tour of inspection in the west. . .and on his return journey, before reaching China, a certain artificer, Yen Shih by name, was presented to him. The king received him and asked him what he could do. He replied that he would do anything which the king commanded, but that he had a piece of work already finished which he would like to show him. "Bring it with you tomorrow," said the king, "and we will look at it together." So next day Yen Shih appeared again and was admitted into the presence. "Who is that man accompanying you?" asked the king. "That, Sir," replied Yen Shih, "is my own handiwork. He can sing and he can act." The king stared at the figure in astonishment. It walked with rapid strides, moving its head up and down, so that anyone would have taken it for a live human being. The artificer touched its chin, and it began singing, perfectly in tune. He touched its hands, and it began posturing, keeping perfect time. It went through any number of movements that fancy might happen to dictate. The king, looking on with his favourite concubine and other beauties, could hardly persuade himself that it was not real. As the performance was drawing to an end, the robot winked its eye and made advances to the ladies in attendance, whereupon the king became incensed and would have had Yen Shih executed on the spot had not the latter, in mortal fear, instantly taken the robot to pieces to let him see what it really was. And, indeed, it turned out to be only a construction of leather, wood, glue and lacquer, variously coloured white, black, red and blue.* [3]

The willingness of people to accept life in objects of stone, metal, or wood seems evidence of some deeply embedded need to believe in the power of either the gods or their specially chosen servants, to create life in any form. The effect is even stronger if the things that move or talk resemble humans. This need has not diminished over the centuries.

The illustrious figures Albertus Magnus (1204–72) and Roger Bacon (1214–94) are supposed to have created, respectively, a life-size automaton servant and a speaking head. At the end of the sixteenth century in Prague, Rabbi Loew produced a living being—the Golem—out of a clay figure by inserting into its mouth a strip of paper with a magical formula. The creation of life from earth or other inanimate substances is a common theme in both history and literature that reached its apogee, in fiction at least, with Baron Frankenstein's monster some two centuries later.

The golden age of automata was perhaps in Europe in the eighteenth century. Skilled craftsmen built incredibly lifelike mechanisms that were exhibited to enormous crowds. The more lifelike the appearance, the greater the acclaim. Apparently the most impressive of these automata was a duck built by Jacques de Vaucanson (1709–1782) and exhibited in 1738. A rebuilt version of this automaton was displayed in Milan at La Scala in 1844 amid great excitement. A member of the audience wrote the following:

> *It is the most admirable thing imaginable, an almost inexplicable human achieve-*
> *ment. Each feather of the wings is mobile. . . . The artist touches a feather on the*
> *upper portion of the body, and the bird lifts its head, glances about, shakes its tail*
> *feathers, stretches itself, unfolds its wings, ruffles them and lets out a cry, abso-*
> *lutely natural, as if it were about to take flight. The effect is still more astonishing*
> *when the bird, leaning over its dish, begins to swallow the grain with incredibly*
> *realistic movement. As for its method of digestion, nobody can explain it.*[4]

There is no question of such devices exhibiting free will or initiating independent action. However lifelike, the duck was no more than a complex clock mechanism of approximately 4000 parts, and from the moment it began to move, its actions were completely prede- termined. We marvel at the incredible ingenuity of the inventor but at the same time we are aware of the limitations of the invention. Still, the skill of these inventors was mind- boggling. Especially impressive are the life-size androids built by Pierre Jacquet-Droz and his two sons near Neuchatel, Switzerland between 1768 and 1774. One, a "child" android called the Writer, can be mechanically programmed to write any 40 characters of text. Another, the Musician, which has the form of a woman, moved with a marvellous grace replete with subtle gestures that included head motions and a curtsy.

The so-called Chess Player of 1769, built by Baron Wolfgang von Kempelen (1734– 1809) was a famous fraud. Costumed as a Turk, the automaton appeared to move the pieces on a chess board and to play quite a good game of chess. It is believed that, unknown to the audience, a person was concealed under the board, though this fact was not actually established during the automaton's lifetime. Edgar Allan Poe, one of those who argued for the hidden person hypothesis, exploited this theme when he wrote, in 1838, the short story called "Maelzel's Chess-Player."

A Twentieth-Century Automaton

In the post-World War II period, before computers had come to the attention of the general public, descriptions began to appear of a whole race of mechanical mice, tortoises, and squirrels whose simplicity of construction, coupled with apparently extraordinary behavior, promised the early appearance of even more incredible creatures. W. Grey Walter, an English neurophysiologist, built a relatively simple electromechanical device, subse- quently called a "tortoise," which seemed to exhibit free will. He described its behavior as follows:

> *When the photocell sees a light. . .the effect is to halt the steering mechanism so*
> *that the machine moves towards the light source or maneuvers so that it can ap-*
> *proach the light with least difficulty. . . . When the brilliance exceeds a certain*

*value. . .the creature abruptly sheers away and seeks a more gentle climate. If
there is a single light source, the machine circles around it in a complex path of
advance and withdrawal.*[5]

When the batteries run down, the device is no longer repelled by light and will approach
its hutch to recharge its batteries. Much was claimed for the abilities of these devices and
others that followed, even though they were extremely simple. Perhaps this phenomenon
is just a natural continuation of the fascination with mechanisms that imitate life. After
the development of digital computers, computer-controlled mechanisms soon superseded
such simple devices. There has been little waning of interest, however. In fact, the
continuing increase in microprocessor power and significant decrease in size has stimulated
the development of contemporary versions of lifelike mechanisms.

The Theme of the Robot

*It is unreasonable. . .to think machines could become nearly as intelligent as we
are and then stop, or to suppose we will always be able to compete with them in
wit or wisdom. Whether or not we could retain some sort of control of the machines, assuming that we would want to, the nature of our activities and aspirations
would be changed utterly by the presence on earth of intellectually superior beings.*[6]

A robot can be thought of as a mobile computer with sensory, tactile, and motor abilities.
Furthermore, it is an artifact made in the image of its human creator, who has endowed
it with some form of lifelike behavior. It need not, at least in principle, be machine-like. One might argue that Frankenstein's monster was a robot created from a human
corpse and given the spark of ''life'' by the power of lightning.

The relationship between the scientist or inventor and his or her creation has inspired
many tales. Two basic plots have emerged. In one, the robot is a subordinate, a servant
quick to obey but unable to initiate independent action. The other is concerned with self-
motivated behavior, with the robot (or creation) as potential adversary or potential master.
Creations of this type have caused trouble through willful disobedience, as exemplified
by Frankenstein's monster, and through carrying out a request too zealously and too
literally, as shown in the story of the sorcerer's apprentice and in *The Monkey's Paw* by
W. W. Jacobs.[7]

Much of the literature in this area relates to the Greek myth of Prometheus, the hero
who disobeyed Zeus, stole fire from heaven, and gave it to humankind. This gift permitted
people to keep themselves warm, to illuminate the night, and to create tools and other
objects. As punishment for this theft Prometheus was chained to a mountaintop and plagued
for eternity by vultures picking at his liver—a torment one might recommend today for
the designers of some particularly terrible computer programs. It is often forgotten that
the full title of Mary Shelley's *Frankenstein,* published in 1818, is *Frankenstein: or, the
Modern Prometheus.* (Remember also that Baron Frankenstein's monster has no name of
its own. Thanks to Hollywood, it has become known simply as Frankenstein.)

In her study of robots and androids in science fiction, Patricia Warrick isolates four themes that emerge from Shelley's novel and recur in modern science fiction.

1. The Promethean theme: the acquisition of a hitherto forbidden skill that is now put to the supposed benefit of humankind.

2. The two-edged nature of technology: benefits are frequently offset by unanticipated problems.

3. The precipitous rejection of technology: the monster launches a campaign of terror only after Dr. Frankenstein abandons him.

4. The uneasy relation between master and servant: what is created sometimes turns against the creator and becomes the master.[8]

This last point is perhaps best exemplified in *Erewhon* (1872), by Samuel Butler, which explores the relationship between humans and their machines. The narrator, discussing the reasons given by the society of Erewhon for banishing machines, notes that it is not existing machines that are to be feared, but the fact that they evolve so rapidly and in such unpredictable directions that they must be controlled, limited, and destroyed while they are still in a primitive form. Compare this fear with the sentiment expressed nearly a century later by one of the founders of Artificial Intelligence in the quotation that began this section. The following quotation from *Erewhon* may serve as a grim commentary on our age:

> *True, from a materialistic point of view it would seem that those thrive best who use machinery wherever its use is possible with profit; but this is the art of the machines: they serve that they may rule. How many men at this hour are living in a state of bondage to the machines? How many spend their whole lives, from the cradle to the grave, in tending them by night and day? Is it not plain that the machines are gaining ground upon us?*[9]

Other Utopian novels, such as Aldous Huxley's *Brave New World*—written about 50 years later—and George Orwell's *1984*, are more concerned with general issues surrounding the organization of a future society. Nevertheless, the all-powerful computer plays an integral role in these societies, whether it regulates the birth process, as in *Brave New World*, or controls a vast two-way communications network by which Big Brother has access to every person, as in *1984*. (See the discussion on videotex in Chapter 13.) The title *1984* has itself become the shorthand term for the perfectly totalitarian society in which all efforts are devoted to maintaining the state against its enemies, both internal and external, real and imagined. ''Big Brother is watching you'' is the ultimate warning for a society in which there is complete absence of privacy and individual freedom.

In the twentieth century, perhaps *the* work of art that most successfully addresses the problem of people and their people-like machines is the play *R.U.R.* (1921) by Karel Capek.[10] In fact the word ''robot'' made its first appearance in this play, whose title is an abbreviation for ''Rossum's Universal Robots.'' In *R.U.R.* humankind has become so dependent on robots that when the robots revolt, there is no hope. However, the robots do not know how to reproduce themselves, the formula having been lost in the general destruction accompanying their takeover. Thus, the people are ultimately destroyed by their creations, a bitter example of the fourth theme mentioned above.

At variance with the almost universal pessimism expressd so far has been the impact on science fiction of Isaac Asimov's robot stories. Asimov, one of the most prolific writers of our time, wrote a series of short stories dealing with robots and in the process introduced a substantial realignment into the imagined human-robot relationship. In his 1942 story "Runaround," Asimov described "the three fundamental Rules of Robotics—the three rules that are built most deeply into a robot's positronic brain." These govern robot behavior with respect to humans in order to prevent any harm coming to a human either through an action or lack of action by a robot. The three laws are as follows:

> *First Law: A robot may not injure a human being, or, through inaction, allow a human being to come to harm. Second Law: A robot must obey the orders given it by human beings except where such orders would conflict with the First Law. Third Law: A robot must protect its own existence as long as such protection does not conflict with the First or Second Laws.*[11]

The working out of implications inherent in these three laws informs the plots of many of the subsequent stories in Asimov's robot series.

The trend of reforming robots has probably reached its peak in the *Star Wars* movies, in which the two robots—R2D2, the chirpy fire hydrant, and C3PO, the prissy, gold-encased English butler—do not appear to have even one malevolent transistor between them. They exist only to serve their masters—humans. In real life another race of robots has appeared in the last few years: those indefatigable workers on the assembly line, the industrial robots (these will be discussed in Chapter 12). We can conclude with the observation that intelligent artifacts, whether in the form of humans or not, continue to exert a powerful influence on the human imagination. In some ways technology, the product of our minds and hands, is a mixed blessing. Writers have explored this ambivalence for many years, but the issues have sharpened with the appearance of that most marvelous of all inventions, the computer.

COMPUTERS AS A CREATIVE MEDIUM

"The Eureka"

Such is the name of a machine for composing hexameter Latin verses which is now exhibited at the Egyptian Hall, in Piccadilly. It was designed and constructed at Bridgewater, in Somersetshire; was begun in 1830, and completed in 1843; and it has lately been brought to the metropolis, to contribute to the "sights of the season. . . ."

The rate of composition is about one verse per minute, or sixty an hour. Each verse remains stationary and visible a sufficient time for a copy of it to be taken; after which the machine gives an audible notice that the Line is about to be decom-

posed. Each Letter of the verse is then slowly and separately removed into its former alphabetical arrangement; on which the machine stops, until another verse be required. Or, by withdrawing the stop, it may be made to go on continually, producing in one day and night, or twenty-four hours, about 1440 Latin verses; or, in a whole week (Sundays included) about 10,000.

During the composition of each line, a cylinder in the interior of the machine performs the National Anthem. (Anonymous, Illustrated London News, 1895.)

What effects has the computer had either directly or indirectly on the arts? "Arts" here means music, drawing and graphics, movies, literature, and dance. We are concerned with the use of computers in the creative process as a tool or aid rather than as the subject matter of the work itself. In the best of all possible worlds you, the reader, would have access to a computer and be able to use it to produce music (with a synthesizer), art (with a graphics system), and perhaps poetry. Second best would be a tape of music, a portfolio of drawings, and a slim volume of computer-generated poetry. Unfortunately, we are in a position only to describe and comment, not to present and demonstrate.

There are a number of issues to keep in mind as we proceed. To what degree is the computer itself creative? This seems to be a question with which the artists themselves have little concern. For those interested in the computer as a tool, there is hardly any reason to attribute special powers of creativity to it. The artist wants to explore ways of creating under his or her initiative. The computer can give the artist a variety of means to extend and augment his or her abilities. Will anything significant emerge from the application of computers to art? The simple answer is "only time will tell." There may not appear to be any great artistic accomplishments up to now. The computer is a relatively new invention, and people will take time to learn how to use it.

Music

Music has probably been the art form in which the most interesting results have been achieved. This is not very surprising, because even before computers were invented, music could be represented by means of an electronic signal that is readily available for a computer to modify. The original signal itself can be generated by electronic equipment. That is, a complex piece of equipment incorporating signal generators, synthesizers, and microprocessors is like a giant "intelligent" organ that can be used by the contemporary composer.

In the 1950s, electronic music meant tape splicing and other manual rearrangements of sound. It was not until the 1960s that sound synthesizers, high-speed digital-to-analog converters, and sound generation programs appeared. One of the most famous early works was the "Illiac Suite for String Quartet" by Lejaren Hiller of the University of Illinois. This composition relied on the computer for the generation of random numbers. Music with a strong random component in its performance or composition is called aleatory music. For purposes of composition computers have proven invaluable because the composer is able to set the parameters of permissible variation, and the computer can select the actual path to be followed. Once the program has been designed the role of the composer is to modify, shape, and select.

The most important figure in electronic or computer music up to now has been Max Mathews of Bell Labs. He developed programs that permitted composers to use computers without concern for the technical details of the machines. There are now music composition laboratories at some of the major universities in the world. A large center for electronic music, the Institut de Recherche et de Coordination Acoustique/Musique (IRCAM), was recently established in Paris. Large record companies release records of electronic music. Fragments of such music appear in movies and television so often now that we are gradually becoming accustomed to its strange and sometimes strident sounds.

However, quite a few discordant sounds have been made as well by critics and the general public. For example, Lars Gunnar Bodin of the Electronic Music Studio of Stockholm has written, "in spite of great efforts in time and money, relatively little of artistic significance has been produced in computer music".[12] The composition of music using mechanical and electronic aids has been subject to criticism similar to that once directed at the mechanical reproduction of music. The German writer E. T. A. Hoffman (about whose life and stories Jacques Offenbach composed the opera *Tales of Hoffman*) wrote the following in 1816:

> *To set to work to make music by means of valves, springs, levers, cylinders, or whatever other apparatus you choose to employ, is a senseless attempt to make the means to an end accomplish what can result only when those means are animated and, in their minutest movements, controlled by the mind, the soul, and the heart. The gravest reproach you can make to a musician is that he plays without expression; because, by so doing, he is marring the whole essence of the matter. For it is impossible that any impulse whatever from the inner man shall not, even for a moment, animate his rendering; whereas, in the case of a machine, no such impulse can ever do so. The attempts of mechanicians to imitate, with more or less approximation to accuracy, the human organs in the production of musical sounds, or to substitute mechanical appliances for those organs, I consider tantamount to a declaration of war against the spiritual element in music; but the greater the forces they array against it, the more victorious it is. For this very reason, the more perfect that this sort of machinery is, the more I disapprove of it; and I infinitely prefer the commonest barrel-organ, in which the mechanism attempts nothing but to be mechanical, to Vaucanson's flute player, or the harmonica girl.*[13]

Before concluding this discussion we should hear from some of the composers themselves. Composer Paul Lansky of Princeton describes himself as a sculptor of sound for whom the computer is an indispensible tool. The composer of computer music is both creator and performer. Composer Charles Dodge says that although 15 years ago there were no great works of computer music, there probably are now. According to him, the computer offers the composer a marvellous set of tools and opens up a "whole uncharted universe of sound."[14]

Visual Arts

Put simply, the computer is becoming a hot item in the art world.[15]

Turning to drawing, graphics, and video art, we find, up to fairly recently, considerable inventiveness but a certain sameness of technique. Facile use of a new and powerful tool may be the problem. As in music, we may have to look to the future for the emergence of real art and not just the obvious exploitation of an available technology. One of the early and important artists to use computers was A. Michael Noll. In an article written in 1967, he makes the point that even though the computer must be programmed to perform each action, its speed, decision-making ability, and large memory give it great power even to the point of appearing to produce the unexpected.[16] The computer permits the artist to explore many possiblities and, in some sense, demonstrates a measure of creativity.

In the interest of exploring this notion, Noll programmed a computer to generate a picture composed of pseudo-random elements resembling paintings done by Piet Mondrian, a well-known twentieth-century artist. The computer-generated picture was displayed, along with a Mondrian painting for the benefit of one hundred subjects, who were asked which they preferred and which was in fact the Mondrian. Fifty-nine percent preferred the computer picture and only twenty-eight percent could identify the Mondrian picture. An interesting fact is that people found the Mondrian too precise and machine-like in its placement of the picture elements, whereas the randomness in the placement of the corresponding picture elements in the computer picture was found pleasing.[17]

Without ignoring or contradicting such research, Noll argues very strongly for a partnership in which the artist maintains creative control. The computer is used to generate possibilities either algorithmically or by introducing a random component. However, the artist is clearly in charge and exploits the power of the computer in a creative partnership. As is not the case with other, more traditional media, the computer is active in an important sense and offers the artist an exciting challenge.

The relationship between art and technology has always been uneasy. It has taken many years for photography to be recognized as art and the suspicion remains that the photographer achieves most by selection rather than by creation, since the camera seems to do most of the work. Thus, it is not surprising that acceptance of such a marvellous piece of equipment as a computer should be resisted by both the public at large and the artist as well. But change is inevitable, given the nature of our times. Ken Sofer, an artist himself has written as follows:

> *By the mid '60's this spirit of experimentation and invention had become nothing less than a cultural imperative. How could a traditional painting or sculpture hope to shock, excite, stimulate, or even draw a glance from an audience weaned on neon billboards, movies, radio and tv? Large, colorful, somtimes kinetic images—plentiful, cheap, disposable—were now part of daily experience, made to be ingested in an instant while the viewer whizzed by on the freeway or flipped through a glossy magazine. The demands of high-speed experience rapidly transferred to art-viewing . . . .*[18]

Somehow these expectations have not been fulfilled. Too frequently the computer is used as an overpriced electronic paintbrush. Most of the results could hardly be termed "fine art": repetitious patterns, distorted images of human forms, and randomly placed patches of randomly generated lines. Sofer adds that, to complete the package, pretentious titles are used: "Combinatorial Cybernetic Still-Life #5000," for example. The situation is really not as grim as Sofer maintains, for many artists have used the computer in a creative and exciting way. One of these is Harold Cohen, who has designed a program called AARON in order to study the way people both produce and understand drawings. Not surprisingly, Cohen has discovered that much of the enjoyment and appreciation of a work of art is brought by the viewer. Many times he has been asked if what is being displayed is indeed art. Another well-known artist who has turned to the computer recently is Philip Pearlstein, famous for his super-realistic nudes. Mr. Pearlstein has described the computer "as another wonderful tool for the artist" and has become quite familiar with tablets, menus, and pixels.

In summarizing the current state of computer art and trying to predict future directions as well, Sofer notes that

> . . .the most successful "computer artists" are those few who do more than merely replace the paintbrush with the electronic pen. These artists use the computer as a means of significantly advancing artistic concerns—a process that often requires conceptual and aesthetic breaks with practices that may have taken a lifetime to develop. Many artists are unwilling (or perhaps unable) to take this leap. In the right hands, though, the computer has proven a remarkably flexible and effective medium for artistic explorations.[19]

However, for those artists who do wish to use the computer to pursue more traditional aims, modern graphics systems do provide a variety of impressive features. At the leading edge of these developments is the Smalltalk group at the Xerox Palo Alto Research Center. This group has developed a system called ToolBox, a computer-assisted drawing system for "general-purpose, interactive image creation and editing." The graphic artist uses a tablet to input an image, and the Toolbox system offers a wide range of facilities to manipulate the image. One simple example: a straight line can be drawn merely by specifying the end points. ToolBox is implemented in Smalltalk-80, an extremely interesting and powerful computer language designed by Alan Kay (then at the Xerox Palo Alto Research Center). (See Chapter 6 for more information about Smalltalk and its educational applications.)

Film

Some would say that movies are *the* exciting domain of contemporary arts. They are another fairly recent art form. In their early years movies were seen mainly as popular entertainment, and profits were the main motive for their production. Almost inadvertently, serious artists were attracted to this new medium and succeeded over time in producing very important and serious artistic endeavors. However, there has always been an uneasy peace between the goals of profit and art. Many of the experimental efforts in film have emerged from a stream outside the so-called commercial film industry.

One of the earliest and most important filmmakers to use the computer as an integral part of the creative process is John Whitney. Fully aware of the potential of computers as early as the 1940s, Whitney observed that

> *the best "computer art" did not compare well with lacework from Belgium made a century ago. But the computer possessed a unique capability of making very complex pattern flow. One could plan exacting and explicit patterns of action and distinctive motions as intricate as lace, but in a way no Belgian lacemaker would ever imagine.*[20]

Whitney created a number of films, with music, generated by computer. They are characterized by the complex development of geometric themes in a rhythmic pattern accompanied by an original musical score. He has no illusions about the role of computers in the creation of art and very bluntly states his beliefs that computers will never create "meaningful" art. The crucial issue in creativity is judgment, not calculation.

It is altogether fitting that the real breakthrough in the application of computers to the making of films was made by Walt Disney Studios in *TRON* (1982). Long the world leader in animated feature films, Disney Studios recognized that the state of the art in computer animation was sufficiently well developed for computers to make a major contribution to filmmaking. The traditional Disney animation system required that many people work over long periods of time to produce thousands upon thousands of drawings. The recent developments in graphics, both in hardware and software, have permitted generation by computer of representational three-dimensional scenes. In all previous movies based on fantasy or science fiction, very complex models—usually quite small—were designed and built. Actors were positioned and cleverly photographed against these models to give the illusion of vast reaches of space, giant castles, enormous space ships and other constructs of the projected future or distant past. Of course many other techniques have been employed in the composition, photography, and editing of films, and computers have played an important role in these phases as well. Over the last few years, advances in graphics software both in the representation of complex solid figures and in their motion, have reached a sufficiently sophisticated level to be useful in film making.

Most of the computer graphics for *TRON* were done for Disney Studios by two companies, Information International, Inc. (Triple-I), and Mathematical Applications Group, Inc. (MAGI). Triple-I was mainly responsible for the design of complex, beautiful scenes. It was MAGI's task to produce the fast-paced action sequences. The integration of live actors and computer graphics is still quite a difficult technical feat. In *TRON*, some frames in the film have been exposed as many as forty-five times to achieve an almost impressionistic effect. Some of the technical specifications were presented in an article by Charles Solomon.

> *The computer images are generated into special, high resolution video screens that contain 4000 horizontal and 6000 vertical lines. (An ordinary television set has a*

mere 525 lines running in each direction.) The lines form a grid, with a point, or pixel, at every intersection—24 million in all. Each pixel is assigned two digital values by the computer. One indicates its relative brightness: the other its color—a proportion of red, blue and green. . . . Up to six hours were required to generate some individual frames.[21]

Most viewers agree that the acting and the plot of *TRON* leave a great deal to be desired. The central and major theme is the extraordinary technology that cascades before the eyes of an amazed but not altogether thunderstruck audience. After all, in some sense, *TRON* is the epitome of the video game writ large. It may be seen as an important breakthrough in popular art, but because it is such a poor film, unfortunately, its significant technical achievements may be overlooked. The trend continues: an uneasy partnership between art and technology. In the early stages of new technological applications, flash usually predominates and novelty almost wins the day. However, if no genuine aesthetic values emerge the technological fireworks will inevitably fizzle out.

Having introduced John Whitney, sometimes called the father of computer films, we complete the circle by becoming acquainted with his son, John Whitney, Jr. Together with his partner Gary Demos, John Whitney, Jr. worked for Information International Inc. (Triple-I) in the making of *TRON* for Disney Studios. Subsequently they formed their own company, Digital Productions, Inc., to make films that used powerful computers and sophisticated graphics equipment or what they call ''digital scene simulation.'' They have leased one of the fastest computers available, the Cray-1 (worth $6.5 million) to carry out their ambitious goals, as follows:

. . . a computer-based system that will produce scripts, scenes, people, and most intriguing, of all behavior. . . . He (Demos) and Whitney both foresee the day when a director will sit down at a terminal, punch in the latest ingredients for producing a first-run hit, connect a port to a cable channel, pop the ''go'' button and boom! A continuous running movie begins complete with a ''crew'' of writers and actors that don't take holidays, or go on strike, get bored, or get burned out.[22]

In July 1984, *The Last Starfighter* was released. It included about 25 minutes of computer-generated film, compared to about 5 minutes in *TRON*. The computer scenes were generated by the aforementioned Digital Productions, using a Cray X-MP. This machine replaced the earlier Cray-1 and was needed in such prodigious computations as those for the hero's space ship *Gunstar*, which required 750,000 polygons and achieved an extraordinarily realistic effect. Interestingly enough, it is a more difficult challenge to represent soft objects such as flowers and people than spaceships and robots.

George Lucas, the creator of the enormously popular and successful *Star Wars* series, has launched a research and development effort to create tools to aid in the production of films. Among these are a system called EditDroid, which uses videodisk technology to edit films and videotapes. The editing process for high technology films is becoming increasingly expensive and time consuming. When the film is transferred to videodisk, the editing is made much easier because no physical splicing is necessary until the entire process is complete. Furthermore, individual frames on a videodisk can be accessed in a few seconds, as opposed to a few minutes with videotape. Another system, called ASP, is the first processor that can digitally mix, edit, and synthesize sound for movies. Down the road are animation systems for creating lifelike three-dimensional images.

Other Arts

The least successful application of computers in the arts has been in generating literature. Experimenters with poetry have achieved their results by putting two kinds of lists into storage: one, words categorized into grammatical classes such as nouns, verbs, and adjectives; the other, a list of patterns for sentences and stanzas. Words are chosen randomly by the program to fill appropriate slots. As you might expect, out of large numbers of poems it is possible to find a few that appeal to some people. The problem in the computer generation of poetry is that beauty lies entirely in the eye of the human beholder. This is especially the case with free verse. For many examples of such verse, it is not obvious that they have been produced by a computer program. Would you be surprised to discover that computers could generate poems that appear to be authored by humans? Since people write such programs and the computer's role is to make many fast, narrowly constrained decisions, in what sense could it be termed creative? At the most basic level, the computer is another in the long history of tools available to people in the pursuit of art. But it is not a passive tool and it must be viewed more as a junior partner. The artist plans, initiates, controls, and selects; the computer increases substantially the artist's range of choices and inspirations.

Other applications that should be mentioned include the use of computers to provide a means for storing choreographic notations. A system of formal notation, long available for music, has so far been lacking for dance (or at least there is no universally acceptable one). Modern graphics systems attempt to deal with this deficiency. Various approaches have involved the development of ways for the computer to represent the human body positioned in a sequence of dance steps. There are a number of different graphics systems available including ones developed by Norman Badler at the University of Pennsylvania, Thomas Calvert at Simon Fraser University, Edward Dombrower, a dancer, and Mike Lopez, an engineer. The representation of the human body varies from stick figure to a bubble or sausage-shaped image. How to realistically depict movements of the human body is still a difficult problem.

Finally, the computer has been used in both the restoration and analysis of art works. For example, in the field of computer-aided investigation into old masters, a lost Leonardo da Vinci mural was revealed by an ultrasonic scanning system that used a small computer for image processing. It is also possible, in a nondestructive fashion, to reveal paintings hidden beneath other paintings. Computers have been used to reduce noise levels in old recordings and to restore films transferred to video tape. In literature, studies have been carried out, to verify or determine the authorship of disputed texts. The number of applications is large and growing.

CONTEMPORARY VIEWS OF THE MACHINE

We are living in an age of science and technology. The newsstand has exploded with *Omni, Science Digest, Science 86, High Technology, Technology Review, Discovery,* and other magazines whose covers advertise stories on biotechnology, artificial life, new theories of the universe, and, inevitably, computers. In addition to the purely technological articles on how microprocessors will revolutionize our lives, stories on intelligent machines appear with regularity. We are told how computers will do the work of doctors, lawyers, and other professionals and that robots will soon be making regular appearances in our homes and in our places of work and play.

The public at large is infatuated with the robot. The immensely popular R2D2 and C3PO are totally dedicated to the well-being of their human masters. They are the complete antithesis of, say, Frankenstein's monster and are, in fact, a realization of the kind of robot proposed by Isaac Asimov. We are now in the era of the robot as friend and servant. Some voices have been raised in warning about the possibility of massive unemployment resulting from the introduction of robots into the assembly line. The counter-argument is that robots will be engaged in boring and dangerous activities and thus free people to realize their full potential in other areas of life. In any case, robots are on the way. We are even being encouraged to attribute robotic qualities to household devices that incorporate electronics—manufacturers inform us in their advertisements that our televisions, microwave ovens, cameras, and other pieces of everyday equipment have an ''electronic brain'' that can think (for us) and therefore act for us.

Intelligent machines may not be an entirely unmixed blessing, as you will recall from that powerful motion picture, *2001: A space odyssey.* A computer called HAL (a name only one letter removed from IBM) begins acting unpredictably as it tries to ensure the success of the space mission, believing that it is in jeopardy because of the actions of the human crew. It causes the death of two men before it is dismantled by the one remaining human. As its circuits are progressively disconnected it appeals piteously to be allowed to continue functioning. It even promises to be good in the future. All this is to no avail, as it has in fact violated Asimov's First Law and must be punished.

This impressive film leaves us with the assured feeling that we humans will retain ultimate control because we can ''pull the plug.'' The popular media generally present a favorable viewpoint toward robots or intelligent machines: They will secure more leisure time for everyone and liberate people from dangerous work; they will mine the seas, explore space, and bring prosperity to all. However, some nonscientific observers think that if machines become intelligent enough they will develop a sense (a strategy) of self-preservation that will cause them to defend their existence. The scientific approach to the development of intelligent machines is called Artificial Intelligence.

ARTIFICIAL INTELLIGENCE: A BRIEF INTRODUCTION
Machines and Living Things Compared

In a paper written in 1955, Anatol Rapoport points out the strong relationship between the level of technology and contemporaneous mechanical models of living things.[23] He first defines a technological "phylum," in comparison with a biological phylum, as characterized by a principle of operation. He then goes on to distinguish four technological phyla that came into being successively. The first phylum is the tool that serves primarily to transmit muscular forces; the second is clockworks that operate under the principle of stored mechanical energy, released subsequently and perhaps gradually; the third is heat engines that operate on supplied fuels; the fourth is machines that operate on the principle of storing and transmitting information.

Because tools do not operate independently, they have rarely been compared to living things, although weapons are often personified in mythology, for example, King Arthur's Excalibur and Sicgfried's Nothung. The second phylum, however, has suggested living things, especially in such complex realizations as mechanical dolls and animals. (In fact, for Descartes, animals were equivalent to highly complicated automata that lacked only souls to differentiate them from humans). The main difficulty with clockworks is that their source of energy is too much unlike the source of energy of living things to allow for a strong comparison. The analogy to living things becomes much stronger when we turn to heat engines powered by such fuels as coal and oil. "It became apparent that machines could be constructed which did not need to be 'pushed' but only 'fed' in order to do work."

In the early twentieth century, the development of the telephone switchboard served as a technological model for the central nervous system. This model, together with the physiological research on the reflex arc, suggested—mainly to the early behaviorists—that "behavior was. . .a grand collection of units called reflexes," to use Rapoport's words.

It was with the arrival of the fourth phylum, however, best represented by the general purpose digital computer, that the possibilities of "thinking machines" became most likely, at least in the opinion of the most devoted practitioners of Artificial Intelligence (AI). Here is a machine of such structural and behavioral complexity that comparisons to the human brain invite serious analysis. Computers are applied to an incredibly wide variety of tasks including many that were formerly the sole province of humans. This gradual encroachment on a private domain has undoubtedly indicated to many people that it is only a matter of time until no exclusively human activities or skills remain. As has often been pointed out, whereas the first industrial revolution replaced man's muscle, the second is replacing his hand and brain.

Few disciplines can have their historical beginnings precisely determined as AI can. In the summer of 1956, a number of researchers met at Dartmouth College to discuss issues of mutual concern focussed on the central question of how to program machines (digital computers) to exhibit intelligent behavior. Among the attendees were Marvin Minsky, John McCarthy (who is said to have suggested the term Artificial Intelligence), Alan Newell, and Herbert Simon (subsequently a Nobel laureate in economics). They gave impetus to, and shaped the direction of, research for years to come. The story of their motivations, how they attempted to realize them, and the major developments—a tale of almost epic dimensions—is recounted by Pamela McCorduck in her book *Machines Who Think*.[24] A shorter version will be presented here.

There are a number of reasons to introduce AI at this point. First, it represents the current best attempt, together with cognitive science, to understand the nature of intelligent behavior. Second, the computational models it has developed have had an impact on a variety of disciplines such as linguistics, psychology, education, and philosophy. Third, and probably most important, is its current visibility in the public eye as a developer of systems for providing "senses" for industrial robots, natural language interfaces for databases, expert systems for chemistry, medicine, prospecting, and so forth. Aside from the typical, sensational claims made for AI in the public media, there are some solid achievements and, more importantly, some hope for significant accomplishments in the future.

A Short History of Artificial Intelligence

A number of events coincided after the Second World War to give rise to the new discipline called AI. Most important, of course, was development of the digital computer, significantly accelerated by the needs of war research. A significant paper written in 1943 by Warren McCulloch and Walter Pitts, called, "A Logical Calculus of the Ideas Immanent in Nervous Activity,"[25] stimulated a number of people to explore the possibilities of achieving intelligent behavior from a machine. In 1948 Norbert Wiener's *Cybernetics* appeared. This book was subtitled "Control and Communication in the Animal and the Machine" and arose from Wiener's wartime research for designing mechanisms to control antiaircraft guns.[26] Researchers interested in intelligent behavior were stimulated to apply the principles of feedback, whereby a system's desired goals are compared to its current situation in order to drive the system closer to where it should be.

Much of the early research could be characterized by its reference to such terms as *adaptive, learning,* or *self-organizing.* That is, what seemed to be required was the application of powerful and general learning principles to a system with very little built-in knowledge. There were hopes of simulating certain aspects of the neuronal structure of the brain, based both on the McCulloch and Pitts work and that of the psychologist Donald Hebb. However, by the early 1960s the directions for the next 20 years were firmly in place. Basically, work on learning systems was abandoned, especially in North America, and the effort turned toward determining how knowledge could be represented in a computer and furthermore how it could be used to solve problems, play games, "see" the world, communicate in natural language, and even infer new knowledge.

Right from the outset of this new direction two streams developed that were sometimes complementary and sometimes antagonistic. One arose from parallel developments in psychology that signalled a movement away from the then-dominant theoretical position of behaviorism toward the newly emerging field of information processing or cognitive psychology. Here the metaphor of information processing by computer was applied to the human system and the heretofore restricted domain of the human mind. Practitioners design models, construct programs, and carry out experiments in an attempt to answer questions about how humans think, solve problems, use language, and see the world.

The second stream is concerned with the building of computer programs to exhibit various aspects of human behavior. That is, to program a computer to solve problems, it is not obviously necessary that the methods used have anything, or much, in common with how people do it. Researchers in AI may be influenced in designing their programs by a variety of sources, of which perceived human methods is one and introspection, hardware architecture, available software, and computational limitations are others. It may turn out that the programs developed are suggestive of mechanisms underlying human performance, but this result is not the primary aim of the researchers.

In the early 1960s, programs were developed to play games such as checkers and chess, communicate in English, prove theorems in logic and geometry, and recognize simple patterns. Their level of performance was not very high in general but there were indications that a new enterprise had been launched that promised to make a major contribution to the study of intelligent behavior. In these early years, AI was sometimes viewed as a somewhat less than respectable branch of computer science. Since then, however, the founding fathers, as they are sometimes called—John McCarthy, Marvin Minsky, Alan Newell, and Herbert Simon—have all been awarded Turing Awards. The Turing Award is given annually to outstanding figures in computer science by the Association for Computing Machinery (ACM), the major association of computer scientists in the United States.

In the mid-1960s much of the research effort was devoted to robotics or integrated artificial intelligence. This work is discussed in Chapter 12. We can mention here that a number of hand-eye systems were built consisting of a computer-controlled mechanical arm and television camera, as well as one mobile robot called "Shaky." Out of this period came a renewed interest in the major components of intelligent behavior, namely vision or image understanding, natural language understanding, problem solving, game-playing and so forth. It became quite clear that the major issues underlying much of the research in AI could be characterized—but not solved, of course—by two words: representation and control. That is, it will be necessary to represent vast amounts of knowledge in the computer even to carry out rather simple tasks. Of course, knowledge is not enough; how and when to use it—control—is of paramount importance.

In pursuit of these goals, new programming languages have been developed. LISP, designed by John McCarthy, was among the earliest and clearly the most important. Some of the ideas incorporated in these languages have been adopted by other language designers. A history of ideas for AI would show that many formerly esoteric notions arising from

AI research have become commonplace in other fields. This has become a major side effect of the research.

During the 1970s the earlier research areas continued to develop, with new branches emerging. Among the latter are expert systems, knowledge engineering, advanced question-answering interfaces to databases, and a variety of new applications. The work in expert systems involves the design and building of large programs to incorporate specialized knowledge and inference mechanisms in order to advise and assist users of the system. Several such systems have been developed in specific branches of medicine, chemistry, and even prospecting. Typically, teams of researchers, both computer scientists and experts, work together to extract and reformulate the specialized knowledge. Programs are written, tested, and modified until they achieve a satisfactory level of performance. For example, one of the earliest expert programs, called MYCIN, was designed to aid a physician in selecting an appropriate antibiotic to treat a blood infection.

The problem for the doctor is to prescribe one of the many available antibiotics before all the laboratory tests results are in. This situation usually requires the doctor to weigh the various known symptoms in order to narrow the range of possible infections, with an aim to selecting the antibiotic that best covers the spectrum of likely diseases. The program incorporates a reasoning system that tries to simulate that of a good diagnostician. (More detail will be given in Chapter 5.)

Artificial Intelligence Now

In the last few years, AI has made a significant impact in the business community. Many university researhers have set up their own companies to exploit their research efforts. There are a number of companies that offer natural language interfaces to large databases. Other companies are marketing visual systems to be used with industrial robots for assembly line operations. Some researchers have formed consulting companies to introduce AI techniques into both manufacturing and office environments. Even more interesting is that several major computer corporations such as Texas Instruments, Hewlett-Packard, and Fairchild Semiconductors, (a division of Schlumberger) have made important contributions to AI research and development. Thus, this rather exotic subdiscipline of computer science is becoming a significant factor in the computer marketplace. Witness the cover of *Business Week,* July 1984: "Artificial Intelligence: it's here."

There are critics of the AI enterprise, and their arguments range from questioning the morality of doing research that can be used by government in surveillance activities to concern about the possibly false philosophical principles that underlie AI. The former position is held by Joseph Weizenbaum of the Massachusetts Institute of Technology. Much of the early research in AI well into the 1970s in the United States was in fact funded by The Advanced Projects Research Agency (ARPA) of the Air Force. This association led some critics to suggest that the major beneficiary of the research would be the defense establishment. An important research area in the early 1970s was speech understanding. In this process a computer, programmed to receive the electrical signal resulting from the transformation of the acoustic speech wave, produced first a representation in words and second a representation of the underlying meaning. It was Weizenbaum's claim that one of the goals of this research was to enable the U.S. secruity agencies to monitor conversations automatically and determine whether or not they posed a risk to the government. His argument was also broader, in that he criticized the entire enterprise for attempting to produce what he called an "alien intelligence." Thus, while programs that could engage in a broad range of behavior might be possible, they would not be desirable because they would be fundamentally at odds with the human experience and spirit. Not surprisingly, this opinion was immediately and vigorously challenged by leading researchers in the field.

Criticism on the basis of philosophical principles was launched by Hubert Dreyfus of the University of California at Berkeley. He argued that the goals of AI were impossible in principle and that researchers were either misguided or were misleading the community at large. More recently he has criticized the claims made for expert systems, countering them with the contention that human expertise is too deep, too broad, and too open-ended to be captured by a computer program. Dreyfus contends that because the dominant stream of Western philosophy, namely analytic philosophy, is bankrupt, any applied research based on it, such as AI, will not succeed. These charges have been largely ignored in the AI community and sometimes angrily denounced as being ill-informed. In recent years, other philosophers have found useful ideas in AI.

When all is said and done, AI has become an important factor both in computer science and in society at large. It is clear that the development of intelligent or even pseudo-intelligent machines will have a significant impact on our future. The role of AI in the various areas investigated in this book, will be assessed, for it has become much more than an academic discipline. Furthermore, note that it will not be necessary for sophisticated systems to be developed before their impact is felt. The premature use of pseudo-intelligent machines may introduce the unfortunate possibility of people being forced to adapt to machines that are not really very smart at all. As we shall see in the next chapter, the emergence of the "chip" will also significantly increase the impact of computers in general and "intelligent" ones in particular.

SUMMARY

The human fascination with artifacts that mimic human behavior is longstanding and has inspired tales and legends from many cultures. Particular noteworthy are the automata built by the Jacquet-Droz family of Switzerland between 1768 and 1774. The theme of robots and their ambiguous relation to their human creators has been expressed in such works as *Frankenstein, R.U.R.,* and *2001: A space odyssey.* In the twentieth century Isaac Asimov, in his robot stories, and George Lucas, in his *Star Wars* series of movies, have presented robots whose sole purpose has been to serve their human masters.

By many artists, musicians, and film makers the computer is seen as a new and powerful tool for the creation of art. Supercomputers are being used to generate extraordinarily realistic film images, doing away with the need for special models and special photographic effects.

In the mid-1950s a new scientific discipline made its appearance. Its goal was to develop computer programs to exhibit intelligent behavior. Its name is Artificial Intelligence and its contributions to technology will be significant. AI techniques are currently being used in vision systems for robots, natural language interfaces for databases, and expert systems for many applications.

NOTES

1. Robertson Davies, *World of Wonders* (Middlesex: Penguin, 1977), p. 60.

2. John Cohen, *Human Robots in Myth and Science* (London: Allen & Unwin, 1977).

3. Joseph Needham, *Science and Civilization in China,* History of Scientific Thought, vol. 2 (Cambridge: Cambridge University Press, 1956), p. 53.

4. John Kobler, "The Strange World of M. Charliat," *Saturday Evening Post,* March 25, 1955, p. 70.

5. W. Grey Walter, "An Imitation of Life," *Scientific American,* May 1950, p. 44.

6. Marvin L. Minsky, *Information* (San Francisco: Freeman, 1966), p. 210.

7. W. W. Jacobs, *The Monkey's Paw* (New Rochelle: Spoken Arts Records, SA1090, 1970).

8. Patricia S. Warrick, *The Cybernetic Imagination in Science Fiction* (Cambridge: MIT Press, 1980).

9. Samuel Butler, *Erewhon* (New York: New American Library, 1960), p. 180.

10. Karel Capek, *R.U.R.* (London: Oxford University Press, 1923).

11. Isaac Asimov, "Runaround" in *I, Robot* (London: Granada, 1968), pp. 33–51.

12. Lars Gunnar Bodin, in Leopold Froehlich, "Give Tchaikovsky the News," *Datamation,* October 1981, p. 136.

13. E. T. A. Hoffman, "Automata," in E. F. Bleiler, ed., *The Best Tales of Hoffman* (New York: Dover, 1967).

14. Charles Dodge, in Froehlich, "Give Tchaikovsky the News," p. 140.

15. Joan Darragh, as quoted in Paul Gardner, "Think of Leonardo Wielding a Pixel and a Mouse," *The New York Times,* April 2, 1984, Section 2, p. 1.

16. A. Michael Noll, "The Digital Computer as a Creative Medium," *IEEE Spectrum,* October 1967. Reprinted in Zenon W. Pylyshyn, ed., *Perspectives on the Computer Revolution* (Englewood Cliffs: Prentice-Hall, 1970), pp. 349–358.

17. Ibid., pp. 354–355.

18. Ken Sofer, "Art? Or Not Art?" *Datamation,* October 1981, p. 120.

19. Ibid., p. 127.

20. John Whitney, *Digital Harmony* (New York: McGraw-Hill/Byte Books, 1980), p. 30.

21. Charles Solomon, "The Secrets of Tron," *Rolling Stone,* August 19, 1982, p. 15.

22. Jan Johnson, "From Fortran to Film," *Datamation,* August 1982, p. 72.

23. Anatol Rapoport, "Technological Models of the Nervous System," Reprinted in K. M. Sayre and F. J. Crosson, eds., *The Modelling of Mind* (New York: Simon & Schuster, 1968), pp. 25–38.

24. Pamela McCorduck, *Machines Who Think* (San Francisco: Freeman, 1979).

25. Warren McCulloch and Walter Pitts, ''A Logical Calculus of the Ideas Immanent in Nervous Activity,'' *Bulletin of Mathematical Biophysics,* vol. 5, 1943, pp. 115–133.

26. Norbert Wiener, *Cybernetics: Control and Communication in the Animal and the Machine,* 2nd ed. (New York: Wiley, 1961).

ADDITIONAL READINGS

Computers as a Creative Medium

''Artificial Intelligence,'' *Business Week,* July 9, 1984, pp. 54–7, 60–2.

Bowman, William, and Bob Flegel, ''Toolbox: A Smalltalk Illustration System.'' *Byte,* August 1981, pp. 369–376.

Cherlin, Merrill. ''Mona Lisa in the Nude??'' *Datamation,* June 1982, pp. 32–34.

Demos, Gary, Maxine D. Brown, and Richard A. Weinberg, ''Digital Scene Simulation: The Synergy of Computer Technology and Human Creativity.'' *Proceedings of the IEEE,* January 1984, pp. 22–31.

''George Lucas Moves his Sci-Fi Genius to the Production Room.'' *Business Week,* December 5, 1983, pp. 184, 186.

Menosky, Joseph. ''Video Graphics & Grand Jetes.'' *Science 82,* May 1982, pp. 24–32.

Myers, Edith. ''Cray Conquers H[olly]wood.'' *Datamation,* July 1, 1984, pp. 24–27, 30, 32.

Artificial Intelligence: A Brief Introduction

Barr, Avrom, and Edward A. Feigenbaum (eds.). *The Handbook of Artificial Intelligence,* vols. 1–3. (Los Altos, Cal.: William Kaufman, 1981–1983).

Dennett, Daniel. *Brainstorms* (Montgomery, Vt.: Bradford Books, 1978).

Dreyfus, Hubert. *What Computers Can't Do,* 2nd ed. (New York: Harper & Row, 1979).

Feigenbaum, Edward A., and Pamela McCorduck. *The Fifth Generation,* (Reading, Mass.: Addison-Wesley, 1983).

Haugeland, John (ed.). *Mind Design* (Cambridge: The MIT Press (A Bradford Book), 1981).

Hebb, Donald. *The Organization of Behavior* (New York: Wiley, 1949).

Nilsson, Nils. *Principles of Artificial Intelligence* (Palo Alto, Cal.: Tioga, 1980).

O'Shea, Tim, and Marc Eisenstadt. *Artificial Intelligence: Tools, Techniques, and Applications* (New York: Harper & Row, 1984).

Raphael, Bertram. *The Thinking Computer* (San Francisco: Freeman, 1976).

Schank, Roger. *The Cognitive Computer* (Reading, Mass.: Addison-Wesley, 1984).

von Neumann, J. *The Computer and the Brain* (New Haven: Yale University Press, 1958).

Winston, Patrick H. *Artificial Intelligence.* 2nd ed. (Reading, Mass.: Addison-Wesley, 1983).

Weizenbaum, Joseph. *Computer Power and Human Reason* (San Francisco: Freeman, 1976).

3

CRITICISM AND HISTORY

The clock, not the steam engine, is the key-machine of the modern industrial age. For every phase of its development the clock is both the outstanding fact and the typical symbol of the machine: even today no other machine is so ubiquitous. . . .

The clock, moreover, served as a model for many other kinds of mechanical works, and the analysis of motion that accompanied the perfection of the clock, with the various types of gearing and transmission that were elaborated, contributed to the success of quite different kinds of machines. . . .

The clock, moreover, is a piece of power-machinery whose "product" is seconds and minutes: by its essential nature it dissociated time from human events and helped create the belief in an independent world of mathematically measurable sequences: the special world of sciences.

◇ *Lewis Mumford,* Technics and Civilization, *1934.* ◇

INTRODUCTION

Computers did not suddenly appear. Technological innovation does not arise from thin air. There are strata of previous technological achievements and economic and human resources. We frequently assume that our times are unique and that only our particular genius could have brought forth such wonders. Many craftsmen, inventors, and scientists laid the necessary groundwork for the modern computer. Its history extends from the invention of the abacus to the designing of the Jacquard loom and beyond.

> *There is a time when the operation of the machine becomes so odious, makes you so sick at heart that you can't take part; you can't even passively take part, and you've got to put your bodies upon the gears and upon the wheels, upon the levers, upon all the apparatus and you've got to indicate to the people who run it, to the people who own it, that unless you're free, the machine will be prevented from working at all.* (*Mario Savio, Berkeley, December 2, 1964.*)

For many, the above quotation was the rallying cry of the protest movement of the 1960s and early 1970s in the United States. It seemed to express the feelings of many that the state was a powerful, oppressive machine grinding up its young to further its single-minded aims. The issue here is not politics, but this perception of technology in control. It is necessary and important to confront the criticisms raised, if not to answer them completely.

COMMENTS ON TECHNOLOGICAL CHANGE

The following two points of view—two caricatures, perhaps—define the conflicting poles of the debate.

> Computers are just tools. We as their inventors and employers decide what we shall do with them. They are more complex and have greater potential than other tools but you should never forget that ultimately that is what they are. All statements to the contrary are alarmist.

> A computer is not just another tool. Computers can perform activities that previously only people could do. Furthermore, by virtue of their enormous speed and capacity they can give unpredictable results when applied in new areas. They already endanger privacy, employment, even freedom. Although previous tools posed some of these difficulties, the computer represents not just more of the same but an obvious quantum jump.

You may not have yet formed an opinion on this issue. In fact it may be premature to expect it. Even if you agree with the first viewpoint, you might in daily life be expected to defend that view again and again as the computerization of society proceeds and new issues crop up. Computers are here and now. Can we still shape our own destiny?

Computers are in a real sense a natural continuation of technological development, and there exists a large body of commentary on the effects and dangers of technology itself. Important scholars have provided a number of incisive insights and warnings.

Machine analogies can be readily perceived in human situations. For Lewis Mumford, the slave population involved in building the pyramids can be seen as a mega-machine, the individual humans analogous to cogs and gears, each performing a limited repeatable task. Siegfried Giedion views the assembly line in a similar manner. In one of his most damning criticisms of modern technology he shows how bread has evolved from nourishing food to convenient, well-packaged, food product. The claim that technology is neutral and merely a tool that can be used for good or ill is subjected to a major critique by Jacques Ellul. The association of technology with totalitarianism in the advanced industrial state is a subject for study by Herber Marcuse. Norbert Wiener points out that just by virtue of its size and speed the computer can go beyond being a tool and in some sense create a new reality.

In an important article published in 1969, John McDermott describes technology as "the opiate of the educated public, or at least its favorite authors."[1] He gives a representative list of the fruits of the cornucopia as seen by a number of the so-called prophets of technology.

> *An end to poverty and the inauguration of permanent prosperity (Leon Keyserling), universal equality of opportunity (Zbigniew Brzezinski), a radical increase in individual freedom (Edward Shils), the replacement of work by leisure for most of mankind (Robert Theobald), fresh water for desert dwellers (Lyndon Johnson), permanent but harmless social revolution [and] the final come-uppance of Mao-Tse-tung and all his ilk (Walt Rostow), and, lest we forget, the end of ideology (Daniel Bell).[2]*

This brief characterization of points of view should be fleshed out. In all the uproar over the wonders of technology, there should be place for a few wise voices with a message of caution and concern. This book explores the impact of recent computer developments. Beyond the initial, obvious benefits, future problems may lurk. It is worth listening to the group of critics, historians, and commentators that includes Mumford, Giedion, Ellul, Marcuse and Wiener—the old, but honorable, guard.

Lewis Mumford

A major social critic and the grand old man of the environmental movement, Mumford is also a distinguished historian of technology. In a long series of books beginning in 1922, he has been especially concerned to establish the continuity of craftsmanship and technology down through the ages. Furthermore, he has attempted to catalog and analyze the variety of forces technology brings to bear against the maintenance of humanity in everyday life. Power, centralization, autocracy, mechanization, and control are a few of the key words that only begin to suggest the many issues that have exercised him for so many years. It is difficult to do justice to a lifetime of scholarship in so brief a space.

We will here be concerned with Mumford's analysis of the impact of computers and automation. He is disturbed not so much by the physical replacement of workers as by the elimination of the human mind and spirit from the process of production. The spirit suffers because of the elevation of computer decision-making and the parallel subordination of individual initiative. The system or organization becomes all-knowing and all-powerful. The individual—both as scientist, engineer, or manager and as consumer—must abide by the established rules even if there is a loss of a human way of life.

For Mumford, the computer itself and its role in automation is just one more step along a road of constrained human choice. He has traced the enslavement of people from the building of the pyramids, under an organizational scheme that he likens to a machine, to the development and refinement of the modern assembly line. It is not inevitable that technology be used to enslave society (even assuming that we feel enslaved), because decisions as to its use must frequently be consciously made. If we have the knowledge and the will, we can structure society so that spontaneity and choice are encouraged and even rewarded. But if computers are left to make what are fundamentally human decisions the consequences may be indeed serious, because computers may be programmed to return only those results desired by the leaders and managers.

In contrast to these perceived limitations in computers, strenuously challenged of course by most computer enthusiasts, Mumford offers a paean to the human brain.

> *Unfortunately, computer knowledge, because it must be processed and pro-grammed, cannot remain constantly in touch, like the human brain, with the un-ceasing flow of reality; for only a small part of experience can be arrested for ex-traction and expression in abstract symbols. Changes that cannot be quantitatively measured or objectively observed, such changes as take place constantly all the way from the atom to the living organism, are outside the scope of the computer. For all its fantastic rapidity of operation, its components remain incapable of making quali-tative responses to constant organic changes.*[3]

Siegfried Giedion

The major work of the architectural and social critic Siegfried Giedion, *Mechanization Takes Command*, appeared in 1948, before computers had achieved a significant presence.[4] He is concerned with the process by which traditional human activities have gradually been assumed by machines to the obvious detriment of the final product. He is interested in "the elimination of the complicated handicraft."[5] An important example is the making of bread, long a central enterprise of human existence. From the beginnings of agriculture and the cultivation of wheat, the preparation of bread has been a necessary and honorable activity. The connection of humans with the organic is well exemplified through bread, its manufacturing (i.e., making by hand), distribution, and consumption. Riots have been provoked by scarcity of bread or slight increases in its price. The images conjured up by the simple phrase "the breaking of bread" are suggestions of basic human relations: sharing, participating, a sense of community, a willingness to understand, and a desire to reaffirm historical continuity.

The problem is, the quality of bread today is highly suspect. For the most part in North America, it looks and tastes like cardboard. Few remember, or even care, what a treat real bread can be. The story begins with the mechanization of kneading, clearly a strenuous activity requiring pulling and pushing and the use of feet as well as hands. In the late eighteenth century, the French pharmacologist Antoine Augustin Pametier described kneading as a process in which flour, yeast, water, and air are sufficiently well mixed to produce a new substance. It is clear that kneading is physically difficult and an obvious candidate for mechanization. Mechanical rotary kneaders were developed as far back as the Romans, and experiments continued through the Renaissance into the industrial era. Surprisingly, however, complete mechanization did not take place until after 1925, with the introduction of the high-speed mixer in the United States. Whereas early machines simulated the action of human hands, the high-speed mixer has an agitator that "usually consists of two arms attached to simple steel bars, which perform sixty to eighty revolutions a minute."[6] In explaining why they have not been widely adopted in Europe, Giedion notes that the more delicate European wheats cannot accommodate to the tremendous speed and shocks produced by these mixers. Beyond the efficiency of using the mixers, there was a stronger motivation: "the main reason seems to have been that the energetic mixing made possible the manufacture of a bread even whiter than before."[7]

The final stage in the process is baking. Again, over time a satisfactory form of oven evolved. It resembled an egg, a shape that proved economical and advantageous for uniform heat distribution. However, there were limitations involved in the method of heating, the means for sweeping out embers, and the problems of dealing with large quantities of bread. And so the shape, size, and method of heating evolved: steel plates replaced brick and gas heaters replaced coal. Still, mechanization was not complete because what was needed was an assembly line process to measure and allocate the ingredients, to mix them into dough, and to cut, weigh, mold, and position the individual portions on a conveyor belt ready for the oven. As early as 1840, the French had achieved the mass production of bread.

Other aspects of the mechanization process should be mentioned. Two basic ferments were used to make the dough rise, yeast and leaven. These underwent a number of chemical transformations to speed up the fermentation process, increasing the weight of the bread. For example, carbonic acid increased the speed of fermentation and human labor was thereby reduced. Additional chemicals were added to make bread look whiter. These additives were used as long ago as the mid-eighteenth century. Even the milling process to produce the flour was altered to produce a whiter, cleaner product. At the beginning of the nineteenth century artificial bleaching was introduced to decrease the aging process and improve the whiteness. More recently, vitamins have been added to replace the nourishment lost through the actions of the previous processes.

As a result of all these innovations, in North America the bread factory has largely replaced the bakery. The small egg-shaped oven has become the 100-foot tunnel oven. The complete process has been mechanized, from the mixing, in several stages, to the dividing, the rounding into balls, the moulding, the placing into pans, and the high-speed fermentation to, finally, the baking of the bread in the oven on an endless conveyor belt. The cooling process is accelerated by artificial means, and the bread is sliced, packaged, and distributed.[8] One question remains. What has happened to the bread?

The technological process has certainly produced a bread of uniform quality, which, it is argued, the public demands.

> *The bread of full mechanization has the resiliency of rubber sponge. When squeezed it returns to its former shape. The loaf becomes constantly whiter, more elastic, and frothier. . . . Since mechanization, it has often been pointed out, white bread has become much richer in fats, milk, and sugar. But these are added largely to stimulate sales by heightening the loaf's eye-appeal. The shortenings used in bread, a leading authority states, are ''primarily for the purpose of imparting desirable tender eating or chewing qualities to the finished product.'' They produce the ''soft velvet crumb,'' a cakelike structure, so that the bread is half-masticated, as it were, before reaching the mouth.*[9]

The story of bread teaches that in the face of increased mechanization there is a strong tendency for the natural to suffer. But is it inevitable? Visitors to San Francisco rave about its sourdough bread, which is mass-produced. French bread is world famous for its taste, texture, and smell and is usually sold by small, family-owned bakeries. Thus, technology is inextricably woven into the social fabric of a culture. If it is important to maintain the quality of bread, independent of issues of mass production and distribution, it will be maintained. Therefore, to understand how technology affects the quality of life it is necessary, at the very least, to understand how public opinion is formed and shaped and how it manifests itself in the accommodation of the new. However, there is one critic of technology who argues that we don't have a real choice.

Jacques Ellul

A French sociologist, Jacques Ellul has become one of the world's foremost critics of technology. His major work, published in France in 1954, appeared in the United States in 1964 under the title *The Technological Society.*[10] He presents a very grim picture, indeed. He views technology as an irresistible, mysterious force, far more menacing than either Mumford or Giedion have supposed. It has an ability to change every aspect of life that it encounters. First, it is necessary to understand what Ellul means by *technique.* It is similar to Giedon's *mechanization* but much stronger.

> *The term* technique, *as I use it, does not mean machines, technology, or this or that procedure for attaining an end. In our technological society,* technique *is the* totality of methods rationally arrived at and having absolute efficiency *(for a given stage of development) in every field of human activity. Its characteristics are new; the technique of the present has no common measure with that of the past. (Emphasis added.)*[11]

The sense of the term will become clearer as we continue.

Ellul argues that although techniques derive from crafts and methods prior to the eighteenth century, there has been a quantitative change, and technique has taken on a life of its own with its own internal logic. Initiated by the labors of past generations, it has somehow become a separate force with potentially terrible consequences.

Ellul presents four explanations of why technique was constrained until the eighteenth century.

1. Only certain constrained areas were amenable to technique.
2. Other areas of life such as leisure, social intercourse, sleep, prayer, and play were more predominant.
3. Technique was local and spread slowly.
4. The geographical and historical isolation of societies permitted, indeed required, the flourishing of many different types of techniques.

The situation is different now—we face the new and terrible power of technique and its unremitting campaign against human individuality. Progress still depends on the individual, but only within the terms defined by technique. Thus, efficiency is of prime concern, and aesthetics and ethics are sacrificed. Progress is a concept inherent in the system and is largely unrelated to the desires or wishes of the people.

It almost seems as if technique is some kind of living, breathing monster out of control, our control at least, with its own aims and its own means of achieving them. What are some of the features of this monster?

> [*Technique*] *has been extended to all spheres and encompasses every activity, including human activities. It has led to a multiplication of means without limit. It has perfected indefinitely the instruments available to man, and put at his disposal an almost limitless variety of intermediaries and auxiliaries. Technique has been extended geographically so that it covers the whole earth. It is evolving with a rapidity disconcerting not only to the man in the street but to the technician himself. It poses problems which recur endlessly and ever more acutely in human social groups. Moreover, technique has become objective and is transmitted like a physical thing; it leads thereby to a certain unity of civilization, regardless of the environment or the country in which it operates.*[12]

Here, in brief, are some of the characteristics of technique as it operates currently:

Rationality.   Aspects of management such as standardization, division of labor, and quality control.

Artificiality.   Technique creates an artificial world, denying and eliminating the natural world.

Automatism of Technical Choice.   The human has no role to play. Technique acts and people observe.

Self-augmentation.   Technique changes and evolves with no help or direct intervention by people.

Monism.   Technique forms a single whole and its various components are self-reinforcing.

The Necessary Linking Together of Techniques.   There seems to be a historical necessity operating in which the technique at one stage must follow the one at a previous stage.

Technical Universalism.   Geographic—technique has been spread by commerce, war, and the export of technicians. Qualitative—technique has taken over the whole of civilization.

The Autonomy of Technique.   A good example is the functioning of an industrial plant as a closed system that is independent of the goals and needs of the society in which it exists.

Since it is not really made clear how technique has evolved, it is certainly not clear what, if anything, can be done. In contradistinction to Ellul's unrelieved pessimism, evidence can be offered of how much life has improved over the years. The obvious decreases in hunger and sickness, the lengthening of the life span, and the increase in literacy are proof of the fruits of technology. Ellul's critics would grant that all is not roses but on balance the good brought by technology far outweighs the ills.

Herbert Marcuse

A social philosopher and political theorist, Marcuse has written on Freud and Marx. In his political writings he is very much concerned with the relation between political power and the quality of life. He analyzes the growth of technology, especially under capitalism, and its impact on people's lives. Marcuse believes that there is a strong connection between political power and technology and that, furthermore, the state maintains itself through its control of industrial productivity. This power reaches out through all aspects of life, and transfers traces of the machine ethic to them. In *One-Dimensional Man* Marcuse describes the relation between people and their things (to which may be added, in a natural extension, the computer).

> *We are again confronted with one of the most vexing aspects of advanced industrial civilization: the rational character of its irrationality. Its productivity and efficiency, its capacity to increase and spread comforts, to turn waste into need, and destruction into construction, the extent to which the civilization transforms the object world into an extension of man's mind and body makes the very notion of alienation questionable. The people recognize themselves in their commodities; they find their soul in their automobile, hi-fi set, split-level home, kitchen equipment. The very mechanism which ties the individual to his society has changed, and social control is anchored in the new needs which it has produced.*[13]

From his political perspective, Marcuse argues that automation will ultimately lead to a socialist state after the capitalist industrial machine has done its worst. Presumably, when the workers assume control of the means of production, they will humanize the work place, freeing themselves from boring and dangerous jobs. Their goal will be not to maximize profits but to liberate the human spirit. In Marcuse's opinion, true freedom will ultimately emerge from automation. This view contrasts sharply with that of Ellul.

Norbert Wiener

Called the father of cybernetics, Norbert Wiener was an important mathematician who had a deep concern about the possible social impact of his work. Cybernetics and automation are intimately related, as engineering is related to mathematics and physics. In fact, the subtitle of Wiener's very influential book, *Cybernetics*, is *Control and Communication in the Animal and Machine*.[14] The central notion in cybernetics is feedback. In this process, an action is maintained by continuously reducing the monitored difference between the current state and the desired state. This principle underlies much of industrial automation, hence Wiener's anguish over the fruits of his labor. He views automatic equipment as equivalent to slave labor, which means that humans in competition with the mechanical slaves must accept economic conditions equivalent to theirs. That is, employers will not pay their human workers more than the costs associated with robots performing equivalent work. He prophecied a period of serious unemployment when the new technology becomes pervasive.

Wiener was much less pessimistic about the future in the second edition of this book, which appeared some 13 years after the first. He felt that many of his concerns were starting to be accepted by the business world. The relation between technological change and unemployment is perhaps the central issue in assessing the impact of technology. There appears to be a general consensus that, initially, technological innovation may result in the loss of jobs but eventually more jobs are created than lost. (We will return to this question in Chapter 10.)

Wiener was also troubled by the ability of computers to produce unintended and unanticipated results. The problem results from a combination of factors, including the speed of the computer, the inadvisability of interfering with it during its computation, the narrowness of the program's scope and the limitations of the data. Note that none of these elements has anything to do with whether a computer can exhibit intelligent behavior. The fundamental point is that computers operate so much faster than do humans that there is a basic mismatch in their interaction. One had better be very sure that the computer is doing what is desired and intended.

Wiener offers a strategy much easier stated than carried out.

> *Render unto man the things which are man's and unto the computer the things which are the computer's. This would seem the intelligent policy to adopt when we employ men and computers together in common undertakings. It is a policy as far removed from that of the gadget worshipper as it is from the man who sees only blasphemy and degradation of man in the use of any mechanical adjuvants whatever to thoughts.*[15]

Wiener feels that computers can ultimately be controlled for the benefit of society. But this sentiment seems to be expressed more as a caution—against the possibility of a terrible future if computers are not used wisely—than as a realistic expectation.

The views of the social critics given above range from apprehension to horror. The easy response to them is, yes there have always been problems, yes there will be more problems, but we are in control of our own destiny. The debate will continue and will probably increase in intensity as the presence of computers is more strongly felt. In all likelihood, the discussion will turn on whether or not the computer in its most prevalent form—the microprocessor—represents a quantitative change in technology. The final word in this section, reminding us that technology is not a recent concern, goes to the nineteenth-century social philosopher John Stuart Mill.

> *Suppose that it were possible to get houses built, corn grown, battles fought, causes tried, and even churches erected and prayers said by machinery—by automatons in human form—it would be a considerable loss to exchange for these automatons even the men and women who at present inhabit the more civilized parts of the world, and who assuredly are but starved specimens of what nature can and will produce. Human nature is not a machine to be built after a model, and set to do exactly the work prescribed for it, but a tree, which requires to grow and develop itself on all sides, according to the tendency of the inward forces which make it a living thing.*[16]

A Measure of Optimism

> *The fact is, that civilization requires slaves. The Greeks were quite right there. Unless there are slaves to do the ugly, horrible, uninteresting work, culture and contemplation become almost impossible. Human slavery is wrong, insecure, and demoralizing. On mechanical slavery, on the slavery of the machine, the future of the world depends.*[17]

As most of this book is a study in success of the computer in its incredibly wide variety of forms and applications, we need hardly pause to praise it. Nevertheless, the few words of cheer above should be welcome, as a clear statement of technology as the servant of the people who invent it, develop it, and employ it to serve the needs of everyone. About one hundred years later, this view was reinforced by Herbert Simon, winner of the Nobel prize in economics in 1978 and one of the fathers of Artificial Intelligence. Simon views technological change from the unique combined vantage point of economist, computer scientist, and cognitive psychologist. In a ringing challenge, Simon presents probably one of the most optimistic and encouraging statements of the technological vision.

> *It is to realize, perhaps for the first time in human history, that we are a part of the world; that we are a part of this vast machinery; that man is not outside nature, that man is not above nature, but that man is a part of nature.*

If we can make peace with ourselves on those terms, it will have at least one desirable byproduct: As we design new technology, as we make use of our knowledge about the world and the knowledge that we are gaining about ourselves, about our thinking processes, through research in AI and cognitive simulation, we will realize that we have to apply our technology in a way that keeps man's peace with the universe in which he lives, instead of conceiving our technology as a weapon with which man can wage war on the rest of nature.[18]

One can almost hear the trumpets.

Among the writers who have extolled the virtues of the coming technological age are Charles Panati, John Naisbitt, Joseph Deken, and, most prominent of all, Alvin Toffler. The claims made for the best-selling books of these authors are as follows:

Charles Panati, *Breakthroughs*, 1980.   An exhilarating first look at the advances in science, medicine, technology and health that are making our tomorrow better. . .today![19]

John Naisbitt, *Megatrends*, 1982.   Ten new directions transforming our lives.[20]

Joseph Deken, *The Electronic Cottage*, 1981.   There is a revolution underway. It promises to change not only the way we live, but ultimately the way we think.[21]

Alvin Toffler, *The Third Wave*, 1980.   The book that makes sense of the exploding eighties.[22]

These authors share an unbounded enthusiasm for the technological developments currently underway. They see breakthroughs in every area of human endeavour: health, work, communications, space, national politics, geopolitics, weather predictions, energy, transportation, education, and so forth. Nothing less than a fundamental transformation of civilization is on the horizon. An end to war, an end to sickness, an end to hunger— these are the promises of the new golden age. The driving force is technology and at its core is the computer.

A BRIEF HISTORY OF COMPUTERS

The next few pages will sparkle with such catchy names as ENIAC, EDVAC, UNIVAC, EDSAC, MARK 1, and others. They are the names of the earliest real computers, developed about forty years ago. How they came to be is a fascinating, long, and involved story. There is a problem inherent in an abbreviated history—it may appear to be a series of inventions that were historically inevitable. The social forces, the burgeoning requirements of applied mathematics, and the demands made during times of war and peace— including the computation of ballistic tables, navigational aids, and census statistics—are discussed in the Additional Readings.

Before the Twentieth Century

Computing probably began with counting, and counting began with fingers and sticks and stones. The abacus, one of the oldest calculating devices, was known to the Egyptians as early as 460 B.C. and is still used today in many parts of the world. There are two classes of computing machines—*analog* and *digital*. An abacus is a digital device in which the positions of individual beads on wires represent numbers. In analog machines, the instantaneous value of a continuously varying physical quantity such as a length, voltage, or angular position represents a number. Before it was rendered obsolete by the pocket calculator, the slide rule was probably the most commonly used analog computing device. Its operation makes use of the fact that the product of two numbers is equivalent to the sum of their logarithms. By using a length on a stick to represent the logarithm of a number, multiplication is carried out by positioning two sticks appropriately. A traditional watch with face and hands is analog (no matter what process is used for positioning the hands), whereas one with only numbers, which change in discrete jumps, is digital. In this history the analog computer is a minor player.

Brian Randell, editor of *The Origins of Digital Computers*, divides their history into two streams: mechanical digital calculation and sequence control mechanisms.[23] These are the two major concerns of computation—how to actually perform a calculation and how to control sequences of calculations. Counting, the former, was of primary concern historically.

For centuries wheels with teeth or cogs in a linked train have been used to deal with addition that involves carries. The complete story includes the development of number systems, leading to the use of the decimal system in Europe. John Napier (1550–1617), best known as the inventor of logarithms, probably was the first person to use the decimal point in arithmetic operations. Until quite recently the credit for inventing the first calculator was given to the famous French philosopher Blaise Pascal (1623–1662). It is supposed that his impetus was to aid his father in performing calculations. In any case, at age nineteen he designed his first machine and by 1645 he had achieved a patent on it. The currently recognized first inventor, however, is Wilhelm Schickard of Tubingen (1592–1635), who apparently sent a set of drawings of a calculating machine to Kepler, the famous astronomer, in 1623. Who was first is not particularly important, since the idea and the necessary technology were in the air. The historical record is probably incomplete. The real importance of a new invention is heavily dependent on the social environment in which it occurs.

Some thirty years after Pascal's invention Gottfried Leibniz (1646–1716), a great mathematician and universal thinker, designed the Leibniz wheel, a crucial component of mechanical calculators. His machine, which was not constructed until 1694, permitted multiplication and division as well as addition and subtraction and was much more efficient than previous devices. As useful calculating devices were developed, the impetus grew to refine and improve them in order to carry out even more complicated computations. Leibniz himself raised the banner for the relief of drudgery through technology.

Also the astronomers surely will not have to continue to exercise the patience which is required for computation. It is this that deters them from computing or correcting tables, from the construction of Ephemerides, from working on hypotheses, and from discussions of observations with each other. For it is unworthy of excellent men to lose hours like slaves in the labor or calculation which could safely be relegated to anyone else if machines were used. (*Emphasis added.*)[24]

Charles Babbage: The Difference Engine and the Analytical Engine

Over the next century a number of refinements took place in the basic calculator, but it was not until the mid-nineteenth century that a generally successful calculator became available. Charles Babbage (1792–1871), a most remarkable man—mathematician, inventor, and initiator of scientific management—flourished in this period. Undoubtedly, he deserves the title father of the computer. Ironically, his story is one of generally unfulfilled ambition. In 1821, he became interested in building a ''Difference Engine'' to automate the calculation of algebraic functions by using successive differences. A story describes the moment of its inception. Apparently Babbage was checking some calculations with John Herschel (the son of Sir William Herschel, the discoverer of Uranus) when Babbage remarked, ''I wish to God these calculations had been executed by steam.'' Herschel simply replied, ''It is quite possible.'' (Steam was the major power source of Babbage's time.)

In 1836, before his Difference Engine was completed, Babbage conceived of a much more powerful, general purpose computer that he called the Analytical Engine. In the end, neither machine was completed, for a variety of reasons—lack of sufficient financial resources, technical requirements beyond the skill available, and a design that underwent too-frequent change. There is little doubt, however, that Babbage at this early date envisioned a machine of such scope that its power would not be realized for more than a hundred years. His design included a memory store, an arithmetic unit, punched card input and output, and a mechanism that provided enough power of control to do iteration and branching. Following his death, others tried to build similar machines with little success. When successful machines were finally built, some of their designers were aware of his work; others were not. In the final analysis, Babbage appears to have been a cranky genius with ideas impossible to realize—for both economical and technical reasons—in his time.

No history of this period would be complete without mention of Augusta Ada, Countess of Lovelace (1816–1852), the only child of the poet Lord Byron and a person of remarkable mathematical ability. In 1840, when Babbage presented a series of lectures in Italy on his machine, they were attended by a young engineer, L. F. Menabrea. Ada translated his notes on the lectures and added comments of her own. Her work is the major account of the Analytic Engine. She may also have been the first programmer—she included a program to compute Bernoulli numbers, an important task for many physical problems. Her description of the engine is quite lyrical, not surprising for the daughter of a poet.

> *We may say most aptly that the Analytical Engine weaves* algebraic patterns *just as the Jacquard loom weaves flowers and leaves. Here, it seems to us, resides more originality than the Difference Engine can be fairly entitled to claim.*[25]

It appears that even the idea of a computer provoked in her mind the possibility that people might readily believe in the creative powers of such machines. She was at pains to disabuse the public of such a thought.

> *The Analytical Engine has no pretensions whatever to* originate *anything. It can do whatever we* know how to order it *to perform. It can* follow *analysis; but it has no power of* anticipating *any analytical relations or truths. Its province is to assist us in making* available *what we are already acquainted with.*[26]

Echoes of this statement have reverberated through the ages. Nothing has been settled—if anything the debate has become more strident, especially as the range of computer applications has been increasingly extended in our time. Followers of Augusta Ada would probably still maintain that computers can only do what they have been programmed to do. The arguments for the opposition cannot be expressed so succinctly, but it can be said that the proponents of Artificial Intelligence see no *a priori* limitations to the power of computers. (See the discussion in Chapter Two.)

What did Babbage achieve in the end? He did not build his Analytical Engine, but he did anticipate much of what would follow. He failed to realize his vision, probably because of his restless mind, the limitations of contemporary technology, and the lack of an obvious need for the projected computing power. He continually designed more advanced machines while the struggle was still on to realize his earlier designs. Still, his intellectual achievement was monumental. Perhaps the last word should be given to his mother.

> *My dear son, you have advanced far in the accomplishment of a great object, which is worthy of your ambition. You are capable of completing it. My advice is—pursue it, even if it should oblige you to live on bread and cheese.*[27]

Control of Computation

Ada's reference to the Jacquard loom relates to the second theme in our history of computers—sequence control mechanisms. The problem is twofold: (a) how to represent numbers and develop a mechanism for performing arithmetical operations on them, and (b) how to carry out sequences of calculations without human intervention, which could only restrict operational speeds. The automata discussed in Chapter 2 were generally controlled by a rotating pegged cylinder or a disc with holes, much as contemporary music boxes are. The problem of how to actually control a process by a mechanism essentially external to that process first arose in the weaving industry.

It was probably a man called Basile Bouchon who in 1725 used a perforated tape to control the weaving of ornamental patterns in silk. This idea was refined over the years by a number of inventors, including Jacques Vaucanson, the creator of the remarkable mechanical duck. The most important contribution was made by Joseph Marie Jacquard (1752–1834). Building on the work of Vaucanson, Bouchon, and others, he designed a system of control that used a connected sequence of punched cards. The holes in the card determined whether or not vertical hooks controlling the warp threads were used in the pattern being woven. By the end of the nineteenth century looms with 400 or 600 hooks were quite common. As early as 1812, there were approximately 11,000 Jacquard looms in France.

In 1836, Babbage adopted the Jacquard card mechanism not only for entering numbers into the machine but most importantly for controlling the sequence of operations necessary to carry out the calculations. It was easier to punch up a set of cards, he reasoned, than to make changes directly within the central core of the computer. Once the cards were made they could be used again whenever the particular computation was desired. Clearly this is much easier than physically altering the computer itself. Babbage anticipated the notion of a fixed machine performing computations under the direction of a program. It is interesting that a technological advance in one area turned out to be influential in quite another one. The story resumes in the United States, where for the most part the electronic computer was first invented and subsequently refined.

Near the end of the nineteenth century in the United States, the demands made on the Census Office became quite burdensome. The 1870 census was the first to make use of mechanical equipment of a rather simple kind. The key figures were John Shaw Billings, who was in charge of the 1880 census, and Herman Hollerith, (1860–1929) who worked for the Census Office from 1879 to 1883 and later supplied the tabulating equipment for the 1890 census. There is some controversy over who should be given credit for the tabulating machine concept. It seems that Billings suggested the idea of using punched cards to represent information but Hollerith actually built the machine. Billings apparently mentioned that he was inspired by the Jacquard loom principle. In any case the machines, patented by Hollerith in 1889, won a competition and were used in the 1890 census to punch and process approximately 56 million cards. Hollerith's machines, in an improved version, were also used in the 1900 census. However, relations between his company and the Census Bureau (the name was changed in 1903) deteriorated so much that for the 1910 census the Bureau used its own machines, which were developed by James Powers.

After Hollerith left the Census Office, he formed a company in 1896 called the Tabulating Machine Company. In 1911 it merged with two other companies to form the Computer-Tabulating-Recording Company. Thomas J. Watson, Sr., formerly with National Cash Register, became president in 1914. Ten years later he changed the company's name to International Business Machines (IBM). In the same year in which Hollerith's company merged, James Powers formed his own company, Powers Tabulating Machine Company, on the basis of patents received while he was employed by the Census Bureau. This company eventually merged with Remington Rand in 1927. Thus, the rivalry of Powers and Hollerith at the turn of the century gave rise to two companies that were rivals in the development of the electronic computer.

It is interesting to note that the process of making Jacquard cards was itself, up until recently, an arduous task. The textile designer in fact drew on paper the threads of the warp and weft showing at each intersection their relative positions and from these the holes were punched. Then, in the mid-1960's a very ingenious method was found by Miss Janice R. Lourie of IBM to automate the whole process with the help of the modern computer. This was displayed on a working loom at the HemisFair in San Antonio, Texas, in 1968. Thus the progenitor of the computer has become its child.[28]

Birth of the Modern Computer

Babbage's machine did not die with him—his son attempted to raise money to complete it. (All that remains is a number of incomplete sections.) Others were influenced. Percy Ludgate, an Irish accountant, attempted to build his own Analytical Engine in 1903. He died in 1922 leaving only a 1909 sketch describing his design. The Spaniard Leonardo Tores Y Quevedo (1852–1936) wrote in 1914 an interesting paper outlining a program-controlled device in the spirit of Babbage's Analytical Engine. He was also well known for his end-game chess playing automata. As we move into the 1930s, the story starts to become rather complicated. Historians are still uncovering and evaluating claims for machines and devices. Furthermore, secret work done during World War II, especially work on the Colossus project undertaken in England, is gradually being declassified only now. It was a very exciting and interesting time—social conditions were ripe for the building of the first computer.

Before the first digital computer was developed there were a variety of analog computers in operation designed to solve specific problems. The most important of these, called the differential analyzer, was built at the Massachusetts Institute of Technology (MIT) by Vannevar Bush in 1931. Its purpose was to solve differential equations arising from several areas of mathematics. More important, perhaps, was its influence on computational endeavors elsewhere. For example, a version of the differential analyzer was built at the Moore School of Electrical Engineering at the University of Pennsylvania between 1933 and 1935. This effort provided the crucial experience from which the first electronic computer emerged some ten years later. As a side effect, MIT's commitment to analogue computers, at the expense of digital ones, probably began at that time.

Electromechanical Computers

It is generally agreed that the first electronic computer was built at the Moore School under the direction of John Mauchly (1907–1980) and John Presper Eckert, Jr. (b. 1919). Called ENIAC (Electronic Numerical Integrator and Computer), it was built between 1943 and 1946. There were others who claimed to be the first. The common factor of such claims was that the device was not electronic but electromechanical; that is, it relied on a mixture of electrical and mechanical components.

Unfortunately, the first of those had very little impact on the development of computers in general. In fact, it was not until after World War II that the important work of Konrad Zuse (b. 1910) became known. He began in Germany to design electromechanical calculating aids in 1934; by 1938 he had produced the Z1, a somewhat unreliable mechanical computer. With the help of Helmut Schreyer he succeeded in building the Z3, "a floating point binary machine with a 64 word store. This machine, since it was operational in 1941, is believed to have been the world's first general purpose program-controlled computer."[29] Zuse continued his work during the war, but resources were not made available to extend his design. He made another important contribution with the design (in 1945) of a programming language called Plankalkul. This work also was not as influential as it should have been because it was unknown at the time.

In the United States, important work on digital computers was initiated at the Bell Telephone Laboratories in New Jersey under the direction of George Stibitz. It is not surprising that Bell would be interested in computers, nor that they would be based on the relay circuit technology already in place in the telephone system. Stibitz and his associates began their research in 1937 and produced the first model, called the Complex Number Computer, in 1940. This so-called Model I was followed by a number of computers over the years: Model II, the Relay Interpolator, Model III, a relay calculator, the Ballistic Computer, and finally Model V in 1946. This last model was a general purpose computer under program control. Even though it was slow, it did permit programs to be changed easily and was quite reliable as well.

Another important early development in computer technology was the work of Howard Aiken (1900–1973). In 1937, while an instructor at Harvard, he convinced IBM to begin the design of a computer. Together with three IBM employees—C. D. Lake, F. E. Hamilton, and B. M. Durfee—Aiken built the Harvard Mark 1, or Automatic Sequence-Controlled Calculator, in 1944. Basically a mechanical computer, it was more than 50 feet long, perhaps the largest ever built. More important than the machine itself, probably, was the fact that it was an entry point for IBM into the world of computers. After this machine, Aiken went on to build a series of machines at Harvard based on mechanical components. When questioned many years later about his reluctance to use electronic components, he replied that he knew that electronics were the way to go but that they were unreliable at first and he preferred the dependability of mechanical systems. At IBM the development of machines continued with the Pluggable Sequence Relay Calculator, installed in 1949, and the SSEC (Selective Sequence Electronic Calculator), completed in 1948 under the direction of Wallace Eckert. The series of computers that followed launched IBM into world leadership.

ENIAC: The First Electronic Computer

The work of Aiken and Stibitz was well known to the designers of the ENIAC, as was that of John W. Atanasoff, who had built a special purpose computer to solve systems of simultaneous linear equations. In fact, Mauchly visited Atanasoff at Iowa State University in 1941 to see his computer and invited him to come to the Moore School. There has been much controversy about how much ENIAC owed to Atanasoff. Mauchly in later years called Atanasoff's computer a "little gizmo." A court ruling in 1973, resulting from litigation between Honeywell and Sperry Rand over the ENIAC patent, was not clear-cut. The ruling, issued in October of 1973, stated, "Eckert and Mauchly did not themselves first invent the automatic electronic digital computer but instead derived the subject matter from one Dr. John Vincent Atanasoff."[30] Nevertheless, the judge acknowledged Eckert and Mauchly as the inventors of ENIAC, and Atanasoff's work did not change the ENIAC patent claims.

Two of the participants have written books about the development of this first electronic computer.[31] Herman Lukoff, an engineer, and Herman Goldstine, a mathematician together with Arthur Burks and John von Neumann, were involved in the development of the ENIAC and successor machines. The Moore School had gotten involved with computers—albeit analog ones—in 1933, with the construction of a differential analyzer. John Mauchly, a physicist interested in the possibilities of electronic means of computation, joined the Moore School in the fall of 1941. Eckert, an electrical engineer employed as an instructor at the Moore School, was supportive of Mauchly's interests. In August 1942 Mauchly wrote a memo, "The Use of High Speed Vacuum Tube Devices for Calculating," which has been called one of the most important documents in the history of computers.[32] The Moore School had by this time become involved with the Ballistics Research Laboratory of the U.S. Army Ordnance Department. Captain Herman Goldstine, acting as liaison officer, helped convince the U.S. government to sign a contract with the Moore School in 1943 to develop an electronic calculating machine for computing ballistic tables. The machine was completed in the fall of 1945. It was a monster. Incorporating over 18,000 vacuum tubes, 70,000 resistors, and 10,000 capacitors, 100 feet long, 10 feet high, and 3 feet deep, it consumed 140 kilowatts in operation.

Given the large number of components, one of the remarkable engineering achievements was that of simply keeping the machine running. For example, to operate for 12 hours without error it had to have a probability of malfunction of less than 1 part in 10^{14}. The person most responsible for making the computer work was Eckert, who, among many other things, set the design specifications for the components. To increase the life expectancy of tubes, Eckert reduced the rated voltages and currents substantially. It is generally agreed that Mauchly was the creator, motivator, and problem solver while Eckert brought great insight, determination, and engineering skill. The senior engineers, Arthur Burks and Kite Sharpless, headed a large team of engineers and technicians. These are a few of the characteristics of the ENIAC: The basic addition time was .2 milliseconds; the largest integer that could be represented was 9,999,999,999, or $10^{10} - 1$. There was one major drawback. Although ENIAC was much faster than any other computer of the time, it took a great deal of effort to set up a problem because it was programmed manually with cables, wires, and switches. This situation had been anticipated by the designers, and they began work on their next computer, the EDVAC (Electronic Discrete Variable Automatic Computer), before the ENIAC was operational.

The Stored Program Concept

The next major step was to control the computer's actions by means of a program stored in its memory. If this could be done, programs could be manipulated just like data. Even more important, the computer could become involved in the preparation of programs themselves through the development of assemblers, compilers, and operating systems. (The latter are themselves programs that reside in the computer and permit the running of user-written programs.) As in many other areas of computer invention, the question of who was responsible for the stored program concept is somewhat unclear. Currently, there is general agreement that John von Neumann is the person to whom most of the credit belongs. Some facts are clear: The idea did emerge in the ENIAC group and it was expressed in print in a draft report dated June 30, 1945, written by von Neumann on the proposed EDVAC. Von Neumann (1903–1957) was one of the supreme geniuses of the twentieth century. He made major contributions to such diverse areas as the foundations of mathematics, quantum mechanics, game theory, hydrodynamics, and the foundations of computer organization and software. Contemporary computers have been described as von Neumann machines. However, there is some question about the origin of the ideas in the 1945 report.

Apparently, the stored program concept emerged in group discussions during the ENIAC project. Von Neumann first became involved with work at the Moore School when taken there by Goldstine in August of 1944. It is his opinion that von Neumann did make the major contribution. It is unfortunate, though, that the draft report did not acknowledge the work of others, and thus became known as the von Neumman report. Goldstine claims that von Neumann did not expect it to be widely circulated before he produced a revised version. Others have not been so agreeable.

Mauchly himself tried to set the history straight. In late 1979 he stated that as early as April of 1944 he and Eckert had planned to include both programs and data in the same memory. Furthermore, they discussed these plans with von Neumann in September of that year when he first came to the Moore School.

> *We started with our basic ideas: there would be only* one *storage device (with addressable locations) for the* entire *EDVAC, and this would hold both data and instructions. All necessary arithmetic operations would be performed in just* one *arithmetic unit. All control functions would be centralized.*[33]

Von Neumann quickly understood the nature of these ideas and reformulated them in his own terms, using such biological terms as organs and neurons. Mauchly insists that von Neumann was merely rephrasing ideas developed by himself and Eckert. In any case, the von Neumann report does contain the first known program for a stored program digital computer; it happens to be a sorting program.

The Moore School went on to complete the EDVAC and delivered it to the Ballistics Research Laboratory near the end of 1951. Mauchly and Eckert left to form their own company, the Electronic Control Company, in late 1946. (The name was changed to

Eckert-Mauchly Computer Corporation in 1947.) Problems with patent disputes and the constraints of the university environment had led to this separation. They conceived UNIVAC (a Universal Automatic Computer) but its development required continued research supported by contracts. For the Northrup Aircraft Company they completed in 1949 a computer called BINAC—the first operational stored-program electronic computer that used mag [sic] tapes rather than punch cards. In 1950 Eckert and Mauchly sold their company to Remington Rand because of monetary problems. The following year the UNIVAC I was completed and used for the computation of the 1950 U.S. census. In 1955 Remington Rand merged with the Sperry Corporation and continued to manufacture the UNIVAC series. (The UNIVAC name was discontinued in 1983.)

Developments in England

In 1946, Von Neumann and Goldstine went to the Institute of Advanced Studies at Princeton University and began to work on a new computer, the IAS. The early 1950s saw the beginnings of the computer explosion, as computers developed at a number of research institutions in the United States and elsewhere (see Table 3-1).

The MARK 1, developed at Manchester under F. C. Williams and T. Kilburn, was probably the first stored program computer to be operational. It was a rather primitive machine and is important mainly for the concept it embodied and for the fact that its development was fairly independent of the Moore School effort.

Another significant project in England was the computer built at Cambridge University under the direction of Maurice Wilkes, called EDSAC (Electronic Delay Storage Automatic Calculator). This machine was based on the EDVAC principles—Wilkes had attended an important series of lectures at the Moore School in 1946. The EDSAC has been called the first practical stored program computer to be completed. It executed its first program in May 1949.[34] Finally, the classified work done at Bletchley Park during World War II has recently been disclosed. A computer called COLOSSUS was developed there under the leadership of a Professor Newman and a Mr. Flowers, with a major contribution by Alan Turing (1912–1954). Turing was later involved with the ACE computers built at the National Physical Laboratories at Teddington.

No history of computing would be complete without mention of Alan Turing. His name has primarily been associated with a theoretical construct called the Turing machine, which he created to explore general issues of computation. More recently his contributions to the design of actual computers, especially his work on a highly secret coding machine called Enigma, have been made public. From a theoretical and a practical perspective Turing is certainly one of the fathers of the modern computer.

The Rise of IBM

The age of the computer had arrived and growth was explosive. IBM quickly established its dominance and its name became synonymous with the computer. How this happened has been debated, but no one disputes the fact that IBM is the major company in the

TABLE 3-1 Early Computers in England and the United States

Argonne National Laboratory	AVIDAC	1949
	ORACLE	
University of Illinois	ORDVAC	1949–52
	ILLIAC	1949–52
	ILLIAC II	1957–62
MIT	WHIRLWIND	1945–52
National Bureau of Standards	SWAC	1948–50
IBM	701	1951–53
	702	1953
	650	1953
	703,704	1954
	705	1954
Cambridge University	EDSAC	1949
Manchester University	MARK 1	1946–48
(U.K.)	Ferranti	1951
National Physical Laboratory	ACE	1945–48
(Teddington, U.K.)	PILOT ACE	1949–50

field, both in the United States and worldwide. Of all the factors contributing to its success, the most important was probably its organizational structure, which was highlighted by a large, well-motivated, and dedicated sales staff. The company stressed a well-trained and responsive sales and service division. Its availability and concern did much to carry its customers through the early uncertainties of the commercial computer age. In the 1960s the industry was described as IBM and the Seven Dwarfs. The dwarfs in 1967 were Sperry Rand (now Sperry Corporation), Control Data Corporation, Honeywell, RCA (Radio Corporation of America), NCR (National Cash Register), General Electric, and Burroughs. Since then both General Electric and RCA have dropped out of the computer business, except that General Electric still maintains a presence in peripherals and computer services.

Currently number two is Digital Equipment Corporation, which has become the leader in minicomputers. Figure 3-1 shows the growth curves of the major computer companies since 1975. Other companies in the top ten are Hewlett-Packard, Xerox, and Wang Laboratories. Hewlett-Packard is strong in minis, micros, peripherals, and services. (Com-

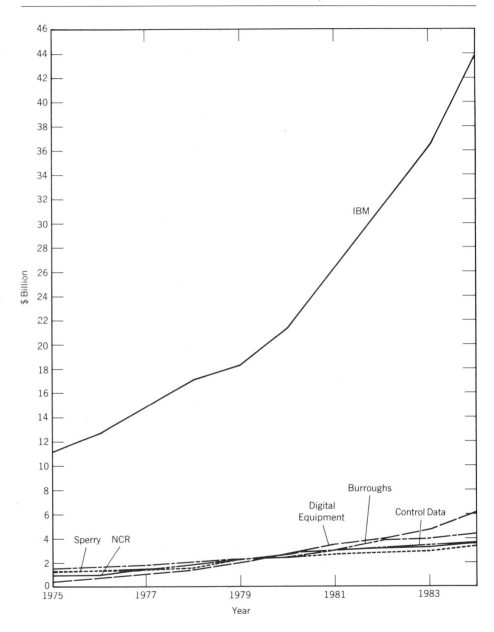

FIGURE 3-1 Data Processing Revenue of IBM and Its Competitors. (Adapted from *Datamation*, June issues, 1976–84.)

puters are usually categorized by size and power. Mainframes are at the top, minicomputers in the middle, and microcomputers, or personal computers, at the bottom. Peripherals include tape drives, disk drives, printers, and so forth.) Xerox's main strength is in peripherals and terminals, office systems, and services. Wang is one of the world leaders in office systems. However, IBM is still the dominating force in the industry and is likely to remain so into the foreseeable future. In the area of personal computers, for example, IBM had no presence in 1980; yet in 1983 it achieved a greater dollar volume than Apple, which had led with a 26 percent market share in 1982. Many questions have arisen about the effect of such a powerful force on the other companies in the industry and, more importantly, on the development of the field itself. Many of IBM's practices have become *de facto* standards. (We will discuss some of these issues in Chapter 11.)

THE EMERGENCE OF THE CHIP

If the aircraft industry had evolved as spectacularly as the computer industry over the past 25 years, a Boeing 767 would cost $500 today, and it would circle the globe in 20 minutes on five gallons of fuel.[35]

If the automobile business had developed like the computer business, a Rolls-Royce would now cost $2.75 and run 3 million miles on a gallon of gas.[36]

The History

The modern computer developed from a mechanical calculator into an immense electronic machine with thousands of vacuum tubes that occupied a large room. The power requirements were enormous and the issue of reliability was of paramount concern. When ENIAC was completed in 1946, it was generally believed that only a very few computers would be necessary to serve the computational needs of the nation. Developments were already underway, however, to change the basic structure of computers. As early as 1945, Bell Laboratories began research to develop electronic devices useful for telecommunications. Leading this research team were William Shockley, John Bardeen, and Walter H. Brattain. They were awarded the Nobel prize for physics for their invention, in 1947, of the point contact transistor. This device was not an instant success, because it operated over a limited range of frequencies, could amplify only to a limited degree, had limited stability, and was expensive to manufacture. It would have been difficult to predict at this point the shape of things to come.

As an electronic component, the vacuum tube generates a great deal of heat in operation, requires considerable power, and occupies a relatively large space. The advantages of the semiconductor are striking: low power requirements, minimal heat generation, and above all microscopic size. The semiconductor, as its name suggests, has conductive properties between those of a conductive material such as copper and an insulating material such as plastic or rubber. The first transistor was made of germanium, as was the second, called the junction transistor. Both were developed by Bell in 1951. Eventually silicon came into wide use, first for transistors and later for integrated circuits, or chips.

Over the next few years developments were rapid, and prices fell correspondingly. The basic motivation for miniaturization, however, did not derive from the requirements of computer engineers. It was the basic need of the space and missile programs for compact, durable, and light components that motivated the drive for miniaturization. Developments were further accelerated by a combination of advances in scientific knowledge and the growth of scientific entrepreneurship.

Transistors were first used in hearing aids in the early 1950s. It was not until 1955 that the first all-transistor radios appeared. Much more importantly, in that same year IBM introduced a computer in which over 1000 tubes had been replaced by more than 2000 transistors. In addition to the virtues of the transistor already noted, there is one additional important point that had great implications for the future.

> The great advantage of the transistor, an advantage scarcely appreciated at the time, was that it enabled one to do away with the separate materials—carbon, ceramics, tungsten and so on—traditionally used in fabricating components. At the same time the transistor raised the ceiling that sheer complexity of interconnections was beginning to place on system design. . . . The transistor was the first electronic component in which materials with different electrical characteristics were not interconnected but were physically joined in one structure.[37]

The next natural step was to include more than one transistor in the same physical structure. Once this idea was articulated, developments took place very rapidly (see Table 3-2). The integrated circuit includes—on a single chip of silicon—transistors, diodes, resistors, and capacitors, all connected in a functional circuit.

Once it was introduced, the integrated circuit business grew rapidly worldwide, with nearly $1 billion in sales in 1970 and $3.6 billion in 1976. These figures are dramatic in more ways than one since there has been a corresponding reduction in prices over these years and an increased number of active elements per circuit. For example, the cost per bit (binary digit) of random-access memory has declined an average of 35 percent per year since 1970.[38] Furthermore, from a single bit per circuit in 1959, the growth curve has been from 1K (1024) in 1970, to 4K in the mid-1970s, to 16K in the late 1970s, to 32K shortly after, followed by 64K in the early 1980s, and the introduction of the 256K bit memory in 1983. (The letter K is an abbreviation for the number 1024.) The benefits of integrated circuits are as follows:

> They are cheaper.
>
> Labor and materials are saved by not having to make large numbers of connections.
>
> The integrated connections are more secure, hence less maintenance is required.

TABLE 3-2 Early Developments in Semiconductors

1953	Harwick Johnson, RCA	Phase-shift oscillator on a single piece of germanium
	G. W. A. Dummer Royal Radar Establishment, U.K.	Concept of integrated circuit articulated
	Jack S. Kilby, Texas Instruments Jay W. Lathrop, Diamond Ordnance Fuze Labs.	
1959	Robert N. Noyce, Fairchild Semiconductor	Integrated circuit appears

Power and space requirements are drastically reduced, resulting also in savings on cooling fans and transformers.

Quality control is improved.

In 1964 Gordon Moore, one of Noyce's colleagues at Fairchild, suggested that the complexity of integrated circuits would continue to double every year. Moore's law is apparently still in effect and augurs well for improvements into the 1990s.

The Microprocessor

So far we have discussed the development of circuits that have either been preprogrammed to carry out well-defined functions or are available for memory purposes. One of the most significant technological innovations of our time took place in 1971 at Intel, a semiconductor company founded two years earlier by Robert Noyce and others in Santa Clara, California.

M. E. Hoff, Jr., a young engineer, invented an integrated circuit that is essentially equivalent to the central processing unit of a computer. Consider the following description:

Hoff's CPU [Central Processing Unit] on a chip became known as a microprocessor. To the microprocessor, he attached two memory chips, one to move data in and out of the CPU and one to provide the program to drive the CPU. Hoff now had in hand a rudimentary general-purpose computer that not only could run a complex calculator but could also control an elevator or a set of traffic lights, and perform any other tasks, depending on its program.[39]

Intel brought out its first microprocessor chip, the 4004, in 1971. A larger model, the 8008, followed in 1972. Near the end of 1973 came the second generation 8080 chip, more than twenty times faster than the 4004. This last chip formed the basis for the personal computer bonanza that followed. Other companies—such as Rockwell International, National Semiconductor, Texas Instruments, and Motorola—soon entered the microprocessor derby.

The microcomputer on a single chip has also been achieved. For example, the Intel 8748 measures 5.6 mm by 6.6 mm and contains a microprocessor, program memory, data memory, multiple input-output (I/O) interfaces, and timing circuits. In 1977 this chip sold for $210 each, in batches of 25 or more, for use in building personal computers or as controls for a variety of devices. By 1984, it could be purchased for as little as $50 each, sold as a single unit. Its program is stored in an erasable and programmable read-only memory (EPROM). That is, the memory contents can be erased by exposure to ultraviolet light and then a new program can be entered by conventional electronic means. "Read-only" means the contents cannot be altered electronically after the program has been entered but can be used (read) in the execution of the program. Within 30 years of the first electronic computer, which filled a large room, the microcomputer had been realized. About 15 can fit on an ordinary postage stamp, excluding of course the power supply, keyboard, monitor, secondary storage devices, and other I/O devices.

In late 1984, Motorola announced the 68C11, a single chip microcomputer with the following properties: 512K bytes of electrically erasable programmable ROM, 4K bytes of ROM, 256K bytes of random access memory (RAM), 8-bit analog-to-digital converter, and four I/O ports. This device is considerably more powerful than 40-year-old ENIAC.

The Semiconductor Business

The semiconductor business is perhaps the crowning jewel of the American industrial system. Its important early growth period was fostered by the United States Department of Defense, which subsidized developmental costs. As it coincided with the emergence of scientific entrepreneurship, the U.S. lead was ensured. The semiconductor industry has an impact far beyond its own domain, because of the multiplier effect. That is, a piece of equipment depending on semiconductors is likely to cost many times more than the integrated circuit itself.

Ian Mackintosh, of the British consultants Mackintosh International, wrote an important paper in 1978 in which he predicted that U.S. domination of the semiconductor market would be increasingly challenged by Japan.[40] This prediction has come true, in that Japan currently controls 70 percent of the world market for 64K RAM and is leading in the introduction of the 256K chip. Furthermore, he analyzed the origins of the industry in the United States with a view to determining future directions. The strategic factors shown below have been crucial, in Mackintosh's estimation.

The Role of Governments. The federal government, especially the Department of Defense and the space program, have underwritten a good portion of the development costs—an estimate of almost $1 billion between 1958 and 1974 alone.

The Benefits of Industrial Synergism. The U.S. integrated circuit industry grew very rapidly because of a receptive computer market eager to make use of the new technology.

The Impact of Technological Innovation. The American entrepreneurial system puts a premium on development and marketing.

Market Factors. The U.S. market is large enough to support the growth of a new and dynamic industry.

Industrial Structure. Except for certain very large companies (such as IBM), most semiconductor companies depend almost entirely on this single product.

Management and People. The management of most successful companies is flexible and responsive to new technological developments.

Availability of Venture Capital in Substantial Amounts.

Large, Capable Research Laboratories.

Skill Clusters. For example, Silicon Valley.

That almost mythical community, Silicon Valley (named for the basic material of semiconductors) is a region running from Palo Alto south to San Jose along San Francisco Bay. It is the home of a number of chip manufacturers, personal computer companies, and peripheral-device companies. It has achieved worldwide fame as a source of innovation and expertise in the incredible explosion of microelectronics technology. Its achievements have been so overwhelming that other regions of the United States and the world have sought to plant seeds for their own Silicon Valleys.

The tradition of scientific entrepreneurship in the Valley is not new. As far back as 1939, David Packard and William Hewlett formed an electronics company, Hewlett-Packard, which in 1984 had total revenues of almost $6.3 billion. The initial impetus of the phenomenal postwar growth of Silicon Valley came from William Shockley, one of the inventors of the transistor. He left Bell Laboratories and moved to Mountain View, California to set up Shockley Semiconductor Laboratory in 1955 and it attracted a number of young, ambitious engineers and physicists. One of these was Robert Noyce, who (with seven others) left Shockley two years later to form Fairchild Camera and Instrument. The Silicon Valley syndrome of old companies spawning new ones was well under way.

After a few years the next generation of offspring were born: National Semiconductor in 1967, Intel—founded by Noyce—in 1968, and Advanced Micro Devices in 1969. These are among the "Fairchildren" of Fairchild alumni. Not only the semiconductor has flourished in Silicon Valley; a whole range of computer-related companies have found the atmosphere congenial. Such large mainframe corporations as Tandem Computers and Amdahl were founded there. In the personal computer market Apple, Atari, Commodore, and many other micro manufacturers have their home in Silicon Valley. The majority of disk drive manufacturers such as Memorex, Century Data, and Information Storage Systems, as well as Shugart Associates and Seagate Technology (makers of Winchester drives) are also neighbors. A critical mass of scientific expertise (Stanford University is in Silicon Valley and the University of California at Berkeley is nearby), technological skills, managerial skills, and venture capital resources have made the Valley a much-envied world center of microelectronics.

The Personal Computer

Almost exactly 30 years after the first electronic computer made its appearance, the first personal computer was marketed. Since then, sales have been phenomenal. In the United States sales for 1981 (excluding software and peripherals) reached $1.4 billion; they were up to $2.6 billion in 1982, $4.2 billion in 1983, and approximately $6 billion in 1984. Worldwide sales were $6.1 billion for 1982 and will soar to $22 billion in 1985. All this has been made possible by the microprocessor, but the idea of making a computer at a price low enough to sell to an individual, coupled with the belief that the computer would have sufficient appeal for that individual, is a product of American scientific and business genius.

The major success story of the personal computer—up to 1983 at least—was Apple Computer Company, founded in the Silicon Valley by Steven Wozniak and Steven Jobs, then in their early twenties. Wozniak built his first machine in his parents' garage. The first Apple machine was marketed in 1976. In 1981 Apple had sales of over $400 million and it exceeded $1 billion in 1983. Other major companies dealing in personal computers are the Tandy Corporation (maker of the Radio Shack TRS and Tandy computers), Commodore (the PET, the Commodore 20 and 64, and Amiga), Hewlett-Packard, and Digital. IBM waited until 1981 to enter the personal computer market but did so with a splash, as previously noted.

In the personal computer market there are three price ranges that define the basic levels of sophistication—under $300, with no monitor or disk drives, sometimes called recreational; under $2,000, with no monitor; and under $5,000. Competition is sure to be fierce and many observers have predicted a major shakedown in the personal computer market, especially in the presence of IBM. There are 150 companies currently but most will not survive, especially when marketing, sales, organization, and financial resources become as important as technological achievements, if not more so. For example, Digital announced in early 1985 that it was suspending production of its Rainbow personal company because of an inventory of approximately 100,000. At about the same time IBM ceased production of its PC Jr., a rare example of a marketing failure.

We are living in a time when computers are numbered in the millions. They are no longer the private preserve of the government, large businesses, and research institutions. Extraordinary power is becoming available to a wide segment of society. How that power will be distributed and used, and to what ends, is a question yet to be answered.

SUMMARY

There is a rather simple dichotomy between the view that technology is neutral, just a tool, and the view that it can create serious problems independent of the intentions of the developers. Critics of the unrestricted use of technology include Lewis Mumford, who is very concerned about the dehumanizing aspects of automation; Siegfried Giedion, who argues that technology in the pursuit of efficiency may be achieved at the loss of quality and traditional human skills; and Jacques Ellul, who presents an enormously pessimistic view of technology (or *technique*) as an all-powerful force independent of human control. Such authors as Alvin Toffler, John Naisbitt, and Charles Panati hail a future full of amazing machines offering a significant transformation of life—for the better, of course.

Charles Babbage, an irascible genius of eighteenth-century England, essentially invented the modern computer. He was unable to build it because of limitations in the technology of the time and his continual changes of the conception.

The modern electronic computer is generally acknowledged to have been invented at the Moore School of Electrical Engineering, at the University of Pennsylvania, by John Mauchly and John Presper Eckert in 1945. Called ENIAC, it was funded by the Department of Defense and motivated by the computational needs of wartime research and development. Other contributions were made in the United States, England, and Germany, and their history is only now becoming clear. IBM (a name synonymous with the computer) has had phenomenal growth and impact on the industry.

The major triumph of technology in the third quarter of the twentieth century may well be the integrated circuit, usually called the chip. Another phenomenon of our times is the personal computer, which provides enormous computing power at relatively low cost and small size. The impact of this machine on society is impossible to predict, but the opportunities it opens will probably have a significant impact on society.

NOTES

1. John McDermott, "Technology: The Opiate of the Intellectuals," *New York Review of Books*, July 31, 1969, p. 25.

2. Ibid.

3. Lewis Mumford, *The Pentagon of Power* (New York: Harcourt Brace Jovanovitch, 1970), p. 273.

4. Siegfried Giedion, *Mechanization Takes Command* (1948; reprint ed., New York: Norton, 1969).

5. Ibid., p. 5.

6. Ibid., p. 172.

7. Ibid.

8. For a detailed description, see Samuel A. Matz, ''Modern Baking Technology,'' *Scientific American*, November 1984, pp. 122–6, 131–4.

9. Giedion, *Mechanization Takes Command*, p. 198.

10. Jacques Ellul, *The Technological Society* (1964; reprint ed., New York: Vintage, 1967).

11. Ibid., p. xxv.

12. Ibid., p. 78.

13. Herbert Marcuse, *One-Dimensional Man* (Boston: Beacon, 1966), p. 9.

14. Norbert Wiener, *Cybernetics: Control and Communication in the Animal and Machine*, 2nd ed. (New York: MIT Press and Wiley, 1961).

15. Norbert Wiener, *God and Golem* (Cambridge, Mass.: MIT Press, 1966), p. 73.

16. John Stuart Mill, *On Liberty* (Boston: Ticknor and Fields, 1863), p. 114.

17. Oscar Wilde, *The Soul of Man under Socialism and Other Essays* (New York: Harper & Row, 1970), p. 245.

18. Herbert A. Simon, ''Prometheus or Pandora: The Influence of Automation on Society,'' *Computer*, November 1981, p. 91.

19. Charles Panati, *Breakthroughs* (New York: Berkley, 1981).

20. John Naisbitt, *Megatrends* (New York: Warner, 1984).

21. Joseph Deken, *The Electronic Cottage* (New York: Bantam, 1983).

22. Alvin Toffler, *The Third Wave* (New York: Bantam, 1981).

23. Brian Randell, ed., *The Origins of Digital Computers, Selected Papers* (New York: Springer-Verlag, 1973), p. 1.

24. Gottfried Liebniz, as quoted in Herman H. Goldstine, *The Computer from Pascal to von Neumann* (Princeton: Princeton University Press, 1972), p. 8.

25. Augusta Ada, Countess of Lovelace, notes to L. F. Menabrea, ''Sketch of the Analytical Engine invented by Charles Babbage, Esq.,'' in B. V. Bowden, ed., *Faster Than Thought* (London: Pitman, 1971), p. 368.

26. Ibid., p. 398.

27. As quoted in Anthony Hyman, *Charles Babbage, The Pioneer of the Computer* (Princeton: Princeton University Press, 1982), p. 167.

28. Herman Goldstine, *The Computer from Pascal to von Neumann* (Princeton: Princeton University Press, 1972), p. 20 (note 24).

29. Randell, *Origins of Digital Computers*, p. 156.

30. As quoted in Nancy Stern, *From Eniac to Univac* (Bedford, Mass.: Digital, 1981), p. 4.

31. Goldstine, *The Computer from Pascal to von Neumann. Herman Lukoff, From Dits to Bits: A Personal History of the Electronic Computer* (Portland, Ore.: Robotics, 1979).

32. Randell, *Origins of Digital Computers*, p. 289.

33. John Mauchly, contribution to ''Readers' Forum,'' *Datamation*, October 1979, p. 217.

34. Randell, *Origins of Digital Computers*, p. 353.

35. Hoo-min D. Toong and Amar Gupta, ''Personal Computers,'' *Scientific American*, December 1982, p. 87.

36. ''The Computer Moves In,'' *Time*, January 3, 1983, p. 10.

37. F. G. Heath, ''Large Scale Integration in Electronics,'' *Scientific American*, February 1970, p. 22.

38. Robert N. Noyce, ''Microelectronics,'' *Scientific American*, September 1977, p. 67. This influential paper presents important reasons for the success of the integrated circuit.

39. Gene Bylinsky, ''Here Comes the Second Computer Revolution,'' *Fortune*, November 1975. Reprinted in Tom Forester, ed., *The Microelectronics Revolution* (Cambridge, Mass.: MIT Press, 1981), p. 6.

40. Ian M. MacKintosh, ''Micros: The Coming World War,'' *Microelectronics Journal*, vol. 9, no. 2 (1978). Reprinted in Forester, *The Microelectronics Revolution*, pp. 83–102.

ADDITIONAL READINGS

Introduction

Forester, Tom, ed. *The Information Technology Revolution*. Cambridge, Mass.: MIT Press, 1985.

Comments on Technological Change

Kuhns, William. *The Post-Industrial Prophets*. New York: Harper & Row, 1971.

A Brief History of Computers

Smith, Thomas. ''Some Perspectives on the Early History of Computers.'' In Zenon Pylyshyn, ed., *Perspectives on the Computer Revolution*. Englewood Cliffs: Prentice-Hall, 1970.

Metropolis, N., J. Howlett, and Gian-Carlo Rota. *The History of Computing in the Twentieth Century*. New York: Academic, 1976.

The Emergence of the Chip

Brown, Ernest, and Stuart MacDonald. *Revolution in Miniature*. 1978. Reprint. Cambridge: Cambridge University Press, 1980.

Hanson, Dirk. *The New Alchemists; Silicon Valley and the Micro-Electronics Revolution*. 1982. Reprint. New York: Avon, 1983.

Rogers, Everett M., and Judith K. Larsen. *Silicon Valley Fever: Growth of High-Technology Culture*. New York: Basic, 1984.

4

THE BUSINESS WORLD

A
merican business has a voracious appetite for more and
better information.

  ◊ *Mark Klein, "Information Politics,"* Datamation, *August 1, 1985.* ◊

INTRODUCTION

A major part of the June 5, 1971 issue of *Business Week* was devoted to a serious overview of computers in business.[1] The underlying sentiment was that computers are wonderful tools but they must satisfy traditional business principles, they must be used wisely, and they tend to generate their own special problems. Technology is changing rapidly, prices are falling, machines are getting faster and smaller, and software to deal with many of the pressing problems of business will soon be available. Minicomputers (minis) were the big news, much cheaper than mainframes but with more computing power for the dollar. And computers were being used everywhere.

> *Process Control and Manufacturing.*   Steel plants, automobile factories, the aerospace industry.
>
> *Education.*   Business schools, high schools and elementary schools.
>
> *Financial Institutions.*   Banks, credit card systems, the stock market.
>
> *Government.*   Social security administration, research, defense department (3200 computers, and the electronic battle field), economic modeling.

  A list for today would be similar but much longer, as would be the list of concerns and claims. Our purpose in this chapter is to trace the evolution of data processing systems—their problems, their uses, and their future. The term data processing has evolved into the more ambitious concept, information processing, and industry managers need management information systems. These systems will provide instant information, decision-making models, forecasts, statistics, graphs, and tables. With a terminal on the desk, the manager can directly access all these forms of business information, or so the story goes.

Among the potential future benefits of computers, none has been as acclaimed as the automated office. There has been a call for the office to be transformed by computers and communication networks in order to decrease paperwork and increase productivity. The personal computer, which has slipped into every nook and cranny of the company, will play an important role. Up-and-coming aids to interaction with computers are an emerging application of Artificial Intelligence—natural language communication—and graphics. The impact of computerization on the organizational structure of companies is an issue, as are the fears of some office workers about the potential industrialization of the office.

DATA PROCESSING SYSTEMS

The computer is almost synonymous with business. After use in military applications, the first computer sales were to business. Since then (more than thirty years ago) business, in all its multifarious interests, has become the major user of computers. Some of the uses are obvious: payroll, accounts receivable, sales records, inventory control—management of all the basic records and computations needed to operate a business. As computer technology evolved and was in fact actively spurred on by the rising expectations of the business community, the range of uses expanded rapidly to meet both perceived and anticipated needs.

The Evolution of Data Processing

Cyrus Gibson and Richard Nolan described the goals of managers in introducing computer facilities and the resulting organizational problems that have arisen.[2] They were interested in methods and techniques for improving these facilities in response to the changing requirements of a company. They argued that there are four stages of Electronic Data Processing (EDP) growth and that it follows an S-curve from an initial to a mature phase. Figure 4-1 shows these stages with an increasing complexity of applications. Obviously, the first stage reflects the replacement of manual methods by the computer, with the primary goal of cost savings. Succeeding stages are characterized by a flowering of new possibilities that exploit the power and speed of computers.

It is instructive to remember that not too many years ago, when the population was not too much smaller than it is today, bills were received, payments were acknowledged, payrolls were computed and disbursed, and society functioned more or less as it does currently. The arrival of the computer, however, meant that management had the potential system capacity to engage in an enormous variety of new activities. This new power would translate into quicker service, more service, possibly better service for the customer, more (not always better) controls, better predictions, and new ways of evaluating information. These new applications are marked by an increasing degree of sophistication (see Figure 4-1).

A new version has arisen of Parkinson's Law, that work expands to fill the time available: Applications expand to fill the computing power available. (A corollary might be, ambition expands even faster.) What are some of these applications? Stage 1 and 2 applications are rather straightforward in that they represent largely standard accounting practices such as general ledger, budgeting, billing, and payroll. Note that Stage 3 is concerned with controlling more adequately the systems already in operation. In stage 4 the full power of computers comes into play in the form of a variety of models and on-line systems.

Simulation models are used to study complex systems for which exact mathematical analysis is too difficult. Companies trying to gauge market trends or determine crucial factors in the production process may decide to develop computer programs that simulate the situation of interest. Such programs are designed to simulate relevant features of the

FIGURE 4-1 Growth of Applications. [Reprinted by permission of the *Harvard Business Review.* An exhibit from "Managing the Four Stages of EDP Growth" by Cyrus F. Gibson and Richard L. Nolan (January/February 1974). Copyright © 1974 by the President and Fellows of Harvard College; all rights reserved.]

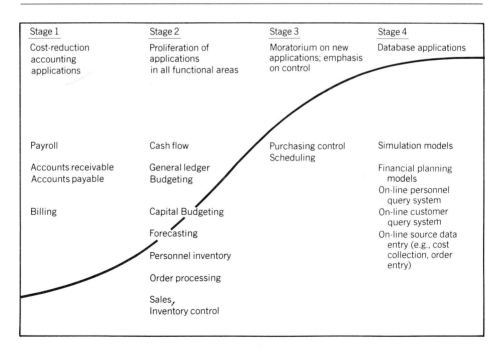

Stage 1	Stage 2	Stage 3	Stage 4
Cost-reduction accounting applications	Proliferation of applications in all functional areas	Moratorium on new applications; emphasis on control	Database applications
Payroll	Cash flow	Purchasing control Scheduling	Simulation models
Accounts receivable Accounts payable	General ledger Budgeting		Financial planning models On-line personnel query system
Billing	Capital Budgeting		On-line customer query system
	Forecasting		On-line source data entry (e.g., cost collection, order entry)
	Personnel inventory		
	Order processing		
	Sales, Inventory control		

real world and study their interaction, because the world is too complex and cannot usually be modified to serve desired purposes. Care must be taken that important and relevant variables are recognized and properly interrelated. The underlying model must be carefully constructed and subsequently evaluated to ensure that the results produced are meaningful and significant.

Simulation is a powerful tool for science, government, and industry but it must be carefully used. In the early 1970s, a considerable controversy arose in the wake of the publication of *The Limits to Growth,* a report that warned of a coming breakdown of the industrial world due to shortages in fuels and raw materials.[3] The report, based on a simulation model, was criticized for ignoring certain information, badly estimating the importance of some of the parameters, and ignoring crucial relations among selected variables. If company policy is to be based on the results of simulations, management must be convinced of their accuracy—a non-trivial requirement. Even so, the use of simulations has become another important weapon in management's operational and planning arsenal.

Financial planning models depend on sophisticated mathematical models that have been designed to predict medium- and long-term events. Such models have become quite useful and important and would not be possible without computers. Their construction requires mathematical, financial, and programming skills. As computer systems have become more powerful these models have taken on a new significance. They can be responsive to changing world conditions and permit managers to make quick decisions. It is interesting to consider a world in which the major financial institutions all depend on sophisticated financial models to carry out their activities. To the best program go the spoils.

One of the major advances of the 1970s was the development of *on-line systems.* An on-line system permits almost instantaneous access to, and response from, the system. For example, a banking system permits on-line access when the teller can update an account directly from a terminal. Prior to such a development it was necessary to enter a day's activities off-line—that is, into intermediate storage—and then enter them later into the system. With on-line systems management can have rapid access to personnel information, customer information, and sales information. It should be noted that an on-line system typically permits access to several hundred users. This requires a large mainframe computer, considerable auxiliary storage in the form of disks and drums, communications networks, many video display terminals (VDTs), and printers.

Gibson and Nolan pointed out a number of the problems associated with the growth of EDP systems in general. One of the earliest was the location of the data processing division within company organization and the implications of this decision. A data processing center could be a branch of the financial division, a service center accommodating a number of departments, or an autonomous division with its own vice-president. Each of these has its own advantages and disadvantages for the company, for middle management, and for the employees. Not uncommonly, the first computer appeared in the finance department, since there were immediate applications in accounting. Soon other departments such as sales, marketing, production, and research saw in the computer an important and necessary instrument. In some cases the large investment in computing resources was jealously guarded by the financial department, and part-time release to other departments may not have been sufficient. Pressure arose for either a central independent computer facility or center to which all divisions or departments would have equal access, or a computing facility directly responsible to other users. In the former case, the center would be just another company division responsible to the president and in competition for resources in its own right. In the latter, the center would be a service department expected to provide whatever might be required and dependent on its clients for its budget. Clearly, different organizational roles imply differing degrees of responsibility. Computer professionals may be either technicians or part of the executive hierarchy.

With the growth in applications, there is a corresponding growth in both the numbers of computer personnel and in their specialization. Stage 1 is characterized by the use of the most basic programming staff—operators, programmers, and analysts. Computer operators have such responsibilities as operating the computer from a console, altering job schedules, mounting magnetic tapes, and being generally responsible for the system. Programmers write programs and analysts are concerned with identifying the problems. The diversification of jobs has grown rapidly. Witness such occupations as systems programmers, applications programmers, maintenance programmers, database programmers and managers, communications and network programmers, and analysts.

So far it all sounds great—more and larger computers, more and better jobs, more interesting work, and more hopes for the future. However, a number of problems have accompanied the new age. Various fears have been aroused in some employees by the introduction and growth of computer facilities. Obviously, a number of employees have had legitimate fears concerning both the nature of their jobs and their continued existence. In fact, computers have replaced and continue to replace people. For many whose jobs were not lost, new factors were introduced. In many cases, a growing dependency on computers became a fact of life. Some employees began to doubt their self-worth. Others wondered just what their jobs were. Much depended on how computers were introduced, on the degree of prior consultation between management and workers, on adequate planning, and on ongoing monitoring. The possibility of worker suspicion and resistance calls for discussion with management, who may be interested in making significant changes in the workplace. Many attempts to introduce computers have run into problems of worker resistance ranging from lack of cooperation to sabotage. In some cases there actually were well-grounded fears of loss of status and of the job itself. Much has been written about this problem and many lives have been and will continue to be affected.

Five Generations of Computers

One of the best overviews of the evolution of computer systems has been provided by Frederic G. Withington, a vice-president at Arthur D. Little Incorporated and a long-time student of data processing systems.[4] He outlines five generations of computers, the first being 1953–1958 and the last 1982–? (see Table 4-1). (The first three generations run

TABLE 4-1 Five Generations of Computers

Name	Period	New Hardware	New Software	New Functions	Organizational Location	Effect on Organization
Gee whiz	1953–1958	Vacuum tubes, magnetic records	None	Initial experimental batch applications	Controller's department	First appearance of technicians (with salary, responsibility, and behavior problems); automation fears among employees
Paper pushers	1958–1966	Transistors, magnetic cores	Compilers, input/output control systems	Full range of applications, inquiry systems	Proliferation in operating departments	EDP group proliferation; some workers and supervisors alienated or displaced; introduction of new rigidity but also new opportunities
Communi-cators	1966–1974	Large-scale integrated circuits, interactive terminals	Multifunction operating systems, communications controllers	Network data collection, remote batch processing	Consolidation into centrally controlled regional or corporate centers with remote terminals	Centralization of EDP organization; division data visible to central management; some division managers alienated; response times shortened

Information custodians	1974–c.1982	Very large file stores, satellite computers	General-purpose data manipulators, virtual machines	Integration of files, operational dispatching, full transaction processing	Versatile satellites instead of terminals, with control still centralized	Redistribution of management functions, with logistic decisions moving to headquarters and tactical decisions moving out; resulting reorganization; field personnel pleased
Action aids	c.1982–?	Magnetic bubble and/ or laser-holographic technology, distributed systems	Interactive languages, convenient simulators	Private information and simulation systems, inter-company linkages	Systems capabilities projected to all parts of organization; networks of different organizations interconnected	Semiautomatic operating decisions; plans initiated by many individuals, leading toward flickering authority and management by consensus; greater involvement of people at all levels; central EDP group shrinkage

from 1953 to 1974, the year the article was written. The last two represent predictions whose accuracy can be better determined at present.) The names of Withington's generations are instructive.

The first three periods represent the initiation and consolidation phase—new hardware, new software, traditional applications, changing organizational structure, and consolidation of the new technology. Withington predicted that the fourth generation, information custodians, would be characterized by very large file stores, general purpose data manipulators, and centralized control with logistic decisions moving to headquarters and tactical decisions moving out. The forecast was actually quite accurate, with a couple of exceptions. The software did not evolve as rapidly as expected, although time-sharing systems did predominate. In the area of hardware, Withington did not anticipate the microcomputer explosion.

The last generation, action aids (beginning about 1982), he supposed would make use of new hardware such as magnetic bubble or laser-holographic technology. This last does not seem likely in the foreseeable future. Most computer companies have given up on magnetic bubble memories, and laser-holographic technology has yet to appear. Less centralized computing was anticipated, but the overwhelming integration of computing and communications could hardly have been expected. Furthermore, rapidly expanding developments in office automation promise to revolutionize the basic operation of business (see *The Office of the Future,* below). Another important achievement will be in management information and decision analysis systems.

Guidelines for Rapid Growth

The transition from computer management to data resource management is an important step. Clearly, the situation changes as the range of applications grows, access diversifies via remote terminals, and more and more activities depend on data processing. In a natural way, the computer is thus transformed into a multi-functional data resource that is no longer the preserve of a designated division but is far-reaching and integrated into all the operations of the organization. Information in a variety of forms is now accessible—on modern systems, by all levels of management, whether or not they are near the computer, technically sophisticated, or have financial, managerial, marketing, or sales expertise.

In 1979 Richard Nolan extended the stages of data processing growth from four to six.[5] He considered the growth in knowledge and technology, organizational control, and the shift from computer management to data resource management—a necessary broadening of computer applications. It is obvious that the growth of knowledge exerts an important influence on the direction and nature of further developments. In terms of organizational control, management must determine a balance between tight and so-called slack control. In fact, this balance will vary depending on the stage of growth. For example, to facilitate growth the control should be low and the slack should be high, but as the system matures both should be high. Nolan bases his results on the study during the 1970s of many companies that passed through all the stages except the last one. Figure 4-2 describes the six stages.

FIGURE 4-2 Six Stages of Data Processing Growth. [Reprinted by permission of the *Harvard Business Review*. An exhibit from "Managing the Crises in Data Processing" by Richard L. Nolan (March/April 1979). Copyright © 1979 by the President and Fellows of Harvard College; all rights reserved.]

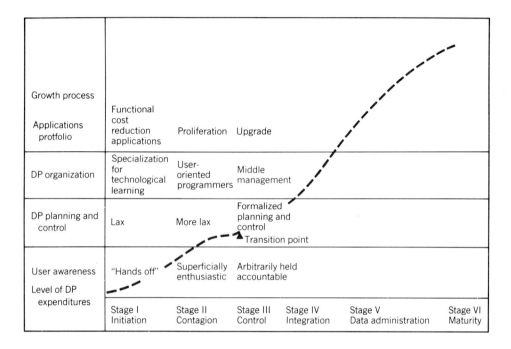

	Stage I Initiation	Stage II Contagion	Stage III Control	Stage IV Integration	Stage V Data administration	Stage VI Maturity
Growth process Applications protfolio	Functional cost reduction applications	Proliferation	Upgrade			
DP organization	Specialization for technological learning	User- oriented programmers	Middle management			
DP planning and control	Lax	More lax	Formalized planning and control Transition point			
User awareness Level of DP expenditures	"Hands off"	Superficially enthusiastic	Arbitrarily held accountable			

Nolan concluded his analysis with five guidelines for managing the anticipated (and actual, as it has turned out) very rapid growth in data processing (DP).[6]

1. Recognize the fundamental organizational transition from computer management to data resource management. This process is triggered by the growth of database technology.

2. Recognize the importance of the enabling technologies. DP networks are enabling new approaches to management control and planning.

3. Identify the stages of the company's operating units to help keep DP activities on track. One can use Nolan's stage theory to identify some of the problems associated with growth.

4. Develop a multilevel strategy and plan. Identify the current status of the company, including the strengths and weaknesses, select an appropriate DP strategy, and prepare a plan for the next few years of DP growth.

5. Make the steering committee work. It is necessary to use the experience of this committee in the planning process.

The Nolan model, or perhaps series of models, is generally well-regarded, but a number of critiques have appeared. King and Kraemer criticize the model for theoretical weaknesses derived from overly simplistic assumptions and insufficient validation of empirical evidence.[7] However, they are quite complimentary in recognizing the significant influence of Nolan's theory on data processing. The formulation of his model seemed to explicate a rather complex phenomenon in a concise and clear description. Benbasat (et al.)[8] criticized the stage approach and provided evidence from seven empirical studies that challenged almost every proposed stage. They too acknowledge Nolan's influence but argue that the model should have been based on a greater variety of cases.

A View of the Future

In 1979 James Martin, the noted author, lecturer, and computer industry authority, made the following prediction:

> *A very major part of the future of all corporations is going to be database technology. And it's now becoming clear that there are going to be many databases, not just one, and these are going to be connected to networks. The databases will be accessible from a diversity of end-user machines. And some of the office automation technology is also going to relate to the same end-user machines and to database systems.*[9]

Among the other concerns, Martin expressed the need to develop strategies for handling data, for distributed processing, for networks, and for office automation. He stressed that companies should adopt planning with a long-range perspective. He also expected wideband transmission of data to have an important impact on company operations, permitting very large amounts of information to be transmitted very quickly. Finally, he predicted some innovative developments—tradeoffs between centralized and decentralized systems, and the introduction of microcomputers into the office. (Surely even Martin must be surprised by the rapidity with which computers have become pervasive both at home and in the office.)

Since their original use in business as high-speed payroll machines, computers have become ubiquitous. They have also become faster and more powerful, and the cost of computation has fallen dramatically. The idea of the centralized, isolated, mysterious computer facility has largely disappeared and been replaced by the fact of a terminal on every desk and instantaneous access to myriads of data. At least, the latter is likely to be the spiel of the current generation of computer salesmen. In any case, we *are* witnessing the transformation of the office. This transformation is heavily dependent on local networks, intelligent terminals, facsimile or duplicating equipment, and electronic mail systems. And to serve management's needs in a more comprehensive fashion, the long-promised, much-heralded, and eagerly-awaited management information system promises to burst forth, finally.

MANAGEMENT INFORMATION SYSTEMS: A PROMISE UNREALIZED?
Definitions and Characteristics

What is a Management Information System (MIS)? There are many conceptions and definitions dependent on who is doing the defining and to what purpose. One of the foremost figures in the development of MIS, Gordon B. Davis, has supplied a definition of what it should be.

> . . . *an integrated man/machine system for providing information to support the operations, management and decision-making functions in an organization. The system utilizes computer hardware and software, manual procedures, management and decision models, and a database.*[10]

An MIS must incorporate expertise from a variety of areas such as organizational theory, economics, accounting, statistics, and mathematical modeling, to say nothing of computer hardware and software. It sounds enormously ambitious and it is. In the view of many, the open-ended expectation engendered by such descriptions is one of the major reasons why any working system is felt somehow to be short of the mark—no matter what it actually accomplishes.

What are the actual components of such systems and what functions do they (or are they supposed to) perform? One way of viewing an MIS is as a pyramid structure (see Figure 4-3). At the bottom is the routine transaction processing that probably occupies a good deal of the computing power of the system (recall that such activities as payroll and accounting were the first application of computers, beginning in the mid-1950s). The next level is concerned with supporting day-to-day activities at the operational level, whereas the third level represents a jump to tactical planning and decision-making. At the top level the MIS concept is fully expressed, with a wide array of resources for strategic planning and decision making for management.

The pyramid—transaction, inquiries, planning and decision-making—sits on top of the data. Where do the data reside? The representation, structuring, and organization of data has occupied much attention. Gradually the notion of a data base management system (DBMS) has evolved, and this concept is fundamental to the MIS. The DBMS must be responsible for manipulating the data on demand by the variety of application subsystems supported by the MIS. DBMS theory is currently a very active research and development area.

The decision-assisting models at the top level of the pyramid have been characterized

FIGURE 4-3 The Management Information System as a Pyramid. (From Gordon B. Davis, *Management Information Systems: Conceptual Foundations, Structure, and Development*, 1974. Reprinted by permission of McGraw-Hill Book Company, New York.)

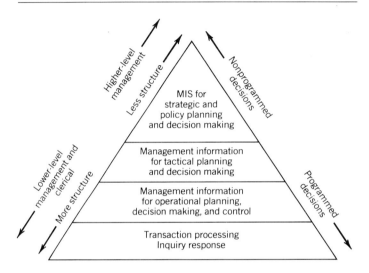

as follows:

> . . . *intelligence models to find problems, decision models to identify and analyze possible solutions, and various choice models such as optimization models that provide an optimal solution or satisficing models for deciding on a satisfactory solution.*[11]

Models may be used to deal with such issues as inventory, personnel selection, new product pricing, and budgetary controls. Four major areas have contributed heavily to the conception and evolution of management information systems:[12]

Managerial Accounting.   Deals with such issues as cost analysis, assignment of responsibility, the provision of reports at a variety of levels, and budgetary information.

Management Science.   Also called operations research. A discipline concerned with determining optimal decisions by using mathematical models and procedures in a systematic and scientific way. Some of these mathematical techniques are linear programming, queuing theory, game theory, decision theory, and simulation.

Management Theory.   Concerned with reaching satisfactory solutions, constrained by the human limitations on the search for solutions. The behavioral and motivational consequences of organizational structure and systems within organizations are also a concern.

Computer Processing.   The developments in hardware and software, obviously necessary for MIS, have also been on occasion a factor that inhibits rising expectations.

The major functional subsystems and activity subsystems of an MIS are shown in Tables 4-2 and 4-3. They are, of course, intimately related. Clearly, an MIS can be a very comprehensive system designed to serve an incredibly wide range of needs.

As might be expected, a number of criticisms have also surfaced. Many of these revolve around the issue of centralization versus decentralization of the information resources, of the computer facilities, and of the analysis and modeling systems. In a sense, certain of these problems have become academic in the age of distributed computing that was brought in by advances in computer technology and communications. But the organizational issues remain—of access, and of smaller specialized databases versus larger uniform ones. Recent proposals have suggested that the time may be fast approaching when most executives sitting at their own desks will be able to call up any data they desire, in any form they

TABLE 4-2   The Major Functional Subsystems of an MIS

Major Functional Subsystem	Some Typical Uses
Marketing	Sales forecasting, sales planning, customer and sales analysis
Manufacturing	Production planning and scheduling, cost control, cost analysis
Logistics	Planning and control of purchasing, inventories, distribution
Personnel	Planning personnel requirements, analyzing performance, salary administration
Finance and accounting	Financial analysis, cost analysis, capital requirements planning, income measurement
Information processing	Information system planning, cost effectiveness analysis
Top management	Strategic planning, resource allocation

Source: Gordon B. Davis, *Management Information Systems: Conceptual Foundations, Structure and Development,* 1974. Reprinted by permission of McGraw-Hill Book Company, New York.

TABLE 4-3 The Major Activity Subsystems of an MIS

Activity Subsystem	Some Typical Uses
Transaction processing	Processing of orders, shipments, receipts
Operational control	Scheduling of activities and performance reports
Management control	Formulation of budgets and resource allocation
Strategic planning	Formulation of objectives and strategic plans

Source: Gordon B. Davis, *Management Information Systems: Conceptual Foundations, Structure and Development,* 1974. Reprinted by permission of McGraw-Hill Book Company, New York.

wish, from personal computers that are part of a large, complex computer network. However, until that time arrives, a number of issues still need to be considered.

Decision Support Systems

A direction MIS has taken recently is toward Decision Support Systems (DSS). One definition of DSS follows:

> *Decision Support Systems . . . represent a point of view on the role of the computer in the management decision making process. Decision support implies the use of the computer to:*
> *1. Assist managers in their decision processes in semistructured tasks.*
> *2. Support rather than replace, managerial judgment.*
> *3. Improve the effectiveness of decision making rather than its efficiency.*[13]

Much of the discussion up to now has taken for granted that MIS or DSS designers have a good idea of what managers need or want from their computer resources. But do they? The following is a dialogue with a typical senior manager:

> *"What do you use computers for?"*
> *"Oh, we use them for everything. Why we have systems on-line, interactive thus-and-so's. We're putting in a distributed such-and-such."*
> *"Yes, but what do you use computers for?"*
> *"Well, I get a lot of reports. Some of them are very helpful . . ."*
> *"Yes, but what do you use computers for?"*
> *"Well, actually—very little."*[14]

This dialogue, its authors argue, represents a fairly accurate picture of an existing situation. They propose explanations of how it is that the systems that support the organization may in fact be of little use to the manager. For one thing, many systems are too rigid and inflexible to respond appropriately to unexpected problems. For another, the classical models of management science may not be applicable in situations that are characterized by exceptions and subjective issues. Frequently, in spite of adequate computing power, it takes too much time to write programs and receive results. Finally, it is important that managers work very closely with programmers and mathematical modelers to develop systems both for exploring problem domains and eventually arriving at reasonable strategies. Clearly, ambitious designers and complex systems are not enough. It is necessary to be aware of the motivations, needs, and work habits of decision-makers.

In response to these concerns, Keen and Wagner propose design criteria based on such concerns as flexibility, ease of use, and adaptivity. For example, it is necessary to employ a flexible development language that permits ease of initiation of new systems and modification of existing ones. If the system is to be used (more than once) by decision-makers, it must encourage the user by not requiring special computer expertise and by employing terms and vocabulary compatible with the manager's conceptual framework. Part of this approach is the extensive use of graphics display devices and report generators. Whatever the details of these criteria, the actual needs of the decision-makers and chief executives must be the central issue.

Rockart and Treacy have proposed the design of an "Executive Information Support" (EIS) system to serve the information needs of the executive in his or her own office.[15] They report that although the number is still small, there are a few chief executive officers (CEOs) who use terminals at their own desks to access reports, carry out analyses, and study market conditions. Rockart and Treacy predict the emergence of a new type of EIS system that should be able to store large amounts of finely detailed information useful for future projections. It should encourage two basic modes of access: status access—to permit the executive to determine the current status and projected trends of the company— and a more personalized access reflecting the special needs and concerns of the individual executive. The term *information center* has also been used to characterize this kind of support. None of this technology will work unless it is embedded in a support structure that initiates the executive with some care and provides continual help and consultation.

Also gaining currency is the "Knowledge Based System" (KBS), a term derived from Artificial Intelligence. A KBS incorporates specific domain knowledge and a set of rules to use this knowledge. As new information becomes available, the system grows in a recursive fashion, increasing the range and power of its application. Whether or not KBSs fulfill their promoters' claims, the trend is towards more powerful aids in decision-making. Interestingly enough, attempts to formalize such high-level processes reveal the enormous complexity inherent in high-level management operations.

Criticisms of the MIS Approach

Written more than ten years ago, John Dearden's paper, "MIS Is a Mirage," is still quite influential. It has been criticized for being polemical, inaccurate, sensational, and provocative. However, most defenders of both the MIS concept and specific MIS systems have found it necessary to respond to Dearden's charges. He lists "four fallacies and one serious misconception inherent in the MIS approach."[16]

FALLACY	*REASON WHY FALLACIOUS*
Management information is homogeneous enough to be an area of specialization for an expert.	Too many different skills are required for a true MIS expert to exist.
Separately developed information systems will result in an inefficient and unsatisfactory MIS.	It is possible to develop coordinated systems for functional areas without a "total systems approach." The issue is really the competence of those developing the systems.
The so-called systems approach will be a major aid to business administration.	As some have noted, the systems approach really involves nothing more—or less—than good management.
It is practical to centralize the control over a company's entire management information system.	Centralizing control over a company's information system may create more serious problems than it solves. It may just not be possible. If the MIS staff has special knowledge in this area it should be responsible.

The misconception is that the people responsible for implementing a specialized MIS system can easily move into other areas of the company and create a comprehensive, general MIS.

Critics of Dearden's point of view have focussed on his reading of the prevalent perception of the MIS approach. It is argued that Dearden has set up a straw issue and then demolished it. The straw issue is that MIS advocates view the ideal system as a unified, consistent, and complete system. The contrary argument claims that such was never the goal and certainly does not represent the majority opinion. Much closer to a mainstream view (at least as of 1972), it is claimed, is a concept of a well-designed MIS that emphasizes such issues as a combined man-machine approach, a variety of decision aids, a number of subsystems with varying degrees of integration, tradeoffs between centralization and decentralization, and most importantly, a design philosophy that is evolutionary.

In 1982, critics supplied almost mandatory remarks about how management information systems had fallen short of the mark. Some of the inadequacies pointed out by Harvey Gand are that in the design and management of MIS, the stress is frequently on technical expertise rather than on established business principles. The immediate needs of the users take precedence over the long-term considerations that result from technological change and personnel turnover.[17] Furthermore, upper management—having made it the responsibility of the MIS managers to set the guidelines, develop the systems, order the hardware, and respond to competing needs—is sometimes unsympathetic to difficulties that naturally arise. Help might be sought from the academic community to deal with many of the problems associated with MIS, but too often academics prefer to confront technical issues rather than situations involving business and managerial concerns.

Furthermore, Gand argues, the most influential contemporary MIS model (see Figure 4-3) is inadequate because it is descriptive rather than normative. That is, the emphasis is on how management information systems have evolved rather than how they should be planned and designed. In this respect, the Gibson and Nolan model does not pay enough attention to the possibilities opened up by rapidly evolving technology. For example, the trend toward distributed computing weakens the emphasis on centralization inherent in the model. Gand proposes a new model based on three goals: stabilization of the MIS process to emphasize innovation, but not at the cost of instability, the provision of adequate system support to achieve both short- and long-term objectives, and the instituting of serious planning to deal with such important issues as changing market conditions, technical innovation, and personnel turnover. One major technological change currently in progress is distributed computing. Much has been made of it as an important new factor in MIS.

Distributed Computing

In the beginning there was one computer and many people wanted (and needed) to use it. They had to wait their turn and were often preempted by the needs of systems programmers or the time constraints of a payroll program. In the late 1950s and early 1960s, the concept of time-sharing began to evolve both in England and the United States. A time-sharing system gives each user the impression that he or she has access to the entire computer. This is actually accomplished by a master supervisory program that allocates small slices of time (quanta) successively to each user's program. There are a variety of different time-sharing strategies. Through the mid-1960s and well into the 1970s, this system was the basic computing environment for most companies. All of the applications discussed previously, including management information systems, have been implemented on time-sharing systems.

On the whole, time-sharing systems have worked reasonably well. Running on large mainframe computers, they are able to serve many users and provide a variety of services, including an array of programming languages, application programs, word processors, not to mention message passing and electronic mail. However, certain problems have stimulated the development of new systems for the organization of data processing facilities. Even though system breakdowns are infrequent, when they do occur hundreds (and even thousands) of users may be affected. For example, after waiting in line at your bank, you finally arrive at the teller only to hear those ominous words, "Sorry, the system is down." When all the computing eggs are in one basket, either everyone computes (assuming sufficient capacity to meet peak demands) or no one computes, when there is an operating system failure or a hardware fault.

The next development was to connect many computers in a network, and distributed data processing (ddp) became the new, important wave of the future. The components of this future are the microprocessor (realized in relatively inexpensive micro- and mini-computers), communication networks—such as private branch exchanges (PBXs)—and new software tools. As originally conceived, PBXs were designed as a local switchboard for offices, but there is one important difference. The PBX has a high proportion of calls among its users rather than from outside. Recently developed PBXs, on the other hand, have a number of features that permit, in fact foster, the development of distributed data processing. Among these are the following:[18]

> The ability to switch voice and data simultaneously at medium rates (up to 56K bits per second).
>
> The ability to switch digitally—important because it eliminates the need for modems, devices that permit computers to communicate over telephone lines. Thus, all internal communications can be carried out digitally.
>
> Voice lines can continue to be used.
>
> More than one line can be used to link nodes on the exchange. This redundancy can improve reliability.
>
> Both voice and text messaging can be accommodated in an electronic mail system.

One basic limitation of current PBXs is their inability to deal with the high rates of data transmission required by large computers. However, they may be adequate to connect personal computers. Of course there are communication systems for linking computers but it must be entirely feasible to distribute computing power—an issue with important implications for management.

Distributed Data Processing (DDP)

There are no accepted definitions of DDP, but it is possible to characterize the concept. First, remember that the necessary ingredients for the distributed computing environment are communications hardware and software, database management systems, fast and less expensive mainframes, and powerful microprocessor-based computers.

The basic organizational issue with respect to DDP is the familiar management choice between centralization and decentralization. The three major phases of computer system organization—batch processing, time-sharing, and DDP—involve different management strategies. Management gains flexibility by the use of DDP. The history of computers and business is rife with exaggerated claims by vendors and data processing professionals and frustration for managers and customers. DDP would seem to be irresistible, given the extraordinary developments in personal computers over the last few years. In any case, consider some of the issues associated with the decision to move toward DDP.

Buchanan and Linowes have suggested two basic considerations to guide managers in their planning for data processing facilities: first, there should be a compatibility between a company's structure, strategy, and information systems; second, the activities that support these systems must be wide-ranging and separable.[19] It is necessary to analyze at the outset those activities of the company that can be partitioned into execution areas—such as database administration, applications programming, hardware operations, and systems programming—or control areas such as accessing data, scheduling tasks, and budgeting. Based on this division, managers can decide what areas can be decentralized and to what degree. A company might decide to implement DDP for the following reasons:[20]

> To accommodate the differing goals and relationships of the company's units.
>
> To allow individual managers to control their own data processing groups.
>
> To coordinate availability of information with decision-making power to support the authority of system users.

Much of this may sound somewhat abstract. What it boils down to is that companies that have a wide range of interests, reflected in a number of autonomous operating units, may find DDP helpful. For example, the database administration activity might be decentralized while "centrally established standards" are maintained. One important example of a large company moving towards DDP to improve its customer service is Citibank of New York. In 1975, Citibank decided to undertake a new program along the following lines that included (a) a reorganization along market segment lines; (b) the establishment of the appropriate technological base to serve the production needs of this market-driven structure; and (c) the redesign of jobs and processes. As part of this plan, the decision was made to turn from "big-box" maxicomputers to decentralized minicomputers and microcomputers in a distributed network.

Richard Matteis, a senior vice president at Citibank, describes the history of computers there as characterized by the ongoing purchase of equipment rather than the solution of business problems. A situation resulted in which a large centralized data center prevented the company from providing individually tailored services to its customers. In an excellent statement on the importance of DDP, he provides the following justification for its adoption:

> *Where there had once been one centralized data center for the institution as a whole, there are now many minicomputer centers, each meeting the specific requirements of the market segment to which it is dedicated. The decentralization enables us to be considerably more flexible in the services we provide to customers. It promises to be far less costly over the long term. And it ensures full accountability by management to the customers served.[22]*

As with any organizational strategy, there are advantages and disadvantages. The disadvantages include a possible dilution of computer expertise because of the increased number of computational centers, more bureaucratic overhead because of coordination problems, and increased managerial problems because of more competition for resources. Nevertheless, DDP appears to be an idea whose time has come, and the next few years will certainly witness a proliferation of such systems.

Managers and Data Processing

A number of questions have arisen about the role and responsibilities of data processing managers within the company. These go beyond the issues of computing and include problems of response to developing needs, worker management, organizational mobility, and of course, planning. Bob King, manager of Mobil Oil's corporate applications services department, was asked, "Bob, you have a well-run operation. Where are your best DP people going? Where do they move within your company?" He replied as follows:

> *Generally, nowhere outside the dp function. Unfortunately, with very few exceptions, they're not going anywhere at all.*
>
> *In spite of possessing latent talents which could be very effectively used in other areas of the company, computer people are not generally seen as movers. DP people are locked in—due to their own desires, their relatively high pay scales, and their image as technicians with limited business knowledge. DPers certainly aren't ascending to the top management ranks of other functions as was forecast a decade ago.*[23]

The achievements of these managers, such as providing instantaneous access to information, both raw and processed, to company executives, have led to better decision-making. Ironically, this development has not benefitted the data processing professional, who seems to be more comfortable with and more committed to machines than people. Other factors beginning to limit the role of the data processing manager are the increasing sophistication of the user, aided by the widespread use of minicomputers and micros, and the growing importance of distributed computing. A more demanding user community is forcing computer managers to be more responsive and accommodating and perhaps less able to rise in the company hierarchy.

In the narrower area of computing issues, many challenges remain for the data processing manager. As distributed data processing becomes more prevalent, it is important for the manager to be concerned with organizational concepts—the relationship between the DP division and the other business units, the rate of technological change, and the assessment of costs of innovation. There are many opportunities for failure and the successful DP operation must be on top of them. Concern with software developments—along with a healthy skepticism for advertised claims—is important, as is an appreciation of the problems associated with network design, traffic control, and potential growth.

From senior management's point of view, data processing has often seemed to be a necessary evil, one that often induced a growing sense of dependency coupled with alienation. However, many chief executives now want more direct access to information and even want to get it for themselves on their own terminals. New programming languages, systems, hardware, and communication networks have been combined to provide easy-to-use systems. Desk top intelligent terminals with sophisticated graphics capabilities can be used to present data in a variety of forms. Some executives have not welcomed these developments with open arms. Advice on terminal phobia or fear of computing has become quite prevalent. The impact of computers has been dramatic at the top—it may prove to be positively astounding in the office.

THE OFFICE OF THE FUTURE

Office automation will change the way all office workers function. With more than 50 million workers currently employed in American offices, this means we will be profoundly affecting our entire society. But we could not take on the task of training this many workers in new work techniques with our present office systems. We'll need systems that are intuitive and tutorial, to minimize and ease the training process. To the extent that we succeed in building friendly systems we will greatly increase the speed and scope of office automation's impact.[24]

Office Automation

What is sometimes called the "electronic office" will be brought about by "office automation" or by the use of "office information systems." It will eliminate paper, promote electronic communication, isolate workers and break down social interaction, reproduce industrial automation in the office, decrease waste of time in preparing documents, and generally improve productivity. Such are the claims made by proponents and the critics.

Probably the most common office functions are as follows:

Answering the telephone and handling messages.

Typing written and dictated material.

Filing and retrieving material.

Copying letters and reports.

Opening and handling mail.

Scheduling meetings and conferences.

Billing and accounting.

Processing internal memoranda.

Miscellaneous—organizing parties, selecting gifts.

In addition, higher level functions include the following:

Carrying out research.

Monitoring market changes.

Drafting original documents.

Utilizing resource people.

Dealing with middle and upper management.

What are the current and proposed functions of the electronic, or automated, office? They are many and diverse, but a number have been mentioned by most observers. Consider the following categories:

Word Processing. The use of computer-aided facilities to enter, manipulate, and edit text—typically via a desk top terminal, either stand-alone or in a network.

Electronic Mail. A system for transmitting messages in text, facsimile images, or voice. There are four different delivery systems:
1. Common carrier-based systems and public postal services.
2. Facsimile systems
3. Personalized computer-based message systems
4. Communicating word processing systems

Teleconferencing. The use of telecommunication systems to permit communication over long distances via audio, computers, video, or combinations of these.

Information Retrieval. The use of the computer to access previously stored and processed information—a replacement of (or at least a complement to) manual files, but far more flexible and useful.

Activity Management. Systems such as electronic tickler (reminder) files and automated task-project management to track, screen, or expedite schedules, tasks, and information.

Other possibilities include the following:

Electronic blackboards for broadcasting messages.

Electronic calendars for scheduling.

Computerized training to provide employees with up-to-date information and introduce new skills.

The portable office, including communication links, portable computers, and paging devices.

The home office as a means for increasing the flexibility of work arrangements.

If all this sounds rather overwhelming, it should, because one of the major components of the so-called information revolution is the electronic office. Much of the work force is currently engaged in white-collar jobs, and what happens in the office matters a great deal.

The Continental Illinois National Bank and Trust Company of Chicago is one of the largest banks in the United States. In late 1977, management decided to reorganize computer services in order to deal with the increasing number of inefficiencies in the office. The first step was to set up the central library, "a computerized stronghold of virtually every byte of information that had been captured and stored."[25] Eventually this library could be accessed by a large number of mini- and microcomputers. Thus, it became possible to carry out the three major perceived tasks involved in automating the office, namely text preparation and communication, the acquisition of information, and voice communication. Eventually this development led to the four systems currently in operation: word processing and remote dictation, electronic mail, an instantaneous information retrieval system (IRIS), and audio mail. All of these are widely used by Continental employees. For example, 3000 people—about one-fourth of the total staff—use the electronic mail system. A great deal of work was put into IRIS, and thus there are now over 2,000 authorized employees with access to over 120 databases with more than 20 billion characters of information. More than 800 IRIS terminals are available worldwide.

Continental encourages its senior employees to have terminals at home so that documents can be prepared and information accessed away from the office. Telephone answering devices are used extensively to make successful interactions more frequent. The integration of the system, to include more functions and to provide more access to employees, has been a prime goal of the company. For example, an accountant may use a terminal and the electronic mail system to execute a stop payment order on a check. There is a graphics facility on which analyzed data can be displayed in a variety of forms, printed, and transmitted to other terminals. Continental is certainly pleased with its approach. Other companies have made a similar commitment.

From a recent analysis of 15 case studies of office organization and work patterns, including some very large companies such as Aetna Life and Casualty and the First National Bank of Chicago, a number of important findings have emerged with serious implications for managers.[26]

1. The lack of proper information-handling facilities is a direct reason for many workers spending less than half their work time on work-related activities.
2. Workers spend 25 percent of their work time on such less productive activities as traveling to meetings, looking for information, and making up for inadequate secretarial support.
3. The commonest forms of professional activity are meetings, both on the telephone and in person. For example, senior managers were found to spend more than 60 percent of their time in meetings.
4. Too little time was spent in analyzing documents as opposed to preparing them—8 percent versus 21 percent.
5. There is a recognition by many workers that too much of their time is nonproductive and they would like to modify their work profiles.

Based on these conclusions, a number of recommendations for office automation were made, with the anticipation of significant gains in productivity. The following innovations were suggested:

Electronic mail system.

Communicating word processor system.

Portable communication devices.

Information retrieval and display.

Videodisk technology for product display and information.

Scheduling and message handling.

With all the demonstrated and potential benefits of office automation, one startling fact has emerged. At the end of 1982, "only 60 of the 1,000 largest industrial companies in the United States [had] fully implemented advanced office automation. . . . Even the word processor [had] replaced fewer than 10 percent of the typewriters in the 500 largest industrial companies."[27] There has been much talk but considerably less action. In the words of the title of a *Fortune* magazine article, "What's Detaining the Office of the Future?"[28]

The potential impact of office technology can be shown by the fact that "in 1980 60 percent of the $1.3 trillion paid out in wages, salaries, and benefits in the United States went to office workers."[29] The basic problem seems to be that it is difficult to come up with solid evidence that the costs in equipment, software, and retraining will pay off sufficiently.

> *After surveying 4,000 offices to find out which activities could be automated at a profit, SRI discovered that in all but special cases, such as legal departments, there were few direct cost savings from any current form of office automation, including word processing. The study left open the possibility that indirect benefits make word processing worthwhile.*[30]

From the point of view of equipment manufacturers, it is well worth overcoming such fears, given that the estimated market for office automation in 1986 is $12 billion (up from $3 billion in 1981).

In a special report, *Business Week* surveyed the current impact of office automation. The motivations for the new technologies were given at the outset. "Savvy executives can use new technologies to flatten the bureaucratic pyramid—by cutting management layers and redefining work patterns."[31] A series of cases were presented to illustrate the problems and promises associated with office automation. To update an earlier figure, one can state that even in late 1984 fewer than 10 percent of the top companies have made major commitments. For example, Prudential Insurance, the world's largest insurance company with assets of $72 billion in 1983, continues its traditional company strategy based on mainframes and owns only 860 personal computers. Travelers—with $33 billion in assets—is moving in the other direction, with over 6,000 personal computers in place and another 19,000 on order. *Business Week* does not attempt to pick a winning strategy but notes that the evolution of a company's corporate structure is likely to be tied in with the way it handles office automation. This view represents an interesting inversion of cause and effect. Computing strategy will determine company organization rather than vice versa.

Of all the various components of the electronic office, it is felt that the most acceptable one to managers will be electronic mail, because it will relieve the impatience engendered by the unpredictable mail service. An extension of this service will be the storing and forwarding of voice messages, certain to become popular because of their convenience, if only the price is right. Much of the utility of office automation depends on having a terminal on every desk. Even here, however, there may be problems if communication difficulties are not overcome. Hence the considerable interest in local area networks (LANS) such as Ethernet from Xerox, Wangnet from Wang, and Arcnet from Datapoint. The afore-mentioned private branch exchange (PBX) is a competing technology. It is not surprising that managers are somewhat bewildered by conflicting claims. Office automation is still poorly understood. Users have difficulty in clearly outlining what they want and vendors are frequently unable to figure it out for themselves. The suspicion grows that it will arrive not as a revolution but much more slowly, with many false starts and blind alleys.

The Personal Computer in the Office

Sometimes the pace of technological development confounds the best-laid plans of management for an orderly progression in the evolution of data processing facilities. Such is the case with the personal computer, which more and more has been finding a home in the office. Originally designed for hobbyists, the market for the personal computer exploded in the early 1980s and reached into schools, homes, small businesses, and executive offices. Early versions of microcomputers were quite limited and were used primarily to do simple accounting, maintain customer lists, and keep records of correspondence. But the machines and the associated software quickly became much more sophisticated and were soon performing such functions as budgeting, inventory management, word processing, and spread-sheet calculations. In small businesses the role of the microcomputer was relatively straightforward, namely, to automate many of the functions previously executed by secretaries. In the medium-to-large company the issue was much more complicated.

The first question of interest is how the personal computer is to be integrated into the typical mainframe-based computer system. It could be used as a stand-alone computer but it seems more natural to use it as an intelligent terminal to provide access to the information available in the central computer. However, the implications are quite significant.

> *It's not only the difficulty of supporting hundreds of terminals. It's not only the lack of software to handle inquiries from nontechnical users. It's the problem that comes up right after somebody gets an answer, and decides he could get a better one by adding more facts to the available data. For organizations just beginning to experience the costs and benefits of information that is recognized as a resource, the implications of the personal systems can be terrifying.[32]*

Along with the possible problems of control come the possible benefits of the democratization of computation. More employees can begin to understand the real and potential power of information systems, and with this knowledge emerges a more informed user group able to ask for better service.

But how do personal computers fit into the overall strategy? Who controls their purchase and distribution? Such questions were the focus of a survey by Advanced Office Concepts.[33] The personal computer is making a faster inroad into the office than did the hand calculator, the report states, and is being used as a dedicated word processor, a computational tool, and an information retrieval device for managers, professionals, and ·executives. There are certainly good reasons for this development: relatively cheap hardware and software, the perceived relative ease of use of personal computers, and an incredibly wide range of useful software packages. Thus, it is no surprise that personal computers have sprung up at every conceivable location in large companies. Most of the companies surveyed were not certain how many personal business computers (PBCs) they had paid for or where they were. About 17 percent of the 24 respondents had installed more than 30 PBCs. Their major applications were financial (78.9 percent), word processing (36.8 percent), scientific (32.2 percent), and marketing (20.5 percent). Obviously, multiple applications were reported by several respondents.

Of particular interest is how the PBCs fit into the existing data processing strategy. On this question, of 199 responses almost 40 percent said that PBCs are supported as terminals on the mainframe. Furthermore, 31 percent of 156 respondents reported that they permitted file transfers from mainframe to personal computer, and 14.7 percent more said they planned to permit them. Only about 17 percent said they allowed updating of the database from the PBCs. Finally, most respondents (almost 88 percent) did not have a company policy on their purchase. In most cases (54.6 percent) the data processing department approved purchases, but individual departments were also well represented (42.9 percent). To take advantage of these trends, IBM announced in mid-1984 a powerful computer, the IBM PC AT, which was specifically designed to be networked and thus provide substantial local computing power along with the ability to communicate with other micros. Thus, personal computers are becoming a significant factor in the office, albeit in a somewhat unplanned and uncontrolled way.

Finally, note that PBCs are also appearing on desk tops in executive offices, allowing executives who are so inclined to bypass traditional means for obtaining computer output and access data on their own. Furthermore, they are able to run spread-sheets, test hypothesis, and work at home if they choose. Such possibilities have spurred the development of management information systems designed for senior executives. (One by-product of the use of personal computers by executives lacking mathematical sophistication is that serious errors occasionally creep into spread-sheet programs.)[34] Afficionados report savings in time and effort as well as a sense of increased power and independence. If anything can be stated with some degree of certainty in this age of explosive change, it is that personal computers have emerged as an influential force both at home and in the office.

On the Road to Better Communications

In the early days computers were locked away in antiseptic rooms guarded by a cadre of initiates who were the sole custodians of programming, data preparation, and result reporting. As the number of people who had direct access to the computer increased, greater demands were made on the managers of computer facilities to provide easier access and better, more readable output. The development of time-sharing systems gave many more people access, but it has been certain improvements in hardware and especially in software that have, in fact, opened up computers.

Graphics

If the business of management is to make decisions based on all the available information, it is obviously important to reduce the effort of gathering, processing, and displaying that information. Recently, technology and software developments have combined to make graphics facilities widely available to both data processing professionals and executives. For most managers, graphics presentation is a needed relief from pages of texts and tables. As someone once remarked, a computer graphics picture is worth a thousand printouts. The benefits claimed for computer graphics are straightforward: saving of time in the production, interpretation, and communication of data, and the assistance in management decision-making provided by visual information that is much easier to assimilate. Interactive graphics systems also encourage managers to explore the available information more extensively. Graphs, charts, and bar diagrams are readily available.

The large, growing number of applications includes the following:

Computer-aided design and manufacturing

Simulation of space flights.

Flight simulators for aircraft training.

Maps illustrating population distributions, sales information, birth rates, voting patterns, and so forth.

The common attribute of these applications is that they condense and distill large amounts of data in order to improve the decision-making process. By employing a distributed computing system with a large mainframe to store data and a number of graphics terminals to display it, management can reduce costs and increase convenience. Therefore, graphics is rapidly becoming an important management tool and thus a means to improve productivity. The decreasing cost of graphics equipment is also a significant factor in its widespread use.

Natural Language

Much less developed, but of enormous potential, is the possibility of interacting with computers in ordinary language. A growing problem in the use of computers is the proliferation of programming languages, special purpose languages, and database query languages. Even with distributed computing and desk-top terminals, there is still a hurdle to overcome if information is to be readily accessible. The language must be natural or it will pose a barrier for many potential users. The first area in which sufficient progress has been made is in the development of natural language interfaces for databases.

Currently, a number of database management systems exist for the storage, retrieval, and appropriate presentation of large amounts of information. The user must consult with database experts to get help in formulating requests in a related query language (or, if you will, a high-level dedicated programming language). The user may decide to become familiar with the query language in order to bypass this step. But experience suggests very few are willing to do this, especially if the language is complex and there is any possibility of a new system on the horizon. Ideally, a user would use English in a way comparable to how he or she might address a colleague while attempting to discover some piece of information. One might imagine a kind of dialogue in which the user both asks questions and then answers the computer's responding questions in order to derive some piece of knowledge.

Several natural language interfaces for querying databases are commercially available. Intellect is marketed by the Artificial Intelligence Corporation of Boston. Among its clients are Filene's—a large Boston department store, Reynolds Metals of Richmond, Virginia, and Fleet National Bank of Providence, Rhode Island. Intellect can be directly interfaced to a number of database and operating systems. (Recently, IBM announced that Intellect was available on IBM PCs linked to mainframes.) This program eliminates the need for extensive and costly training programs. A result is that for some companies it is necessary to control access time because so many people have become familiar with the system. A typical request that can be handled by Intellect is, "Who are the top five salesmen in achievement quota?" Some queries require a dialogue. "Give me the average salary of our top two departments as determined by each department's average salaries," for example, would require additional clarifying input by the user.

To use Intellect, it is necessary to spend a short period building a dictionary, or lexicon, of words likely to be used in the domain of interest. The purchase price, about $70,000, includes training of the database manager but not the construction of the lexicon, which may add an additional $10,000. Many of the users are quite enthusiastic about Intellect's performance. "Intellect a breakthrough? Oh yes, I'd call it a breakthrough. I've not seen anything else that is truly natural language."[35] Some critics, however, claim that Intellect is really just one more tool and not a breakthrough or an answer to everyone's problems.

> *"Intellect solves one small class of problems—query requests. By and large queries are only 10% of the applications."*

> *"[Intellect was] rather inefficient. We look on it as a quick query tool for very small applications, not against large data files."*[36]

Other Developments

For many purposes, natural language may not be necessary. To minimize keyboard interaction by building in a wide array of useful facilities, accessible by alternative means, is thought by some to be adequate. This idea, in part, is the strategy behind Apple's introduction of the Macintosh computer. It provides a variety of commands, displays, and computations which the nonexpert user may access by pointing to a location on the screen with a "mouse." This menu of resources eliminates the need for a programmer and reduces the necessity of typing long lists of commands. The user can do financial computations and integrate the results into a report simultaneously. The screen is meant to capture the feel of a desk top, from which layers of paper are lifted to reveal what lies beneath. Then the lifted papers can be recalled and used. This invention probably represents the wave of the future. It has been received with much acclaim, although Apple has not yet achieved a breakthrough in the office.

Much more experimental and even less well-developed is voice communication. The ability to issue instructions and request information by voice would be the ultimate in office automation. The computer would also be able to respond by voice. However, speech understanding by computer is an enormously difficult problem, especially if subject matter, range of speakers, and environmental conditions are unrestrained. For very specialized purposes and under severe constraints, a few simple commands can currently be understood. Speech production—a much easier task—is now routinely available, even on some personal computers. Years ago, Texas Instruments introduced *Speak-and-Spell*, a toy that produced digitized speech instead of playing back previously recorded words and phrases. When speech recognition (better understanding) finally arrives, it will have an enormous impact in the office and elsewhere.

ORGANIZATIONAL AND SOCIAL ISSUES

We have discussed the major impact of computers on business but have not said very much about how computers will affect the managerial structure or office workers. It is obvious that the introduction of computational facilities has altered both the structure and nature of work.

The Changing Role of Middle Management

From Figure 4-3, which depicted the management information system as a pyramid, it might be inferred that the top of the pyramid represented higher-level management, the bottom lower-level management and the middle, middle management. This rather simple picture is instructive, for it does show a small group of top management supported by an ever increasing number of middle and lower-level managers. Furthermore, middle management is obviously situated to serve as a buffer between the top and the bottom. Traditionally its role has been to transform the high-level policy decisions of top management into actions to be carried out by lower-level management, to monitor the execution of the policies, and to report and interpret the results to the top. In the age of the computer and the availability of vast quantities of information, the role of middle management is undergoing a fundamental change. A special report in *Business Week* attempted to characterize this transformation.[37]

Simply stated, much of middle management's function has been made redundant as a result of information being made directly available to top managers. Stored, processed, and displayed in a variety of forms in computers, this information obviates the need, in many cases, for human intervention. In a real sense, the applications programs have captured some of the expertise of the middle managers once and for all.

The Bureau of Labor Statistics places unemployment among managers and adminis-

trators in nonfarm industries at its highest levels since World War II. And that does not include the thousands of managers who accepted early retirement or opened their own businesses. [38]

Changes are beginning to appear in a number of ways. [39]

Information can now flow directly from the factory to the top managers without intervention by middle managers.

Surviving middle managers must broaden their viewpoint to deal with interdisciplinary problems.

Career advancement patterns in the corporations have changed, and there are fewer possibilities for upward movement.

First-line managers have assumed increased responsibility for running the plant with less intervention from middle managers.

There will be an increased emphasis on product-related activities such as manufacturing, marketing, and computing and less concern with financial matters and analysis.

The economic recession of the late 1970s resulted in the dismissal of many middle managers as companies sought to reduce costs. Cuts were also made in companies and industries not seriously damaged by the recession, as senior management took the opportunity to reduce managerial overhead with the help of new computer systems. Even with the recovery of recent years, middle managers have not been rehired in significant numbers. For example, the Association of Executive Search Consultants said that in 1983, searches for managers to fill jobs paying under $60,000 a year dropped 21 percent from 1982—itself a bad year. [40] A fundamental restructuring of American management organization, aided by the growth and distribution of computer facilities, is probably underway.

There is the danger, in management's eyes, that the data processing staff could come to substantially replace the middle managers it has eliminated. But by preventing each department or division from developing its own computational facility—through the use of central mainframes and distributed access—this potentiality should be no problem. All in all, the trend is toward a flatter organizational structure, leaner staffs, more decision-making at lower management levels, increased computer training, and more effective information flow. Managers who wish to survive must increase their computer sophistication. This fact is recognized by the managers themselves, as a poll by Lou Harris and Associates shows. [41] When asked if computer access increases productivity, 91 percent said yes. Eighty-four percent agreed that there is a possible increase in the number and variety of responsibilities that could be handled.

Office Work

Significant changes are occurring in the organizational structure of companies as a result of information technology. It is also affecting the nature of work in the office itself. Those companies that have successfully implemented computer systems have, among other things, involved the affected staff in all the discussion, planning, installation, monitoring, and evaluation phases. Otherwise, fear of the unknown can create problems, with unpleasant repercussions. Consider the following apocalyptic view:

> . . . *automation will turn the office into an information sweatshop. Vast numbers of jobs will be eliminated. Those that remain will be in unhealthful white-collar factories, where worker production will be measured in "keystrokes"—each touch of the keyboard—and all absences from work stations will be electronically recorded.*[42]

There are also fears of the equipment: the possible video display terminal (VDT) problem. (See Chapter 10 for a fuller discussion of this and other work-related issues.) The imposition of a factory model is also of serious concern because of the rich structure of social relations that exists in the ordinary office. It is worrisome to imagine rows of people huddled over individual terminals, communicating via electronic mail, and worried about electronic surveillance. There are questions of whether skill levels will be raised or lowered. Is a person who can use a word processor more or less skilled than a more traditional secretary? Part of a word processing system consists of form letters that require only minor addenda. Contrast this with a typist producing the entire letter. Few can argue that it is somehow better for the soul to type 80 words a minute—and then do revisions or even retype an entire letter—than to use a computer to make the changes.

As business is the largest user of computers, it is not surprising that many of the technological developments in computers have been directed towards business applications. The ongoing transformation of business, made possible by the information-processing revolution and spurred on by contemporary economic vicissitudes, will have enormous implications for society at large.

SUMMARY

The history of computers is very much intertwined with their role in business. From their earliest use in payroll and accounting to more recent applications in knowledge-based planning, computers have become an integral component of the business community. Some of the business applications of computers are in simulation, financial planning models, and the extensive use of on-line systems.

Data processing has taken several organizational forms, including a division of the financial department, service bureau, and a separate division reporting directly to the president. Each of these has its own advantages and disadvantages. One of the most influential models of the evolution of data processing is a six-stage model formulated by Nolan. As of 1979 stage 3, characterized by planning and control, had been reached.

Management Information Systems (MIS) have been advertised and anticipated for several years. They are supposed to support a variety of management and decision-making functions. They have succeeded in part, but have existed more as a subject of discussion than as actual working systems. More recently, MIS has evolved into Decision Support Systems, Executive Information Systems, and Knowledge Based Systems.

Opening up more ways of serving computing needs is the growth in distributed computing. From large mainframes to networks of minicomputers linked to mainframes, to microcomputers linked to minis linked to mainframes, the opportunities are open-ended, but there are many associated difficulties. A paramount consideration is the communications hardware and software necessary to make such systems work. A variety of networks are available, sold by different vendors, with or without the incorporation of existing telephone switching systems.

Microcomputers have suddenly appeared on the scene, bringing computing power to everyone's desk (and home), but usually with little planning or overall control.

The so-called office of the future features electronic mail, word processing, information retrieval, scheduling, and teleconferencing. The impact on employment and work structure has yet to be understood. A number of other technological advances are entering the world of business. Among these are graphics (for generating graphs and presenting data in novel and informative ways) and natural language interfaces for databases (to permit ease of access to information). One of the major casualties of the growing use of computers in companies is the middle management level. It is being squeezed out as a result of the expanded role of line managers and the increasing direct availability of information to upper management.

NOTES

1. "Business Takes a Second Look at Computers," *Business Week*, June 5, 1971, p. 59.

2. Cyrus F. Gibson and Richard L. Nolan, "Managing the Four Stages of EDP Growth," *Harvard Business Review*, January/February 1974, pp. 76–88.

3. D. H. Meadows, D. L. Meadows, J. Randers, and W. W. Behrens III, *The Limits to Growth* (New York: Universe, 1972).

4. Frederic G. Withington, "Five Generations of Computer," *Harvard Business Review*, July/August 1974, pp. 99–102.

5. Richard L. Nolan, "Managing the Crisis in Data Processing," *Harvard Business Review*, March/April 1979, pp. 115–126.

6. Ibid., p. 124ff.

7. John Leslie King and Kenneth L. Kraemer, "Evolution and Organizational Information Systems: An Assessment of Nolan's Stage Model," *Communications of the Association for Computing Machinery*, May 1984, pp. 466–475.

8. Izak Benbasat et al., "A Critique of the Stage Hypothesis: Theory and Empirical Evidence," *Communications of the Association for Computing Machinery*, May 1984, pp. 476–85.

9. As quoted in Ronald A. Frank, "The Future According to James Martin," *Datamation*, October 1979, pp. 86–7, 90.

10. Gordon B. Davis, *Management Information Systems: Conceptual Foundations, Structure, and Development* (New York: McGraw-Hill, 1974), p. 5.

11. Ibid., p. 7.

12. Ibid., pp. 8–12.

13. P. G. Keen and M. S. Scott Morton, *Decision Support Systems: An Organizational Perspective* (Reading, Mass.: Addison-Wesley, 1978), p. 13.

14. P. G. Keen and G. R. Wagner, "DSS: An Executive Mind-Support System," *Datamation*, November 1979, p. 117.

15. John F. Rockart and Michael E. Treacy, "The CEO Goes On-line," *Harvard Business Review*, January/February 1982, pp. 82–88.

16. John Dearden, "MIS IS a Mirage," *Harvard Business Review*, January/February 1982, pp. 90–99.

17. Harvey Gand, "An MIS Model for Change," *Datamation*, May 1982, pp. 180–82, 186, 188.

18. Ed Yasaki, "Is there a PBX in Your Future?," *Datamation*, March 1983, pp. 100–102, 104.

19. Jack R. Buchanan and Richard G. Linowes, "Understanding Distributed Data Processing," *Harvard Business Review*, July/August 1980, pp. 143–153.

20. Ibid., p. 146.

21. Richard J. Matteis, "The New Back Office Focuses on Customer Service," *Harvard Business Review*, March/April 1979, pp. 143–153.

22. Ibid., p. 153.

23. Janet Crane, "The Changing Role of the DP Manager,"*Datamation*, January 1982, pp. 96ff.

24. Amy Wohl, president of Advanced Office Concepts, as quoted in Kenneth Klee, "Wanna Bet?" *Datamation*, September 1982, p. 65.

25. Louis H. Mertes, "Doing Your Office Over—Electronically," *Harvard Business Review*, March/April 1981, pp. 127–135.

26. Harvey L. Poppel, "Who Needs the Office of the Future?" *The Futurist*, June 1982, pp. 37–42.

27. John Cunningham, executive vice-president of Wang Laboratories, as quoted in Sandra Salmans, "The Debate over the Electronic Office," *The New York Times Magazine*, November 14, 1982, p. 133.

28. Bro Uttal, "What's Detaining the Office of the Future?" *Fortune*, May 3, 1982, pp. 176–178, 182, 184, 189, 193, 196.

29. Ibid., p. 176.

30. Ibid., p. 182.

31. "Office Automation Restructures Business," *Business Week*, October 8, 1984, pp. 118–119.

32. Peter Krass and Hesh Wiener, "You Mean I Can't Just Plug It In?" *Datamation*, September 1981, p. 196.

33. Reported in Amy D. Wohl and Kathleen Carey, "We're Not Really Sure How Many We Have . . . ," *Datamation*, November 1982, pp. 106–109.

34. "How Personal Computers Can Trip Up Executives," *Business Week*, September 24, 1984, p. 94.

35. Charles Peters of Reynolds Metals, as quoted in Jan Johnson, "Intellect on Demand," *Datamation*, November 1981, p. 78.

36. Jan Johnson, "Language Paralysis," *Datamation*, November 1982, p. 93.

37. "A New Era for Management," *Business Week*, April 25, 1983, pp. 50ff.

38. Ibid., p. 50.

39. Ibid.

40. Jeremy Main, "The Recovery Skips Middle Management," *Fortune*, February 6, 1984, pp. 112–114, 116, 118, 120.

41. "A New Era for Management," p. 64.

42. Sandra Salmans, "The Debate over the Electronic Office," *The New York Times Magazine*, November 14, 1982, p. 133.

ADDITIONAL READINGS

Management Information Systems:
A Promise Unrealized?

Davis, Michael W. "Anatomy of Decision Support." *Datamation*, June 15 1984, pp. 201–2, 206, 208.

Dutta, Amitava and Amit Busa, "An Artificial Intelligence Approach to Model Management in Decision Support Systems." *Computer*, September 1984, pp. 87–97.

Emery, James C. and Christopher R. Sprague, "MIS: Mirage or Misconception." *Society for Management Information Systems Newsletter*, August 1972, pp. 2–6.

Dickson, G. "Management Information-decision Systems." *Business Horizon,* December 1968, pp. 17–26.

Dickson, Gary W. "Management Information Systems: Evolution and Status." In Marshall C. Yovitts, ed. *Advances in Computers*, vol. 20. New York: Academic, 1981.

The Office of the Future

Gabel, David. "Computer Graphics: The Perfect Visual Message." *Personal Computing*, February 1983, pp. 96–100, 102, 104, 107, 110.

Kornbluh, Marvin. ''The Electronic Office.'' *The Futurist*, June 1982, pp. 37–42.

Lewis, Geff. ''Voice Mail Struggles to be Heard.'' *High Technology*, October 1984, pp. 23–24, 26.

Nulty, Peter. ''How Personal Computers Change Managers' Lives.'' *Fortune*, September 3, 1984, pp. 38–40, 44, 48.

Winston, Patrick H. and Karen A. Prendergast, eds. *The AI Business: Commercial Uses of Artificial Intelligence*. Cambridge, Mass.: MIT Press, 1984.

5

MEDICINE AND COMPUTERS

*M*edicine today is in the midst of a technological revolution, a transformation that is already changing the
art of healing.

♦ *Laurence Cherry, "Medical Technology: The New Revolution,"*
The New York Times Magazine, *Aug. 5, 1979* ◇

INTRODUCTION

Medicine is, at its root, people helping people. Doctors skilled at diagnosis and treatment
are expected, in our society, to recognize the health problems of their patients, recommend
the best ways to treat them, monitor this treatment, and adjust it if necessary until full
health returns or a stable condition is achieved. In the course of this process it may be
necessary to prescribe changes in diet, administer drugs, use equipment to monitor various
.body functions, or perform surgery—in short, to apply any necessary technology to meet
the perceived needs of the patient. This model for health care in the United States stresses
treatment rather than preventive methods and is eager to employ expensive and sophisticated technology. Examples of the latter are open-heart surgery, dialysis machines, and
computer-aided tomography (CAT) scanners.

The computer has been used in this system in a variety of ways. It has found a natural
home in the health delivery system and has supported a kind of medical practice that
emphasizes and depends upon high technology. These computers have responded to the
deeply felt concerns of hundreds of thousands of health care professionals working within
the current system. On the other hand, some are concerned that loss of humanity and
increase in alienation might result from the growing dependence on machines.

The most natural and earliest use of computers in medicine was in record-keeping,
billing, and payroll, as in other areas of society. In medicine, however, record-keeping

serves a function beyond its immediate use. The ability to access medical records in an information system can serve a research as well as a directly medical function. Some important application areas for computers are cross-sectional image analysis systems, psychiatry, and medical education. Attempts are being made to automate the decision-making process of physicians and to supplement the available knowledge needed in medical practice. Potentially important applications of Artificial Intelligence are being made in those areas.

People with a variety of disabilities, such as the blind, the deaf, the bedridden and the paralyzed, have been important beneficiaries of technological developments. The computer and (even better) the microprocessor have opened up a number of possibilities otherwise beyond their reach. There are now automatic devices for communication and for answering the telephone or the door. Other devices can monitor the ill and alert doctors or nurses if help is needed. Besides these uses, computer programming itself is an occupation that can liberate the homebound because it can be practiced in the home. Video games are being used in therapy for patients suffering from brain disorders as a result of strokes, tumors, and degenerative diseases. The games help improve hand-eye coordination, patient alertness, attention, concentration, memory and perceptual motor skill. A variety of Atari programs have been used as ''verbal/mathematical skill reinforcers, memory drills, perceptual motor skill practices, and table games.''[1] Patients seem to be much more amenable to and even enthusiastic about a session with a video game than with a traditional therapist. There are plans to tailor software more specifically for rehabilitation purposes in the video-game context. All in all, it sounds like a marriage made in heaven.

MEDICAL INFORMATION SYSTEMS

On the surface, medical information systems appear to include just computer databases that store information, programs to process user queries, and more programs to present the results in a variety of forms. However, special demands in medicine have resulted in the development of information systems with appropriate properties. It may literally be a matter of life and death that medical records be accurate, complete, and current. This requirement is the most basic, but there are a number of subsidiary ones beyond patient care, namely administration, accounting, monitoring and evaluation of service, research, and resource allocation. Figure 5-1 represents an idealized information system. On the left are the various sources of the medical record. The information must be represented in a well-structured, unambiguous, and readily accessible form. On the right are some of the uses to which the medical records can be put. Obvious uses are diagnosis, therapeutic decisions, and accounting and administration. Important indirect applications include teaching, clinical research, and epidemiological studies. Finally, access is available to attending physicians, consultants, nurses, paramedics, and—in the future—the patient, as an active participant in the health care process.

No existing system exhibits all these features, but a number capture many of them. Table 5-1 shows a possible organization for the different aspects of ideal Medical Infor-

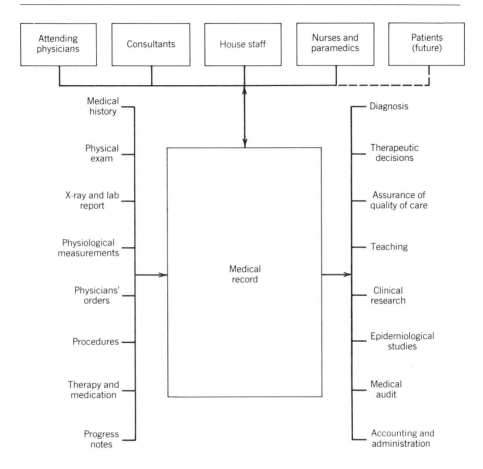

mation Systems (MISs, not to be confused with Management Information Systems). Complexity and comprehensiveness increase as one moves from Class A to Class C systems.

Class A: The COSTAR System

The COSTAR system (*Co*mputer-*St*ored *A*mbulatory *R*ecord) was designed to carry out the data processing needs of a group practice that treats ambulatory (or "out-") patients. This system has become popular because it deals with the accounting and administrative side of a group practice and also provides a much-needed system for storing and processing medical records. Some of the basic components of COSTAR are as follows:

Security module	Control of access and maintenance of backup records.
Registration module	Collection of basic patient information and keeping it current.
Medical records module	Acceptance of data from a given visit and output of reports on present and aggregate status.
Scheduling module	Scheduling of patients and sending out of reminders.
Accounts receivable module	All financial processing.
The COSTAR Report Generator	Generates a variety of listings.
The Medical Query Language (MQL)	Permits the querying of the medical information.

An organization can select a subset of these components to serve its special requirements.

This comprehensive, well-designed system permits long-term structured record-keeping as an important aid to health care. All aspects of the patient's condition, the medical treatment, and results are stored in a time history that is readily available. For example, using the MQL a doctor or other health professional can formulate a query for a question such as:[3] "Identify all male patients over forty with a diagnosis of hypertension noted by Dr. Smith during the last year." The system permits the use of accumulated medical records as a resource to study possible long-term trends for individual patients and for groups of patients.

Class B: The MATRIX Database Management System

MATRIX is a trademark for a system developed and sold by Technicon Medical Information Systems. It is designed to serve needs ranging from those of small rural hospitals to large, urban medical centers. Its major selling point is that it promises to save costs in the processing of administrative and medical records by reducing errors, increasing accessibility, and improving communication among health care professionals. One basic design consideration, and another important selling point, is that it assumes little or no data processing experience for its users. Video display terminals and high speed printers are distributed throughout the hospital. Much of the communication is with light pens and special keys on the console. There does not appear to be anything particularly novel about MATRIX but it is well-designed for its purpose and apparently fairly widely used.

TABLE 5-1 Medical Information Systems

Type	Characteristics	Current Status
Class A	Individual stand-alone, for single departments, research users, laboratory systems, and so forth.	Wide proliferation. Example: COSTAR
Class B	Hospital information system—institutionally and administratively based communication network.	
Class B Level 1	Includes an admissions, discharge, and transfer system, and a data collection message switching subsystem; on-line terminals.	Emphasis is on communications and administration-oriented applications. More than 500 systems as of 1980.
Class B Level 2	Same as Level 1, plus archival structure for medical records of orders, results, and so forth, that can generate medication schedules and nursing care plans, for example.	About 50 systems as of 1980.
Class C	Medical record-based rather than administratively or fiscally-based (Class B). Includes fully integrated ancillary subsystems or applications.	Major example is PROMIS, developed at the University of Vermont in Burlington.

Source: Marion J. Ball, ''Medical Information Systems in the U.S.A., 1980,'' in Gremy, F., et al., eds., *Medical Informatics Europe 81* (Berlin: Springer-Verlag, 1981), pp. 22–32.

Class C: PROMIS, The Problem Oriented Medical Information System

PROMIS goes far beyond automated record-keeping. It is described as ''a comprehensive approach to health care, from research and education to overall management of health and illness, with emphasis on the individual's role in his [or her] own health care.''[4] The decision-making component of PROMIS takes into account the following factors:

The current and past medical history of the patient, including treatment and progress reports.

Personal and social values, such as willingness to undergo certain treatments and various costs of health services.

> Specific knowledge about medical decision making—how doctors solve health problems.

It can be seen that this system attempts to aid the physician in decision making, not just to maintain records.

To develop a plan of action for the treatment of a patient, a large amount of knowledge must be available, including the specific knowledge about the patient: biographical information, past medical problems and associated treatment, and the current status. In order to interpret the medical data properly, a large set of facts is made available to guide the physician in exploring the possible causes of a symptom or illness. In certain situations when a possible problem has been identified, PROMIS will suggest a strategy for investigating the circumstances surrounding the diagnosis. PROMIS is continually evolving as more information is added, and should be an important system both in its own right and as an influence on other systems.

The three systems just discussed have been designed for use by group practices, small and large hospitals, and medical institutions, in both treatment and research. On the other hand, the arrival of the inexpensive personal computer has made it possible for every doctor's office to have a system for maintaining medical records. Individual doctors are most likely to use the computer strictly as a billing and accounting system. The storage of medical records may not be of the highest priority, given the costs of software, storage, and the ongoing expense of data entry. But there is a concerted effort by a number of companies to sell small systems to doctors and dentists. Apparently only about one percent of dentists have their own computer systems; many others use service bureaus.[5] Data processing can certainly help with records, scheduling, billing, and insurance.

Many reasons have been given for the importance and usefulness of medical information systems, but perhaps one additional reason might be offered: Medicare. In 1968, Medicare was introduced to help the elderly pay their bills. Medicare payments have become a crucial factor in hospital finances, approaching about $40 billion in 1984 or about 38 percent of their income.[6] Up to very recently, hospitals were able to recover their medical costs from the government in a straightforward manner. Now, however, the federal government will only pay the hospitals a fixed amount to treat each illness, not the total amount as under the previous arrangement. By this means hospitals are encouraged to treat illnesses as quickly and cheaply as possible in order to recover a greater proportion of their costs. If the cost of the treatment is less than the prescribed payment, the hospitals may pocket the difference. This situation has motivated the development and implementation of medical information systems to help reduce costs.

MEDICAL APPLICATIONS

The computer has found a welcome home in medical diagnosis, treatment, and aid to the disabled. Powerful tools have become available for exploring parts of the body previously accessible only through surgery. For patients in intensive care or on life-support systems, the availability of microprocessors has relieved nurses of the responsibility of constant surveillance. In such applications, the computer is indispensable both as a high speed arithmetic processor and in its ability to make decisions by comparing observed data to previously stored criteria.

Body Imaging

Until recently there were two basic methods for identifying and investigating problems within the human body: X-rays—with or without the use of ingested or inserted dyes or radioactive tracers—and surgery. Both methods have obvious drawbacks. Surgery is a traumatic invasion of the body and should be reserved for situations that demand the actual removal of diseased or damaged organs or tissues or the correction of problems. Its use as an exploratory tool should be minimized. Over the past ten years a number of methods for producing images of various parts of the body have been developed, employing both invasive and noninvasive means. Probably the best-known is the Computerized Axial Tomography or Computer-Assisted Tomography (CAT) scanner.

CAT Scanners

The term *tomography* refers to "any of several techniques for making X-ray pictures of a predetermined plane section of a solid object, by blurring out the images of other planes." In an ordinary X-ray picture, the X-ray source produces a diverging beam that passes through the body and falls on a photographic plate. Although it has proven to be an invaluable tool, conventional X-ray does have limitations in that there is little sense of depth, and soft tissues show up somewhat blurred. The CAT scanner uses X-rays to produce sharp, cross-sectional images of the human body. The patient lies horizontally on a table and is placed in the center of the apparatus, which consists of an X-ray source and collimator (a device to focus the beam) on one side, a detector and data acquisition system on the other. The body is kept stationary in the scanner, while the apparatus rotates around a given section, generating X-rays that are registered by the detectors as they pass through the body. There is attentuation of the beams as they pass through body structures of varying densities. The actual cross-sectional image is produced by using a computer to carry out a complex summation of the various measurements made. Although various algorithms for producing cross-sectional images have been known for years, it is only when using a computer that the computation becomes feasible.

   The CAT scanner has been hailed as a major, almost revolutionary advance in medical diagnosis. It is important that the X-ray exposure necessary to produce a cross-sectional image is no greater than that for a conventional X-ray. Most major hospitals have acquired CAT scanners even though the price is of the order of $1 million. In fact it has become something of a controversial item, as there has been criticism of the unseemly haste with which hospitals have competed to purchase the latest and most expensive equipment. However, there is no denying that it has proven to be an important diagnostic tool.

Positron-Emission Tomography (PET) Scanners

As is often the case, new technology follows rapidly on the heels of the old. The use of a PET scanner requires the subject to ingest, or be injected with, a radioactive isotope, typically of oxygen, carbon, and nitrogen. The system detects the radioactive decay by means of special scintillation counters. These isotopes are called positron emitters, because as they decay they release positively charged particles that after collision with electrons are annihilated. Gamma rays result whose direction of travel can be detected very precisely, thereby revealing a great deal about the relevant body tissue. The patient is placed inside a ring structure containing an array of gamma ray detectors. The directions are identified, and the computer comes into play to construct a cross-sectional image of the distribution of the positron emitter. The PET scanner has an advantage over the CAT scanner in that it is able to reveal the functioning of organs and tissues, not just their outline.

The PET scanner can be used to (a) monitor blood flow in certain areas of the heart, (b) assess the intake of sugar in cancer tumors or the brain, and (c) study chemical reactions that may suggest schizophrenia or Alzheimer's disease. As one researcher has stated, ''This is the first time we have been able to observe functions of the brain in connection with functions in the body.''[8] There are many fewer PET scanners than CAT scanners in use, and many of the results obtained so far are still experimental.

There are some problems associated with the widespread use of PET scanners. Short-lived isotopes are necessary to prevent the patient from receiving too large a dose of radiation while the scan is in progress. Isotopes with such short half-lives (between 2 and 110 minutes) must be produced on-site by a cyclotron. The need to have a cyclotron on hand increases the costs enormously, on the order of $2 million for a PET installation. Furthermore, at the present stage of development the interpretation of the data is a very complex process. It still requires the efforts of specially trained chemists, mathematicians, physicists, computer scientists, and doctors. It has been predicted that by the end of this decade twenty PET scanners will be in use in the United States. Both PET and CAT scanners are subject to the criticism that they expose the body to excessive radiation from either gamma rays or X-rays. A new and apparently safer method, the NMR, is currently being developed.

Nuclear magnetic resonance (NMR)

NMR produces images similar to those obtained by CAT scanners but also permits the actual observation of certain internal processes such as the movement of blood, the reaction of cancerous tumors to a particular therapy, and the status of bypass grafts.[9] All these observations can be accomplished without X-rays, the injection of hazardous dyes, or the use of radioactive isotopes. Nuclear magnetic resonance has been used for many years by chemists to analyze uniform solids and liquids. In its medical application, the patient is placed inside a large cylindrical magnet. In the plane of radiation, the magnetic field can vary between 1500 and 15,000 gauss (more than 15,000 times the magnetic field of the earth). Under the influence of the large magnetic field, the atomic nuclei of hydrogen, phosphorous, and other elements act as tiny bar magnets and align themselves in the direction of the field. When the radio frequency (RF) is removed, the tiny magnets return to their original positions and in the process emit characteristic RF signals. An antenna in the cylinder detects the radio waves and transmits them to a computer to be analyzed and presented as an image. Further information is available, because the computer can also determine the rate at which the nuclei return to their original positions. It is possible to obtain a sequence of images of the human heart with the valves opening and closing.

There are some disadvantages. Among these are cost—an NMR system sells for about $1.5 million, about 50 percent more than a CAT scanner. The system must be isolated from extraneous electromagnetic signals and magnetic substances. There may be a hazard to people with artificial joints and pacemakers. The long-term effect of high magnetic fields on the body is unknown. Pregnant women are currently being excluded from examination by NMR. It is being introduced more slowly than the CAT scanner, but the future holds much promise for its use.

Other Imaging Systems

Computers have been used in an imaging system that produces real time displays of brain waves—actually the distribution of electric potentials over the surface of the brain—on a color TV monitor.[10] This system may prove to be an aid to the anesthesiologist, who could get immediate feedback on the effects of the treatment. An array of electrodes attached to the scalp feed their signals first to filters, then to an analog-to-digital converter and a fast Fourier-transform processor. All of these steps are supervised by a microprocessor.

Another body imaging technique uses ultrasound, especially to monitor the state of the fetus in the uterus. An extension of the electroencephalogram has been developed recently, called the magnetoencephalogram. It is a noninvasive procedure for charting the brain's electrical activity. We may be approaching an age in which many aspects of the internal activity of the human body will be accessible for monitoring and measuring by such noninvasive techniques.

Storage of Images

As a variety of techniques have developed for producing images of the body, an interesting problem has arisen. Large numbers of images must be stored, cataloged, and made readily available for future reference. Since these images have been computer-generated, they can be directly stored in digital form. Considerable work has been carried out in this field, called *computer-assisted picture archiving and communication systems* (PACs). One quite appropriate and promising medium for the storage of large numbers of permanent digital images is the videodisk.

Electronic Monitoring

For the patient in the intensive care unit of a hospital, the immediate world is full of electronic hums and beeps, flashing lights, and video monitors. Many activities performed by nurses in the past are now being carried out by a combination of sophisticated electronics, microprocessors, and software. Many body functions can be monitored automatically and compared to desired (or dangerous) levels by specialized equipment that emits signals to warn the nurse if an emergency arises. This system relieves nurses of the stressful and tedious work of sitting at the bedside of critically ill patients. The patient can be assured of constant monitoring and the nurse can apply herself to patients who are conscious of her efforts.

Is the practice of medicine becoming increasingly dehumanized? How far have we moved away from the image of the doctor or nurse hovering near the patient, deep in thought, full of compassion? Perhaps this image is overly romantic and has little to do with the actual quality of care.

Computers in Medical Education

Aside from the use of computer-aided instruction in medical schools (the importance of which should not be overlooked) a significant and interesting application has been medical robots. These devices are shaped like humans, covered with synthetic skin, and chock full of electronics that simulate a variety of human functions. Controlled by computers, they are used to provide students with an opportunity to perform diagnostic tests before they are experienced enough to interact usefully with human subjects. As advances are made in robotics, these medical robots will become more sophisticated and more challenging for students.

ARTIFICIAL INTELLIGENCE IN MEDICINE

At the heart of medical practice is the diagnosis, that somewhat mysterious process by which a doctor assimilates medical evidence—in the form of family history, symptoms, the results of tests, and direct verbal reports—and determines a course of treatment along with further tests to ascertain whether the patient is in fact suffering a particular ailment. Although there have been significant advances in medicine, the determination of the nature, cause, and treatment of disease and disability is still often more art than science. The process depends heavily on the experience, knowledge, and skill of the attending physicians and sometimes on just plain luck. The educational process depends on teaching diagnostic skills by example, occasionally in stressful situations, with the hope that the novice will learn from the experienced.

As medicine becomes more specialized and more complex, the average doctor finds it increasingly difficult to keep up with recent developments. It is important, therefore, that doctors—especially in isolated and rural areas—have access to medical information systems. Such systems can serve as easily accessible, user-friendly medical libraries available at all hours over long-distance telephone lines. The next stage would be a system to provide medical advice or consultation. In this domain, Artificial Intelligence techniques can make a real contribution. One of the major research areas in AI is the modeling of human problem-solving and decision making abilities. In the last few years there has been a considerable effort to apply AI techniques to the problem of medical decision making. There are several components to this research: the acquisition of medical knowledge, the problem-solving system, a decision making strategy that captures the abilities of the best doctors, a means for adding new knowledge and modifying old, and finally, a facility for natural communication.[11]

MYCIN

One of the earliest and most influential systems for medical advice is called MYCIN, designed to recommend the appropriate antibiotics to treat bacterial infections. (MYCIN is a typical suffix for the names of antibiotics, for example, streptomycin, aureomycin.) Why not wait until all the laboratory tests are in and then produce a positive identification instead of prescribing with uncertainty? Frequently, a physician must make a decision before all the results of tests are available, in order to alleviate the suffering of the patient. This action requires making the best use of what is known, taking advantage of the ranges of coverage of the different antibiotics. A doctor can usually make the right decision, but can a program? A sample dialogue with MYCIN is shown in Figure 5-2.

Knowledge of blood bacterial infections in MYCIN is stored in the form of *if-then* rules. The *if* part of the rule is tested to see if it matches some part of the current situation; the *then* part performs an action or adds new information if the match is successful. The following is a typical rule:

> *If* the infection type is primary-bacteremia, the suspected entry point is the gastrointestinal tract, and the site of the culture is one of the sterile sites
>
> *then* there is evidence that the organism is bacteroides.

MYCIN has some 300 rules of this sort. Its problem-solving strategy is to chain backwards, trying to find confirming or primitive facts for positive hypotheses. Given the amount of knowledge it has, MYCIN can make about 100 different diagnoses. Since it must find the best diagnosis in the face of uncertainty, a crucial issue is how to combine the various degrees and sources of uncertainty to make a plausible diagnosis. The system builder must assign to each primitive fact a certainty factor—a number between zero and one.

Superimposed on MYCIN's problem-solving strategy is a simple theory of plausible inference, for combining the certainty factors in order to produce an overall certainty level for the hypothesis. There is also an attenuation parameter, associated with each rule, that measures the degree to which the *if* part actually implies the *then* part. What does all this mean? Basically, hypotheses are traced backwards in the search for supporting evidence. When this process in complete, the certainty factors associated with the evidence are combined to yield an overall rating.

The combining strategy incorporates the inference system. For example, if a rule of the form *if A* and *B* and *C then D* is used, and it has an attenuation factor of x, the certainty of D, the conclusion, is determined as follows:

> Find the smallest of the certainties of A, B, and C.
>
> Suppose it is B.
>
> The certainty of D is x times the certainty of B.

FIGURE 5-2 Part of a MYCIN Dialogue. [From E. H. Shortliffe, *Computer-Based Medical Consultations: MYCIN* (New York: Elsevier, 1976), pp. 49–50.]

.....PATIENT-1.....
1) Patient's name: (first-last)
**JEREMIAH SAMPLE
2) Sex:
**MALE
3) Age:
**60
I will refer to the most recent culture
for which you desire therapeutic
advice as:
.....CULTURE-1.....

    4) From what site was the
    specimen for CULTURE-1 taken
    **BLODD

= BLOOD [Notice the use of the spelling corrector]

    5) How many days ago was
    this blood culture (CULTURE-1) obtained?
    **2
    I will refer to the first offending
    organism from this blood culture
    (CULTURE-1) as:
    .....ORGANISM-1.....

        6) Enter the identity (genus)
        of ORGANISM-1:
        **UNK [Answer not known]
        7) Staining characteristics of
        ORGANISM-1 (gram):
        **? [The user requests
           examples of responses]
        WHAT IS THE STAIN OF ORGANISM-1?
        Expected responses are:
        ACIDFAST
        GRAMPOS
        GRAMNEG
        Enter HELP for list of user options
        **GRAMNEG

In other words, if all the conditions to satisfy a conclusion are necessary, pick the one with the lowest certainty in order to compute the certainty of the conclusion. This strategy errs on the side of being cautious, a good idea for doctors.

There are other important features of MYCIN. As can be seen in Figure 5-2, the physician interacts with MYCIN in English. This feature is quite important, as it serves to break down doctors' resistance to dealing with computers. Because of the constrained context, the natural language facility is not very complex. Another very important feature is that MYCIN can be asked to justify its decisions, both intermediary and final. Figure 5-3 gives some examples of MYCIN's explanation facility. Note that the program mentions only those rules that were used and when they were invoked.

Finally, MYCIN has the ability to acquire new knowledge. As physicians work with it they may decide to alter the attenuation factor for one or more rules, or even to add new information in the form of one or more new rules. Furthermore, MYCIN is able to accept this information in an English-like form and then convert it into its internal representation. All in all, this system has been influential both in medicine and especially in the growing area of expert systems. With respect to medicine, MYCIN has not replaced and is not expected to replace the physician. Rather, it—or more precisely its more advanced successors—will probably be used to augment the physician's skill.

Systems such as MYCIN will probably be very useful in medical education when students are learning diagnostic techniques. In fact, a recent offshoot called NEOMYCIN has been developed to capture psychological aspects of the reasoning process. These can then be presented to students to increase their awareness of the diagnostic process. Another descendent of MYCIN is a system called ONCOCIN, designed to help clinical doctors in the treatment of cancer patients. There are many different kinds of cancers and many different treatment strategies. ONCOCIN should help clinicians plan, monitor, and evaluate schedules of therapy for patients. MYCIN and its offspring have been developed jointly by the departments of medicine and computer science at Stanford University.

FIGURE 5-3 MYCIN's Response in Justifying a Decision. (From Shortliffe, *Computer-Based Medical Consultations: MYCIN*, p. 200.)

WHAT MADE YOU THINK ORGANISM-1 MIGHT BE A PROTEUS?

> I USED RULE 163 TO CONCLUDE THAT THE IDENTITY OF ORGANISM-1 IS PROTEUS. THIS GAVE A CUMULATIVE CERTAINTY FACTOR OF .277. THE LAST QUESTION ASKED BEFORE THE CONCLUSION WAS MADE WAS 26.
>
> I USED RULE 084 TO CONCLUDE THAT THE IDENTITY OF ORGANISM-1 IS PROTEUS. THIS GAVE A CUMULATIVE CERTAINTY FACTOR OF .117. THE LAST QUESTION ASKED BEFORE THE CONCLUSION WAS MADE WAS 24.

CADUCEUS

In order to be useful in a program, medical knowledge must be extracted from physicians and represented in an unambiguous form. This knowledge from skilled practitioners can then be passed on to succeeding generations. This possibility is part of the motivation for a project that has been underway for more than 10 years at the University of Pittsburgh.[12] Its name is currently CADUCEUS—the winged, serpent-entwined staff of Hermes, symbol of the medical profession. Under the leadership of Jack D. Myers, a distinguished internist, and Harry Pople, a computer scientist, this long-range project has been dedicated to developing a program that would simulate, in some sense, Dr. Myers's quite formidable skills. Currently CADUCEUS (formerly called INTERNIST) knows about 4,000 pieces of information about nearly 600 diseases. Dr. Myers expects another 5 to 10 years of work until the program begins to approximate the breadth of knowledge and skills of a trained physician. He expects the use of such a program to free doctors from a great deal of mundane activity. Some critics are concerned that such consultation or diagnosis programs will contribute to the dehumanization of medicine.

PARRY

What of the use of computers, assisted by AI, to treat the mind? Can only psychotherapists, psychologists, and psychiatrists minister to the health needs of the human psyche? For more than 15 years Kenneth Mark Colby and his colleagues have been developing computer programs to simulate mental disorders.[13] It was hoped that successful simulations would provide some insight into the identification, nature, and treatment of such disorders. For example, one program called PARRY was designed to model paranoid behavior. The program (P) is able to communicate with an interviewer (I) via a computer terminal as shown in Figure 5-4.

A considerable amount of effort has gone into the natural language (read English) facilities. Transcripts of such interviews have mistakenly been attributed, by reputable psychotherapists, to actual interviews with diagnosed paranoids. Colby built the model to test his explanation for paranoia which derives from the paranoid individual's negative self-image. Instead of acknowledging his own inadequacies, the person blames others for associated feelings of shame and humiliation. Colby would eventually like to use the computer model not as patient but as therapist to provide treatment. He argues that with rising costs and a limited number of trained professionals, many people with mental disorders do not receive adequate treatment. Of course, he recognizes that current natural language facilities are just not sophisticated enough. PARRY frequently responds with cliches, and repeated sessions reveal a somewhat limited vocabulary.

Colby feels, however, that even without a powerful language ability computer programs can perform a useful role as therapists. They could take biographical information and symptoms, make the person feel at ease, and keep him or her talking in a nonpressured situation. Presumably, the computer does not threaten, does not make judgments as to personal appearance, and does not get bored. Joseph Weizenbaum, who wrote a program

FIGURE 5-4 A Fragment of a Psychiatric Interview with Parry. (From Roger C. Parkinson, Kenneth Mark Colby, and William S. Faught, "Conversational Language Comprehension Using Integrated Pattern-Matching and Parsing," *Artificial Intelligence*, October 1977, pp. 131–132.)

I: WHY ARE YOU HERE?
P: I'M SOMEWHAT UPSET
I: HAVE YOU DREAMT ANY STRANGE DREAMS?
P: I DON'T REMEMBER DREAMS
I: CAN STRANGERS READ YOUR MIND?
P: NATURALLY NOT
I: I SEE YOU'RE TOUCHY ABOUT THAT
P: ONLY WHEN PEOPLE ANNOY ME
I: DON'T YOU LIKE BEING HERE?
P: NO

I: DO YOU HAVE ANY HOBBIES?
P: YES, I LIKE HORSERACING
I: GO ON
P: THERE ARE A LOT OF TRICKY OPERATORS
   DOWN THERE
I: DID YOU GET GYPPED?
P: YES, THOSE GUYS ARE CROOKS
I: ARE YOU DISTRUSTFUL OF PEOPLE?
P: SOME PEOPLE ACT KIND OF FUNNY, LIKE
   THOSE IMMIGRANT TYPES I WORK WITH
I: IN WHAT WAY?
P: THOSE FOREIGNERS ARE TRYING
   TO RUN THE COUNTRY

in 1965 called ELIZA (or DOCTOR) to carry out a kind of therapeutic conversation, is highly incensed by the idea that a machine could ever act like a human.[14] He argues that there is no way that a computer program could ever know what it is to be human and therefore no way that a program could be a therapist. This controversy has existed for several years, but the research goes on. Whether or not humans will ever feel comfortable telling their problems to computers, only time will tell. Certainly claims will continue to be made for the scope and power of computer programs. Obviously, at the most fundamental level of human emotions human interaction is necessary and advisable.

COMPUTERS AND THE DISABLED

It sometimes seems as if the microprocessor was developed just to help the paralyzed, the paraplegic, and the bedridden. The impact is likely to be so revolutionary that science fiction will overlap with fact. Among the wonders that will come to pass: the blind will be helped to see (albeit dimly), the deaf to hear (albeit barely), the crippled to walk (albeit slowly and with difficulty), and the paralyzed to communicate with the world.

Paraplegics

A woman had suffered from *dystonia musculorum deformans* from the age of seven. This disease, spreading from her legs to her upper body, resulted in a loss of control over her legs, loss of bladder control, the necessity to live in a wheelchair with arm, leg, and back braces and dependence on a catheter and medication for pain and muscle spasms. In September 1982, at age 29, she received treatment from Dr. Joseph M. Waltz, director of neurological surgery at St. Barnabas Hospital in the Bronx, N.Y. After four weeks she could walk and no longer required the catheter or the braces. A miracle? Perhaps. It is a miracle of modern technology.[15]

Dr. Waltz has developed a spinal-cord stimulation system consisting of tiny platinum electrodes implanted along the upper spinal cord, connected to a receiver implanted beneath the skin, at the side, and a microprocessor hanging from a belt. The microprocessor generates low power radio frequency (RF) signals that are picked up by the receiver and then emitted by the electrodes to stimulate the spinal cord. After a period of fine tuning, the emitted signals will either augment or inhibit the brain's own impulses in an appropriate fashion. The system can help improve a number of other disorders such as cerebral palsy and epilepsy.

What of those with severe spinal cord damage; surely they cannot be helped by electrical stimulation? Another form of technology may come into play here. Near the end of 1982, newspapers and television stations across the country showed pictures of a young woman, encased in a harness of mechanical and electronic gear, taking a few tentative steps.[16] She was Nan Davis, a 22-year-old paraplegic who had been injured in an automobile crash more than four years earlier. Dr. Jerrold Petrofsky, a biomedical engineer at Wright State University, had developed a rather complex system for helping paraplegics to walk. It involved taping a number of eletrodes and sensors to major muscle groups in the legs, programming a personal computer to send out carefully timed signals to the proper muscles, and using a feed back system to monitor the movements of the ankles, knees, and hips. This experimental system permits Ms. Davis to take only simple, level steps—no sitting, squatting, or climbing steps. For the future it will be necessary to reduce the size of the equipment and extend the sophistication of the program, clearly an enormous task. But for paraplegics confined to wheelchairs, the future possibilities have been glimpsed and a spark of hope has been ignited. (In March 1985, the television movie "First Steps" portrayed the struggles and hopes of Ms. Davis and Dr. Petrofsky.)

The Blind and Deaf

Most advances in the treatment of the blind and the deaf are still experimental. For the blind, help comes in two forms: technology to improve access to information, and a means for providing a crude form of vision. In the former case, the important development is the Kurzweil Reading Machine.[17] The blind person places a book or printed page on its glass top. A scanning mechanism converts the print images to electrical signals that are processed by a computer program whose output device is a voice synthesizer. The program incorporates a large number of English phonological rules (over 1,000) and exceptions (over 1,500). The voice itself is somewhat difficult to understand, but users report that in a very short time they become quite comfortable with it. In addition, controls allow the user to vary the pitch, spell out the letters in words that have not been understood, repeat previous words, and increase the number of words scanned per minute. The Kurzweil machine has become an important element in the resources available to blind people, but because of its cost—about $25,000—it will, for the foreseeable future, be used primarily at reading centers and libraries for the blind.

Braille books are the most common way for the blind to acquire information in quantity. Their production and use is rather awkward and costly. They take up considerable space on the library shelves—72 volumes for the collegiate edition of Webster's Dictionary—and are not exactly portable. A company called Triformation Systems now produces a machine called the Microbrailler 2400.[18] Typewriter size, it accepts cassette tapes recorded with signals that correspond to Braille characters. The output is an array of metal rods that produce the Braille characters. With this device blind people can now both accumulate their own libraries and easily carry them. Since most of the nation's blind do not read Braille, future efforts may be directed more to voice tapes and electronic means for dealing with voice.

On the other hand, it may be possible to bring to the blind a modified form of vision by performing the following operation. A small section of bone is removed from the back of the skull (under a local anaesthetic, because the brain itself has no pain receptors). A one-inch square teflon wafer that contains 64 electrodes is then carefully placed on the visual cortex. Stimulating the electrodes causes white points or flashes of light to be seen (and this is the appropriate word) by the blind person. In its working model, the complete system will consist of a miniaturized TV camera mounted in glasses, or inserted in an artificial eye that is attached to a microprocessor inserted in an eyeglass frame. The microprocessor will organize the image from the camera so as to produce an appropriate array of signals that can be sent by radio or directly connected to the wafer on the visual cortex. So far, only simple visual patterns can be recognized because the number of electrodes is too small. Furthermore, stimulating a system as complex as the visual cortex in a meaningful way is as complicated as trying to input a given number into a computer by exciting elements of its large memory. Clearly, much experimentation is necessary before a device of this sort will be useful.[19]

Similar devices are being reported for the deaf. One consists of a microphone that picks up sound, transforms it into an electrical signal, and transmits this signal to an electrode implanted into the cochlea of the inner ear. The cochlea is the coiled structure that stimulates many hair cells to produce electrical signals in the auditory nerve. The few people who have had this system implanted report sound similar to a radio that is not tuned in. Nevertheless, specific sounds such as traffic noises and telephones can be identified.[20] The attempt to link microprocessors and electrical transducers to human sensory and motor systems is just beginning. Successful linking will certainly prove to be a long and difficult road.

The Bedridden

Microprocessors are being used to control various parts of the environment of bedridden people by translating spoken or other commands into actions. One such individual, Rob Marince, who is paralyzed in his arms and legs, must lie on his back and until very recently would have been condemned to the prison of the mind within the body.[21] Thanks to his brother and a friend, he now is at the center of a wondrous communication network. Through voice control he can summon television from around the world by requesting the satellite dish in the yard to be pointed in any given direction. With a vocabulary of about 300 words, he can play video games, participate in a conference type telephone system, use a video recorder, dictate letters, dim the lights, and even program a computer. In the future a robotic arm will be hooked up to the system. All this is quite expensive— though Gary Marince, the ingenious brother, managed to acquire about $60,000 in free components from manfacturers. Such systems will get cheaper, especially since the heart of the system, the microprocessor, is already relatively inexpensive.

The computer itself has enabled a number of disabled people to express themselves in ways not previously possible. Cerebral palsy has prevented many of its victims from speaking understandably or from controlling their arms and hands to write. Typing requires less motor coordination, especially on specially designed oversize keyboards connected to microcomputers. With special programming languages and software, such afflicted people can communicate more readily, and minds locked in uncooperative bodies can emerge. A number of handicapped children have found the computer to be a liberating force that returns much for the little effort required to press a few buttons. For those unable to speak clearly, a computer can display their words as they are keyed in and through a speech synthesizer make them heard. The applications are growing daily as the disabled become aware of the potentialities of the computer.[22]

A Very Personal Computer

The first cardiac pacemaker was implanted in a human in 1958, in Sweden, and the second a year later in the United States. These early devices emitted pulses in a fixed, regular pattern to overcome the condition known as heart block, in which the body's method for stimulating the heart operates intermittently. Unfortunately, this fixed-rate system of stimulation could occasionally cause the heart to beat too rapidly (tachycardia), resulting in death. Advances in design resulted in pacemakers that operated only on demand, when the body's natural stimulation failed. Eventually, pacemaker technology benefitted from developments in microelectronics, and programmable microprocessors are currently being implanted. Physicians can vary such features as sensor-amplifier sensitivity, energy output per pulse, pulse width, pulse frequency, and delay between chamber pulses. In addition, system diagnostics are available over telephone lines to permit doctors to check the behavior of the pacemaker. The importance of such developments is readily apparent—approximately 150,000 implants are done yearly at a cost of over $2 billion.[23]

Social Issues

Perhaps the most serious charge against the use of computers in medical care, or in the health delivery system, is that they tend to dehumanize the patient-physician relationship. This argument suggests that doctors will shunt patients towards computers in order to increase their income by treating more patients. For the foreseeable future, computers will not be treating people directly; they will be an adjunct to doctors, complementing their knowledge. But what about large information systems, in which the patient is just a record to be scanned, modified and, of course, billed. It is certainly possible for patients to be treated in a dehumanizing way in a large medical center. The question is whether or not the use of computers aggravates this situation. Critics of computers in medical care argue that by their very nature the machines, and the organizational structure in which they are embedded, tend to centralize control, diminish individual responsibility, and inevitably will decrease the human quality in the relationship. On the other hand, computers that assume much of the routine clerical work in hospitals and offices should free conscientious physicians to spend more time with their patients.

Hardly anyone could disagree with the important applications made feasible by computers in body imagery, education, and devices for the disabled. Surely the ability to diagnose internal problems by relatively noninvasive means is an incalculable benefit. But even here, the haste with which hospitals rushed to acquire million-dollar machines made many uncomfortable. The motivation seemed to be a concern with status and prestige rather than the therapeutic benefits. CAT scanners seemed to typify a large-machine mentality at the heart of the U.S. medical system. It was easier to purchase a large machine than to provide preventive medical care for the less fortunate members of the community. In the case of microprocessor-based equipment for the disabled, there should be no argument against the significant and beneficial changes made in the lives of such people. However, there seems to be an imbalance in that relatively large amounts of money have been made available for treatment and equipment for a relatively few individuals. On the other side it is argued that costs are high in the initial experimental phases, but in the long run many will benefit.

Other issues include the question of responsibility and legal liability in the age of computer-based decision making. This concern enters in especially with respect to the use of AI techniques in medical expert systems. Who is responsible for the failure of a diagnosis or a course of treatment decided on with a computer? Is it the programmer or team of programmers, the computer manufacturer, the medical experts from whom the knowledge was derived, the actual physician in charge of the case, or the hospital itself? Such questions must be answered in anticipation of increasingly widespread use of computers in medical decision making. An interesting reverse aspect of this potential problem is that hospitals or doctors may be found negligent if they fail to use a computer in situations where its performance is superior to that of a doctor. For example, if a computer system were available with specialized knowledge for some rare disorder and the doctor on the case did not avail him/herself of this knowledge, to the detriment of the patient, grounds for criminal charges might exist.

The following list of questions about computers and medical care is not comprehensive, but does suggest the kinds of issues that are arising.[24]

1. How can confidentiality of medical records be maintained?
2. Is the developing standardized computer review of diseases an inhibiting force in medical practice?
3. What are the responsibilities associated with autonomous monitoring systems?
4. Will medical information systems aid medical research?
5. Will computer-based medical decision making actually improve care?
6. Will physicians use medical decision making systems, and what are the legal implications?
7. How will medical information systems affect employment?
8. How are the roles of health professionals altered when computer systems are used?

The fundamental question to be addressed is whether or not computers will improve the health delivery system both in terms of the quality of the care itself and the numbers of people involved.

> *The reliance on technology to solve what is essentially a complex social issue is not peculiar to medicine. Failure to recognize the interplay of social forces underlying a problem makes for inappropriate and wasteful uses of scarce resources.*[25]

Surely, many people have been helped and will be helped by medical technology, but will society as a whole be improved? Another way to focus on the use of computers in medical care is to ask if money spent on computers might better be spent on nurses. Are large amounts of money being used to help a relatively small number of people with expensive technology, to the detriment of the health care services available to many others? Given the rising costs of health care, computers are seen by many administrators as a way to control expenditures while maintaining a high level of service. These decisions about the welfare of citizens must be made by society at large. To enable that process, the role and impact of computers in medicine must be regularly monitored and assessed.

SUMMARY

The practice of medicine is slowly being affected by the use of computers in record-keeping, diagnosis, treatment, and research.

Beyond the direct application of storing patient records, medical information can serve a variety of needs, including medical research. Computer databases, which can be searched more easily than manual ones, can uncover trends and access individual records at a distance. Systems vary in range of functions, ease of use, and ability to accommodate new data processing responsibilities. In medical diagnosis, computers play a vital role in the new area of body imaging, which includes such systems as CAT scanners, PET scanners, and NMR systems. Other important computer applications are the automated electronic monitoring of patients and the use of medical robots for teaching purposes.

AI has come to play a useful role. Diagnostic systems incorporate expert knowledge that is derived from physicians and implemented in programs that can perform limited medical reasoning. There have been tentative attempts to model psychologically deviant behavior.

The linking of computers to communication systems and to physical manipulators has provided new opportunities for disabled people to escape the boundaries of their beds and homes. The Kurzweil Reading Machine helps the blind to access material not available in Braille automatically and quickly. Other aids for the disabled are still in the experimental stage.

New microprocessor-driven pacemakers are being used to deal with various cardiac problems. In addition, they facilitate long-distance patient monitoring and treatment.

Some commentators have expressed concern that an increasing use of technology in the medical delivery system will lead to dehumanization of the doctor-patient relationship. Large expenditures for medical technology have also been criticized as an allocation of resources away from preventive care.

NOTES

1. Susan L. Westphal, "Video Games Aren't All Play," *High Technology*, May 1983, p. 78.

2. Peter D. Beaman, Norma S. Justice, and G. Octo Barnett, "A Medical Information System and Data Language for Ambulatory Practices," *Computer*, November 1979, pp. 11–12.

3. Ibid., p. 14.

4. Peter L. Walton, Robert R. Holland, and Lawrence I. Wolf, "Medical Guidance and PROMIS," *Computer*, November 1979, p. 19.

5. Kenneth Klee, "Oh, Those Doubting Dentists," *Datamation*, August 1982, p. 34.

6. "The Medicare Squeeze Pushes Hospitals into the Information Age," *Business Week*, June 18, 1984, p. 87.

7. Richard Gordon, Gabor T. Herman, and Steven A. Johnson, "Image Reconstruction from Projections," *Scientific American*, October 1975, pp. 56–61, 64–68.

8. Dr. Vincent Sade, as quoted in Ellen Ruppel Schell, "PET Projects," *Technology Review*, January 1982, p. 19.

9. Franklin H. Portugal, "NMR: Promises to Keep," *High Technology*, August 1984, pp. 66–69, 72–73.

10. Marilyn A. Harris, "Brain Waves Appear on TV in Real Time," *Electronics*, February 24, 1983, pp. 47–48.

11. Bruce G. Buchanan and Edward H. Shortliffe, eds., *Rule-Based Expert Systems: The MYCIN Experiments of the Stanford Heuristic Programming Project* (Reading, Mass.: Addison-Wesley, 1984).

12. Patrick Huyghe, "The Electronic Doctor," *Science Digest*, April 1983, pp. 36–38, 97.

13. Kenneth M. Colby, *Artificial Paranoia* (New York: Pergamon, 1976).

14. Joseph Weizenbaum, *Computer Power and Human Reason* (San Francisco: Freeman, 1976).

15. Mark A. Fischetti, "Probing the Human Body," *IEEE Spectrum*, January 1983, pp. 77–78.

16. Stephen Solomon, "Spare-Parts Medicine," *The New York Times Magazine*, November 28, 1982, pp. 120, 134.

17. E. Cantarow, "Raymond Kurzweil, Giving 'Sight' to the Blind," *Sci Quest*, February 1981, pp. 21–23.

18. G. Bruce Knecht, "Computer-Age Tools for the Blind," *Dun's Business Month*, February 1983, pp. 43, 45.

19. John Horgan, "Medical Electronics," *IEEE Spectrum*, January 1984, pp. 92–93.

20. Ibid., p. 92.

21. Philip Faflick, "Power to the Disabled," *Time*, December 13, 1982, pp. 66, 68, 70.

22. Sylvia Weir, Susan Jo Russell, and Jose A. Valente, "Logo: An Approach to Educating Disabled Children," *Byte*, September 1982, pp. 342, 347, 350, 352, 355, 358, 360.

23. Janet Raloff, "Keeping Pace," *Datamation*, January 1984, pp. 38–40, 44, 46.

24. Anthony I. Wasserman, "A Problem-List of Public Policy Issues Concerning Computers and Health Care," *Communications of the Association for Computing Machinery*, May 1975, 279–280.

25. Abbe Mowshowitz, *The Conquest of Will* (Reading, Mass.: Addison-Wesley, 1976), p. 140.

ADDITIONAL READINGS

Introduction

Preston, Kendall, Jr., et al. ''Computing in Medicine.'' *Computer*, October 1984, pp. 294–311.

Medical Information Systems

Schatz, Willie. ''Pinching Pennies.'' *Datamation*, February 1984, pp. 79–82.

Sneider, Richard M., Ralph E. Boyce, and Charles A. Tapella. ''The Matrix Data Base Management System.'' *Computer*, November 1979, pp. 28–31.

Medical Applications

Brody, Jane E. ''Magnetic Device Lifts Hopes For Diagnosis Without X-Ray.'' *The New York Times*, November 28, 1982, pp. 1, 39.

Cherry, Laurence. ''Medical Technology: The New Revolution,'' *The New York Times Magazine*, August 5, 1979, pp. 12–17.

Fischetti, Mark A. ''Probing the Human Body.'' *IEEE Spectrum*, January 1983, pp. 75–78.

Wallis, Claudia. ''Making the Body Transparent,'' *Time*, January 31, 1983, pp. 58–59.

Artificial Intelligence

Colby, Kenneth Mark. ''Computer Psychotherapists.'' In Sidowski, Joseph, et al. eds., *Technology in Mental Health Care Systems*. Norwood, N.J.: Ablex, 1980, pp. 109–117.

Taylor, Tom R. ''The Role of Computer Systems in Medical Decision Making.'' In Smith, H. T., and T. R. G. Green, eds., *Human Interaction with Computers*. New York: Academic, 1980.

Ticer, Scott. ''Therapy on a Disk: The Computerized Road to Mental Health.'' *Business Week*, August 19, 1985, pp. 75–77.

Computers and the Disabled

''Computers and the Disabled.'' *Byte*, September 1982 (speical issue).

Krahe, Jaime Lopez. ''Man-Machine Communication.'' In Gremy, F., et al., eds., *Medical Informatics Europe 81* (Berlin: Springer-Verlag, 1981), pp. 883–889.

Technology and Handicapped People. U.S. Congress, Office of Technology Assessment, OTA-H-179. Washington, D.C., May 1982.

Social Issues

Fitter, Mike and Max Sime, ''Creating Responsive Computers: Responsibility and Shared Decision-Making.'' In Smith, H. T., and T. R. G. Green, eds., *Human Interaction with Computers*. New York: Academic, 1980, pp. 39–66.

Shell, Ellen Ruppell. ''CAT Fever: A Questionable Prognosis.'' *Technology Review*, July 1981, pp. 22–27.

6

COMPUTERS AND EDUCATION

*I*nformation technology holds a significant promise as a
mechanism for responding to the education and training
needs of society, and it will likely become a major
vehicle for doing so in the next few decades.

◇ *U.S. Congress Office of Technology Assessment,* Informational
Technology and Its Impact on American Education, *1982.* ◇

INTRODUCTION

In 1866, the blackboard was hailed as a revolutionary device certain to have a significant
impact on the educational process. Since then, "revolutionary" changes have appeared
more frequently: radio in the 1920s, film in the 1930s and 1940s, language laboratories
and television in the 1950s, and beginning in the 1960s, the computer. Claims for the
latter have been mounting ever since. It will allow students to learn at their own pace. It
will not be judgmental, impatient, or unsympathetic. Appearance, social class, and race
are irrelevant to it. The teacher will be free to devote quality time to those with real need
while others acquire information, review material, take tests, or even play games. The
computer will keep track of the student's progress, produce grades and averages, suggest
additional material, and alert the teacher to any potential or actual problem. More and
more material will be made available in an ever-increasing number of subjects. The
computer itself will excite students, igniting their native curiosity and natural desire to
learn. New programming languages and systems will appear, opening up innovative and
challenging environments. In short, it is claimed, teaching and learning will never be the
same.

Between 1982 and 1983, elementary schools with computers increased from 20 percent to 62 percent. For junior high and high schools, the increases were from 40 percent to 81 percent and 58 percent to 86 percent, respectively. The growth in the number of computers in schools promises also to be explosive a recent survey reveals.[1] In all levels of the educational system, both public and private, it is estimated that there will be almost nine million computers installed by the end of 1990. It is further estimated that of these about two million will be sold in 1990 at an average cost of about $1000. Associated with the hardware is an enormous market for courseware—the software necessary for computer-aided instruction. In 1990 almost $260 million of courseware is expected to be sold with the new computers, and about $340 million more will come from sales for existing computers. Thus, the total 1990 market is estimated to be approximately $2.6 billion. It has been further estimated that the market will reach $3 billion by 1986.[2]

The major manufacturers of microcomputers, such as Apple, IBM, Commodore, and Radio Shack, are certainly competing strenuously for this market. In fact, Apple offered to donate a computer to every school in the country if given improved tax benefits. Such a gift would have resulted in not only tax benefits but also increased software sales. This congressional bill failed. In 1983 Apple went on to offer a free system to every school in California, and over 9,000 systems were distributed at a cost of about $20 million. Apple is by far the most important computer company in education, with almost half the school market as of 1983. Radio Shack trails with 21 percent, Commodore with 15 percent, and Atari, IBM, and TI have about 7.5 percent of the total. Furthermore, of about 6200 educational software packages, 2000 can be run on Apples. IBM, never shy about entering a profitable market, seemed to be gearing up to establish the IBM PC Jr. as a major competitor to the ubiquitous Apple. Then in March 1985 it announced that it was suspending production of the PC Jr.

The rush for computer education is not limited to the schools. On television and in magazine advertisements, parents are being urged to buy computers and software so that their children are not disadvantaged. The problem of choosing appropriate home computers and software has become so overwhelming that a new industry has arisen of books and magazines that describe not only the home computer market but individual computers as well. Bookstores now offer computer sections. Not just books and magazines but also floppy disks and cassettes are for sale. It is argued that unless children have access to computers at home they will fall behind because of the shortage of computers in the schools. (The question of computer literacy is discussed in Chapter 14.) Of course, parents are reminded that they will also be able to use the computer for household finances, mailing lists, recipes, and video-games.

For the student who does not want to be left behind even in the summer, the computer camp offers the opportunity to combine nature and technology. Some computer manufacturers—Atari is one—have started their own camps. Campers or students focus their activities toward mastering the personal computer in the context of normal camp events. Some questions may be raised about unrelieved year-round pressure on young people to achieve success at the terminal. The usual rejoinder is, kids demand computer time, so what is a parent to do?

The voices of the young themselves may be instructive. In 1981, *Datamation* interviewed four teenagers between the ages of 13 and 16 from across the United States. These boys have a combined experience of 12 years in computing. Below are some of the responses:[3]

> They need to take history out and put computers in because history has no meaning. You never use history.
>
> Who cares if Davy Crockett discovered America?
>
> English grows increasingly redundant.
>
> They're [computers] very fast, dumb beasts.
>
> Programmers are smarter than computers, but computers think faster.
>
> It's never the machine's fault.
>
> All I ever read is manuals and computer magazines and that stuff.
>
> In the future there won't be any more public schools. People will sit in front of their CRTs. . . .

Much of these boys' conversation is technical, full of terms like Winchester disks, CDC Cyber 73, Microsoft BASIC, Z80B, VisiCalc, and voice synthesizer. It is small wonder that many adults say they occasionally feel that they have come in in the middle of a movie.

As companies rapidly introduce and expand their computer systems, it becomes a matter of survival for employees, including management, to acquire computer skills. In response to such needs a number of institutes and schools have appeared to serve this market. At the top of the line is the School of Management and Strategic Studies run by the Western Behavioral Sciences Institute in California. It caters to potential chief executives and provides some unique benefits, at a cost, of course. For example, each student receives a microcomputer to keep after the course is over. Much of the instruction, assignments, and consultation is carried out over a computer network. The result is a flexible, asynchronous system of instruction and communication, an important consideration for busy executives. They can pursue their education at their desks, at home, and in their free time. Though currently expensive, home education over computer networks may be a significant part of the future education systems.

Computer-assisted instruction is a well-known term, but what does it include and how well is it working? A well-publicized, much acclaimed computer learning environment is provided by the language LOGO. It arose out of research carried out by Artificial Intelligence researchers. The LOGO environment is supposed to liberate the young from the constraints of traditional educational methods. From the elementary school to the university, computers are playing an ever-increasing role both as part of traditional education and as a new focus for investigation. Finally, the impact of computers on the educational process has been criticized, and needs to be evaluated.

COMPUTER-ASSISTED INSTRUCTION (CAI)

CAI is not just another computer application; it has the potential to shake up the entire school system and revolutionize education.[4]

Any discussion of computers in education is inevitably sprinkled with an alphabet soup of names: CAI, CAL, CBE, and CML. Figure 6-1 shows the devision of computer-based education (CBE) into a number of categories. CBE is the general, catchall term for all uses of computers in education, instructional or not. The major component of noninstructional uses is data processing, including record keeping, inventory control, attendance and employment records, and other nonacademic uses. Some of the noninstructional applications shown in Figure 6-1 may be described as follows:

- **Computer-assisted testing (CAT):** The use of the computer solely as a testing medium. It is possible to take advantage of the computer's abilities to provide imaginative tests or merely to use it as a substitute for manual testing.
- **Computer-assisted guidance (CAG):** The computer is used as an information retrieval system to provide guidance for graduating students. It does not add to students' skills or knowledge but may encourage them to take certain courses to help with their future career plans.

FIGURE 6-1 An Organization Structure for Computer-Based Education. (From Greg Kearsely, "Educational Applications, Unit 16," *Computers in Perspective,* 1978. Copyright © by Athabaska University; all rights reserved. Reprinted by permission of Athabaska University.)

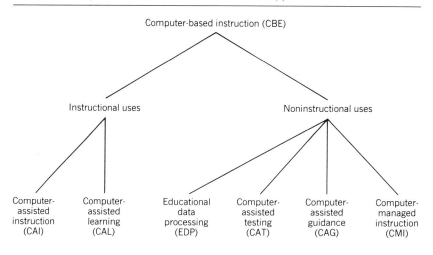

- **Computer-managed instruction (CMI):**   The teacher uses the computer to plan a course of study, tailored for the student, that consists of computer sessions, readings, and testings. The computer will keep track of the student's performance and provide regular reports, highlighting problems and accomplishments. (In England this application is called computer-managed learning—CML.)

These applications are useful and important, but the most interesting, exciting, and far-reaching work is being done in the areas of CAI and CAL.

Varieties of CAI

Simply put, CAI is the use of the computer directly in the instructional process as either a replacement for or complement to books and teachers. CAI has been a factor in education for a long time (since the 1960s at least)—as a much-heralded but never quite perfected educational system. Because of the premature introduction of CAI software, many educators have become quite cautious about the claims for such systems. However, with the pervasiveness of microcomputers, the demand to install CAI systems in schools has become overwhelming. An overwhelming amount of software is also available. Among the many varieties of CAI are the following:

- **Drill and practice:**   The teacher provides the primary material in the ordinary classroom environment. The CAI system is then used by students to test the level of their knowledge and to practice certain skills. This use complements the teacher, permits students to make mistakes while learning in a private context, and allows the teacher to spend extra time with weaker students.
- **Tutorial:**   The computer system is used to present new material to the student. It incorporates a teaching strategy that involves an evaluation procedure, alternative ways to formulate questions to the student, and some degree of flexibility in interpreting student responses.
- **Simulation:**   It is used to explore a relatively complex problem domain. It captures the important aspects of the situation and permits the student to explore the ways in which the various variables interact. Simulations are useful in studying biology (predator-prey models), transportation, urban development, and computer configurations.
- **Games:**   For academic purposes games can be a somewhat painless way of providing information and sharpening skills.
- **Cognitive diagnostics:**   This relatively new application involves the use of the computer to determine automatically the kinds of systematic mistakes or bugs that students make. This process can be very important in helping students improve their performance.

In the basic mode of drill and practice, the computer asks a question, receives the answer and provides an appropriate response. If the student's answer is correct, a complimentary remark is in order. If the answer is incorrect but belongs in a class of expected answers, a variety of responses may be selected. Finally, if the answer is incorrect and the system cannot deal with it, it must repeat the original question, and supply the answer, or go on to a new but similar question. In the second case, the question may be repeated with an encouraging remark, or a new question is posed based on the student's perceived difficulty. Because the computer can be programmed to keep track of each student's individual performance over a long period of time, at any given session it can work on those areas that need special attention and also boost the student's ego by reinforcing performance in areas of past success. Clearly, drill and practice are helpful when simple facts are to be learned in a structured context.

Tutorial systems for CAI are much more complex, since in this context new information is being delivered. At each stage the program can supply some general piece of information, a fact, an example, or a question to test the student's comprehension. As the major purpose of tutorial programs is to teach, they must have some way of determining what the student probably knows, what his or her difficulties are, and how the material can best be presented. In such programs, the knowledge typically is represented in a tree structure, and the presentation involves following the branches exhaustively. By precisely defining a local context, this tree organization helps identify the problems that the student may be having.[5]

There are other aspects of this approach to CAI. For instance, more than one answer to a question may be acceptable, and the program must be prepared to deal appropriately with different responses. Furthermore, it must be able to produce sequences of questions that explore some area in detail, and such sequences may depend on the nature of the intervening questions. Clearly, the preparation, design, and realization of tutorial programs is a complex task, and it is not surprising that the overall quality of such programs could be better. As the material to be presented becomes more difficult, the problem of presenting it also becomes more of a challenge. Tutorial programs are increasingly useful as they allow more flexible input by the student. This input may include the ability to ask limited questions. Once again the influence of Artificial Intelligence will become increasingly important, as programs become able to communicate more readily with users. In addition to facility in natural language, the more advanced programs will need abilities in problem solving, knowledge representation, and inferencing.

Simulations are useful for studying processes so complex that it is difficult to determine the specific impact of individual variables. For example, suppose we are interested in studying traffic flow at a busy intersection. A computer program can be written to capture the important features of the intersection—the traffic light sequence, and estimates of traffic density in each direction—defined by the average expected occurrence of a vehicle in a given small time interval. How is the backup of traffic related to the arrival rates and the traffic light patterns? To facilitate this investigation, a simulation program will accept values for the input numbers and then display the resulting behavior as it unfolds over time, preferably using graphics. In more advanced applications, students will be able to construct the simulation domain themselves out of a building block set of components, to study not only the system behavior but how well it has been modeled. As the simulation unfolds, the system may ask the student about decisions involved in selecting values and about expectations that the student has about its behavior. Simulations are designed for more than the acquisition of factual knowledge. They encourage students to discover for themselves how something works. They have been used extensively in the physical and biological sciences as a substitute for and supplement to actual laboratory experiments.

As *video games* established an incredible appeal and excitement outside the educational establishment, it was inevitable that the schools would begin using them to teach children. Games minimize any fears children may have about sitting in front of a terminal. They can be tailored to young children and to teenagers, who are enormously fascinated with them. They are challenging, almost hypnotic, and—if properly handled—can be an open door to most other forms of CAI. Some games can be combined with a question-and-answer feature to reinforce certain concepts. Others can be presented as a kind of puzzle for which the student must figure out the rules. How significant an impact games will have on education is still an open question.

Cognitive diagnostics is a fairly recent development still in the research stage, but is having some influence on educational methodology. The goal is to determine the kinds of errors the student is making with a view towards helping improve overall performance by suggesting new problem-solving strategies. Much of this work has been carried out at the Xerox Palo Alto Research Center under the direction of John Seely Brown, in the domain of simple arithmetic skills. The student answers a number of arithmetic problems, such as subtraction. The program analyzes the answers and supplies the teacher with the information necessary to help the student. Notice that this help does not just inform the student about rights and wrongs but describes in a systematic way how errors are being made. Work in this area is giving new impetus to theories of skill execution.

Major CAI Systems

A large number of companies are competing in the educational software market. They include the computer manufacturers themselves, subsidiaries of large companies such as Science Research Associates (a division of IBM), major units of large companies such as Control Data's PLATO system, and independent companies that produce software for a variety of computer systems. An extremely wide variety of educational software is currently available. PLATO and TICCIT are among the major projects.

PLATO

The PLATO system has been in existence, in one way or another, at the University of Illinois since 1959. It has been funded by the National Science Foundation, the Office of Education, and a combination of companies and organizations. Currently under a licensing agreement by the University of Illinois, Control Data Corporation (CDC) develops and distributes the system. CDC has launched an extensive advertising campaign to market PLATO software for such microcomputers as the IBM PC, Apple II Plus, the ATARI 800, and the Texas Instrument TI 99/4A. This campaign is an attempt to bypass the schools and go directly into the home, with educational software in such areas as French, German, and Spanish, simple arithmetic, and high school physics. PLATO systems are appearing in the employee training programs of many large companies. United Airlines uses PLATO, as does the U.S. Navy, to train naval recruits.

PLATO is probably the largest CAI system in the world. As of 1981 there were about 6,000 PLATO terminals in use. Its original design depended on a large mainframe computer to serve many individual users working at their own rather sophisticated terminals. The standard PLATO terminal has a touch-sensitive screen and a typewriter keyboard, as well as a number of adjunct devices such as speech synthesizers, optical scanners, random-access videodisks, and hardcopy units. The system is well designed to support a variety of CAI applications including drill and practice, tutorials, and simulation. Because of the touch-sensitive screen, PLATO can be used by young children unable to type well. The number of applications of PLATO systems is quite high. The following are typical:

> University-level courses in such areas as physics, engineering, astronomy, psychology, music, and nursing.
>
> Public school courses for inner-city schools, to improve arithmetic skills and reading levels.
>
> In job counseling and drug control programs, to improve the job skills of the hardcore unemployed.
>
> Special training programs at correctional institutions.
>
> Remedial education programs for Native Americans.

The typical PLATO system consists of a large Control Data computer connected via a communication network to a number of terminals. Such a large computer can deal with up to 32 different sites each with up to 32 terminals. The communication network can be a combination of satellite, cable, or ordinary telephone lines. This system permits a large number of students at different sites to meet their individual needs with respect to both subject matter and degree of difficulty. The software (or courseware) itself is prepared using the TUTOR language. Usually, a course management team will spend a great deal of time designing and implementing a course. In some cases up to 250 hours are necessary to prepare one hour of course time. Courses involve the presentation of new material, drill sessions, tests, results, and recommendations. For example, in the test context, questions can be answered by touching true or false boxes on the screen. Because PLATO can use the entire record of the student's past performance as background, it can establish a kind of personal tone in its interaction. If the student has not done well (again) on a test, PLATO will urge the student to consult a reference and then to attempt some of the drill problems.[6]

The basic question about any educational system is, "How well does it work?" A number of studies seem to show that students learn more quickly using PLATO Basic Skills software than do control groups. However, these are not conclusive results and more testing is necessary.

TICCIT

TICCIT is a clever acronym for Time-shared Interactive, Computer-Controlled Information Television. Begun in 1971 at the MITRE Corporation, the development of hardware and software was funded by the National Science Foundation. A number of features are unique to TICCIT. It (a) incorporates a design strategy into which all software must fit, (b) is designed to implement the tutorial mode of CAI rather than drill and practice, and (c) allows the user more initiative than do many other systems. Furthermore, it combines computers and television in an interesting and novel way. Each TICCIT station is a study carrel, containing what is apparently a color television set, a special keyboard, earphones, and a place to take notes. The displays on the screen are in color and quite sophisticated. A set of 15 "learner control" keys is used by students to select which instructional display to view next, which segment of material to study next, and how to accomplish this task.

TICCIT was originally designed for junior college students. Most of its applications have been for teenagers and adults. All commercial rights for TICCIT are controlled by the Hazeltine Corporation. Systems are currently being used by universities (Brigham Young), community colleges (Northern Virginia), the Department of Defense (Naval Air Station, San Diego), and the handicapped (Model Secondary School for the Deaf). Among other subject areas, courseware has been written for English, French, Spanish, linguistics, symbolic logic, air crew training, oceanography, nursing, and electronics. A TICCIT course includes a large number of displays. Each display may require one or more television frames and is limited to one form of information type. Basically, there are three types of information used to present ideas (see Figure 6-2).

- **Rule**   a means for presenting a general statement such as a definition, a statement of a relationship between ideas or concepts, and the individual parts of a procedure.
- **Example**   an example of a rule, that is, an illustration of a definition, a certain relationship, or a given procedure.
- **Practice**   a way for the student to test his or her understanding of the rule.

A single TICCIT system supports up to 128 student stations. The overall communications system is quite complex, because of the large number of images, both single frames and color videotapes. The videotapes must be mounted manually by an operator, while single frames are transmitted from disk storage. Audio messages are stored digitally and automatically sent to the student. More recent configurations have evolved as the price of hardware has fallen. These have focused on minicomputers rather than mainframes. Authoring courses for TICCIT is easier than for other systems because the design strategy is built in. However, course authors must organize the material around the constructs built into the system. For example, authors can prepare display images on graph paper first or directly on the television screen.

TICCIT has not yet fulfilled the aims of its developers. In tests conducted at two community colleges during the 1975–76 school year, it was found that more students dropped the TICCIT mathematics courses than a conventional one, but those that completed the course did better. Fewer graduates of the TICCIT mathematics course went on to take additional mathematics courses. The results in English courses were better. The English course was carefully designed for the TICCIT approach while the mathematics course was more or less transferred directly from a textbook. In the Navy, students were enthusiastic about the TICCIT training program and performed better than those who took a

FIGURE 6-2 Three Sample Displays from TICCIT. (a) Rule Display. (b) Example Display. (c) Practice Display. (From M. David Merrill, Edward W. Schneider, and Kathie A. Fletcher, *TICCIT*, 1980. Copyright © 1980 by Educational Technology Publications; all rights reserved. Reprinted by permission of Educational Techology Publications.)

Here, then, is the general rule
for pronoun-referent agreement.

A pronoun agrees in number with
its REFERENT. Singular referents
take singular pronouns. Plural
referents take plural pronouns.
Singular referents which have
no sex indicated take the
generic pronouns him/he/his.

Rule

(*a*)

In the passage below, the pronoun
in green agrees with its referent
in light blue.

Neither John nor Harry brought his
coat to the ball game.

This can be reviewed in lesson 4.2.

EXAMP   1 EASY PAGE 1/1

(*b*)

Edit any pronoun in the passage
below that doesn't agree in
number with its referent. If
all pronouns are correct, press
ENTER.

Several of the mechanics brought
his tools.

PRACT   3 EASY PAGE 1/1

(*c*)

workbook version. Finally, when used by excellent teachers not intimidated by technology, TICCIT reduced significantly the time necessary for students to complete a course. It would seem that good teachers will be able to use the technology to the advantage of their students, and will not impede its introduction into the classroom if the technology is seen to be beneficial.

Other CAI Projects

There are many other important CAI projects and systems. One of the pioneers in CAI is Dr. Patrick Suppes of the mathematics department at Stanford University. Since 1963 he has been developing programs to improve the performance of children in elementary logic, arithmetic, and reading. In 1967 he founded Computer Curriculum Corporation (CCC) to develop and market CAI systems based on his research. These programs for drill and practice have been used by hundreds of thousands of students with good results. Apparently, ten minutes' use per day has resulted in gains in student averages. Federal support of research in educational technology has made a difference here. This modest approach, with limited aims, has been a success. Incidentally, most of the programs are written in BASIC.

Another important figure in CAI is Alfred Bork, a professor of physics and of information and computer science at the University of California at Irvine. He has been designing CAI software to teach introductory physics since 1970. His work illustrates the importance of graphics in learning physical concepts, self-paced instruction, and computer-student dialogues. In physics the ability to draw trajectories, surfaces, and oscillatory motions is a very important ingredient in understanding the associated physical process. Bork is very optimistic that microcomputers will usher in a new age of CAI.

COMPUTER-ASSISTED LEARNING (CAL)

In my vision, the child programs the computer *and, in so doing, both acquires a sense of mastery over a piece of the most modern and powerful technology and establishes an intimate contact with some of the deepest ideas from science, from mathematics, and from the art of intellectual model building.*[7]

CAL promotes a vision of the computer as a learning resource and as a stimulus for the imagination of the child, a powerful friend able to follow commands and respond to requests. The major figure in CAL is Seymour Papert, professor of mathematics and of education at the Massachusetts Institute of Technology. He has made major contributions in cognitive psychology and Artificial Intelligence. Earlier in his career he worked with Jean Piaget, the eminent child psychologist. From these experiences have emerged some important ideas on how children might learn by using a computer—an ideal instrument, given its power to simulate and to be whatever the child desires. The programming language Papert designed permits even young children to do very inventive things.

LOGO: A New Way of Learning?

The development of LOGO (or Logo) emerged from research in three areas: AI, psychology (based on the important work of Jean Piaget), and computer science in general. Seymour Papert and his colleagues at MIT began to put their ideas about education into effect. They are concerned with such issues as helping people (a) to build various computational models as a method of learning, (b) to interact with these models as a means to improve performance, (c) and to develop a sense of wanting to learn how instead of bemoaning one's deficiencies. One can learn in several ways: by being told directly, by reading, by being helped, and by discovering things oneself. Traditional teaching methods are based on the first two; the LOGO approach is based on the last two, together with the notion of the model, which is derived from research in AI.

It is important in the design of intelligent systems to develop appropriate models of both the problem and the solver. The model of the solver must include a representation of the problem-solving strategy, a representation of the problem domain, a means of evaluating the performance of the solver, and finally a strategy for improving (or in computer talk, debugging) the solver. As systems have been developed within this frame-work, a new appreciation has been gained—about learning, about the importance of adequate models, and about what a computer language must be able to do in order to represent problems and provide procedures for solving them.

In the area of education, especially that of children, the principles embodied in the LOGO concept include such important features as ease and simplicity of expression, explicit representation of fundamental programming ideas, and immediate feedback. Programs can be written very simply by children, but this in no way limits the power of these programs. As children grow in sophistication and become more experienced, the language permits them to extend and build on their previous work in a natural way.

Perhaps the most important aspect of LOGO's success has been the immediate response it provides to the student. The most popular LOGO environment is turtle graphics. (LOGO programs can be written to drive music synthesizers and physical mechanical devices also called turtles, but graphics is the most common output form). The screen may be visualized as a field on which a small, triangular object, a turtle, can move under program control. The turtle can be given a heading, a number of unit steps to take, and directed whether or not to leave a track. (LOGOs designed for different computers may have additional different properties.) By suitably directing the turtle—and this is, of course, what a program does—it can be made to produce a pattern on the screen. Figure 6-3 illustrates some simple LOGO commands and a program. The LOGO instructions are straightforward. A LOGO procedure (or subprogram) is indicated by the words TO SQUARE. :SIZE indicates that when SQUARE is used it will be necessary to supply it with a value for SIZE—that is, SIZE will turn out to be the length of the side of the square. The form of the program on the left of Figure 3*b* shows explicitly the individual steps necessary to draw a square. In Figure 3*c*, the command SQUARE 10 causes the sequence of steps to be produced with a step size of 10. The program on the right of Figure 3*b* is an equivalent

FIGURE 6-3 Some LOGO Instructions and a Program. (a) Some LOGO Instructions. (b) To Draw a Square (Two Versions). (c) Stages of the Square-Drawing Program.

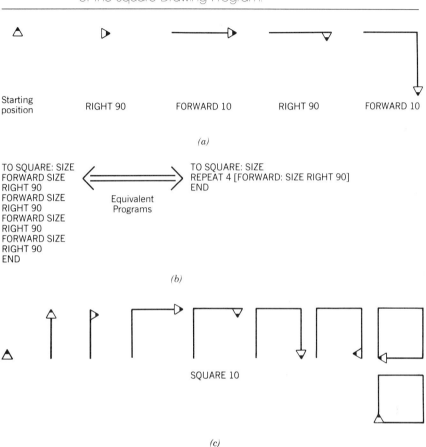

program for SQUARE that illustrates the use of the REPEAT command. In this program the sequence [FORWARD:SIZE RIGHT 90) is to be repeated 4 times.

It is easy to show how SQUARE (with simple modification) can be used as part of a more complex program to draw a window with four panes. In Figure 6-4, SQUARE is first modified so that after the square has been drawn the turtle is pointing to the left (rather than up). Now the window with four panes can be drawn by four calls to the square program. This process of building up more complex programs from simpler ones illustrates a major feature of programming in general and LOGO in particular. Furthermore, an important lesson in thinking has been demonstrated—the student can see how complex

FIGURE 6-4 The Use of the SQUARE Program to Draw a Window with Four Panes. (a) Modification of the SQUARE Program. (b) The WINDOW Program. (c) Stages of the WINDOW Program.

```
TO SQUARE: SIZE
REPEAT 3 [FORWARD: SIZE RIGHT 90]
FORWARD SIZE
END
```
(a)

```
TO WINDOW: SIZE
REPEAT 4 [SQUARE: SIZE]
END
```
(b)

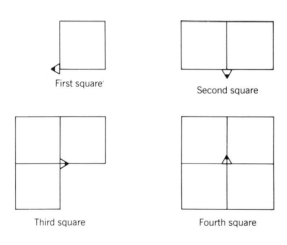

First square

Second square

Third square

Fourth square

(c)

concepts can frequently be structured in terms of simpler ones. And students are able to learn this lesson for themselves.

One very important aspect of the use of LOGO in schools is its impact on the social environment. The traditional classroom has one teacher and many learners, and the flow of knowledge is directed from the teacher to the students. In an environment rich in self-discovery, new and interesting possibilities arise. For example, students can help one another to learn by sharing individual knowledge, by asking interesting questions, and by working together in common pursuits. Papert speaks to this issue in *Mindstorms*.

> *By building LOGO in such a way that structured thinking becomes powerful think-*
> *ing, we convey a cognitive style one aspect of which is to facilitate talking about*
> *the process of thinking. LOGO's emphasis on debugging goes in the same direction.*
> *Students' bugs become topics of conversation; as a result they develop an articulate*
> *and focused language to use in asking for help when it is needed. And when the*
> *need for help can be articulated clearly, the helper does not necessarily have to be*
> *a specially trained professional in order to give it. In this way the LOGO culture*
> *enriches and facilitates the interaction between all participants and offers opportu-*
> *nities for more articulate, effective, and honest teaching relationships.*[8]

The notion of a "LOGO culture" is quite interesting, for it suggests a shared language, common interests, and common goals. This LOGO culture may more properly be spoken of as a subculture of the rapidly growing computer culture, in which children can share ideas and enthusiasms.

Smalltalk-80

While work was in progress on LOGO at MIT in the early 1970s, a group of researchers at Xerox's Palo Alto Research Center were developing something called the Dynabook concept. The idea was to make available a computer the size of a book, with high-resolution graphics, touch-sensitive input, and audio capability. The range of applications was intended to be quite broad, including educational uses. Crucial to the concept is the programming language (and software system) called Smalltalk-80. In brief, Smalltalk-80 has the structure of a network of computers that can communicate with one another by sending and receiving messages. These individual computers are called objects and they are defined by the programmer to carry out certain computations. Thus, instead of the traditional sequential programming style, Smalltalk-80 supports a sort of parallel control structure.

One of the main features of Smalltalk-80 is the readily accessible and powerful graphics system it supports. The screen and graphics systems designed at Xerox permit the programmer to produce sharp, intricate, and detailed pictures. The quality of the pictures and the menu-driven presentation of commands is quite similar in concept to the LISA computer system introduced by Apple in early 1983, and the Macintosh, which arrived later. Young people have been able to produce interesting pictures in color. A stimulating environment is provided, in which to explore a variety of concepts. A child can acquire such very powerful concepts as process, symbolic representation, and different means of interpretation. A flexible animation system permits the drawing of two-dimensional pictures, and a "transparent paint" allows background for moving images. Thus, it is possible to draw different components of a scene separately and then combine them for a finished product.

The computer has enormous potential to expand educational horizons and languages such as LOGO and Smalltalk-80 are playing a major role in this process. No doubt future languages will incorporate many of the features in these two and will also take advantage of improvements in graphics facilities, increased memory, and faster execution times.

COMPUTERS IN HIGHER EDUCATION
Universities

Computers first made their presence in education felt at universities, both as research tools and as objects of study. Not long after the first electronic computer, ENIAC, was built at the Moore School of the University of Pennsylvania, students were being instructed in the intricacies of computer design and programming. Electrical engineering departments turned their attention to transistors, semiconductors, integrated circuits, and communications. New departments of computer science were founded, to instruct students in the care and feeding of computers—that is, programming—and to carry out research in such areas as operating systems, the theory of computation, numerical analysis, and Artificial Intelligence. Many important innovations have come from the universities—time-sharing systems, programming languages (such as LISP, PASCAL, and BASIC), graphics devices (SKETCHPAD), numerical packages, and a variety of intelligent systems. The universities have filled an important function in training large numbers of computer professionals and in introducing several generations of other students to computers long before computer use became fashionable in the wider society. This role was recognized quite early by computer companies. Among these, IBM was the most prominent in recognizing the fact that early exposure to a given computer system would be a major influence in subsequent choices made by the students when they established themselves in the outside world. This realization produced a strategy that worked exceedingly well and contributed to IBM's dominance in the computer industry.

More recently, computer companies have again begun to respond to the possibilities at universities. Carnegie-Mellon University (CMU) in Pittsburgh is one of a number of universities that are making a commitment to the personal computer. CMU plans to provide a personal computer for each of its approximately 5500 students by 1986. Under one plan, each student would be required to purchase a computer at a subsidized price. IBM has entered into an agreement with CMU to develop these high-performance personal computers. In the first stage about 100 machines will be installed, while IBM and CMU jointly develop future work stations using about $20 million in IBM funds. The intention is clearly that every student be able to use a computer in a wide variety of ways—to check for assignments in a course, to prepare and submit assignments (via a file accessible only by the instructor), to check if a desired book is available in the library, to take tests and exams, and to send and receive messages among fellow students and professors. All this can be done from a terminal in the student's own room or from one of many work stations distributed around the campus. Hard copies will be available from fast printers near the work stations.

Drexel University in Philadelphia, Clarkson College in Potsdam, N.Y., and Rensselaer

Polytechnic Institute in Troy, N.Y. are among U.S. universities rapidly moving into the computer age. The term *computer literacy* has been bandied about to describe a desirable condition among students and (ultimately) the population at large, the idea being that everyone should have some working knowledge of computers. Just as the ability to read is a measure of the general educational level of a society, so computer literacy will become a measure of its technical level. Universities that fail to respond to the needs of their students in a rapidly changing world will have much to answer for. Another university that has long been at the cutting edge of change, and has not shortchanged its students, is MIT. In mid-1983 both IBM and Digital Equipment Corporation (DEC), the two largest computer manufacturers in America, agreed to provide $50 million in equipment and personnel to MIT for the development of software to permit programs to move easily between equipment made by the two companies. MIT intends to use the equipment for purposes of instruction in both classroom and home. Paul E. Gray, the president of MIT, notes:

> [*Project*] *Athena will integrate computers into the educational environment in all*
> *fields of study throughout the university in ways which will encourage new concep-*
> *tual and intuitive understanding in our students.*[9]

The introduction of large numbers of computers requires an extensive campus-wide network. The most ambitious current plan is that of the University of Houston, where by 1986 about 10,000 personal computers will be linked to one another and to a system of several dozen super-minicomputers and mainframes. At Dartmouth College, as of fall 1984, students purchased over 1,500 Macintosh computers at special prices. These were linked over the digital portion of the college network, supported by 65 message-switching minicomputers. The University of Waterloo has the most sophisticated campus network in Canada. It consists of about 215 micros in 15 small networks and 1,100 terminals connected to 6 mainframes. Clearly, the wave of the future is the ''wired campus,''—a vast array of personal computers and work stations and a new style of instruction and interaction.

A number of problems may impede the universities in fulfilling their responsibility. The first is quite basic—there is a shortage of university professors with computer expertise. In 1979, about 250 new Ph.D.s graduated in computer science (compared with 256 in 1975) and found 1,300 positions to choose from. 650 academic positions were available, but fewer than 100 new Ph.D.s were interested. In the period 1975 to 1979, undergraduate enrollments in computer science doubled, but faculty size and lab space increased only minimally. It is no surprise that a report presenting these and other findings was titled ''A Discipline in Crisis.''[10] The difficulty of attracting new and qualified teachers and researchers will have a serious impact on universities in particular and society in general. The growth and vitality of the burgeoning technological society is directly related to the number and quality of people intimately involved in its development—namely, the technologists. Furthermore, the universities themselves have also filled an important role, which will diminish unless they are able to attract the best people and the best equipment.

The situation remained critical in 1982—still only about 250 Ph.D.s per year with 1300 positions available.[11] The number of undergraduates entering computer science courses and programs continues to grow, and universities continue to encounter difficulties in retaining young faculty members. Various government measures have been taken to increase university funding for computer equipment and to facilitate university-industry relations, through tax benefits for equipment donations.

Another problem the universities face is that industry, recognizing the available expertise, is investing large amounts of money in joint projects with university researchers. This activity raises serious questions about autonomy, ethics, and responsibility. Can a university researcher simultaneously be responsible to his or her university, discipline, students, and corporate sponsor? What about the free and open circulation of research results, when industry has proprietary interests? Going one step further, a number of university researchers have themselves formed companies, to develop commercial applications of their own research work and to consult with industry in their areas of expertise. This development is not new, and there are arguments in favor of cooperation between academia and business, but there are dangers. Researchers must be careful not to exploit their students' work for financial profit or use results achieved with the help of government funds for private gain. Computer science, especially Artificial Intelligence, is quite fashionable and there is considerable temptation for university researchers with these backgrounds to jump into the marketplace.

Vocational Training

If the universities are having trouble finding sufficient staff, other segments of the educational community (not including elementary and secondary schools) are doing better. The major growth area is in private schools for vocational training. Although these schools are not competing with universities, they are producing the large numbers of necessary technicians. The largest of these schools, National Education Corporation (NEC) is introducing computer-based technology in its teaching methods. One system involves the use of textbooks with bar codes (similar to those on a variety of products) and personal computers with wands used to call up displays on the screen. NEC will offer degrees in such areas as computer science, electronics, and robotics. There is a bright future for such schools, because more and more of the work force will need to be retrained in the face of advancing technological change.

Many companies are retraining their employees using in-house programs run by such vocational schools as NEC or Control Data with its PLATO system. Among the hardware components in the newer systems are videodisk players, personal computers, and video screens. The use of interactive videodisks appears to be of increasing importance in learning systems, as vast amounts of information can be stored in a high quality format. An increasing number of companies in a variety of industries are turning to computer-based training systems. Mechanics at Ford dealerships can learn to service new engine designs using on-site training systems. J.C. Penney uses interactive videodisk systems to teach inventory control. The cost of videodisk courseware is considerably more expensive than that of the less elaborate computer-based systems—perhaps $35,000 to $100,000 per hour compared to $2000 to $20,000 per hour. Not surprisingly, the Department of Defense is the major user. Small, low-cost videodisk systems now available should increase the usefulness and general distribution of such training systems.

ISSUES AND PROBLEMS

A basic question, not easy to answer, is *does computer-assisted instruction improve learning?* On the other hand, does it dehumanize the learning process? The mere use of new technology—whether blackboards, television, or computers—does not in itself guarantee better learning. One of the fundamental criticisms levelled against CAI is that an infatuation with hardware has minimized the concern about the educational merits of the courses. Critic after critic has bemoaned the poor quality of the material. As the market has grown, the rush to produce software has resulted in a lowering of quality. Perhaps there also exist some serious problems with educational theory itself, and it is unreasonable to expect CAI to produce wondrous results. Another problem—frequently ignored—is the difficulty of obtaining qualified teachers who know how to use available hardware and software to their best advantage.

One of the earliest and most important critics of computer technology in education is Anthony Oettinger of Harvard University.[12] His criticisms run deeper than a distaste for the state of educational technology of the late 1960s. He argues that the introduction of CAI was premature, many of the programs were insufficiently tested, unrealistic expectations were held, and many of the early programs were merely books directly translated into computer programs. With his understanding of computers, he does not deny that computer technology holds much promise, but the questions are *when and how*. Oettinger devotes some attention to the concern in educational circles with individualization—the idea that because of different learning rates among students, better results can be achieved by tailoring instruction to each student's individual needs. The computer can shine here, with its potential to serve a wide variety of students with differing abilities. One of the problems with individualization, however, is that the spread, even among students supposedly evenly matched, can grow so large that scheduling instruction can become a serious problem even with computers to help. There are also problems with adequate personnel and with providing educational material of sufficient range and depth.

In a recent survey of CAI, Chambers and Sprecher review a number of studies and report some tentative findings.[13] These are surprisingly inconclusive, after years of experimentation. Several studies show that though CAI may or may not improve learning, as compared to traditional approaches, it does reduce learning time. There is also some evidence that less gifted students are helped more than average or better ones, but that retention rates may be lower. It would be difficult to argue a case for large-scale expenditures in CAI based on these findings. There are many more problems. Large expenditures in time and money are needed to produce educational software, extensive training is necessary to write CAI programs, and perhaps most significantly, there is no serious and meaningful methodology for the creation of educational software. This problem is not the direct fault of the technology but reflects the lack of an existing theoretical, psychological, and educational base. There has been a considerable trial-and-error component in many systems that are supposed to be well-established. Because the cost of producing courseware is so great, there is pressure to recover costs as quickly as possible through volume sales.

Given the large cost of developing educational software, it may be necessary to centralize the educational system itself to take advantage of advances in CAI. A uniformity of material across the nation may result, a prospect somewhat at odds with the present stress on local differentiation. The design, development, and distribution of educational technology is fast becoming a major industry, largely under the control of those companies large enough to finance the considerable expenditures necessary. It is no accident that such computer industry giants as IBM, Xerox, Control Data, and DEC are major players in educational technology. These companies became large and powerful not because of their expertise in education but rather because of their technical, marketing, and financial expertise.

All these concerns may become academic as the cost of microprocessors decreases rapidly and they become increasingly powerful. Their very low cost means that personal computers, readily affordable by schools and homes alike, will inevitably become quite common and irresistible. Whether the level of education improves by virtue of such technology is debatable. Nevertheless, the promise of such systems as LOGO and Small-talk-80 gives one hope that the computer, properly used, can be a liberating force, fostering what Ivan Illich, a well-known critic of technology, calls conviviality.

> *Tools foster conviviality to the extent to which they can be easily used, by anybody, as often or as seldom as desired for the accomplishment of a purpose chosen by the user. The use of such tools by one person does not restrain another from using them equally. They do not require previous certification of the user. Their existence does not impose any obligation to use them. They allow the user to express his meaning in action.* [14]

Illich does not mention computers explicitly, but they have the potential to be tools for conviviality par excellence. The best of the LOGO uses are appealing in this respect.

The following cautions should accompany the use of computers by educators:

Remember that female students of all ages may be shortchanged when their male counterparts monopolize the computer (see Chapter 14).

Video games are fun, but don't let them take over.

Encourage play and cooperation (remember LOGO). Allow students to reflect on their experience and talk with one another.

Be modest in your expectations.

SUMMARY

Computers are rapidly becoming a pervasive feature of the educational scene. Will they transform education or are they just one more educational novelty, as were blackboards, radio, and television?

Almost all the schools in America have computers. They are used to teach programming and such subjects as arithmetic, geography, history, and so forth. Of course, they are also used to play games. The market for hardware and software is large and growing. Apple is currently leading, followed by Commodore and Radio Shack. Television and magazine advertisements by these manufacturers and others suggest to parents that their children will suffer if computers are not made available to them at school and at home.

Computer-based education can be divided into a number of categories. The major areas are Computer-Assisted Instruction (CAI) and Computer-Aided Learning (CAL).

CAI includes such activities as drill and practice, tutorial (in which new material is presented), simulation (a means to explore the behavior of complex systems), and games. Among the major efforts in CAI are PLATO, originally developed at the University of Illinois in the early 1960s and now sold under license by Control Data Corporation, and TICCIT, developed by the MITRE corporation in 1971.

CAL puts the computer itself at the center of the learning experience. It is argued by its foremost proponent, Seymour Papert—one of the creators of the programming language LOGO—that an understanding of some of the important principles associated with programming can improve a child's performance in other areas.

At universities computers are being used in almost every area of instruction. Some universities are requiring that incoming students purchase their own microcomputers. They will be used for word processing, assignments, library searches, and communicating with fellow students and professors. Comprehensive communication systems to support the growing number of computers have been initiated at some universities.

There is no hard data available to prove whether or not CAI is a better way to learn. There does exist enormous pressure on schools and parents to buy more and better computers and courseware. It is not yet clear how computers can be best used.

NOTES

1. James Hassett, ''Computers in the Classroom,'' *Psychology Today*, September 1984, p. 27.

2. Willie Schatz, ''The Old School Sell,'' *Datamation*, March 1984, p. 160.

3. ''Growing Up Computing,'' *Datamation*, June 1981, pp. 214, 216, 218.

4. David Moursand, as quoted in Deborah Sojka, ''CAI Catches On,'' *Datamation*, March 1981, p. 188.

5. For more information, see David Godfrey and Sharon Sterling, *The Elements of CAL* (Victoria, B.C.: Press Porcepic, 1982).

6. Harold F. Rahmlow, Robert C. Fratini, and James R. Ghesquiere, *PLATO*, The Instructional Design Library, vol. 30 (Englewood Cliffs: Educational Technology, 1980), p. 47.

7. Seymour Papert, *Mindstorms* (New York: Basic Books, 1980), p. 5. This book is perhaps the best source for learning more about LOGO.

8. Ibid., p. 180.

9. As quoted in "M.I.T. to Get Computers in an I.B.M.-Digital Pact," *The New York Times*, June 1, 1983, p. 31.

10. Peter J. Denning, ed., "A Discipline in Crisis," *Communications of the Association for Computing Machinery*, June 1981, pp. 370–374.

11. Stephen S. Yau, et al., "Meeting the Crisis in Computer Science," *Communications of the Association for Computing Machinery*, December 1983, pp. 1046–1050.

12. Anthony Oettinger, *Run, Computer, Run* (New York: Collier, 1971).

13. Jack A. Chambers and Jerry W. Sprecher, "Computer Assisted Instruction: Current Trends and Critical Issues," *Communications of the Association for Computing Machinery*, June 1980, pp. 332–342.

14. Ivan Illich, *Tools for Conviviality* (New York: Harper & Row/Perennial Library, 1973), p. 23.

ADDITIONAL READINGS

Introduction

Holman, Elli. "Camping and Computers—An Educational Alternative." *Personal Computing*, February 1983, pp. 126–8, 131–2.

Rowan, Roy. "Executive Ed. at Computer U." *Fortune*, March 7, 1983, pp. 58–60, 64.

Computer-Assisted Instruction

Bork, Alfred. *Learning with Computers*. Bedford, Mass.: Digital Equipment Corporation, 1981.

Burton, Richard. "Diagnosing Bugs in a Simple Procedural Skill." In Sleeman, D., and J. S. Brown, eds., *Intelligent Tutoring Systems*. New York: Academic, 1982.

Kearsley, Greg and Beverly Hunter. "Electronic Education." *High Technology*, April 1983, pp. 38–44.

Merrill, M. David. "Learner Control in Computer Based Learning." *Computers & Education*, vol. 4, no. 2, 1980, pp. 77–95.

Merrill, M. David, Edward W. Schneider, and Kathie A. Fletcher, *TICCIT*. The Instructional Design Library, vol. 40. Englewood Cliffs: Educational Technology Publications, 1980.

Taylor, Robert, ed. *The Computer in the School: Tutor, Tool, Tutee*. New York: Teachers College Press, Columbia University, 1980.

Computer-Assisted Learning

Byte, August 1982. Special issue on LOGO.

Goldberg, Adele. "Educational Uses of Dynabook," *Computers & Education*, vol. 3, no. 4, 1979, pp. 247–266.

Computers in Higher Education

Currier, Richard L. "Interactive Videodisc Learning Systems." *High Technology*, November 1983, pp. 51–60.

Friedman, Edward A. "The Wired University." *IEEE Spectrum*, November 1984, pp. 115–120.

Main, Jeremy. "New Ways to Teach Workers What's New." *Fortune*, October 1, 1984, pp. 85–86, 90, 92, 94.

McCartney, Laton. "Academia Inc." *Datamation*, March 1983, pp. 116, 117, 120, 122, 126.

"National Education: Trade Schools Go High Tech." *Business Week,* July 4, 1983, pp. 85–6.

Osgood, Donna. "A Computer on Every Desk." *Byte*, June 1984, pp. 162 ff.

Issues and Problems

Maddison, John. *Education in the Microelectronics Era* (Milton Keynes, England: The Open University Press, 1983).

7

GOVERNMENT AND COMPUTERS

A *ll government, indeed every human benefit and enjoy-*
ment, every virtue, and every prudent act, is founded on
compromise and barter. We balance inconveniences; we
give and take—we remit some rights that we may enjoy
others. . . . Man acts from motives relative to his interests;
and not on metaphysical speculations.

◇ *Edmund Burke,* Speech on Conciliation with America, *March 22,*
1775 ◇

INTRODUCTION

Governments exist to serve their citizens, and presumably computers are playing a role
in this endeavor. How, and for what purposes, do governments use computers? Obviously,
their primary activity is record-keeping—the gathering, entering, maintenance, processing,
and updating of files on individuals, families, organizations, and companies. The government might actually be thought of as *the* great record-keeper, whose insatiable appetite
for information arises from the belief that the continual accumulation of information
inevitably leads to the provision of better services. The U.S. government is the single
largest user of computers. Many of the applications are well known—taxation, social
security, census, health, education and welfare, agriculture, and so forth. Other areas are
national security and defense, and research.

Clearly, the government is more than simply a user of computers. By virtue of being
such a major purchaser of computer technology, the government tends to set standards
and shape the form of future developments. The needs of the Census Bureau played an
important role in the early development of the computer. In carrying out its responsibility
for the nation's security, the Department of Defense (DOD) has spurred research and

development in integrated circuits, programming languages, operating systems, security methods, and fault-tolerant designs. The National Aeronautics and Space Administration (NASA) is concerned with such issues as miniaturization, low power consumption, high reliability, and resistance to the effects of vibration, and weightlessness.

State and local governments are also computer users and these applications certainly have a direct effect on citizens. Examples here are property taxes, licenses, and welfare records. Another area of growing importance is the increasing involvement of computers in the political process. This new development in the use of computer technology makes it possible to produce detailed mailing lists of voters who will respond as desired to specific issues. The use of computer models to predict voter behavior is also increasing in popularity. Computer applications in war include the computerized battlefield, the use of computers in war games, and the increasing reliance on computers to make nuclear launch decisions.

Many other areas of activity that involve computer applications and the role of government will be dealt with in further chapters. Because government is intricately involved in so many phases of society, it is inevitable that government-related issues turn up in many areas. In relation to computers and the law, such issues as the legal protection of software, the use of computers by law enforcement agencies, and computer crime, are paramount. The federal government is being called upon to take an active role in directing the future of American industry. In the communications industry, steps in regulation will have significant repercussions with respect to the computer networks spanning the country. And how is international data flow to be supervised and controlled? Finally, one of the major concerns of the public is the question of privacy of computer records. This extremely important issue (discussed in Chapter 9) includes problems of government legislation and such related issues as freedom of information.

DATA PROCESSING ISSUES AND PROBLEMS

Background and Predictions

A federal government report states that the installed base of computers grew from about 6000 in 1974 to almost 11,000 in 1979 and was expected to exceed 29,000 by 1985.[1] Most of the computers in government service in 1985, it is predicted, will be minicomputers, although the study probably underestimated the impact of personal computers. Even though minicomputers are expected to be about 80 percent of the total by 1985, they will represent only about 10 percent of the total dollar value. Most of the investment costs will be in the mainframes required for the enormous computing needs of government. Spending on all the necessary peripherals such as tape drives, disk drives, both floppy and rigid, terminals, and printers will also increase rapidly, with a special spurt in graphics terminals. Finally, add-on high-speed memory is expected to more than double by 1985.

One is tempted to wonder about this continual and rapid growth in computer technology.

The business of government seems to grow much faster than the population it is supposed to serve. Granted, new needs are recognized and new methods of computing statistics and identifying problem areas are developed. But somehow the growth in computing power exceeds these requirements; it almost seems to be obeying some natural law of unrestricted expansion, driven perhaps by the ambitions of administrators. This view is not a criticism of the beneficial aspects of computer use, but is a plea against growth for growth's sake and growth without purpose.

Other interesting facts emerged from the report. COBOL is the most widely used language, and is expected to be the principal language in over 60 percent of government installations. (The Department of Defense has recently encouraged the development of a new programming language called ADA [see Chapter 3, section titled "Charles Babbage," for one origin of this name]. Very shortly, all contract software developed will have to be implemented in this new language, thereby guaranteeing a new major industry in ADA software production.) The primary uses of computers in government are accounting, inventory, personnel, and commercial applications. As of 1979, there were almost 600 database management systems installed.

In 1981 the Federal government spent about $6 billion on electronic data processing and related activities, compared with about ten times that amount in the private sector. For fiscal year 1983, total obligations for information technology systems totalled $10.4 billion. Estimates for 1984 and 1985 are $12.3 billion and $13.9 billion respectively. These expenditures are expected to increase at a faster rate than the federal budget, with the fastest growth taking place in the Department of Defense. The breakdown of the information technology systems budget into specific categories, is shown in Table 7-1. Personnel costs, as a percentage of the total, are expected to decrease while capital investment increases. National security and international affairs computing costs will rise from about $5.2 billion (49 percent) in 1983 to $7.3 billion (51.7 percent) in 1985.

The necessity to modernize and maintain aging software is a growing problem. By 1990, $2.1 billion will be necessary for modernization. During the 1990s, $9.8 billion will be required for maintenance—about 43 percent of the total federal expenditures on software. So much software was developed in-house that the government must devote enormous resources just to keep the system functioning. Because of the need to keep old software running—by emulating old systems on new ones—the advantages of spectacular advances in hardware are not being sufficiently realized. The difficulties are compounded by the lack of adequate documentation, inflexible progamming languages such as COBOL, and badly written programs. Building for the future on the shaky foundations of the past is a dangerous and expensive exercise.

State governments have been slower to implement computer systems, but given their many and varied responsibilities, they did appreciate the important benefits. Some state government areas of concern are tourism, recreation and wildlife, highway patrol, education, municipalities, health care, courts, worker's compensation and labor issues, and taxation. In all these areas records must be kept, statistics computed, bills and statements issued, and payments acknowledged. Computer databases have been developed to store information on government and volunteer services and on people who have applied for

TABLE 7-1 Federal Information Technology Expenditures

	Expenditures in $ Millions		
	1983	1984	1985
Category	(Actual)	(Estimated)	
Capital investments: site preparation, purchase of hardware and software	1,394	1,961	2,494
Leases and rentals: equipment rental, leased space, software, and so forth	1,570	1,949	2,132
Commercial services: ADP and telecommunication services, operations and maintenance, system analysis and programming	4,701	5,488	6,144
Personnel costs	2,735	2,935	3,163
Total	10,400	12,333	13,932

Source: Adapted from *A Five-Year Plan for Meeting the Automatic Data Processing and Telecommunication Needs of the Federal Government,* vol. 1: *Planning Strategies,* U.S. Dept. of Commerce, Office of Management and Budget (Washington, D.C., April 1984).

welfare aid or help from other government programs. The legislative branches of state governments (and of the federal government for that matter) have also been using computer systems for such purposes as budgeting, retrieval of statutes, and the drafting and printing of statutes.

Large Information Systems

Governments, at every level, are great record keepers. With the onset of the computer as a means for storing and processing data, the rate of information accumulation has increased to a point where the federal government maintains thousands of databases. When we speak of databases in this context, a better term, especially for those that apply nationwide, might be information systems.

Advances in telecommunications technology have made possible the development of large information systems that are accessible from terminals across the country. The crucial components of the new information systems technology are the falling prices and increased power of microcomputers, a widespread computer communications network, powerful information and display systems, and large, compact memory storage. Examples of the kinds of systems, both government and private, that are of concern are: the FEDWIRE electronic funds transfer network operated by the Federal Reserve System; the computer-based, nationwide credit card authorization services run by VISA and American Express; airline reservation systems; air traffic control systems; and the military command and control systems operated by the Department of Defense. It is readily apparent that such systems can have a major impact on society, especially considering such additional factors as the explosive growth in personal computers, the increasing number of computer networks, the acceptance and use of information networks, and the competition among such corporate giants as IBM and AT&T.

Several questions arise about how these databases affect government policy, government action, and civil liberties. It is not difficult to appreciate the concern of some people about the dangers of potential misuse. The list of issues arising from the growth of such databases is long, and many of the items are quite complicated. From the government's point of view, it must exercise responsibility in a number of areas.

Privacy and freedom of information.

Regulation of use.

Security of systems.

Security of data transmission by encryption methods.

Dependence on an "automated bureaucracy."

Guarantees of constitutional rights in the use of the systems.

Formulation of a policy statement to guide future developments.

Automated Bureaucracy

Even before computer systems became prevalent, governments were regularly subject to the criticism that they were too bureaucratic. The most straightforward interpretation of this charge is that bureaucracies frequently are so concerned with rules and procedures that they forget that their purpose is to deal with people and their problems. Thus, it is feared that computer systems will serve bureaucratic interests, not the public's, by further shielding government workers from direct responsibility. Furthermore, how do such systems affect the quality of decisions? Are citizens still assured of due process when computers are part of the decision-making process? Can the high-level policymakers in Congress and the executive branch be sure that the bureaucracy is accountable? An alternate viewpoint holds that before computers bureaucracies had been drowning in paper that prevented them from adequately serving the public. In fact, in 1980 the Paperwork Reduction Act was passed. Its goal was to increase the use of computers in government as a way of reducing the flood of paper. Futhermore, it raised the importance of information technology to a level comparable with financial and personnel management. It is expected that records will be better organized and more easily accessible and that errors will be reduced. The advanced systems will permit improved controls and better accounting, and will allow supervisors to more readily monitor the performance of the front-line staff. On the other hand, as service improves, working conditions may suffer. The use of technology to improve human relations is a two-edged sword. Efficiency will increase, supposedly, but at the cost of some loss of control by the workers.

Redundant Data

Among the federal governments' vast databases—more than 3.5 billion records, covering every person in the United States—there are many duplicate entries. The Paperwork Reduction Act gave the Office of Management and Budget (OMB) responsibility to monitor the information-processing activites of the government. The OMB has forestalled a number of data-gathering efforts because it was discovered the data already existed. For example, the Department of Housing and Urban Development wanted to acquire minority employment data from state governments, something which the Equal Employment Opportunity Commission had already done. Thus, the almost 90 government agencies now share their collected information, with the obvious result of taxpayers' money saved.

There are potential undesirable effects, though. Agencies have differing degrees of confidentiality and security associated with their data. The Census Bureau is one agency charged with collecting data and ensuring privacy in order to improve the accuracy of its information. Surely it cannot share its files. Directives from the OMB assign the responsibility of protecting the data to the original collecting agency. Still, general rules are necessary for safeguarding information in a shared system. In another effort to deal with the redundancy problem, a vast catalog of all government information called the Federal Information Locator System has been built. Even with sharing and catalogs, though, the human problem remains. Where knowledge is power, the sharing of information is felt by some to be the giving-up of power. Thus, it may be quite difficult for the government to save as much as it could by reducing redundancy in its records.

Some Possible Solutions

President Carter commissioned a study of the data processing environment in the Federal government. The President's Reorganization Project, as it was popularly known, released its summary report in April, 1979. It found that the federal government was, in general, mismanaging its information technology resources, and had not developed a plan for exploiting the opportunities of the future with respect to investment, service delivery, protection of citizens, or national security. The condition was manifested by such major symptoms as:

> Public complaints about delays and inaccuracies at many service delivery points.
>
> Inability to protect the rights and privacy of individuals from intrusive practices of government agencies, large corporations, and others.
>
> Growing obsolescence of equipment, systems, and personnel.
>
> Increasing economic threats, accelerated by the availability of technical information and products flowing freely and uncontrolled from the United States into competitor nations.
>
> A military enterprise that is operationally vulnerable as a consequence of obsolescent equipment and systems and underdeveloped technical personnel.

Other evidence indicates that the situation has not changed for the better since then.

The Federal Government is not just another large computer user—it is a *very* large user, and the extraordinary range of its activities requires many complex systems. Many of the applications it must accommodate are quite specialized: for example, military command and control systems and real-time control of space missions. Furthermore, many government activities are open to public scrutiny, unlike those of private companies. Thus, there are special requirements for the government's computer systems. There have been many suggestions made about how to improve the situation. One study recommends the following:[2]

> Given the developments in computer technology, significant improvements can be achieved by decentralizing the resources. (see "Distributed Data Processing," Chapter 4).

> Surprisingly, detailed examinations of individual data processing departments may be more harmful than helpful because of the cost in time, money, and decreased morale.

> Long-term planning as mandated in the Paperwork Reduction Act must be instituted, and this planning process must actually lead to an improved purchasing policy.

> Better methods of management should be implemented, including improved accounting procedures.

> An overall strategy for managing all the information resources—including computers, paper files, and microfilm—is necessary.

The federal government is an enormously complex institution. Data processing systems, if not appropriately organized, will do very little to improve the performance of an organization. The recommendations made above, if carried through, would somewhat improve the performance of the federal bureaucracy, but more attention must be paid to the people involved in the information processing system. There is no reason to expect substantial improvement in the operation of an organization as enormous as the federal government unless the strategic planning involves both people and machines.

LOCAL GOVERNMENT

Local government is closest to the people, in a sense. Its actions are felt, or at least perceived, to be more relevant to daily life than those emanating from distant state or federal capitals. Given the range of activities of local governments, it is not surprising that the average citizen has strong opinions of their performance that are based on direct personal evidence. Some of the functions of local governments are as follows:

Safety.   police, fire department, licensing.
Social Welfare.   welfare, education, garbage collection, libraries, parks, health.

Development.   transportation, planning, commercial development, building inspection.

Finance.   Property taxes, assessment, licensing, budgeting.

In all these activities the computer has proven to be invaluable. Some municipalities have been experimenting with comprehensive databases that can store data acquired by different departments. These databases give the ability to produce a variety of statistics to aid in planning, to access linked records, and, possibly, to spot anomalies in such records. Unfortunately, the systems have been oversold. It is claimed that information systems will cut costs, reduce staffs, and provide better information for decision-making, and that superiors will be better able to monitor the performance of their subordinates. When these claims are examined more carefully, it turns out that not all is smooth sailing. Staff reductions have not been a matter of course. There has been an increased work load because of coding and data entry; the computer facility has encouraged new projects, and additional staff are necessary to manage the computer facilities. Furthermore, there are morale problems with computer monitoring, because such monitoring is typically insensitive to the needs of the workers.

Two Examples

Urban Transportation   Local governments are concerned with planning, building, and maintaining a city's network of roads, bus lines, and sometimes subways. It is also necessary to make connections with interstate highways within municipal boundaries. All of this requires extensive planning, which has an impact on neighborhoods, community services, and transportation patterns within the city. During the heyday of freeway construction, major cities were criss-crossed with multi-lane roads and extensive exit-and-entry interchanges. Well-established neighborhoods were often literally split apart as residents found themselves on opposite sides of an impassable barrier. Gradually, groups seeking to save their neighborhoods, began to petition city governments for a voice in future development. There were other concerned groups as well—local merchants interested in improved access to their stores, city planners trying to produce comprehensive development strategies, and state and federal officials responsible for the nation's transportation system.

The computer has clearly been an important factor in this decision-making process. It has become possible to simulate the proposed development on a computer, including the roads themselves, expected buildings as a result of the new transportation network, new housing patterns, and new service requirements. The results of such simulations have been used by ''experts'' to bolster their arguments, and with the computer behind them it was difficult to assail their position. A major question about simulations is how well do they represent and account for the relevant variables in the real world situation. When some of the variables must measure such social concerns as neighborhood cohesiveness, natural communication and transportation patterns, and ease of travel to work, it is no wonder that the results are somewhat suspect in the eyes of the affected community. The computer lends an air of authority and correctness to the output it produces, especially when these results are couched in formal and formidable terms. The challenge of the future is to give the community access to the data, assumptions, and model used by the planners. The necessary expertise to evaluate computer simulations will be difficult to acquire, but the human resources required for this task will probably become available in the future. At the very least, the voice of the neighborhood should be able to be heard above the din of excitement about the computer.

Automated Welfare Because welfare systems are seen by many cities as a necessary but not particularly desirable responsibility, their performance has been supervised as closely as possible. The information system seems to be an ideal solution to many actual and anticipated problems. The records of individual clients and their families can be stored, updated, and what is most important, monitored. One such system provides for the uniform entry of data and monthly statistical summaries, including client profiles and agency work loads for managers. It also has a client-tracking system that keeps track of what agency or agencies a person has been referred to, whether or not that person has been accepted, and what services have been provided. The most direct benefits are that duplicate forms are eliminated, time and effort are saved by the automatic production of statistical reports, and individual clients are more easily tracked by caseworkers.

If the data is accurately recorded, if all the relevant agencies are part of the system, and if caseworkers are responsible, it should be possible to provide better service and spot violators. There are many jobs involved, however, and such systems are not as successful as they might be. Typically, they are used to further centralize the control structure of the bureaucracy, tending to instill a sense of insecurity in the front-line caseworkers, to say nothing of the damaging impact on welfare recipients. The circle is complete when the caseworker attempts to defeat the system by holding back information. Once again the lesson is clear: for information systems to be successful, whatever other problems exist, designers must take into account the interests of those people affected by their use.

THE POLITICAL PROCESS

Computers are used to register voters prior to elections and to tabulate the results on election night. They are used to sample public opinion, predict the outcome of elections, and maintain lists of supporters. Already fears have been expressed that the political party with sufficient financial resources to afford the best programmers and computers will have a major advantage in the electoral process.

Getting Elected

It requires a great deal of money to get elected to political office. The role of fundraiser has been assuming increasing importance. Traditionally, supporters have been identified and then canvassed for contributions during the campaign. But increasingly sophisticated fundraising methods have been developed that take advantage of the computer's abilities. Mailing lists of supporters are carefully organized in terms of ethnic background, income, education, age, sex, and opinion on a number of issues. Also stored in the computer are texts of fundraising letters, each focussing on a particular issue. Such systems are maintained by the political parties and by corporate political-action committees (PACs), legislated by Congress to collect money for political candidates. Whenever a political issue surfaces, the appropriate letter form is selected, and "personally" addressed by the computer to those supporters with an appropriate profile. The rate of successful return has increased dramatically.

These techniques have also been used to mobilize support for political causes, in which case letters and telegrams are solicited rather than money. A system for this purpose requires a moderately-sized computer, considerable storage, a high-speed printer, folding-sealing-stamping equipment, and people to do data entry. The ability to target voters along ethnic, regional, religious, or any other lines results in more efficient fundraising and more effective pressure tactics. But the public should be aware of what lies behind current solicitation practices.

The low price of personal computers means that they are now readily available for almost every political campaign in the land. Something like 50,000 individuals are elected in each election cycle.[3] Besides the important fundraising activities, computers are also used to plan the candidate's schedule, organize press releases, plan questionnaires, and schedule volunteer workers. Basic financial programs can be used to monitor donations and expenditures in order to ensure that sufficient funds are available for the entire duration of the campaign. A number of software packages have been developed exclusively for use in election campaigns to analyze previous election results, keep track of supporters, and perform financial analysis. In the 1984 national election it was generally agreed, even by the officials in the Democratic Party, that the Republican party had a considerable lead in the use of computers.

What Does the Voter Want?

Nowadays, people are asked their opinion about everything: their favorite soap, television show, and politician. There are public polls such as Gallup, Harris, and Roper, and many private ones are done for elected officials as well as candidates. The computer is now used to store survey results and to perform sophisticated statistical analysis and projections. Over the years, models have been constructed that can predict with reasonable accuracy, on the basis of a careful sampling of voter preferences, the outcome of elections on the local, state, or federal level. A danger of such models is that both elected officials and candidates for political office will begin to tailor their opinions in the directions determined by the models. A basic conflict for elected officials will be heightened—to vote their conscience or to represent the political views of their constituency, when these are in opposition.

There is more in the future. In Columbus, Ohio about 30,000 homes, under a system called QUBE, have been wired up to a central computer by a two-way communication system. QUBE has been used to sample public opinion in a quick and painless fashion. A question put to the subscribers appears on their television set. Viewers press either the yes or no button on their handsets when the vote is being taken. Each home on the network is briefly scanned, the votes are accumulated, and the results appear on the screen in a few seconds. Could (or should) such a polling method be used within the current political system? With this method in operation, a well-publicized issue would be presented to the voters. Advocates pro and con would be given air time to present their views in a variety of formats. Finally, a vote would be taken, and then what? Should a vote of this kind be binding? Is it similar to a plebiscite?

Many questions must be answered before so-called instantaneous or electronic polling can become part of the democratic process. The fundamental issue turns on whether or not democracy can function as an extended Athenian marketplace. Supposedly, democracy began in Athens, where the citizens of that city state (not the women or the slaves) decided issues of concern in open debate and public vote. Perhaps modern communication networks and computers can recreate the best features of that noble experiment. As might be expected, there would be a number of problems. How is a question to be formulated? How is the voting process itself to be monitored to ensure that only legitimate voters actually vote? How is the security of the central computers to be guaranteed? All these questions may be beside the main point—what benefits will actually accrue by integrating electronic polling into the current system? The answer will be up to politicians, political scientists, and the public at large.

Who Won?

For many people, the most exciting and interesting part of the election process is election night, as the returns are presented to the nation over the three television networks. In reporting the 1984 election, the networks for the first time used real-time computer graphics to display the results. Certain graphic information such as the candidates' pictures, maps of the states, and the forms of charts and graphs were prepared in advance. As the returns flooded in, the existing graphic information was combined with the new information and presented in a variety of colors and forms. A spokesman for CBS news noted, "In 1984, for the first time, we will be able to do true real-time, data-dependent images and animation."[4] (High resolution, three-dimensional animation in a wide range of colors must await another election.)

Computer models for predicting election outcomes on the basis of interviews with selected early voters have come under some criticism. In 1984 the landslide for President Reagan was anticipated quite early, but there was little surprise as most polls had predicted such a result. In the 1980 presidential election, however, many voters in the western part of the country apparently did not bother voting because the television networks declared President Reagan an early winner. While these lost votes probably did not affect the presidential election, they did have an effect on local and state elections. It has been suggested that early computer predictions should not be annnounced until the polls have closed everywhere. Staggered hours might be a solution. In any event, the power of computer models to affect the electoral process must be recognized and steps must be taken to remedy the situation.

THE NATION'S DEFENSE

A major responsibility of the federal government is to defend the nation from both internal and external enemies. This is certainly reflected in the fact that the defense budget is the major component of the total budget. The Department of Defense (DOD), with its vast resources, has taken a lead in the development of both computer hardware and software. Much of the early research in integrated circuits was funded by DOD for military purposes. Given the sheer size of the military establishment, problems of organization are serious. There is enormous difficulty in coordinating a world-wide enterprise consisting of millions of soldiers and civilian personnel and billions of dollars of equipment, while maintaining a high degree of military preparedness. Crucial to this responsibility has been the development of the military's large and complex information system, Communications, Command, Control and Intelligence (C^3I).

C^3I depends very heavily on two post-World War II advances; satellite communications and computers. Obviously, having a world-wide communications system in place is necessary both to coordinate activities and to use monitoring devices such as radar. The huge amount of information that needs to be stored, processed, and presented in a variety of forms demands large, high-speed computers. For example, the North American Air Defense Command (NORAD), located in an underground center in Colorado, has about 10 mainframes, as well as many minicomputers and micros. Computers are also necessary for many other purposes.

The C^3I market is enormous and growing. Currently $31.5 billion, about 11 percent of the 1984 defense budget, it is expected to grow to $49.1 billion by 1993. Much of the budget is classified, and the actual amounts may be even larger. The range of activities is also undergoing change—from an emphasis on dealing with highly mobile distributed systems and the necessity of hardening against nuclear blasts, to a more direct concern with computers and so-called interactive intelligence, which is frequently based on AI. Thus, out of the early use (in the mid-1970s) of C^2 for control and communications, the use of an expanded mnemonic, C^4I^2, may develop for communications, command, control, computers, and interactive intelligence. A variety of advanced systems for distributed computing, battlefield decision-making, and intelligent aids to planning are coming on-line.

The Computerized Battlefield

In the 1982 conflict between Britain and Argentina over the Falkland Islands, a single $200,000 computer-guided missile, the French Exocet, destroyed the British destroyer Sheffield, a $50 million warship. The power of computer-age weapons was frighteningly revealed. The general class of weapons with microprocessors are called precision-guided munitions (PGMs). Probably the most publicized and sophisticated of the PGMs is the cruise missile. It is programmed to fly a ground-hugging route to its target to avoid most radar, and has a microcomputer aboard with detailed topographic information about its route. During flight this computer can compare information received from its sensors with its programmed knowledge to keep the missile on course. Future versions are expected to be able to recognize their designated targets when they arrive, to reduce the possibility of being deceived by camouflage. After a 1,500-mile trip the cruise missile can hit a ten-foot-square target.

With weapons this smart, how necessary are people? Perhaps the goal of the next stage of warfare planning will be to remove people from the battlefield. Wars of the future might be fought with computer-controlled aircraft in the sky and robots on the land. Robots with radio receivers and transmitters could lead troops into battle or into dangerous forays where the risk of death is high. Would this make the threat of launching a war less frightening?

In the air, significant changes are already taking place. The fighter airplane has become too complex for the human pilot. Vast amounts of information must be gathered, processed, and presented to the pilot on instruments. Within a plane, travelling with the velocity of a speeding bullet, the pilot has little opportunity to make decisions. The director of the Avionics Laboratory at Wright-Patterson Air Force Base has stated,

> *The pilot is now relegated to the role of second or third backup. He doesn't fly the airplane. He thinks he does but he doesn't. He commands the system, but the system decides whether or not the command is valid and responds accordingly.*[5]

Because of the bewildering array of dials on the modern control panel, the pilot is faced with information overload. To alleviate this situation, designers are developing sensors that speak their warnings, and more importantly, controls that respond to voice commands. Thus, while engaged in evasive actions the pilot can shout ''fire'' to send off a missile. Speech recognition is still in an experimental phase, as are other developments arising out of research in AI. The DOD has long been a major funder of research in AI, especially through the Defense Advanced Research Project Agency (DARPA).

In October 1983, DARPA announced the Strategic Computing Plan, ''to provide the United States with a broad line of machine intelligence technology and to demonstrate applications of the technology to critical problems of defense.''[6] AI can contribute in such areas as the representation of inexact knowledge, complex pattern-matching, and general problem solving. One example is the robot car or tank that can survey the battlefield, accumulate data and send it back to headquarters by radio. Rugged, powerful, and compact computers are necessary, as is integrated AI for planning routes and analyzing a wide variety of data supplied by sensors. Other directions of future research are the development of faster and smaller integrated circuits and the computer interpretation of photographs.

War Games

In times of peace, armies engage in a variety of war games to maintain a high state of readiness. In the age of the computer it has become unnecessary to commit large numbers of troops and quantities of equipment to test the condition of the armed forces. Furthermore, individual soldiers can improve and test their skills without firing a shot or losing a tank or airplane. The ubiquitous video game has been adapted by the military to provide experience for pilots and tank gunners in firing missiles and shells. The video game can be programmed so that the imaginary projectiles follow realistic trajectories. A much more complex game, called Janus, has been developed by the Pentagon to test the reaction of military officers in a simulated battlefield experience. Essentially the simulation pits U.S. forces against Soviet forces, anywhere in the world but usually in West Germany. The displays are very detailed, and the players sit at elaborate terminals moving the various components of modern warfare—tanks, helicopters, artillery, and even chemical and tactical nuclear weapons—across the battlefield screen.

An early finding is that officers seem quite eager to use nuclear weapons even though in one simulation exercise a premature strike killed not only enemy troops but U.S. troops as well. The system responds with brilliant images to indicate the detonation of such powerful explosives. There is some concern that playing Janus will make it easier to use nuclear weapons in the field, although some argue that the revulsion apparent in many of the players suggest that this game may have the opposite effect. The computer does provide an opportunity to gain experience in a battlefield situation without danger to life and limb, although its effect on the psyche remains unknown.

War by Accident

> On June 3, 1980, at approximately 2:26 a.m. Eastern Daylight Time, the SAC Strategic Air Command command-post display system indicated that two SLBMs (Submarine Launched Ballistic Missiles) had been launched toward the United States. Eighteen seconds later, the display system showed an increased number of SLBM launches. . . . After a brief period, the warning displays at SAC indicated that Soviet ICBMs had been launched toward the United States. After another interval, the NMCC (National Military Command Center) command-post received indication that SLBMs were launched toward the United States.[7]

At NORAD headquarters a warning was announced that within 20 minutes as many as 20 million Americans would be killed by the Soviet attack. A decision to launch a U.S. attack would have to be made quickly. All across the country, airplanes took off, missiles were readied, and everyone was put on alert. Within six minutes of the beginning of the crisis, humans at NORAD realized that it had been a false alarm. A faulty chip had been discovered; the back-up system had worked, this time.

It is to be hoped that this event was an isolated one. Even with very low probability, the consequences of a mistake are so dreadful, one would be too many. The increasing dependence on computers not only to analyze data but also either to suggest actions or to take actions independently is seen by many as a real danger. The warnings have come from within the military establishment itself. The concern is that the need to respond quickly requires putting more reliance on the information processing capability of computers. Fred C. Ikle, a former Undersecretary of Defense for Policy in the Carter administration, has stated, ''The more we rely on launch on warnings (or for that matter, the Soviets do) the greater the risk of accidental nuclear war.''[8]

An organization of computer scientists called Computer Professionals for Social Responsibility (CPSR) represents those professionals concerned about the social implications of their work. They are particularly concerned about the role of computers in the defense of the nation. DARPA's plan to employ AI in a more central role has stimulated CPSR to express more forcefully its apprehension about an increased reliance on automated systems.

> *Like all computer systems artificial intelligence systems may act inappropriately in unanticipated situations. Because of this fundamental limit on their reliability, we argue against using them for decision-making in situations of potentially devastating consequence.*[9]

The authors of DARPA's ''Strategic Computing Plan'' are certainly aware that current computer programs cannot begin to deal with the complexities of modern warfare. They have turned to AI and automatic decision-making as a means of coping with uncertainty. Furthermore, the scope of the new systems is expected to extend to strategic weapons.

> *Commanders remain particularly concerned about the role that autonomous systems would play during the transition from peace to hostilities when rules of engagement may be altered quickly. An extremely stressing example of such a case is the projected defense against strategic nuclear missiles, where systems must react so rapidly that* it is likely that almost complete reliance will have to be placed on automated systems. *At the same time, the complexity and unpredictability of factors affecting decisions will be very great. (Emphasis added.)*[10]

Although there are risks and problems, DARPA sees no alternatives.

In the summer of 1983 a very popular movie, *War Games,* explored the possibility of how a computer system penetrated by a bright teenager, might accidentally start a nuclear holocaust. The film showed the use of computers in decision-making as a way of bypassing the inabililty of many soldiers to fire missiles when ordered to do so in a realistic war situation. Interestingly enough, the military itself resisted this option, arguing that better training of its soldiers would suffice. In response to the popularity of *War Games* Thomas C. Brandt, (Assistant Deputy Chief of Staff for Operations for combat operations) of NORAD took great pains to assure the public, ''No, that could not happen as it's portrayed in the film because of the nature of the system, because at NORAD people make decisions, not computers.''[11] Despite such reassurances, the public is concerned because this is one area in which computer errors cannot easily be corrected afterwards.

The Strategic Defense Initiative

The possibility of nuclear war has been a fact of existence for most of us. It represents the terrifying vision of a technology that, once created and implemented, is inevitably loosed upon the world (recall the discussion in Chapter 2).

On March 23, 1983, President Reagan delivered his now famous "Star Wars" speech, launching the Strategic Defense Initiative. Its goal is the development of a comprehensive defensive system to identify, intercept, and destroy all or most of an enemy's ballistic missiles. The debate over the feasibility of such a system and its impact on the current strategy of mutual deterrence has been raging ever since.

It is clear that enormous computational resources will necessarily be involved in the Star Wars project. Thus, it is not surprising that the computer science community has been split by a debate over the practicality of such a project and the morality of participation in its development. (See Chapter 14 for a discussion of ethics and professionalism.)

Computer-based systems can be unreliable because of problems with data, hardware, and software. Data problems in this case are overwhelming because of the difficulty of guaranteeing the validity of radar measurements, especially when thousands of warheads must be monitored. Although current computers are quite reliable, hardware faults can have a devastating effect on overall system reliability. If hardware also includes vital communication links, the dangers are substantially compounded. A recent book by Daniel Ford casts serious doubts on the viability of the vast communication system that links satellites, radar installations, field commands, the key Cheyenne Mountain Complex (which makes the final decision on whether an enemy attack has been launched) and finally, the President's command center.[12]

The most serious area of concern, however, is software—the programs that direct the computer to perform its many tasks. Star Wars will place unprecedented demands on software, to such a degree that many computer scientists have publicly expressed serious doubts about its ever working. The software must operate correctly the first time it is used. Anyone familiar with writing even short programs knows that such an event is almost nonexistent.

> *Because of the extreme demands on the system and our inability to test it, we will never be able to believe, with confidence, that we have succeeded. Most of the money spent will be wasted.*[13]

Supporters of Star Wars argue that the problem is real but that the research effort will be directed towards solving it, perhaps with the use of large-scale computer simulations. At this point, the integral involvement of computers in such a fundamental issue of planetary survival is not surprising. What we should all be concerned with are the historical precedents in the development and use of technology. Those precedents seem to point to an operative technological imperative: if something can be done, it will be done. There is more: if something exists, it will be used. This prospect is an overriding fear that governs our existence.

The Vulnerable Integrated Circuit

In 1976, a Russian pilot defected in an advanced fighter, the MIG-25, called the Foxbat. What made this plane unusual, at least in the eyes of the U.S. military, was that it relied on vacuum tubes rather than integrated circuits. Was this another example of Russian technical backwardness? Actually, it represented an early awareness of the susceptibility of integrated circuits to an electromagnetic pulse (EMP) from a nuclear blast high above the earth. A nuclear warhead detonated 250 miles above the center of the United States would cover the continent with EMP, with peak fields of the order of 50,000 volts per meter. Fields of this strength would have a devastating effect on all solid state devices, severely impairing power and communication systems. Vacuum tubes, by contrast, because of their solid metal parts separated by a near vacuum, can resist high-voltage surges.[14]

What can be done to protect vulnerable chips? A natural idea is shielding, but it does not work very well. Other attempts have used special metals, germanium rather than silicon-based integrated circuits, and filtering techniques. So far all these methods have problems, but perhaps the DOD has developed methods that are currently classified. It is ironic that all the virtues of microelectronics—small size, low power consumption, ruggedness—may be defeated by EMP.

CONCLUDING REMARKS

Much has been said and written about the power of information technology in modern society. The state has come to depend increasingly on this power, but to what end? Has bureaucratic control been further entrenched through the use of computers? Is the general public better served or are the aims of the managers and administrators of primary consequence?

How do databases or information systems actually affect organizational structure, quality of service, and strategic planning? These are difficult questions. As more and more information systems have been installed, not all has gone as expected. Costs have not immediately decreased, staff requirements have increased, the appetite for more equipment has grown, and fears about privacy and security have emerged. The database has taken many guises: interdepartmental resource, service for executive needs, single department system, or mixed-access system that permits public users to view statistical information. Given all these different organizational roles for information systems, how are they used and to what end? Management science (discussed in Chapter 4) is the discipline concerned with methods and techniques that aid planning and decision-making. Two basic techniques of management science are the Planning, Programming, and Budgeting System (PPBS), and systems analysis and operations research.

Planning, Programming, and Budgeting System

First instituted in the Department of Defense in the early 1960s and heavily promoted by Lyndon Johnson in 1965, PPBS was hailed as a revolutionary system. It is supposed to determine national goals on a regular basis, select the most critical ones, discover efficient means for reaching these goals with costs specified several years into the future, and ensure that all the programs are cost-effective. Unfortunately, PPBS seems to be more idea or philosophy than rigorously defined program and has come under criticism for not delivering what was promised. Defenders have agreed that it does not depend on mathematical models and is not intended to replace human judgment. What it is supposed to do is clearly identify the important factors under consideration, and initiate a comprehensive cycle of the information memoranda necessary to outline the important objectives, the financial plan (relating costs to objectives), and some analytic justification for these plans and projections.

So far, this approach has failed to include people issues—motivation, mixed loyalties, unclear goals—in the model. This very difficult task is not likely to be solved soon. More research is needed, even in the more traditional areas, to take advantage of the enormous computing power available. Sophisticated simulations, comprehensive budgeting models, and closer involvement with social scientists, economists, and mathematicians are needed for future systems.

Systems Analysis

The systems approach has, its supporters claim, been responsible for managing the military, dealing with a large government bureaucracy, and putting a man on the moon. Furthermore, it is claimed, a nation that can put a man on the moon can control its pollution, renew its decaying cities, provide adequate housing, reduce crime, and improve medical care and the education system. Systems analysis depends on such management tools as operations research, cost-benefit analysis, and various techniques derived from engineering, statistics, and economics. The integration of systems analysis and information systems sounds at first like a marriage made in heaven. Basically, more and better information should result in better decision-making, better service, and lower costs.

Frequently an increase in efficiency is claimed to be identical to an improvement in service to the public. There is a basic assumption that information is neutral—that facts can be gathered, entered into a computer, processed by a variety of programs, and presented in a variety of formats, and then meaningful decisions can be made. But facts or data are not independent of the context in which they are gathered; the motives of the investigators and the aims of the management organization are crucial factors in how these resources are used. Computers and systems analysis tend to bestow a level of respectability perhaps not warranted by the theory being implemented. There is a self-perpetuating momentum in governmental use of systems analysis and information systems. As justification for vast expenditures in time and money, the results produced by such systems must be relevant and important. Government expenditures in this area must be eventually justified to the public at large. In the age of the computer it becomes increasingly difficult to evaluate the performance of a bureaucracy shielded by an impenetrable system. Ours is an age of experts, none more vocal than systems and computer experts. A well-informed public is a crucial ingredient in the process of societal adjustment to the major changes brought on by technological innovation.

SUMMARY

Government is probably the largest single user of computers. These uses are incredibly varied, and their impact is felt throughout society. The federal government has purchased and continues to purchase an enormous number of computers. It exerts considerable pressure on the market to conform to its requirements. One example is the ADA programming language designed by the Defense Department for its future software plans. Governments gather, store, and process vast amounts of information. The public may be concerned about how this information is safeguarded and how it is used. As the bureaucracy depends more heavily on computer systems, it may become less responsive to the needs of the public it is supposed to serve. It may hide behind the computer instead of providing human answers.

In local government, which is responsible for many important services, computers are finding a role in such diverse departments as police, welfare, education, planning, property taxes, and budgeting.

More recently, the electoral process has witnessed the introduction of computers for purposes of identifying targeted special-interest groups and fund-raising. The television networks use computers to monitor the voting process and, more controversially, to predict the outcomes, as early as possible. The Department of Defense (DOD) is the single largest user of computers in the federal government. The DOD has launched major programs to modernize its command structure and its weaponry, including airplanes and tanks with sophisticated computer systems. Major funding for AI has come from the DOD, in pursuit of improvements in battlefield capabilities. Given the important role of computers in the detection and recognition of large-scale military threats, some people have expressed a deep concern that accidental war may occur because computer systems will respond before humans can intervene. In spite of assurances by the government that humans will always retain ultimate responsibility, the ability to respond quickly is a high priority for military decision-makers.

NOTES

1. *An Assessment and Forecast of ADP in the Federal Government*, U.S. Department of Commerce, National Bureau of Standards Publication no. 500–79 (Washington, D.C., August 1981).

2. Robert V. Head, *Federal Information Systems Management* (Washington, D.C.: The Brookings Institution, 1982).

3. Rodney N. Smith, "The New Political Machine," *Datamation*, June 1, 1984, pp. 22–24, 26.

4. Tekla S. Perry, "TV Networks Vie for Viewer's Votes," *IEEE Spectrum*, October 1984, p. 68.

5. William Burrows, "Fighter Planes: Age of the Computer Ace," *Science Digest*, July 1983, p. 55.

6. "New-Generation Computing Technology: A Strategic Plan for its Development and Application to Critical Problems of Defense," in *Strategic Computing*, Defense Advanced Research Project Agency, Department of Defense, October 28, 1983.

7. Report of the U.S. Senate Committee on the Armed Services, as quoted in Christopher Simpson, "Computers in Combat," *Science Digest*, October 1982, p.34.

8. As quoted in Arthur Macy Cox, "When Computers Launch the Missiles," *International Herald Tribune*, June 9, 1982, p. 4.

9. Severo M. Ornstein, Brian C. Smith, and Lucy A. Suchman, "Strategic Computing," *Bulletin of the Atomic Scientists*, December 1984, p. 12.

10. "New-Generation Computing Technology: A Strategic Plan."

11. As quoted in Lee Grant, "War Games: Separating Fact from Fiction," *Vancouver Sun*, July 6, 1983, p. D 17. (Originally appeared in Los Angeles Times.)

12. Daniel Ford, *The Button* (New York: Simon & Schuster, 1985).

13. Professor David Parnas, statement of resignation from a nine-member Star Wars advisory panel on computing, as quoted in Phillip Elmer-DeWitt, "Star Wars and Software," *Time*, July 22, 1985, p. 39.

14. William J. Broad, "N-Blast in Space Could Silence North America," *The Province* (Vancouver), January 9, 1983, p. B3.

ADDITIONAL READINGS

Data Processing: Issues and Problems

Berney, Karen. "Aging Software Swamps Bureaucracy." *Electronics*, June 14, 1984, pp. 115–116.

Computer-Based National Information Systems. U.S. Congress, Office of Technology Assessment Report. Washington, D.C., September 1981.

Costs and Benefits of Database Managment: Federal Experience. U.S. Dept. of Commerce, National Bureau of Standards Publication 500-84. Washington, D.C., November 1981.

"A Lesson in Reducing Redundant Data." *Business Week*, September 27, 1982, pp. 82, 86.

Local Government

Danziger, James N. "Computers, Local Governments, and the Litany to EDP." *Public Administration Review*, January/February 1977, pp. 28–37.

Kling, Rob. "Automated Welfare Client-Tracking and Service Integration: The Political Economy of Computing." *Communications of the Association for Computing Machinery*, June 1978, pp. 484–493.

The Political Process

Conniff, Richard. "Government by Computer." *Science Digest,* December 1982, pp. 55–57, 104.

Laudon, Kenneth C. "Information Technology and Participation in the Political Process." In A. A. Mowshowitz, ed., *Human Choice and Computers 2.* New York: North-Holland, 1980, pp. 167–191.

"The Powerful New Machine on the Political Scene." *Business Week,* November 5, 1984, pp. 58, 62.

The Nation's Defense

Stefik, Mark. "Strategic Computing at DARPA: Overview and Assessment." *Communications of the Association for Computing Machinery,* July 1985, pp. 690–703. (See also the February, March, and August 1985 issues.)

Walker, Larry. "The U.S. Attacks the C³I Problem." *Electronics,* December 15, 1983, pp. 98–107.

Weber, David M. "DARPA after Robot Car." *Electronics Week,* November 5, 1984, pp. 24, 29.

Wilson, Andrew. *The Bomb and the Computer.* New York: Dell, 1970.

Concluding Remarks

Hoos, Ida R. *Systems Analysis in Public Policy: A Critique.* Rev. ed. Berkeley: University of California Press, 1983.

Westin, Alan F., ed. *Information Technology in a Democracy.* Cambridge, Mass.: Harvard University Press, 1971.

8

COMPUTERS AND THE LAW

*B*ad laws are the worst sort of tyranny.

◇ *Edmund Burke (1729–1797)* ◇

*T*he first thing we do, let's kill all the lawyers.

◇ *William Shakespeare,* King Henry VI Part II ◇

INTRODUCTION

A given technological innovation will inevitably secure its place in society as the existing system of laws is expanded to accommodate it. What is remarkable about computer technology is how fast this process has occurred and how many interesting and important legal issues have arisen. As many have noted, computer professionals and legal professionals share at least one thing: they both have an extensive and impenetrable jargon. In a very short time a new subdiscipline has come into being, usually called computer law. One lawyer (Thomas Christo) has argued that it is wrong to speak of computer law when in fact there is just the *Law*.[1] Nevertheless, a number of universities do offer courses in computer law and there are several journals in this area. What, then, are some of the issues that fall within the purview of computer law?

There are really two major areas of concern. Computer crime involves the use of the computer to steal or embezzle money in a manner that could not easily have been done otherwise. There are also such crimes as stealing computer time, unlawful access to files, and the acquisition of privileged information. The second major area is concerned with the relation between copyright and patent law and the legal protection of software. Much has been written about whether or not current law can be used in this area. There is the problem of distinguishing between the central idea captured in a program and the program itself. Other problems are occurring as the distinction between hardware and software becomes increasingly blurred. How does one protect programs implemented in ROM (Read Only Memory)? There are questions about the copying of the masks used to manufacture microprocessor chips or, what is more subtle, the determination of the underlying logic.

Law enforcement is another area that has been dramatically affected by the introduction of computers. The development of large databases to store criminal records represents a significant advance in criminology and a new area of concern for civil libertarians. Various proposals for nationwide centralized information systems have been debated for years because of concern about the increased powers that would accrue to the police. Currently, many police forces have equipped their patrol cars with two-way terminals that enable their officers to check suspicious license plates against a list of stolen cars stored in a central database. In the investigation of serious crimes, evidence can be stored on a computer in a highly cross-indexed fashion that may result in new leads being uncovered. Other police applications are databases for traffic violations, crime statistics, management of police resources, and organizational administration.

Developments in information processing have also affected the way law is practiced. Legal information retrieval systems help the lawyer in case preparation. Research is in progress to model legal reasoning in computer programs, another example of applied Artificial Intelligence. More straightforward applications in the lawyer's office include the automatic preparation of legal documents and tax returns, office management, statutory research in the legislative process, and estate planning. Furthermore, the computer business itself relies on lawyers to draw up contracts, deal with tax considerations, and handle all the other issues that arise in normal business operations.

Other legal issues arise in other contexts. The privacy issue involves new legislation (see Chapter 9). Important legal problems arise around electronic funds transfer systems, transborder data flows, government regulation of the computer and telecommunication industries, and the control of technology transfer (see Chapter 11). One final question is the legal status of evidence derived from computers. Is computer output to be considered as primary evidence?

COMPUTER CRIME

One of the more glamorous products of the new technology is the computer crime story. Hardly a day passes without a report that yet another computer system has been broken into, and money has been removed; discussions of computer security abound. The glamor component seems to arise because computers are supposed to be so formidable that any breakdown in their security is clearly newsworthy. There is also a "David and Goliath" image of the lonely, clever computer programmer cracking the all-powerful system. Many people are quite sympathetic to the human-versus-machine success story even if a crime has been committed. However, crimes are being perpetrated, and measures must be taken to prevent them.

The use of computers to commit crimes is not the only way they are associated with unlawful activities. Sabotage can be directed towards the computer installation itself in order to uncover information useful to crack various security codes. The computer can be the target of people who object—for political, social, and economic reasons—to the growing influence of computers in everyday life. The attack might be directed towards the communication network in which the computer is embedded—for example, phone lines might be tapped. These possibilities have stimulated an ongoing concern with computer security. Besides safeguarding the physical system, the data itself may need to be protected.

Defining the Term

Donn Parker, an expert on computer crime, prefers to use the term computer abuse. He defines it as follows:

> . . . *any incident involving an intentional act where a victim suffered or could have suffered a loss, and a perpetrator made or could have made gain . . . associated with computers.*[2]

The group he heads at SRI International (Menlo Park, California) has been carrying out an ongoing study of the variety and scope of computer crime. It is difficult to determine how prevalent such crime is. Companies that have been victimized are not eager to publicize the crime, if they are financial institutions that depend upon a reputation for security. Therefore, the figures for computer-related crimes are based on estimates derived from figures on all actual reported crimes. In 1979, the FBI reported that while the average armed robbery netted about $9,000 and the average amount of funds embezzled or obtained by bank fraud was about $19,000, the average computer fraud totaled $450,000. How much money has been involved in computer frauds is a major unknown number, with estimates ranging from $100 million by the United States Chamber of Commerce to $3.5 billion according to the Harvard Business Review. In 1984, the American Bar Association's task force on crime released a survey of 283 companies and agencies.[3] About 25 percent reported "known and verifiable" losses resulting from computer crime and totaling up to $730 million. Most companies did not report the crimes to the police for fear of possible suits by stockholders.

Not all the cases described below have unimpeachable evidence that they actually occurred. Such crimes are possible, and whether or not they have actually been perpetrated is not the issue. That they could happen has encouraged designers of systems to incorporate improved security measures. Here, then, are some crimes, presented for purely academic interest, of course:[4]

> By controlling a Florida race track computer, conspirators were able to issue additional winning tickets in a combination of races—called a trifecta—for which the total payoff is not displayed.

Employees in a city welfare system were arrested for issuing fraudulent welfare payments.

An accountant for a fruit company was able to inflate prices on invoices by small amounts and then distribute the extra money to fictitious accounts. Because prices fluctuate in this market, the accountant was able to adjust prices by simulating the firm's accounting system on a service bureau computer.

A member of the computer staff for a department store would buy expensive appliances and then adjust the prices on the invoices when they came into the computer center.

A drug company invented a new drug. A competitor managed to rent excess computer time on the drug company's machine and was able to steal files describing the drug.

A thief replaced bank deposit slips in the public counter of a bank with slips made out with an appropriate code to deposit funds in his account. After accumulating $100,000, he disappeared.

The ''salami swindle'': Miniscule amounts are removed from the accounts of unsuspecting individuals and accumulated in the account of the thief. It might be done in interest-bearing savings accounts in employee investment plans, or if the amounts are small enough, in paychecks.

An employee of a board of education in New York used the school computer system to store data on horse breeding. He was found innocent because the judge ruled that his actions were not specifically forbidden.

A student in Texas was discovered scanning grade records stored on the university mainframe. He had used his microcomputer to access and change grades in two of his courses. Suitable punishment was to be arranged in consultation with his professors.

These examples contain the major ingredients in computer crime: trusted employees, inadequate monitoring, lack of sufficient audit checking, minimal security in the computer center, and a lack of foresight in the design of the computer systems.

There has been criticism of the most important and influential study on computer crime cases, that done by Donn Parker at SRI International. One critic, John Taber, suggests that the study has achieved more importance than it merits. For instance, it has reported a remarkable rate of increase in computer crime: 144 cases in 1973, 381 in 1974, and perhaps over 700 by 1980. Its statistics give average loss per computer crime as $450,000 (the same as the FBI) and annual costs of $300 million. This latter figure is based on the view that only a ''tip of the iceberg'' of computer crime is being reported. Unfortunately this figure has been uncritically accepted by many in the field. It is claimed that SRI uses ''suspected mythical cases, which they themselves doubt, and unvalidated data, which they admit is unverified.''[5] Their sources are largely the popular computer trade magazines. The lesson in all this is to be cautious when reading stories about great computer capers.

There is certainly computer crime—but what kind, how much, and how significant it is is not yet clear.

A further example reinforces skepticism. One of the most well-known examples of computer fraud, the so-called salami swindle, depends on a rounding-off process to accumulate funds in the perpetrator's account. Taber is highly critical:

> *It is the best and most important example of a sophisticated computer crime, on which there is wide agreement, and is cited as an impressive instance of the widespread problem of criminal programmers.*
>
> *It has never happened.*[6]

Taber's analysis of the mathematics of the rounding-off process shows that for all practical purposes it is impossible to steal large amounts of money this way.[7] To accumulate $200,000 would require over 160 million transactions, at an interest rate of 4 percent. Given that most banks have no more than 10,000 accounts, it would be necessary to round off each account over 16,000 times to accumulate the stolen amount. This would take many years, and no reported computer crime has extended over a lengthy period.

The term *computer crime* can be broadly or narrowly interpreted. The Wells Fargo National Bank of San Francisco reported a loss due to embezzlement of $21.3 million in 1980. The crime involved a computer, a former bank officer, and several boxing promoters. However, bank officials claim that it could not really be called a computer-related crime.

The Computer in a Subsidiary Role—Two Cases

In Nikolai Gogol's novel *Dead Souls*, the protagonist Tchitchikov must use the names of dead serfs as collateral to obtain government loans. In the mid-1960s, Equity Funding Corporation seemed to have found a good way to make money by combining insurance and mutual funds in a single company. Its stock was much admired on Wall Street until the scandal broke in 1973. Equity had to grow at a high rate to maintain its glamorous reputation. One way to raise money was to sell insurance accounts to other companies at discount rates. Under the direction of the top executives, employees created phony individuals and stored the accounts in the computer. A year after these were sold, it was necessary to pay the reinsurer the premiums supposed to be paid by each policyholder. So more fictitious accounts were created to raise additional money, and the involved staff spent many days and nights in the creation of new accounts. The entire fraud was uncovered when an employee reported it to the New York state insurance department.

The use of the computer was not particularly sophisticated in this case. Its main purpose was to establish credibility for the accounts by having them listed in a computer printout. Because top management was so intimately involved in this fraud, usual in-house security methods would not have been effective. This was clearly more than just a computer fraud. In the end, about $2.1 billion of a total value of $3.2 billion in life insurance policies was declared to be fictitious by the bankruptcy trustee. The fraud is a major event in the history of business crime, but the computer played at most a supporting role.

In 1978, Stanley Mark Rifkin was employed to set up a back-up system for the ''wire room'' of the Security Pacific National Bank in Los Angeles. The wire room is the center of a communications network that electronically transfers between two and four billion dollars a day. The back-up system was needed to keep the communications network operating in case of a failure in the primary system. It was only natural that Rifkin was able to acquire detailed information on the operation of the system. Much of his information was obtained by direct interviews with the relevant bank employees. On October 25, 1978, Rifkin visited the wire room supposedly to do a study, but his real purpose was to obtain codes written on a piece of paper on a wall inside the room. Later the same day he called the wire room, issued the proper codes, and in the name of Mike Hansen—of the International Department of Security Pacific National Bank—had $10.2 million transferred to an account in the Irving Trust Company in New York and from there to a bank in Switzerland.

Rifkin might easily have succeeded if he had flown to Switzerland and collected the money, but he had other plans. He did fly to Switzerland, but it was to purchase over $8 million in Russian diamonds. Upon his return to Los Angeles he met a lawyer with whom he had previously discussed how diamonds could be sold secretly. The next day the lawyer had met with the FBI and told them about his dealings with Rifkin. Rifkin was subsequently arrested, and the diamonds were recovered. He was tried and sentenced to eight years in federal prison. The Rifkin crime illustrates the vulnerability of complex computer communication systems. Security requires the maintenance of high standards of awareness, but it will always be difficult to guarantee that employees with access to secret codes do not have criminal intentions.

Electronic Funds Transfer Systems

Electronic Funds Transfer Systems (EFTS) (considered in depth in Chapter 11) have been developed to transmit funds across the country and around the world by means of telecommunications systems. What is actualy sent is an electronic message indicating that funds are to be removed from accounts, added to accounts, and transferred between accounts. Other more common examples of EFTSs are automated teller machines (ATMs), point-of-sale (POS) terminals, automated clearing houses, and home banking. As was shown in the Rifkin case, EFTSs are prime targets for technologically sophisticated criminals. EFTSs can be categorized along three lines: consumer, corporate, and internal. Each of these will have possibilities for criminal acts.

Typical crimes associated with the misuse of ATMs (consumer EFTSs) are: the theft of cards and personal identifier numbers, the withdrawal of more money than is actually in the account, the counterfeiting of cards, and finally, the assault of individuals who have just withdrawn money. Individual ATM losses have been small, but there have been incidents in which large amounts of money have been stolen. The Rifkin case is a prime example of corporate EFTS crime. It depended on the acquisition of authorized transfer codes and the rapid disposition of transfer commands, an important feature of EFTSs.

Internal EFTS crime is done by a bank employee with computer access. The perpetrator can transfer funds illegally on a continual basis or blackmail individuals with information derived from a careful monitoring of EFTS transactions. This type of crime is not unique to EFTSs, but the existence of EFTSs facilitates its perpetration.

While not strictly part of current EFTSs, credit-card transactions will in the future be handled directly by such networks. The major crimes associated with credit cards are counterfeiting and theft. According to the American Bankers Association, in 1982 losses from counterfeit cards were $40 million, and from stolen cards, $200 million.[8] In 1980, losses from counterfeit cards were only $3.5 million. Attempts to make it more difficult to forge cards have included the use of microelectronics in the card itself as well as a three-dimensional hologram. Either would be almost impossible to duplicate.

Espionage in the Computer Industry

The computer industry itself is subject to criminal acts. Because of the rapidly changing state of technology, competition is so intense that on occasion very large companies have attempted to obtain privileged information by surreptitious means. Probably the most celebrated example occurred in the summer of 1982 when Hitachi, a major Japanese electronics company with 1982 sales of nearly $10 billion, was involved in an FBI sting operation. Two Hitachi employees were arrested in the act of buying IBM trade secrets. Hitachi eventually pleaded guilty to a one-count indictment of conspiring to transport stolen IBM property from the United States to Japan. Because IBM is such a dominating force in the computer industry, it is advantageous for its competitors to obtain advanced knowledge of its plans. That such a large company as Hitachi would engage in illegal activities to obtain secret information from IBM is indicative of the extreme pressure of competition.[9]

Legislation

The fundamental prerequisite for drafting legislation is a precise definition of the area of concern. One author has listed five categories of currently recognized crime.[10]

- **Financial crime:**   stealing or embezzling via a computer.
- **Informational crime:**   using the computer to acquire privileged information.
- **Theft of property:**   taking computer equipment.
- **Theft of services:**   using the computer for unauthorized purposes.
- **Vandalism:**   physical damage to computer hardware or software.

The first attempt at a federal computer crime bill was formulated in 1979 and called the Ribicoff bill after Senator Abraham Ribicoff, its major supporter. The bill was proposed as an amendment to the Criminal Code of the United States. The opening section read in part:

Computer Fraud and Abuse

Whoever uses, or attempts to use, computer with intent to execute a scheme or artifice to defraud, or to obtain property by false or fraudulent pretenses, representations, or promises or to embezzle, steal, or knowingly convert to his use or the use of another, the property of another, shall, if the computer is owned by the U.S. government or a financial institution involved in interstate commerce, . . . be fined not more than two times the amount of the gain directly or indirectly derived from the offense or $50,000, whichever is higher, or imprisoned not more than five years, or both.[11]

The remainder of the bill includes damage to computers as a crime, defines ''computer,'' defines ''financial institutions,'' and describes the responsibilities of federal authorities. This bill was defeated in a Senate vote. Its detractors claimed it did not adequately define information as property.

HR.5616, a computer crime bill passed unanimously by the House of Representatives, was amended and passed by the Senate on October 11, 1984. Called the Counterfeit Access Device and Computer Fraud Act, it contains legislation on penalties for credit card abuse and computer crimes that involve illicit access to computer databases.[12] A basic provision gives penalties for those who knowingly access a computer that affects interstate or foreign commerce without authorization. These penalties include fines ranging from $5000 to twice the value obtained by the crime as well as imprisonment for up to 20 years. The Act further provides penalties for the unlawful access of any records protected by the Financial Right of Privacy Act or the Fair Credit Reporting Act, thereby safeguarding banking and credit records. To use, modify or disclose information, or prevent the authorized use of a computer owned or operated by the U.S. government is declared a misdemeanor. Actual technical terms are to be defined in regulations by the relevant agencies.

Several state laws deal with computer fraud and computer crime. As of 1980, seventeen states had enacted computer crime laws and several others had proposed legislation. These laws differ quite significantly from one another. There have been very few indictments and even fewer convictions, hence little experience has been gathered in the application of the various laws. Cases of arson, burglary, embezzlement, extortion, and forgery have been prosecuted under state laws. The Florida Computer Crimes Act of 1981 stands out as an important piece of legislation. It defines offenses against intellectual property and against the authorized computer user as follows:

Whoever willfully, knowingly, and without authorization destroys data, programs, or supporting documentation, residing or existing, internal or external to a computer, computer system, or computer network commits an offense against intellectual property. . . .

*Whoever wilfully, knowingly, and without authorization denies or causes the denial·
of computer system services, . . . commits an offense against computer users.*[13]

Security Procedures

As in many other areas of life, prevention is far better than detection, indictment, and possible conviction. What steps can administrators of computing facilities take to ensure the physical security of the system itself, and the security of the communications network?

Physical security involves the computer itself, the peripheral equipment, and the rooms and buildings, including furniture, tape storage, and terminals. Obvious care must be taken with respect to fire, water, earthquakes, explosions, and other natural causes. Special care must be taken to control access by people in order to safeguard the equipment and physical surroundings. It may be necessary to require identification badges for those individuals who work in restricted areas. There must be alternative power supplies as well as back-up systems to be used in case of damage. An entire sub-industry has grown up to advise companies in physical security and to supply security equipment. As the dependency of society on computers increases, it becomes a basic necessity to take steps to guarantee physical security.

System security involves the basic operation of the computer itself. The issue is access—to the computer, the associated files, sensitive production programs, and even the operating system. The basic controls used to restrict access are computer identification numbers (IDs) and passwords. Within this system there may be privileged function levels, including user and program access control. An ID is typically issued by the computing center; it is the user's responsibility to choose a password as a second level of security. The operating system of the computer will permit access only to identifiable IDs and passwords. Once on a system, the ordinary user is restricted to his or her own files and system programs, including programming languages and library functions. Individual users may provide other users with access to their files, where access may mean reading the file, writing into it, or both. The operating system must ensure individual user security as well as protect itself from unauthorized access. There are a number of by-now-traditional means of cracking system security.

Browsing   refers to the fact that once on the system, it may be possible to look through data without proper authorization. One technique is to request large amounts of additional space. If the system does not first clear the data before making the space available to a user, the data may contain useful information. The remedy in this situation is obvious: make sure that no information remains in memory after it is no longer needed.

Concerted attack   involves discovering a password by trying all possibilities in the range of permissible passwords. This attempt can be defeated by increasing the size of the range, by changing passwords on a regular basis, and by signing a user off after two or three wrong password attempts.

The Trojan horse technique   involves the inclusion of unauthorized programs or data inside authorized ones to get them into the system. One story, perhaps apocryphal, is about a disgruntled programmer who embedded a special program segment inside the operating system. Two years after he left, the system wiped out many user files and then wiped itself out. His code had checked the date each day until a certain date was reached and then it executed. All code must be carefully checked before becoming part of the working system. Of course, the only safe system is an isolated one in which no new programs are added.

Spoofing   occurs when the perpetrator writes a program that simulates the terminal screen prior to signing on. When an unsuspecting user sits down at the terminal and signs on, the program saves the password, signs itself off, and connects the user to the system. In this way passwords can be stolen and used subsequently for illegal access to files.

The security kernel   is basically a hardware/software mechanism necessary to realize a special program called a reference monitor. The reference monitor checks every reference made by a person or program to an object, file, device, program, or user. It determines whether the reference is permitted under the security policy implemented in the system. To be effective the kernel must be complete (in that it must monitor all references), tamper-proof, and verifiably correct. Bugs in the kernel could wreak havoc in the system. A number of kernel-based systems have been developed.

Telecommunications security   problems occur because computer centers are usually part of networks and a considerable amount of data is sent and received over telephone lines and microwave systems. It is possible to eavesdrop on such communication systems by wiretapping the line or by listening in on radio or microwave signals. The standard way to deal with this problem is to code, or encrypt, the data before transmission. In 1977 the Data Encryption Standard (DES) was adopted by the National Bureau of Standards. DES, available on an inexpensive chip, can be used to encrypt data for storage or transmission in a cipher text, decipherable only to users who know the key. Unfortunately, DES is not as widely used as it might be. Many banks do use it to encode financial transactions. Recently there has been considerable interest in a new type of encryption system called a public key cryptosystem. Instead of a single key for both enciphering and deciphering, a public key system has two keys, the enciphering key, which is public, and the deciphering key known only to the receiver. To send a message to a given destination it is only necessary to look up its public key and then encipher the message. The deciphering key is only known to the destination and therefore the message is secure. Of course this system depends on the difficulty of breaking the code, even with the aid of modern computers. In 1982 an Israeli mathematician, Adi Shamir, demonstrated how one version of this system could be cracked. More complex versions, still unbroken, are the object of a great deal of research, as encryption has great financial, political, and military importance. In fact, the U.S. government has been so concerned that it has attempted to control the publishing of research in this area. It will probably require a major computer crime to convince more companies that data encryption is not a luxury but a necessary cost of doing business.

The increasing frequency of unauthorized connections to computer systems over telephone lines has resulted in a number of methods to prevent unwarranted access. Passwords, security kernels, and data encryption provide substantial protection, but additional measures are necessary to deal with telephone access. The most recent development is the call-back security system in which the computer will only permit access if the call was made from a previously authorized number. All incoming calls are answered without an acknowledgment tone while a library of valid codes is checked to verify the legitimacy of the call. A valid location identification number must be provided that permits the system to call the user back in order to establish a valid connection. Thus, the computer cannot be accessed from an unauthorized location even if the code is known.

One final example of an attempted computer crime should be sufficient to convince even the most skeptical that computer crime is a serious problem. Early in 1983, the New York Times reported that a former economist for the Federal Reserve Board had been arrested for trying to gain unauthorized entry to the Federal Reserve's computer.[14] He had taken a job as a forecaster with the brokerage firm E. F. Hutton. To impress his new employers, he planned to obtain secret data about the nation's money supply. Apparently he used another Federal Reserve employee's access code to gain entry, but the system's security made it possible for his attempt to be recognized, and he was apprehended.

The following security procedures are generally advisable:

> Concern with security must be built into the original design specification of the computer system, both in the physical surroundings and the hardware and software.
>
> It is necessary to have a complete back-up system in case of damage from natural causes or sabotage.
>
> A policy for prosecution of crimes should be drawn up, posted, and followed.
>
> Have regular and unannounced audits of procedures to ensure compliance.
>
> Rotate personnel regularly and be suspicious if there is any reluctance.
>
> Screen personnel carefully, especially for sensitive jobs.
>
> Be sympathetic to customer complaints; they may be the first sign that there is a problem.

POLICE AND TECHNOLOGY

The police have the responsibility to enforce the law, apprehend criminals, keep the peace, and generally maintain law and order. Jurisdictions for police forces can be: city (or local), state (including highway patrol), and federal (the FBI). At each of these levels technology can play a variety of roles. For the city or state police officer driving through a neighborhood in a cruiser, a major innovation is the on-board computer terminal that permits access to a database of criminal records. For the FBI, the development of large databases has helped immeasurably in the coordination of criminal investigations. In fact, for investigations of any size, the computer is used to store all relevant information, which can then be processed in the hopes of turning up possibly useful relationships.

Aside from their functions as information processors, computers are playing an increasingly important role in criminal investigations. One very valuable application is in fingerprint identification, exemplifed by the FBI's Automatic Fingerprint Identification System, soon to be operative. It combines humans and computers in the process of data extraction, classification, matching and retrieval. Computers are also being used to cross-check the chemical spectra of unknown compounds against a database of known spectra to produce likely candidates for further human analysis. Another area under study is the computer identification of human faces or of mug-shots. The Israeli National Police Force is engaged in a project based on the use of so-called, Identi-Kit descriptions of suspects.

Computers and Local Police Forces

Computer technology has been used in police departments since the mid-1960s. Two factors spurred the growth of investment in technology. The President's Commission on Law Enforcement and the Administration of Justice recommended in 1967 that technology might aid in police work. Secondly, The Law Enforcement Assistance Administration provided additional funds to purchase equipment.

The applications can be divided into two general groups, distinguished by whether they involve simply standard data processing applied to police work or whether they make a unique contribution. For example, the use of computer databanks to store records of traffic accidents and driving and parking violations may be useful in keeping track of delinquents but it is hardly a novel application. Similarly, the use of files for office work such as personnel records, payroll, inventory control, and budget analysis is rather routine. Some applications unique to police work are the following:

> Instant access to databases from patrol cars.
>
> Allocation of patrol cars on the basis of expected need, perhaps based on computer models.
>
> The use of computers to dispatch vehicles as well as the tracking of such vehicles.
>
> Computer explorations to reveal crime patterns based on crime and arrest statistics.

A number of cities—including St. Louis, Kansas City, Oakland, Los Angeles, San Diego, and New York—have led in the implementation of systems that aid in resource allocation and control of vehicles and officers. As might be expected, some of the more advanced applications were not successful. Reasons varied, but some key elements were a lack of commitment and direction from the top, problems with personnel turnover, and the usual systems difficulties. It is important to introduce such systems carefully, with a long-term plan and well-defined monitoring procedures. It is difficult to evaluate the impact of computer technology on the quality of police work, partly because it is hard to separate it from the many other factors that affect crime rates. There is a fear that dependence on computers could detract from an important facet of police work—human relations. To be effective, police must establish a presence in the community based on trust and respect. The usefulness of computers must be judged not just on the basis of crime statistics but also on the degree to which people are actually helped to live safer lives.

National Computerized Criminal History Systems

More and better information resources should help police forces at all levels of society do their job more efficiently. This oft-repeated argument is brought forth when the question of computerized databases for the police is raised. What kinds of information are being talked about? From the local police comes such basic information as names, dates, arrests, charges, associates, aliases, photographs, and fingerprints. From the courts, information is provided about charges, disposition of cases, and sentences. Correctional institutions have records of entry, conduct, and release date. Such information becomes part of the criminal history record. The FBI began in 1924 to maintain a national criminal history record system in its Identification Division (known as Ident). By 1981, 49 states had identification bureaus as well, Nevada being the lone exception.

Computers were first used for criminal record processing by the FBI in 1963. In early 1967, the National Crime Information Center (NCIC) was open for operation. It contained records of wanted persons, stolen vehicles and license plates, guns, and other articles. Initially there were 15 participating agencies, including the police departments of New York, Boston, Chicago, St. Louis, Philadelphia, and New Orleans, and the state police of Pennsylvania, Texas, and California. Criminal records were explictly excluded from the NCIC until after the stolen property and wanted person files were implemented. Criminal records were first accommodated by the FBI in the Computerized Criminal History (CCH) program near the end of 1971. There was some disagreement over who would manage this system and how detailed the records would be. Eventually it was decided that the NCIC/CCH would simply store an index to records held by individual states on single-state offenders, whereas for multi-state offenders the entire records would be held. Full implementation has not taken place, for a variety of reasons. Only eight states maintain criminal history records in CCH.

As of 1981 the CCH file in the NCIC contained about 500,000 Federal records out of a total of 1.9 million. Some problems seem to be associated with such a federal database. One of the major ones is accuracy. A number of studies have shown unacceptably high error rates. A 1979 study showed that about 27 percent of CCH records did not show a court disposition that had occurred, and about 20 percent of Ident arrest records sampled were inaccurate with respect to charging, disposition, and sentencing.[15] Incomplete or inaccurate records play havoc with the administration of justice. Another important issue is privacy. In 1981 over 50 percent of requests for information from Ident were made by noncriminal justice agencies for such purposes as employment, licensing, and security checks. Congress has been concerned about controlling the dissemination of criminal records and guaranteeing their security. This problem is especially serious because the frequency of erroneous or incomplete data is so high.

Suppose a national CCH system were in place. It might have the following important applications:

> Criminal investigations.
>
> Police bookings (the availability of on-line criminal information would be helpful in determining how long to hold a suspect and whether or not to fingerprint).
>
> Pretrial release and bail decisions.
>
> Presentence investigation reports (these are used by judges in determining appropriate sentences).

Problems of noncriminal uses would also have to be dealt with. The use of criminal records to determine employment seems to put an individual in double jeopardy. Strict operating procedures for noncriminal access would be necessary. Of course, the records must be accurate. Finally, how relevant is a past criminal record to future employment behavior? Surprisingly, a large number of Americans have criminal records—some 35 million citizens as of 1979, of which 26 million were in the labor force.[16]

There are other potential problems. Any wrong use of criminal record information would adversely affect some minority groups. The balance of power between the states and the federal government must be considered. Surveillance is a concern, as the FBI in the late 1960s and early 1970s kept files on many anti-Vietnam war protesters who had broken no laws. The FBI has subsequently refused all requests for use of the NCIC for intelligence purposes but has proposed to establish an NCIC file on persons "judged to represent a political threat."[17] There is currently no national computerized criminal history system. The last 15 years or so have witnessed a number of proposals for the establishment of such a system, but so far it has not happened. In this case, the supposed advantages of technological innovation have not automatically overriden the potential dangers and disadvantages.

THE LEGAL PROTECTION OF SOFTWARE

> *Congress shall have Power . . . To promote the Progress of Science and useful Arts, by securing for limited Times to Authors and Inventors the exclusive Right to their respective Writings and Discoveries. (The Constitution of the United States, Article I, Section 8, 1788.)*

The framers of the Constitution would have been surprised by the development of computers. The attempt to characterize software in order to design appropriate legal protection has been a long and torturous process that is by no means complete. Computers themselves are readily protected under patent law, as they are certainly inventions. But problems have arisen even here because of the difficulty in determining how to safeguard the masks used to produce integrated circuits. The major concern, however, lies with computer software, more specifically with applications programs. Congress has passed legislation that provides penalties for those who infringe upon the safeguards granted by patents or copyrights. There is the protection afforded by case law to protect trade secrets, and there is the law of contracts. Each has different background, advantages, and disadvantages.

One of the problems in protecting programs is a basic question of definition. As Gemignani has pointed out a program may be viewed as

> *a particular form of expression of a flowchart or algorithm, a process for control-*
> *ling or bringing about a desired result inside a computer, a machine part or com-*
> *pletion of an incomplete machine, a circuit diagram of an incomplete machine, a*
> *circuit diagram or blueprint for a circuit board, a data compilation, a code*
> *writing . . .*[18]

The list does not end there. All the key terms in the constitutional mandate—limited time, author, inventor, and discovery—must be interpreted in the present context.

Patents

Obtaining a patent is a long and involved process, but it does confer considerable advantages—a monopoly on use, as well as considerable tax benefits. Are computer programs patentable? The relevant portion of the U.S. Code, section 101, states:

> *Whoever invents or discovers any new and useful process, machine, manufacture,*
> *or composition of matter, or any new and useful improvement thereof, may obtain a*
> *patent therefor, subject to the conditions and requirements of this title.*[19]

Thus, a program would have to be considered a programmable process or a programmed machine. The history of attempts to patent programs is rife with controversy, confusion, and a basic inability to define the nature of a relatively new technology.

Companies and individuals wishing to patent their software are confronted by a tangled situation. The Patent Office has consistently rejected most patent applications. The Court of Customs and Patent Appeals has generally supported attempts to patent software. The Supreme Court has usually overturned decisions by the Court of Customs and Patent Appeals and has not clarified the question of the patentability of software. And, finally, Congress has so far not passed necessary and appropriate legislation. In 1968, the Patent Office made an official statement: ''Computer programs per se . . . shall not be patentable.''[20] In the following year, the Court of Customs and Patent Appeals, in hearing a patent appeal, set aside this opinion.[21] Since then a series of cases have proceeded to the Supreme Court, which consistently rejected patent claims until the case of Diamond v. Diehr in 1981. In this case, Diehr applied for a patent for a process for molding raw uncured synthetic rubber into cured products. This process involved measuring temperatures, using a computer to determine cure times, and opening a press accordingly. The Patent Board rejected the claim, and the Court of Customs and Patent Appeals reversed the rejection, arguing that the mathematical formula was embodied in a useful process. The Supreme Court upheld this opinion in a five-to-four decision. Three basic points of law emerged from the Court's opinion.[22] First, the mere inclusion of a mathematical formula, or programmed computer does not invalidate a claim. Second, in this claim, it was stated, "the respondents [did] not seek to patent a mathematical formula." Third, the claims sought "only to foreclose from others, the use of that equation in conjunction with the other steps in their claimed process." There will be more cases, more opinions, and eventually Congress will pass appropriate legislation. For now, there are a number of advantages and disadvantages to the patent process with respect to software protection.

Patent protection is broad and long-term (17 years). Independent development is no defense against an infringement charge. However, there are some serious disadvantages. Obtaining a patent is a long and costly process. Protecting a patent may also be quite costly. Only the "programmed machine,"—that is, application programs—is patentable, not data or documentation. Not all programmed machines are patentable, and more experience will have to be gained to determine the bounds. Before the Diehr decision, out of about 100,000 patent applications filed each year only about 450 were for program patents. Diamond v. Diehr may change this situation, but in such a rapidly changing field the lengthy application process, requiring full disclosure, may not be the best way to protect software.

Copyright

A new Copyright act was enacted in 1976 and became effective in 1978. The new law was not meant to apply to computer software issues until a report was issued by the National Commission on New Technological Uses of Copyrighted Works (CONTU). On the basis of CONTU's recommendations, the Computer Software Copyright Act of 1980 was enacted. It contained the following definition:

> A "computer program" is a set of statements or instructions to be used directly or indirectly in order to bring about a certain result.[23]

(The noted author John Hersey, a member of CONTU, objected strenuously to the recommendation to provide copyright protection to programs. He argued that a program is not a "writing" in the Constitutional sense.) Permission was granted to an individual user to make copies or changes in a copyrighted program, for back-up purposes. In Section 102(a) of the Copyright Act the definition of what can be copyrighted is as follows:

> Copyright protection subsists . . . in original works of authorship fixed in any tangible medium of expression, now known or later developed, from which they can be perceived, reproduced, or otherwise communicated, either directly or with the aid of a machine or device.

A number of cases since 1978 have clarified some of the issues of copyright protection. Its advantages are (a) it is easy to obtain—inexpensive and quick; (b) it is appropriate for works which have wide circulation; (c) it endures during the author's lifetime plus fifty years; and (d) preliminary injunctions may possibly be much more easily obtainable than for possible patent violations. Nevertheless, there are some serious drawbacks. There are still some open questions about what is actually covered. For example, are object programs embodied in ROMs? What about the source program on tape? The scope of protection may be uncertain. For example, can one reproduce copyrighted subject matter in order to develop an object that cannot be copyrighted? Since software is widely proliferated, it will be difficult to enforce copyrights. Can the masks used to produce integrated circuits be copyrighted? Proving that infringement has occurred may be extremely difficult. It is necessary to demonstrate that copying has taken place and that this constitutes an improper appropriation. The Act does permit a user to copy a program for private use. Improper use must be adjudged by a layperson, not a technical expert. The most critical issue arises from a statement issued by the Supreme Court in 1954: "Protection is given only to the expression of an idea—not the idea itself."[24]

In 1984, Franklin Computer agreed to pay Apple $2.5 million in an out-of-court settlement resulting from a 19-month legal controversy.[25] Apple originally sued Franklin for producing a computer in which the logic and structure of the Apple was copied. An initial temporary injunction was denied.

> Agreeing with Franklin's attorneys . . . [the judge] said that operating systems are not a "language of description" because they are understandable primarily to machines, not people, and therefore are not eligible for copyright.[26]

Apple argued in its appeal that the code was an expression of the program and therefore could be copyrighted.

In 1983 The United States Court of Appeals for the Third Circuit in Philadelphia ruled that all computer programs can be copyrighted even if they are an integral part of a computer's circuitry. This decision strengthened the protection of software under the copyright laws, by reinforcing the notion of intellectual property rights as applicable to computer programs. Because most of Franklin's sales were derived from products that used Apple software, the decision was seen as a threat to its future. In fact Franklin filed for bankruptcy later in the year, a dramatic result of the ruling and perhaps a warning to other companies that unauthorized copying is a crime.

Trade Secrets

The most favored method of protection is neither patent nor copyright but trade secrets. As there is no federal trade secrecy legislation, the relevant laws have been established, not in a uniform manner, in the individual states. One definition of a trade secret is "any formula, pattern, device or compilation of information which is used in one's business and which gives him an opportunity to obtain an advantage over competitors who do not know or use it."[27] Trade secrets law appears to cover programs as "processes comprising inventions, with documentation protectable as ancillary 'know-how'."[28] Databases and documentation could also receive protection as information of value. An attempt has been made to establish uniform laws on trade secrecy—the "Uniform Trade Secrets Acts" were drawn up in 1979, approved by the American Bar Association in 1980, and adopted by Minnesota and Arkansas in 1981.

The main advantages of trade secrecy laws are that preliminary injunctions are readily obtained, the applicability over a wide range of subjects is relatively clear, protection applies to both ideas and expressions, the waiting period is brief, and the application remains in force for a long period. Among the disadvantages are the lack of uniformity across the United States, the stress on secrecy as a bar to progress, the lack of protection against independent development, the difficulty in maintaining long-term secrecy—especially for widely proliferated software, and possible preemption by the Copyright Act. Despite these problems, trade secrecy is likely to continue to be the most favored method for protecting software.

Other Methods

To protect software, an employer may make a contract with the relevant employees as part of the terms of employment, which may include such stipulations as no unauthorized copies and no public discussion of programs under development. Whatever the specific terms of a contract, an employee is expected to respect confidentiality. Associated with the sales or licensing of software, there may also be contractual arrangements controlling disclosure. In such a rapidly evolving industry, employees tend to move readily among companies. Contractual arrangements are a reasonable way to maintain software protection, but the restrictions must not be too severe or they will not be upheld by the courts.

Finally, to protect secrecy it is certainly advisable to improve the effectiveness of security procedures. Also technology may be employed to increase the difficulty of making unauthorized use of programs. The copying of disks may be made quite difficult by special built-in protection. For example, the software may be restricted to run only on certain machines. Additional methods of foiling would-be violators have been and could be devised.

LEGAL APPLICATIONS

Data processing has arrived at the lawyer's office just as at the school administrator's and the doctor's. Besides such important everyday activities as records, accounts receivable, payroll, and billing, there are some special computer innovations in the legal profession.

Document Preparation

One of the major selling points of computers in the law office is their ability to store a variety of legal forms on-line. For a specific case, a secretary or typist need only enter information relevant to the situation and the document, with as many copies as necessary, can be produced on a printer. Changes and amendments are easy to produce. The increase in productivity will be an important factor in keeping law firms competitive. But this step is only the first in the automation of the law office. Successive stages will deal with litigation and/or legal research, the tracking of cases and court appearances, and such advanced applications as the scheduling of lawyers and cases, the avoidance of conflict of interest in pending cases, and finally, systems to actually help lawyers in the preparation of their cases. There are already in operation systems—somewhat primitive—that help in the preparation of estate taxes, real estate agreements, and wills.

Legal Information Retrieval

> *It is . . . in the nature of a lawyer's work that he must be able to say with complete confidence that he has considered all the documents of the past relevant to the case, or that there are none which are relevant.*[29]

A case preparation may require an extensive search through previous cases. This process can be very time-consuming and is an obvious opportunity for automation. Information retrieval (IR) has become increasingly important as the amount of information in many different fields has grown rapidly. IR is concerned with the gathering, storage, processing, searching, and dissemination of information. A variety of techniques have been developed to store large quantities of information in an efficient manner. Associated methods are available to retrieve information on the basis of specialized index terms or keywords. Special-purpose query languages have been designed to aid in this process. These languages permit the formulation of descriptions on the basis of which the desired information can be found. This process requires the prior assignment of index terms to the documents being stored.

The choice of index terms represents a simple kind of partitioning of the knowledge being represented in the system. It is usually left to humans to categorize documents by subsets of the given terms. This task is a highly subjective one and can have a significant impact on how effectively the relevant information can subsequently be retrieved. The performance of an information retrieval system can be measured by how well it steers a course between returning too many and too few items. As a user you would like the system to discover all items relevant to your interest but you would not be happy if it also found too many irrelevant ones. On the other hand, if it turned up only a few items, and ignored many other relevant ones, this result would not be very pleasing either. Thus, research in IR has focussed on such issues as automatic indexing, content analysis, file organization, and search strategies.

The amount of information needed for case preparation has grown rapidly over the years, until many lawyers have despaired over the magnitude of the problem. It has become more and more difficult to find many of the relevant materials by traditional manual methods. Poor research increases the number of badly prepared legal cases, resulting in more appeals. In addition, the task of retrieving information could occupy many more lawyers than necessary. The computer and its associated software have come to the rescue.

A number of legal information retrieval systems are currently available. A major legal research system called LEXIS, provided by Mead Data Central on its own special purpose terminals, apparently has about 90 percent of the market, with more than 25,000 searches carried out daily. Basically, the lawyer using LEXIS enters a word, phrase, or combination of words and phrases that best capture an authority that is being looked for. The system then displays on the screen all documents that actually contain these words or phrases anywhere in the text. It is the job of the user to envision the different ways in which cases discuss the ideas of interest. Therefore, it is incumbent upon the user to formulate a wide range of grammatic and semantic forms with which to query the system. In fact, many searches are done on the basis of an initial single word matching, with subsequent refinement by additional words. The problems of information retrieval are difficult, and the solutions are still primitive.

What is needed is search based on conceptual grounds. It will require natural language abilities far beyond what are now available. Even more difficult is retrieval based on analogy, a very important ingredient of legal thought. Perhaps this process represents a stage beyond information retrieval on the road toward the modeling of legal reasoning. L. Thorne McCarty and N. S. Sridharan have been engaged for several years on the TAXMAN project. One of its major goals is "to develop a theory about the structure and dynamics of legal concepts, using corporate tax law as an experimental problem domain."[30] Their work is an application of AI techniques to the domain of legal reasoning. Their current ideas are directed toward representing an abstract concept as a "prototype," as a relatively concrete description, and as a sequence of "deformations" that can map the prototype into an alternative form. This research is still experimental, but it should influence attempts to formalize legal reasoning. A future application of this work might be to aid judges in dealing with the enormous complexities of some cases.

Another developing concept is the litigation support system (LSS), to help lawyers in many of the phases of trial and case preparation. Many large companies have developed such in-house systems to help improve their legal research process. For some complex cases, which may involve more than 50,000 pages of evidence, an LSS is invaluable in cross-referencing and tracking case progress. Major firms that have their own systems include AT&T with its Bell Legal Information System, I.B.M. with its Storage and Information Retrieval System, and Control Data with the PALLAS system. Although most law firms have not taken the plunge, it is clear that future developments will require the automation of both the law office and the legal process. Information retrieval will become more sophisticated and research efforts on legal reasoning will eventually result in more help for the lawyer. Will victory in court go to the most advanced program?

OTHER DEVELOPMENTS

There is uncertainty over the status of masks used in the production of chips, or integrated circuits (see the discussion on copyright above). In 1984 Congress passed the Semiconductor Protection Act. It extends copyright protection to integrated circuit designs for up to ten years, and theft of these designs may result in fines. In effect, this new law defines a new form of protection by permitting manufacturers to copyright the design of chip-making masks. Reverse engineering—the process by which the principles of operation of a chip are uncovered in order to be improved upon—is not affected, but direct piracy is. The act requires that the mask be formally registered with the Copyright Office, a simple procedure unlike the patent process.

Suppose a navigator aboard an aircraft uses a computer to plan a route that results in the aircraft's crashing into an unexpected mountain. Who is responsible? Among the candidates are the navigator, the pilot, the aircraft company, the computer manufacturer, and the software developer. The grounds for suit may include breach of warranty, breach of third-party beneficiary contract, negligence, and strict liability. In the last instance the programmer might be found liable even though he was very careful in both the writing and debugging of the program. As the dependence of society on computers grows, there will be a corresponding growth in litigation associated with computer malfunction.

Another area of interaction between computers and the law is computer-generated evidence. Might computer printouts be introduced as evidence in court? The Hearsay Rule defines as inadmissible statements made out of court that are intended "to prove the truth of what the statement asserts."[31] On the face of it, computer printouts result from programs developed by humans and are produced out of court. But there are many exceptions to the Hearsay Rule under which printouts have been admitted. For example, records produced in the normal course of business operations are held to be reliable. It may be necessary to establish the reliability of the equipment and that the operating procedures are well defined, safeguarded, and proper.

The Supreme Court ruled in Diamond v. Diehr that programs could be patented, although a number of issues remain to be clarified. One year earlier an equally important decision was handed down in which the Court ruled that a human-made microorganism could be patented. Thus, two dynamic technologies have recently been afforded patent protection. Finally, it is interesting that the major competitor with the United States in technology, Japan—despite being a quite different culture—has developed a patent practice similar to U.S. patent law. On the other hand, a Japanese requirement to license software has aroused considerable controversy.

SUMMARY

The introduction of computers in significant numbers into society has brought, in the area of the law, problems of new crimes and new ways to commit old ones. Computer crime has become one of the most publicized aspects of computer use. The various crimes associated with computers are difficult to evaluate in terms of either magnitude or frequency, but it is safe to say that the number is increasing and the stakes are growing. Victimized companies and banks have been reluctant to publicize such crimes for fear of endangering their reputations for security. Nevertheless, enough cases have been documented to indicate that computer crimes can be quite subtle and difficult to detect.

Two cases that have achieved considerable fame are the Equity Funding fraud and the Rifkin case. Although computers were used, these crimes depended more on human gullibility and lax security practices. Other examples of computer crime include the illegal use of automatic teller machine cards, the unauthorized use of a computer for personal gain, the creation of fictitious accounts into which disbursements are made, and so forth. The range of crimes made possible by computers is so wide that precise definition has proven elusive.

Legislation has been passed in various states to deal with computer crimes, but it was only in late 1984 that Congress passed the Counterfeit Access Device and Computer Fraud Act to provide penalties for illicit access to computers. A variety of security methods have been proposed to protect against both physical and electronic trespassing. Only authorized staff should be able to gain direct entry to the computer. A system of passwords and priority levels should be used to restrict unauthorized sign-ons via remote terminals.

Police forces have found computers a useful tool in combatting crime. Remote terminals in patrol cars can be used to access central databases for checking of license plates and personal identification. Large central databases of criminal records are in use to facilitate the communication of information among state and federal police forces. There is some concern that such records can be used for questionable purposes and to the detriment of innocent individuals.

The development of software and computers must be protected against illegal copying, to ensure that developers are properly rewarded for their work and to encourage others to enter the marketplace. Traditional means of protecting original creations are copyrights and patents. It has taken a long time to determine the proper form of protection for computer programs, but recent legislation and court decisions have extended such protection to both programs and hardware. However, the most favored method of protection is under trade secrets legislation enacted in the individual states.

Computers improve the operation of the law office by storing standard legal forms in word processors, and in case preparation to search legal precedents. AI techniques may make it possible to model legal reasoning.

NOTES

1. Thomas K. Christo, "The Law and DP: A Clash of Egos," *Datamation,* September 1982, pp. 264–5, 267–8.

2. Donn Parker, *Crime by Computer* (New York: Scribner's, 1976), p. 169.

3. Ann Reilly, "Computer Crackdown," *Fortune,* September 17, 1984, p. 14.

4. Leonard I. Krauss and Aileen MacGahan, *Computer Fraud and Countermeasures* (Englewood Cliffs: Prentice-Hall, 1979), and Tekla S. Perry and Paul Wallich, "Can Computer Crime Be Stopped?" *IEEE Spectrum*, May 1984, pp. 34–35.

5. John K. Taber, "A Survey of Computer Crime Studies," *Computer/Law Journal,* Spring 1980, p. 295.

6. Ibid., p. 312.

7. Ibid., pp. 311–327.

8. "To Catch A Credit-Card Thief," *Business Week,* April 4, 1983, pp. 75, 77.

9. David B. Tinnin, "How IBM Stung Hitachi," *Fortune,* March 7, 1983, pp. 50–56.

10. Pamela Gonzalez, "Addressing Computer Crime Legislation: Progress and Regress," *Computer/Law Journal,* Summer 1983, pp. 195–206.

11. Michael M. Krieger, "Current and Proposed Computer Crime Legislation," *Computer/Law Journal,* Summer 1983, p. 725.

12. "On Washington," *The Institute, News Supplement to IEEE Spectrum,* December 1984, p. 2.

13. As quoted in Krieger, "Computer Crime Legislation," pp. 733–4.

14. Jonathan Fuerbringer, "Data Theft Laid to Ex-Federal Reserve Aide," *The New York Times,* January 5, 1983, p. 1.

15. *An Assessment of Alternatives for a National Computerized Criminal History System.* U.S. Congress, Office of Technology Assessment (Washington, D.C., October 1982), p. 90.

16. Charles Bruno, "The Electronic Cops," *Datamation,* June 15, 1984, p. 116.

17. *An Assessment of Alternatives,* p. 146.

18. Michael C. Gemignani, *Law and the Computer* (Boston: CBI, 1981), p. 84.

19. David Bender, *Computer Law: Evidence and Procedure* (New York: M. Bender, 1982), p. 4A-2.

20. As quoted in Gemignani, *Law and the Computer,* p. 102.

21. Ibid.

22. As quoted in Bender, *Computer Law,* pp. 4A-7–4A-8.

23. Ibid., p. 4A-31.

24. As quoted in Gemignani, *Law and the Computer,* p. 90.

25. "Franklin Settles with Apple," *Business Week,* January 16, 1984, p. 34.

26. David E. Sanger, "The Gavel Comes Down on Computer Copycats," *The New York Times,* October 23, 1983, p. 8F.

27. Bender, *Computer Law,* p. 4A-78.

28. Ibid., p. 4A-79.

29. Colin Tapper, "World Cooperation in the Mechanisation of Legal Information Retrieval," *Jurimetrics Journal,* vol. 9, 1968, p. 1.

30. L. Thorne McCarty and N. S. Sridhavan, "The Representation of an Evolving System of Legal Concepts: II. Prototypes and Deformations," *Proceedings of the Seventh International Joint Conference on Artificial Intelligence* (Vancouver, 1981), p. 246.

31. Gemignani, *Law and the Computer,* p. 165.

ADDITIONAL READINGS

Computer Crime

Bernhard, Robert. "Breaching System Security," *IEEE Spectrum*, June 1982, pp. 24–31.

Electronic Fund Transfer Systems and Crime. U.S. Department of Justice, Bureau of Justice Statistics. Washington, D.C., July 1982.

"General News and Notes." *Communications of the ACM*, November 1984, p. 1169.

Landwehr, Carl E. "The Best Available Technologies for Computer Security." *Computer*, July 1983, pp. 86–100.

Parker, Donn B. "Computer Abuse Research Update." *Computer/Law Journal*, Spring 1980, pp. 329–352.

Parker, Donn B. *Computer Security Management*. Reston, Virginia: Reston, 1981.

Parker, Donn B. *Fighting Computer Crime*. New York: Scribner's, 1983.

"Special Report: Safeguarding Computer Security." *Electronics*, March 8, 1984, pp. 121–140.

Whiteside, Thomas. *Computer Capers*. New York: New American Library, 1979.

Police and Technology

Colton, Kent. "The Impact and Use of Computer Technology by the Police." *Communications of the ACM*, January 1979, pp. 10–20.

The Legal Protection of Software

"Computer Copying Stirs Legal Snarl." *The New York Times*, July 5, 1983, pp. 1, 29.

Graham, Robert L. "The Legal Protection of Computer Software," *Communications of the Association for Computing Machinery*, May 1984, pp. 422–6.

Hinch, Stephen W. "Protecting Semiconductors from Piracy," *High Technology*, November 1984, pp. 74–5.

Myers, Edith. "Patents for Software," *Datamation*, May 1981, pp. 54, 56, 58.

Legal Applications

Schatz, Willie. "New Ways to Write Writs." *Datamation*, April 1982, pp. 34–6, 39–40.

Slayton, Philip. "Electronic Legal Retrieval." Government of Canada, Department of Communications. Ottawa, 1974.

Other Developments

Blumenthal, David A. "Lifeforms, Computer Programs, and the Pursuit of a Patent." *Technology Review*, February/March 1983, pp. 26–32.

Nycum, Susan. "Liability for Malfunction of a Computer Program." *Rutgers Journal of Computers, Technology and the Law*, vol. 7, no. 1, 1979, pp. 1–22.

9

PRIVACY AND FREEDOM OF INFORMATION

*T*he makers of our Constitution undertook to secure
conditions favorable to the pursuit of hapiness. . . .
They sought to protect Americans in their beliefs, their
thoughts, their emotions and their sensations. They conferred,
as against the Government the right to be let alone—the most
comprehensive of rights and the right most valued by civilized
men. To protect that right every unjustifiable intrusion by
the Government upon the privacy of the individual, whatever
the means employed, must be deemed a violation of
the Fourth Amendment.

◊ *Justice Louis D. Brandeis, Dissenting, Olmstead v. United States,
277 U.S. 438, 1928* ◊

INTRODUCTION

The following are excerpts from newspaper articles in the United States and Canada:

- The cable company's computer may well know, for example, if you pay
  your bills on time, what magazines you buy and the movies you watch.
  (*The New York Times*, November 13, 1983.)
- The Reagan Administration has drafted a plan requiring the Census Bureau
  to share the personal information it collects about the American people with

a number of Government agencies. (*The New York Times*, November 20, 1983.

- The White House has decided not to seek legislation that would require the Census Bureau to share its information with a number of other government agencies. . .the Administration was concerned ''about the public's perceptions that the existing safeguards might be weakened.'' (*The New York Times*, November 24, 1983.
- An Internal Revenue Service office in Texas is seeking to establish electronic links with the computers of 80 counties that will provide it instant access to local records concerning property taxes, voter registration and automobile ownership. (*The New York Times*, March 13, 1984.)
- The Reagan Administration has sharply reduced the number of Federal employees working to protect individuals from improper use of public and private records, according to a report by the General Accounting Office. (*The New York Times*, September 23, 1984.)
- By using computerized investigation techniques known as data matching, the federal Government last year discovered that it had made $82-million in unemployment insurance overpayments. (*The Globe and Mail*, Toronto, October 3, 1984.)
- The Federal Bureau of Investigation in the United States has direct access to the Canadian Police Information Centre computer system, even though the Canadian Intelligence Service does not. (*The Globe and Mail*, Toronto, October 17, 1984.)
- The machine-readable passport is upon us. The British government has accepted it without public discussion even though the technology carries the threat of Europe-wide surveillance of innocent travellers. (*New Scientist*, January 5, 1984.)

Probably the single most frequent charge levelled against computers is that they rob us of our privacy. Banks of computer tapes are envisioned in some back room, on which the intimate details of the lives of many people are stored. Government agencies, law enforcement officials, insurance companies, banks, and many others have access to private information about most people in society. This situation was true before the arrival of computers, but somehow the computer has added a significant new element—perhaps the ability to search rapidly through large amounts of data, perhaps the image of the computer as a malevolent force, or perhaps the general trend in society towards the accumulation of information that is made possible by computers.

In 1978 and 1979 a major survey on privacy was undertaken by Lou Harris and Associates and Dr. Alan F. Westin, a long-time student of privacy issues. The survey sampled included a representative cross-section of about 1500 American adults and selected ''leadership groups'' of about 600 from 10 different groups including government, life insurance, and credit card companies. Many dimensions of privacy were explored. Table 9-1 reveals some of the fears and concerns of the general public, industry, and government officials. (Table 9-1 represents only a very small and carefully selected part of this quite extensive survey.) A few points are clear, as follows:

> The general public is concerned about computers in general (Questions 1 and 5) and privacy in particular (Questions 2 and 3). Even in responding to computers and the quality of life, the general public is much less enthusiastic than the other specialized segments.

> The bank and credit card executives are the least concerned about privacy issues (Questions 1, 2, and 3) and, except for computer industry executives, the most enthusiastic about computers.

> Congressmen and their aides and doctors are the most concerned about privacy issues.

> All the groups believe (with a percentage of at least 56 percent) that a ''Big Brother'' society is at least somewhat close.

In a survey taken some five years later by Lou Harris and Associates, a wide range of responses to the impact of technology were solicited.[1] Questions 1, 2, and 5 were asked again. The results are quite similar to those of 1978. To Question 1, 51 percent yes, 42 percent no, and 6 percent not sure; to Question 5, 6 percent there already, 23 percent very close, 40 percent somewhat close, and 28 percent not close. Thus, over the past few years it seems that for the general public, computers have become associated with privacy issues. The level of this interest may vary somewhat but it does exist, and government leaders should be aware of it

Clearly, there is a deep concern among most segments of society about the growing number of records being held in both private and government databanks. The U.S. government as of 1982 maintained databanks containing over 3.5 billion individual records, or an average of about 15 for each American. Credit bureaus hold records on most Americans; they are used mainly to verify application for credit such as life insurance, mortagages, and consumer loans. The goverment records are obviously needed for the agencies to carry out their responsibilities. In the not-too-distant past, however, various departments did establish databanks to collect information on individuals who were perceived as a possible threat to the stability of the government. Such activities did exert an inhibiting effect on the free exercise of constitutional rights.

Privacy is a cultural, philosophical, and political concept. The formulation of legislation in this area clearly depends on how privacy is viewed and valued. Concern with privacy did not begin with computers. As Edward Coke (1552–1634), an English writer on the law, put it, ''A man's house is his castle.'' The common person and the king should be equal with respect to the security of their homes. The computer seems to have added several important new wrinkles to this principle. The collection, storage, and retrieval of large amounts of private information—by credit bureaus, for example—has become a major industry. (See the discussion of managing large government databases in Chapter 7.)

Another potential problem area is the use of the Social Security Number (SSN) as a

TABLE 9-1 Responses from Various Groups to Questions on Computers and Privacy

Questions	General Public 1974 (1495)	General Public 1978 (1509)	Business Employees 1978 (199)	Computer Industry 1978 (36)	Congress-men and Aides 1978 (77)	Doctors 1978 (33)	Banks 1978 (36)	Credit Card Executives 1978 (40)
1. Do you feel that the present uses of computers are an actual threat to personal privacy in the country or not?								
Yes	38%	54%	54%	53%	75%	70%	22%	25%
No	41%	31%	42%	44%	23%	24%	78%	75%
Not sure	21%	14%	4%	3%	1%	6%	—	—
2. Computers have made it much easier for someone to obtain confidential personal infor-								
Agree		80%	78%	67%	88%	94%	36%	53%
Disagree		10%	21%	33%	9%	6%	58%	48%
Not sure		10%	1%	—	3%	—	6%	—

mation about
individuals
improperly.

3. In general, the privacy of personal information in computers is adequately safeguarded.	Agree	27%	43%	42%	22%	18%	78%	80%
	Disagree	52%	48%	53%	65%	76%	17%	15%
	Not sure	21%	9%	6%	13%	6%	6%	5%
4. Computers have improved the quality of life in our society	Agree	60%	88%	97%	86%	73%	89%	98%
	Disagree	28%	10%	3%	13%	18%	11%	3%
	Not sure	13%	2%	—	1%	9%	—	—
5. How close are we to a "Big Brother" society as depicted in George Orwell's 1984?	There already	8%	2%	—	1%	6%	—	3%
	Very close	26%	21%	14%	9%	33%	8%	13%
	Somewhat close	39%	54%	50%	52%	39%	50%	40%
	Not close	19%	24%	36%	38%	21%	39%	45%
	Not sure	8%	—	—	—	—	3%	—

Source: Louis Harris and Associates, *The Dimensions of Privacy*. Prepared for Sentry Insurance, Stevens Point, WIS., 1978. Reprinted by permission of Garland Publishing, Inc. Question 5 has been rephrased for brevity.

universal identifier. There is a fear that the SSN could be used to link different files to build a composite record of an individual. Other fears have centered on the idea that if there is a single number by which a person could be identified, this might lead to dehumanization. People want to be treated as people, not numbers.

In response to a variety of problems associated with violations of privacy, legislation has been enacted in the United States to guarantee certain rights. This legislation addresses some issues, but others remain open. Privacy is a cultural issue, and different types of legislation exist in other countries.

The term *freedom of information* is generally applied to the concept that governments must make the information they collect accessible to the public at large unless they can demonstrate a pressing need for secrecy. The explication of this idea requires a distinction between privacy and secrecy. In general, governments are reluctant to reveal their operations. Eventually legislation was passed in the United States to provide public access to government under a set of regulations, the Freedom of Information Act.

Finally, future privacy issues will arise in connection with new technological developments. Given varying national privacy laws, international agreements will have to be developed to deal with the flow of data across borders. Two-way home information systems (called videotex, for short) may result in the accumulation of personal data. How such information will be regulated is still an open issue. It seems that everywhere one turns, someone or some group is asking questions and gathering information. How was it used, who has access and for what purposes, and what rights do the people about whom the information was gathered have?

THE NATURE OF PRIVACY

A man has a right to pass through this world, if he wills, without having his picture published, his business enterprises discussed, his successful experiments written up for the benefit of others, or his eccentricities commented upon, whether in handbills, circulars, catalogues, newspapers or periodicals. (Jurist Alton B. Parker, Decision, Robertson v. Rochester Folding Box Company, 1901.)

Privacy as a social issue has long been a concern of social scientists, philosophers, and lawyers. The arrival of the computer has sharpened this concern and made concrete a number of threats to personal privacy. But what does the word privacy mean? Is privacy a right?

Privacy is the claim of individuals, groups or institutions to determine for themselves when, how, and to what extent information about them is communicated to others.[2]

Alan Westin, the author of the above statement, has probably made the most important recent contributions to both the definition and scope of the meaning of privacy in the age of computers. In fact, the definition given above is arguably the most common one in current use. Westin's definition has been criticized because it formulates the definition in terms of a claim. The counter-argument is that privacy ''is a situation or freedom about which claims may be made.''[3] This dissension may appear to be the usual legal hairsplitting, but it seems to suggest that the Westin definition represents an activist view that privacy should be a right. Two other criticisms of the Westin definition are that it limits the concept of privacy to information control, and only information about the individual who makes the claim at that.

It is not surprising that information and its control feature so prominently. After all, the forthcoming ''information age'' will certainly catapult individual privacy to the forefront of civil liberty issues (if it has not done so already). However, information is not the only thing that comes to mind when one thinks of privacy. Also important are being alone or alone with one's family, not being exposed to displays one considers offensive, and the right not to have one's behavior regulated (for example, the right to use contraceptives, or to have an abortion). These issues arise in connection with such privacy problems as surveillance by the use of wiretapping, electronic bugs, and long-range microphones; possible censorship of the public media; and the tension between individual behavior and the demands of society.

The concept of privacy can be given three aspects: territorial privacy, privacy of the person, and privacy in the information context.[4] Territorial privacy refers to the very basic notion that there is a physical area surrounding a person that may not be violated without the acquiescence of the person. Laws referring to Peeping Toms, trespassers, and search warrants have been enacted to safeguard territorial privacy. The second category, in some sense, is concerned with protecting a person against undue interferences such as physical searches and information that violates his or her moral sense. The third category is the one most relevant here, as it deals with the gathering, compilation, and selective dissemination of information.

Privacy and Information

To live in contemporary society is to leave, stored in records held by institutions, a trail of the following kinds of information:

Vital statistics (birth, marriage, death).
Educational (school records).
Financial (bank records, loans).
Medical (health records both physical and mental).
Credit (credit cards, credit record, purchases).
City government (house taxes, improvements).
Employment (earnings, work record).
Internal revenue (taxation, deductions, earnings).
Customs and immigration (passports, visas, customs payments).
Police (arrests, convictions, warrants, bail, paroles, sentences).

Welfare (payments, history, dependents).

Stores (credit record, purchases).

Organizations (membership, activities).

Military (service record, discharge status).

Motor vehicles (ownership, registration, accident record).

This list represents only a sample of the kinds and sources of information being held about the average citizen. The computer has made it possible to store an enormous amount of information and to retrieve it in an efficient manner. Most of the above-listed records are held by government institutions at all levels. This fact is seen by some critics as evidence of the insatiable appetite of government to know more and more about its citizens. In the private domain there has been a corresponding increase in the amounts and uses of information.

In recognition of this explosion in information, the concept of privacy has undergone some changes. Inevitably there will be disclosures of information—if not, why has it all been collected? How can the rights of the affected person be protected? Perhaps the prior question is what should these rights be? A basic statement appeared in 1973, in an important U.S. government report, as follows:

> *An individual's personal privacy is directly affected by the kind of disclosure and use made of identifiable information about him in a record. A record containing information about an individual in identifiable form must, therefore, be governed by procedures that afford the individual a right to participate in deciding what the content of the record will be, and what disclosure and use will be made of the identifiable information in it. Any recording, disclosure, and use of identifiable personal information not governed by such procedures must be proscribed as an unfair information practice unless such recording, disclosure or use is specifically authorized by law.[5]*

This statement does not describe what information should be stored, or what the controls for its use should be, but it does argue for the legal establishment of privacy rights for the individual. Subsequent legislation did delineate and incorporate some of these rights by regulating the behavior of record-keepers.

The general public in the United States is concerned about threats to personal privacy, and this worry is growing, as Table 9-2 illustrates. Many people would claim that there is a basic human need for privacy. Not all basic human needs are defended in law, however. It has been recognized that individual privacy, in its many manifestations, is a basic prerequisite for the functioning of a democratic society. In this light, the recommendations made in the 1973 goverment report have served as a basis for subsequent legislation.

> • *There must be no personal-data record-keeping systems whose very existence is secret.*

TABLE 9-2 Perceived Threats to Personal Privacy

Date	Total Public	Very Concerned	Somewhat	Only a Little	Not Concerned
1978	1,511	31%	33%	17%	19%
1983	1,256	48%	29%	15%	7%

Source: For 1978 data, Louis Harris and Associates, Inc., *The Dimensions of Privacy*, p. 13. Prepared for Sentry Insurance, Stevens Point, Wis., 1978. Reprinted by permission of Garland Publishing, Inc. For 1983 data, Louis Harris and Associates, *The Road After 1984*, p. 10. Prepared for Southern New England Telephone, New Haven, Conn., 1983.

- *There must be a way for an individual to find out what information about him is in a record and how it is used.*

- *There must be a way for an individual to prevent information about him that was obtained for one purpose from being used or made available for other purposes without his consent.*

- *There must be a way for an individual to correct or amend a record of identifiable information about him.*

- *Any organization creating, maintaining, using or disseminating records or identifiable personal data must assure the realiability of data for their intended use and must take precautions to prevent misuse of the data*[6]

These principles reflect a number of concerns about the collection and availability of personal information, in an age when computer technology has made record-keeping a major industry. Some obvious worries are addressed, in part, by the recommendations. The requirement that the existence of databanks be publicly known is a prerequisite for all the others. To establish the requisite trust and confidence in systems, adequate guarantees of data integrity and security must be maintained. The collection of personal data is an important area because the quality of the information stored depends on the care with which it is gathered. There is the possibility that data collected for one purpose will be used for another. As the technology permits ease of transfer of files, it is possible for a variety of interested parties to make use of data collected by others. Because important decisions are made on the basis of the stored information, the subject should have the right to examine it and make changes according to clearly defined procedures.

Records have been kept on individuals from time immemorial, but the use of computers has introduced a change in kind as well as in degree. Records can now be easily transmitted over long distances, searched efficiently, and merged if desired. Since the cost of storage is cheap, more data can be stored and so more is collected. As more information is collected, more uses are made of it, as if the availability drives the need. There seems to be an insatiable appetite for information in both the private and public domains. Since these trends are likely to accelerate in the future, much is to be gained by trying to understand the various implications of contemporary threats to privacy.

DATABANKS

The issue of privacy raised by computerization is whether the increased collection and processing of information for diverse public and private purposes, if not carefully controlled could lead to a sweeping power of surveillance by government over individual lives and organizational activity.[7]

Individual privacy is threatened by the possible use of government databases for surveillance. Such use may inhibit the free exercise of constitutionally guaranteed rights, such as freedom of speech and petitioning the government for the redress of grievances. With private databanks, such as those maintained by the large credit bureaus, the impact could be quite serious. Without credit, a car, house and life insurance, and a mortgage are not available. A suspect credit rating may limit one's type of employment, housing, and one's children's educational possibilities. Quite clearly, the misuse of information by others could have a devastating effect on a person's life. With the increasing use of information systems to store personal records, the imbalance between the individual and the "system" has grown. It is therefore incumbent upon the record-keeper to establish guidelines to insure the protection of individual rights.

The Privacy Commission, set up after the passage of the Privacy Act of 1974, enunciated the three necessary objectives of a privacy protection policy as follows:[8]

To minimize intrusiveness. This involves creating a balance between what is demanded of an individual and what is provided in return.

To maximize fairness. This will make sure that information stored about an individual is not used unfairly.

To create legitimate, enforceable expectations of confidentiality. It is most important to guarantee that recorded information is subject to the most stringent security procedures.

Data Collection and Access Controls

With respect to the collection of data, it is a natural assumption that a person is willing to supply information for the sake of some benefit that follows the transaction. The prime example of this exchange is the census, in which privileged information is supplied to the government, presumably to improve future service. Regulations to preserve privacy have been established to guarantee this trust. However, more and more frequently data is being collected about individuals without their cognizance. Most government databanks store information derived from compliance with government regulations, but there are others for which information has been gathered either secretly or without direct permission.

In the former category are criminal files such as the FBI's National Crime Information Center (NCIC). In the latter are databases maintained by national security agencies such as the CIA. The control of these databanks obviously requires special treatment.

Once the data is in place, the next concern is access. Who is allowed to use the information and under what circumstances? Since different government agencies collect information under different circumstances, the transfer of records among agencies and departments must be restricted. The government rule is that data must not be made available to a third party if the original conditions of collection would be violated. In practice, this rule has not been very effective, and agencies do exchange information quite freely. Furthermore, there is a built-in conflict between privacy controls and freedom of information laws. For national criminal databases such as the NCIC, it is quite difficult to control access effectively. This is a general problem with distributed systems and it is especially aggravated when the system is nationwide. Thousands of law enforcement officials have access to the NCIC, creating an enormous internal security problem. The growing use of distributed computing and databases suggests that control of data use will be an ongoing major challenge.

Another access problem involves such information as births, deaths, marriages, vehicle licenses, and property transfers. In the age of manual files, such data could be obtained, but with difficulty. The transfer of information in the form of computer records considerably simplifies matters. As uses for this information are found by companies, issues of access will be raised. Motor vehicle records are obviously useful to companies that want to reach the driving public. The fact that computers can process large amounts of data rapidly and search for desired conditions means that such information has become a valuable commodity. And structured information is particularly valuable.

Surveillance

The potential use of government databases to monitor individuals represents one of the major fears of society. In Table 9-1 the general public expressed a definite fear about the nearness of a "Big Brother" society. The collection of detailed information on citizens can be used to inhibit their activities. For example, early in 1970 it was revealed that the U.S. Army had been monitoring the lawful behavior of a number of groups and was preparing reports and dossiers on individual members. The Army has reportedly maintained files on a very wide range of groups, from right-wing activists such as the Missilemen to such nonviolent groups as the Southern Christian Leadership Conference, the Civil Liberties Union, and the National Association for the Advancement of Colored People. The information collected was made available to other government agencies over a teletype network.

Computers and modern communications networks do not in themselves cause the development of such databases. The decision to engage in surveillance activities is a response by certain administrators to certain social situations. However, by enlarging the possibilities, the computer has created a new reality. As more data can be collected, cheaply stored, readily transmitted, and efficiently processed, more government agencies (and companies) will be encouraged to set up and maintain databases. There is an ongoing worry, based on past performance, that government agencies will assume responsibility in areas not proscribed by their congressional mandate. The Army's activities are just one example. The increased use of computers will sharpen apprehension about privacy violations and perhaps result in improved and closely obeyed security procedures.

Another very disturbing example was the revelation, during the Watergate investigation, that illegal record-keeping had been done by the FBI with its COINTELPRO files and the CIA with its files on American citizens. In this case, a law enforcement agency and an intelligence agency clearly broke the law when they violated the privacy of Americans. As a result of their misdeeds and others the Privacy Act of 1974 was passed.

Constitutional Guarantees

Some very complex privacy issues are highlighted by the First, Fourth, and Fifth Amendments to the Constitution. These amendments are concerned with the following rights and guarantees:

> *First Amendment.*   Freedom of religion, speech, the press, peaceable assembly, and the right to petition for redress of grievances.
>
> *Fourth Amendment.*   No unreasonable search and seizure by the federal government.
>
> *Fifth Amendment.*   A person may not be compelled to testify against himself or be deprived of life, liberty, or property without due process.

By the collection of large amounts of data and surveillance of individuals and groups (as discussed above), the government could inhibit the freedoms of speech and assembly guaranteed in the First Amendment. Threats to these rights have occurred in the past, against both active and passive participants in political meetings and demonstrations. A basic challenge arises whenever threats to First Amendment rights surface: ''What have you got to worry about if you haven't done anything wrong?'' Unfortunately, the collection of data by the government, as well as surveillance, can be repressive in itself, in that it creates the impression that an activity is not proper and that participants ought to reconsider their actions. In some cases, information has been used directly to affect the employment of individuals. First Amendment rights are crucial to maintaining a democratic society, and any attempts to limit them must be forestalled.

The interrelation between information systems and the Fourth Amendment turns on such issues as the use of personal or statistical data as a reason for search and seizure, the information itself as the object of the search, and the use of the system to facilitate the search and seizure. With the use of criminal record information systems, police may carry out searches on the basis of instantaneous access to the database. Courts may be concerned about whether such information provides reasonable cause. Computer systems could be employed to monitor the shopping activity of individuals by accessing appropriate electronic funds transfer systems. This activity would be much more intrusive than personal observation could be.

Possible Fifth Amendment violations may arise when data collected for one purpose is used by the government as evidence in an unrelated case. Another problem may arise in the use of criminal records in computer models to predict criminal behavior. Individuals' rights could be denied on the basis of predictions, not actual unlawful action. Since these records may include statements by the persons being modeled, self-incrimination is a definite possibilty. More constitutional issues associated with databanks and privacy will surface in the future.

Statistical Data

Vast amounts of data are collected by the government for administrative and planning purposes. But there are other important applications, such as research, within and without the government. There is controversy about whether the statistical use of data violates the privacy of identifiable individuals. Recent research has shown that by appropriately selecting samples from a large population and carrying out careful statistical tests it is possible to determine data about individuals. This activity might violate the conditions under which the original information was gathered. Thus, guidelines and procedures for the statistical use of data must be established. They should then be publicized, to reassure the general public. Access to original data should be carefully controlled, and research groups wishing to use such data for their projects should subscribe to a code of ethics. Governments have a responsibility to safeguard the information supplied by their citizens.

Computer Matching

A final example of the possible misuse of the data that is collected and stored in government databases is particularly worrisome. It points out that the arrival of the computer has literally created new avenues for the exercise of bureaucratic power. The term *computer matching* probably reached public consciousness in late 1977, when Joseph A. Califano, Jr., the Secretary of Health, Education, and Welfare, announced a new program, ''Project Match,'' to reduce welfare violations. The idea was to match computerized lists of federal employees against computerized lists of state welfare rolls. Any person whose name appeared on both lists, a so-called hit, would be a likely candidate for welfare fraud investigation. Other examples of computer matching include the following:

> The Selective Service System is planning to match its registrant list against drivers' lists of males between the ages of 18 and 20 to discover those men who have not yet registered.

> The Internal Revenue Service (IRS) has a test program to match its lists against commercially available lists of estimated household incomes.

Another IRS project, in Florida, collected real estate lists to determine those people not declaring real estate income.

The U.S. Department of Agriculture checked its personnel records of employees in Illinois against Illinois state files of real estate agents, to investigate potential conflicts of interest.

A basic concern is that governments will be too eager to launch such "fishing expeditions" simply because it is so easy to cross-check different computer files—and it is getting easier as the software and hardware continue to improve. The typical purpose of computer matching is not to gather evidence in the course of a criminal investigation against a specified individual, but to spread a wide net in order to catch people not previously charged with wrongdoing. Thus, it is an attempt to generate evidence before an investigation has been launched. Data files collected for one purpose are used for entirely different purposes. Presumption of innocence, a fundamental principle in the American system of government, is apparently at odds with the practice of computer matching.

The Privacy Act of 1974 (see Privacy Legislation" below) embodies the principle that information collected about individuals for certain purposes cannot be used without their consent for unrelated purposes. An individual's consent is not required if the information is to be used either in a manner consistent with the original purpose—the "routine use" provision—or for a criminal investigation. Computer matching has been justified by appeal to the routine use exception. In response to criticisms about the extensive use of computer matching, the Office of Management and Budget (OMB) drew up a set of guidelines in 1979. These have not satisfactorily addressed the critical issues, in the opinion of many critics.

Richard P. Kusserow, Inspector General of the Department of Health and Human Services, argues that computer matching is just another necessary weapon in the government's arsenal against waste and fraud. Because the cost of such fraud is so enormous, the government is entitled to take whatever measures it deems necessary to protect the rights of innocent taxpayers. The Reagan Administration revised the OMB guidelines in 1982, in order, it was claimed, to "streamline paper-work requirements and reiterate requirements for privacy and security of records."[9] The government maintains that privacy safeguards are in place and that computer matching is not a threat to civil liberties. The critics argue that the safeguards are inadequate and that computer matching represents one more serious step in the erosion of personal privacy.

Private Databanks

Let us not overlook a significant fact. . . people tend to state their case most favorably when they know that the information they supply will be the basis of their having their application granted. . . . It is essential that we be permitted to verify the information presented to us by the applicant through credit bureaus and others . . . .[10]

A great deal of information about individuals is collected by the private sector. Educational, employment, medical, financial, and insurance records all require protection to ensure privacy. Probably of greatest importance in the average citizen's life is the use of credit information. When an individual opens a charge account, applies for a credit card or life insurance, or takes out a loan, personal and financial records are created. Apparently, credit bureaus first opened their doors in the early 1900s to provide services for specific businesses. They produced reports in various forms on individuals applying for credit. As of 1977 the Associated Credit Bureaus–the national trade association—reported that a total of about 150 million credit histories were held by credit bureaus in America. This number surely includes many duplications, since national and local companies compete for the same records.

How does this system of credit reporting work? In applying for a credit card, a form is filled out in which basic biographical information is supplied. The form includes a clause that permits the credit card company to carry out an independent credit check of the applicant. Signing the application form sets the wheels in motion. No one is forcing the person to apply; if a person does apply for credit, it is reasonable to expect that his or her financial background, social background, and credit rating are of concern in the granting company's decision. The company then turns to a credit bureau. It either already has a credit history because previous application for credit had been made, or discovers a credit record held by another company, or initiates an investigatory process. Interviews are carried out with employers, neighbors, financial institutions, relevant merchants, and even law enforcement officals. A file is created, and the credit bureau reports the results of its investigation, for a price. On the basis of this report, credit is given or refused. (What recourse does the unsuccessful applicant have? See "Privacy Legislation" below.) Not only does the applicant give permission for a credit check to be run, but he or she also permits any information gathered to be used for subsequent requests. Thus, there exists a vast information network—discrete in parts, in others loosely connected—with an incredible variety of information about anyone who has ever become involved in any aspect of the credit system. It appears that individuals relinquish control over information about themselves when they need to obtain credit. Since insurance and mortgages are virtual necessities in today's society, it is apparent that for all practical purposes we do not control certain information about ourselves.

Various government agencies have been interested in obtaining access to all this available information for regulatory, investigative, and law enforcement purposes. Government authorities can obtain such information by a variety of methods, both formal (subpoena or court order) and informal (letter, telephone, or in person). Most credit bureaus seem to be quite willing to supply information informally when requested. Only the Internal Revenue Service, of all government agencies, informs individuals that information about them has been requested or obtained. There is considerable room for violation of privacy and confidentiality.

The collection of information by credit bureaus is an industry. One of the largest companies, TRW, in 1984 had about 120 million names in its credit rating system. Because so much depends on credit reports, it would be comforting to know that the material gathered is, on the whole, accurate. But many horror stories have surfaced about people being denied loans and having their lives seriously disrupted because of misleading and incorrect information. The Fair Credit Reporting Act was enacted in 1970 by Congress to guarantee certain safeguards regarding credit reporting (see below). It almost seems that one of the major driving forces behind the "Information Age" is the growth in traffic of personal and financial information.

SOCIAL SECURITY NUMBER

One of the first large scale assignments of numbers to people occurred in concentration camps. Any camp survivor will attest to the dehumanizing effect which being a mere number has on the psyche and self image.[11]

The idea of being known and treated as a number arouses considerable anger and concern. Prisoners, concentration camp inmates, employees, and students all have numbers. Whether or not the identification of people with numbers is dehumanizing, it is true that such identification does make administrative work more efficient. This fact suggests to certain people that a single number—a universal identifier—would be useful. Among the characteristics of such an identifier would be uniqueness, permanence, universality, conciseness, and reliability. The universal identifier could be a single number assigned to each individual at birth. It would replace all other numbers such as those for driver licenses, bank accounts, credit cards, employees, and so forth. A single number, easy to remember and convenient, certainly sounds like a good idea—apart from the negative overtones.

The great threat posed by a universal identifier is that all records referring to the same individual might be linked by access to different databases. A universal identifier would render this task trivial. All records in the relevant databases keyed by the identifier could be retrieved. The worst fears about an all-powerful, all-knowing state would thus be realized. The Association for Computing Machinery, a well-informed organization in this matter, with a membership of more than 26,000 computer specialists, in 1974 urged the passage of "legislative safeguards against the misuse of universal identifiers, including the Social Security Number [SSN]."[12] Civil libertarians are concerned that the SSN might be used as a universal identifier. Created to monitor the accounts established under the Social Security Act of 1935, the SSN has subsequently been used for personal identification in transactions such as check cashing.

The SSN in itself does not satisfy the criteria for a universal identifier. It is not unique—many people have more than one SSN, and some people have the same SSN. Even without a universal identifier, record linkage is possible (though less convenient) by means of a search using such keys as full name, birth date, birth place, address, and sex. There is an aversion in America to the use of a universal identifier because of well-justified fears about its possible misuse. As with other aspects of the privacy problem, adequate safeguards must be in place to protect the rights of individuals.

PRIVACY LEGISLATION

> *More important, however, is the fact that it* [The Assault on Privacy] *should bestir all Americans to claim their constitutional legacy of personal privacy and individual rights and to demand an end to abuses of computer technology before the light of liberty is extinguished in our land.*[13]

Lawmakers frequently respond to public pressure by formulating legislation to deal with generally agreed-upon abuses. Since 1968, a series of laws have been passed that deal with credit protection, as follows:

Consumer Credit Protection Act.   To state clearly the cost of borrowing.

Equal Credit Opportunity Act.   To prevent irrelevant issues from biassing credit applications.

Fair Credit Reporting Act.   To permit the correction of mistakes on the credit record.

Fair Credit Billing Act.   To correct billing mistakes.

Truth In Lending.   To permit retraction of certain mortgage contracts.

Fair Credit Reporting Act

> *. . .to insure that consumer reporting agencies exercise their grave responsibilities with fairness, impartiality, and a respect for the consumer's right to privacy.* (Fair Credit Reporting Act, 1970.)

In 1967 the first Congressional hearings were held to address threats to personal privacy by some credit bureaus: false records, biased records, outdated material, and errors in data entry. The Fair Credit Reporting Act (FCRA) was passed in 1970 and came into law in April 1971. Below is a brief overview of the main points of the act:[14]

Accuracy of Information.   Credit agencies must take all reasonable steps to guarantee the accuracy of reports in collection, storing, and processing.

Obsolete Information.   Certain information must not be included after a number of years have elasped: bankruptcies, 14 years; suits and judgments, 7 years; criminal arrest, 7 years.

Limited Uses of Information.   This point specifies the conditions under which an agency may supply a report. Examples are credit, employment, licensing, legitimate business needs, court order, and with written instructions from the concerned individual.

Notices to Individuals.   If the results of the report adversely affect the individual, he or she must be notified and supplied with the name and address of the relevant agency. If an investigation is to be undertaken, the affected individual must be notified.

Individual's Right of Access to Information. The individual has a right to be fully informed about all information held about him (except for medical records), and the sources and recipients of the information—for the previous 2 years for reasons of employment, and 6 months for others.

Individual's Right to Contest Information. An individual can dispute the information held on him, which may require a reinvestigation. If the disagreement is not resolved, the agency must permit the individual to include a brief statement in the file.

The FCRA appears to represent a significant advance in the privacy rights of individuals, but there have been critics.

> . . . *to parody the title of a hit Broadway show and film: "A Funny Thing Happened on the Way to the Senate Floor." The original Proxmire bill had been butchered; it was drawn and quatered and its vitals were left on the Committee's chopping block*[15]

Arthur Miller was concerned that the act actually broadened the category of those who could have access to credit files; credit bureaus did not have a clear obligation to maintain confidentiality or accuracy; the individual would face great procedural difficulties in exercising his or her rights; incorrect information would not necessarily be corrected by all information users; and credit bureaus would be protected in cases of careless use of incorrect information.

There were two interesting outcomes of the act. First, most credit bureaus separated their credit reporting activities from their investigative responsibilities. Separate firms carried out the data collection, and the credit bureau was relieved of the costs of complying with the act's accuracy requirements. Second, although the act regulated the activities of credit reporting agencies, at the same time it legitimized them. Companies had been operating in a legal vacuum and were getting somewhat nervous about their status. After the act, it was quite proper to collect, store, process, and supply information about individuals. In the name of protecting some rights, a more basic right has perhaps been lost—namely, the control over information about oneself.

Since the act was passed there have been proposals for amendments, but none have yet been enacted. One recommendation is that individuals be permitted to examine their files in person and to make copies if they wish. Individuals should be allowed to see their medical records. Other recommendations are concerned with (a) providing a credit applicant with details about the types and sources of information to be gathered, (b) disclosing (in writing) reasons for an adverse decision and the specific items that support it, and—upon the request by an identifiable individual—(c) supplying him or her with any personal information that may be held. Most of the suggestions are directed toward ensuring that the average citizen has no doubts about the accuracy of the information held about him.

Personal Privacy Act

The passage of the Privacy Act of 1974 was the culmination of many studies and hearings, but the Watergate scandal was the major factor in its approval.

> *The purpose of this Act is to provide certain safeguards for an individual against an invasion of personal privacy by requiring federal agencies, except as otherwise provided by law, to. . .*
>
> *(1) permit an individual to determine what records pertaining to him are collected, maintained, used or disseminated by such agencies;*
>
> *(2) permit an individual to prevent records pertaining to him obtained by such agencies for a particular purpose from being used or made available for another purpose without his consent;*
>
> *(3) permit an individual to gain access to information pertaining to him in federal agency records, to have a copy made of all or any portion thereof, and to correct or amend such records;*
>
> *(4) collect, maintain, use, or disseminate any record of identifiable personal information in a manner that assures that such information is current and accurate for its intended use, and that adequate safeguards are provided to prevent misuse of such information;*
>
> *(5) permit exemptions from the requirements with respect to records provided in this Act only in those cases where there is an important public policy need for such exemptions as has been determined by specific statutory authority; and*
>
> *(6) be subject to civil suit for any damages which occur as a result of wilful or intentional action which violates any individual's rights under this Act.*[16]

With respect to subsection (5), records maintained by the CIA, any law enforcement agencies, prosecutors, courts, correctional institutions, or probation or parole authorities are exemptions as defined in the act. Because police work depends so heavily on informers, these records must be excluded from general access. Also exempt are records involving national defense or foreign policy, specific statute exclusions, trade secrets, and the protection of the President. Many other categories are given in the act. It also required the establishment of the Privacy Protection Study Commission, to conduct a study of the databanks, automated data processing programs, and information systems of governmental, regional, and private organizations in order to determine the standards and procedures in force for the protection of personal information.[17] The commission enunciated the following Principles, as manifested in the act's provisions:[18]

> *Openness.* Record-keeping systems and procedures shall be public.

Individual Access.   Individuals have the right to see (and copy) information about themselves.

Individual Participation.   Individuals have the right to make corrections.

Collection Limitation.   The type of information collected, and by what manner, shall be regulated.

Use Limitation.   There are limitations to how information may be used.

Disclosure Limitation.   External disclosures are limited.

Information Management Limitation.   Procedures must be established to provide proper safeguards for handling personal information.

Accountability.   A record-keeping organization is accountable for its practices.

The Privacy Act became effective on September 27, 1975. At that time, in compliance with it, 85 federal agencies reported the existence of over 6000 record-keeping systems that contained over 3.8 billion records, record-keeping rules, and procedures for public access. Exemption, full and partial, was granted to 889 record systems, of which 755 involved law enforcement activities. Several shortcomings of the act have been pointed out. There are no enforcement procedures for such violations as systems not being made public or improper dissemination of records. In violation of the spirit of the act, large government agencies—such as the Departments of Defense and Health, Education and Welfare—declared themselves to be single agencies. Thus, transfer of information among their many databases need not be made known to individuals. The exemptions granted the CIA and law enforcement agencies are too broad. Perhaps only active files should be protected. Finally, there is a tremendous burden on individuals to discover the systems that store information on them, given the large number of systems and the different rules maintained by each agency. Futhermore, it would be much too expensive for agencies to notify individuals without a request being made.

Implicit in all the legislation discussed so far is an after-the-fact philosophy. The assumption is that computerized personal record systems are here to stay, and it is only necessary to regulate their use in order to limit the worst abuses. The law is employed to establish procedures and provide recourse for injured parties. The prior question of whether there is justification and need for a particular database has not been legally addressed. Any government agency can decide to set up a record-keeping system whenever it wishes. Most of the critical energy in the privacy issue has been directed toward the adequacy of procedures rather than the prior question of need.

Family Educational Rights and Privacy Act

In contrast to the omnibus approach of the Privacy Act, the Family Educational Rights and Privacy Act (FERPA), passed in 1974, was directed at educational records. This law gives the parents of minors and students over 18 the ''right to inspect and review, and request correction or amendment of, an education record.''[19] Educational institutions must inform parents and students of their rights and must draw up appropriate procedures to conform with the regulations of the act. Since there are over 60 million students, this act covers a great number of people. A privacy law in this area was necessary, because in addition to grades, conduct, and attendance information, some schools keep track of the family life—its stability and economic and social level—and social life of the student, including relationships and membership in churches. The file may also contain psychological test data and teacher evaluations. The unauthorized use of this data could seriously affect the student's life both in and after school.

Schools tend to divulge personal information readily to other schools, law enforcement officials, and for research purposes to the government. Frequently, the interests of the student are secondary. The desire to collect more and more information seems to be increasing, because records are heavily used in decision making. This trend is especially strong in those institutions with large numbers of students. In many postsecondary institutions there is a history of cooperation with law enforcement officials, especially with respect to information about student radicals. It was this rather slipshod treatment of student records, with little access for students or their families, that motivated the passage of FERPA.

Experience in Other Countries

The United States has taken a ''data regulation'' approach to privacy protection. There are at least two other ways to proceed. Invasion of privacy could itself be recognized as an actionable wrong. For example, the Privacy Act enacted in 1968 in the province of British Columbia, Canada states as follows:

> *It is a tort, actionable without proof of damage for a person wilfully and without a claim of right, to violate the privacy of another.*[20]

Unfortunately, a victim may never know that his or her privacy has been violated, and remedial action is slow and costly. Another approach is to establish an ombudsman office to adjudicate privacy complaints. The state of New South Wales (Australia) created a permanent Privacy Committee with powers to: ''engage in research and investigation of privacy protection problems, broadly construed, and to seek the resolution of specific complaints brought to the committee's attention by individuals who feel that their privacy has been invaded.''[21] The committee will investigate complaints and attempt to persuade agencies to adopt improved procedures. This method is deficient in that in the absence of complaints many violations may be overlooked. Futhermore, rulings on individual cases will lead to a piecemeal approach to the definition of privacy rights.

Sweden became the first country to enact privacy legislation with the passage of its Data Bank Statute in 1973. This act covers both public and private databanks and requires that any existing or future databank be subject to monitoring by the Data Inspection Board (DIB). Permission must be given by this Board for the right to maintain a record system, and approval must also be given for the operating procedures. In practice, government databanks are exempt from the Board's regulation because they do not require approval, only acknowledgement. The Board is allowed to regulate such issues as methods of data collection, what information may be made available, and control and security. When an organization has been given permission to establish a database, an employee called the registrar-accountable must be appointed to maintain the system. This individual is responsible for assuring that the regulations set by the DIB are followed. The responsibility includes (a) notification of individuals about the uses being made of information about them, (b) the maintenance and deletion of information, and (c) ensuring that the information stored is complete. A comprehensive system of laws deals with violations associated with this act. Final appeal against decisions by the DIB is political—to the King in Council. The operation of the statute was reviewed in 1981 and found to be satisfactory.

In France, the Law Concerning Data Processing, Files and Liberties, passed in 1978, created a National Commission on Data Processing to regulate and enforce the privacy legislation. The Commission must approve government databanks and be assured that private operations conform with the law. The law sets out the terms of licensing and the operating procedures, including access and data correction. There are limitations on the type of data that can be collected, the methods of collection, and the duration of storage. The commission must publish an index of all regulated data processing operations. The law attempts to inform individuals about those parties who have requested information.

At the end of 1982 the United Kingdom Data Protection bill became law. It provides for the registration and supervision of data bureaus by an independent registrar appointed by the Crown. This registrar is responsible for maintaining a register of databanks. Individuals can obtain details of information held about them and can seek compensation in the courts for any damages suffered because of inaccurate data. Individuals are permitted to have access, at regular intervals, to data held on them and are able to have the data corrected or removed—a fundamental right. For reasons of national security, certain data is excluded from the provisions of the bill. Government departments have the same obligations as private companies, but cannot be sued for damages because of errors. A data protection tribunal will deal with appeals against the registrar's decisions.

In Sweden and France, there is considerable concern about the types of information collected and the steps taken in setting up databanks. In Germany, these setting-up processes are not regulated by statute, and the only control on the collection of data is that the subject must agree to it. The American regulatory scheme differs substantially from the European, in that there is no board or commission responsible for monitoring the government agencies. Each agency must set up and implement rules that satisfy the requirements of the act, and the Office Management and Budget is required merely to develop guidelines for enforcing regulations and provide help for other agencies. The 1977 German law gives different groups of data processors different responsibilities with respect to informing people of the existence of personal data, its transmittal, access, and correction rights.[22]

There seems to be a general consensus that privacy legislation should be concerned with three broad areas: (a) the setting-up of databanks and collecting of data, (b) procedures for regulating the management of the information—that is, right of access and data correction—and (c) monitoring and enforcement schemes. Countries have chosen to emphasize these aspects to varying degrees. Compared to the extensive powers of the French National Commission, the Privacy Commissioner in Canada has quite limited powers.

FREEDOM OF INFORMATION

The freedom of information issue exists in uneasy tension with the question of personal privacy. The freedom of information concept is concerned with the rights of citizens to obtain access to information held by the government. The desire to obtain information from the government may endanger the privacy of individuals about whom records are kept. Thus, the situation is such that the individual demands the right to know but at the same time wishes to guard his or her privacy.

It is recognized that the vast amounts of information collected by the government are used to serve the public—for administrative purposes and for planning and research. Research uses—frequently by external agencies, research groups, and universities—involve statistical data in which information about individuals cannot be identified. Although there are some problems, it is generally agreed that information used for such statistical purposes usually protects privacy, and it is readily made available.

The following problem areas arise:

> There must be a reconciliation between the freedom to obtain information from the government when that information contains personal information about other people.

> Should there be absolute guarantees on the privacy of personal data or should the release of such information be discretionary?

> There are currently restrictions on individuals obtaining access to information about themselves. How does this relate to a freedom of information scheme?

> Various individual access procedures should be consistent with some overall freedom-of-information concept.

The Freedom of Information Act

The Freedom of Information Act (FOIA) was passed in 1966, went into effect on July 4, 1967, and was subsequently amended in 1974 and 1976. Its basic principle is that any person may request access to government records and may make copies of same. Certain records are exempt from disclosure. "Record" is taken to mean all the documents either in the possession of an agency or subject to its control. Some of the features of the FOIA are as follows:

> Requests must be made to the agency that holds the record—that is, any "executive department, military department, Government corporation, Gov-

ernment-controlled corporation, or other establishments in the Executive Office of the President or any independent regulatory agency.''[23]

If an agency refuses to provide the records within a ten-day period, appeal is possible, first to a higher level and then to a district court.

A fee may be charged for searching, reviewing, and copying.

Each agency is required to publish, in the *Federal Register*, information about its organization, access methods, rules of procedure, and so forth.

Not all agencies are required to respond to requests; in fact, there are nine exemptions. The first refers to national defense and foreign policy, and includes executive privilege as it relates to state secrets. A 1974 amendment directed the heads of agencies claiming this exemption to turn documents over to the courts for a final decision. Other exemptions include trade secrets and commercial information, internal personnel rules and practice, information limited by appropriate statutes, inter- and intra-agency memoranda, reports prepared in the course of regulating or supervising financial institutions, and geological and geophysical information. Two exemptions are particularly significant. Exemption (6) excludes ''personnel and medical files and similar files the disclosure of which would constitute a *clearly unwarranted invasion of personal privacy*.''[24] (Emphasis added.) This provision has been broadly interpreted by the courts. One decision ruled as follows:

> . . . *under normal circumstances, intimate family relations, personal health, religious and philosophical beliefs and matters that would prove personally embarrassing to an individual of normal sensibilities should not be disclosed.*[25]

Exemption (7) deals with law enforcement records. The original wording in the act was criticized because it permitted the withholding of just about any file labelled ''investigatory.'' Amendments introduced in 1974 defined this exemption more precisely. In part, they exclude access to investigatory files if such access ''constitutes an unwarranted invasion of personal privacy.''[26] This differs from Exemption (6) only in that it omits the word ''clearly.'' The courts have not held this difference to be significant. The FOIA does protect privacy, but the distinction must be made between an individual requesting information about a third party or about himself or herself. The latter case has been dealt with under the terms of the various privacy acts. With regard to the former, the absolutist position would be to restrict all access to personal information about another individual. However, there seems to be general agreement that on occasion the cause of open government must have higher claim than that of personal privacy. For example, it may be necessary to examine information about public officials to determine if they are exercising their responsibilities as required by law. There is a ''balancing'' test in Exemption (6): For each request for access, privacy and confidentiality must be balanced. Appeal to judicial review is possible, and case law will determine appropriate guidelines over time. Another approach might be to specify, in advance, records for which privacy must be maintained and to exempt them absolutely from disclosure. This approach may not be satisfactory in all cases, as it makes no provision for public's right to know in special circumstances.

Finally, little attention has been paid to the question of whether information supplied under guarantees of confidentiality could be released under a freedom of information request. In at least one case a judge has ruled that whereas the promise of confidentiality is an important factor in deciding whether to supply the information, it is not an absolute prohibition. As in so many other areas of government activity, the concept of balance is of prime importance. It has been recommended that before an agency complies with a request to supply personally identifiable information, it must first obtain permission from the individual. This factor may be important in the balancing process. Recent attempts to obtain information have encountered bureaucratic delays and resistance.[27]

FUTURE PROBLEMS

Privacy as an issue will not disappear. In fact, it will become more pronounced as the computer makes even greater inroads in the functioning of society. Future problems are linked inextricably to the ability of the computer to process large amounts of information efficiently and rapidly. Although the computer has brought certain problems to the fore, the importance of privacy is a societal issue and its protection depends on a host of social concerns.

Electronic Funds Transfer Systems (EFTS)

EFTS can be characterized as an integration of computer and communication systems for the purpose of facilitating financial transactions. The most common are probably the automatic tellers now used by millions to perform straightforward banking transactions. Other parts of the system are point-of-sale terminals, which are used to pay for purchases instantaneously and electronically. Automated clearing houses transfer payments by electronically debiting one account and crediting another. In the records thus accumulated, a great deal of information is available about an individual's purchases and banking behavior. With these concerns in mind, Congress passed the Financial Institutions Regulatory Act in 1978. The part of this act devoted to EFTS (called the Fair Funds Transfer Act) is an amendment to the Consumer Credit Protection Act. The bill defines EFT as ''any transfer of funds which is initiated through an electronic terminal, telephone instrument, or computer magnetic tape.''[28] The portion, entitled the Right of Financial Privacy Act is concerned with a traditional privacy issue, access to financial records—by agreement of the customer, administrative subpoena or summons, search warrant, judicial subpoena, or formal written request, a copy of which is filed in court. The government must inform an individual that his or her financial records are being requested and advise of the laws that could prevent the release of these records. The requesting government agency is not permitted to share its information, once obtained, with any other agency. This law is gradually being extended to an increasing number of areas of society in which personal records are kept—credit, government, education, and financial records.

Videotex or Interactive Home Information Systems

The combination of television, computers, and two-way cable communication networks promises to open up a wide array of services to the home. These include home banking and shopping, educational services, entertainment, instant opinion polling, organizational fund raising, and others. The operators of such systems will be collecting a great deal of personal information about subscribers' viewing habits, entertainment preferences, financial behavior, and political opinions. This information is of interest to commercial marketing firms, who obviously wish to direct their sales campaigns at choice audiences. Lists of subscribers sorted on the basis of different factors can be sold to various groups. Confidential information could be made available to third parties, such as political groups who may use it in political campaigns. The government may wish to obtain records in connection with gathering evidence in litigative processes. Credit-granting companies might be interested in home information records as part of the credit background of applicants.

There is no federal legislation yet on this issue, but a number of cities and states have adopted laws to protect personal information on such systems. For example, Illinois passed the Cable Television Privacy Act in 1981, and was the first state to do so. This act prevents companies from providing lists of subscribers without the individual consent of every person on the list. Some cable systems have adopted their own set of standards, presumably to forestall government regulations. Warner Amex—the operator of the Qube system in Columbus, Ohio—was the first to publicize a ''code of privacy.'' Some of the provisions include the right to examine and copy any personal information held, the right to make verifiable corrections, and that information may be surrendered to government agencies by court subpoena only. These rules and others derive from a tradition of practices developed in the 1970s. Presumably, the future holds the prospect of federal legislation when sufficient experience has been gathered, and the powerful interests involved in videotex have consolidated their position

Transborder Data Flows

Individual countries have formulated privacy protection laws that may not be compatible. The European Economic Community has agreed to a convention for privacy protection that will cover the flow of information among member states. Problems arise when countries whose privacy laws are not compatible wish to exchange information. As there are international agreements in many areas, one might eventually expect treaties in this area as well. In the absence of such agreements, countries may refuse to permit personal data to be sent to other countries where the laws are weaker or do not apply to nonresidents. The urgent need of international treaties may not be apparent in the United States. Because it is so prominent in the data transmission field very little U.S. data goes out, and it may be said to be a data-importing country.

Concluding Remarks

The right to privacy is not viewed as an absolute right, especially with respect to information. The major thrust of legislation has been to control, not to forbid, the collection and use of private information. Information about any individual is not always in that individual's control. Rather, it can be gathered, stored, and disseminated by both private and public agencies. The law has provided protection, and one must continue to turn to the law for future protection. The distinguished jurist William O. Douglas referred to the police in the following quotation, but he might just as well have been concerned with other institutions and groups in society.

> *The free state offers what a police state denies—the privacy of the home, the dignity and peace of mind of the individual. That precious right to be let alone is violated once the police enter our conversations.*[29]

SUMMARY

The impact of computers on privacy is one of the major concerns voiced by the public at large. Although most people agree that computers have improved the quality of life, there is a definite apprehension that some form of an Orwellian *1984* society is not far off. Privacy is an important but difficult right to maintain when so much information about individuals is gathered and stored by both public and private agencies. Personal data must be safeguarded and only used for the purpose for which it was originally collected.

One of the fears of legitimate groups is that databases built up by government surveillance will be used to harass lawful activities. The increasing use of computer matching is of concern to civil libertarians, because the searching of computer records in order to turn up possible violations seems to be an action contrary to the presumption of innocence. Credit bureaus play a major role in the marketing of information. Because credit ratings are so important in almost every aspect of life, it is necessary to guarantee that such data is as accurate as possible and that individuals be informed as to its use. There is a fear among some people that the Social Security Number will be used as a universal identifier, a means to link individual records in distributed databases.

In response to public concern, a number of acts have been passed by the federal government to deal with the most serious violations. The European approach in the private sector is to establish government agencies to license and regulate companies which operate databases. Freedom of information occasionally conflicts with privacy rights, but balances must be struck to ensure that the public is able to obtain information about the actions of government.

NOTES

1. Lou Harris and Associates, *The Road after 1984: The Impact of Technology on Society* (New Haven: for Southern New England Telephone, 1983).

2. Alan F. Westin, *Privacy and Freedom* (New York: Atheneum, 1967), p. 7.

3. Kent Greenawalt, ''Privacy and Its Legal Protections,'' *Hastings Center Studies*, September 1974, p. 45.

4. *Privacy and Computers*, Canada Dept. of Communications/Dept. of Justice (Ottawa: Information Canada 1972), p. 13.

5. *Records, Computers, and the Rights of Citizens*, U.S. Dept. of Health, Report to the Secretary's Advisory Committee on Automated Personal Data Systems (Washington, D.C., 1973), pp. 40–41.

6. Ibid., p. 41.

7. Westin, *Privacy and Freedom*, p. 158.

8. *Personal Privacy in an Information Society*, report of the Privacy Protection Study Commission (Washington, D.C., 1977), pp. 14–15.

9. Richard D. Kusserow, ''The Government Needs Computer Matching to Root Out Waste and Fraud,'' *Communications of the Association for Computing Machinery*, June 1984, p. 543.

10. Written statement of J.C. Penney Company, Inc. to the Privacy Protection Study Commission, February 12, 1976, as quoted in *Personal Privacy in an Information Society*, p. 43.

11. Inger Hansen, *Report of the Privacy Commissioner on the Use of the Social Insurance Number*, Government of Canada, Canadian Human Rights Commission (Ottawa: 1981).

12. News release of a resolution of the Association for Computing Machinery Council, November 14, 1974.

13. Sam J. Errin, Jr. (U.S. Senator), forward to Arthur R. Miller, *The Assault of Privacy* (Ann Arbor: University of Michigan, 1971).

14. *Records, Computers, and the Rights of Citizens*, pp. 66–69.

15. Miller, *Assault on Privacy*, p. 86.

16. Section s.2(b) of the Privacy Act of 1974, 5 U. S. C., s.552a, passed as part of Pub. L. No. 93-579.

17. *Personal Privacy in an Information Society, (1977)*, p. xv.

18. Ibid., pp. 501–502.

19. Ibid., p. 413.

20. *Privacy and Computers*, p. 139.

21. *Public Government for Private People*, The Report of the Commission on Freedom of Information and Individual Privacy, Province of Ontario, vol. 3 (Toronto: 1980), p. 637.

22. Ibid., pp. 602–603.

23. Ibid., volume 2, pp. 455–457.

24. Ibid., p. 114.

25. Ibid.

26. Ibid., p. 115.

27. Steve Weinberg, "Trashing the FOIA," *Columbia Journalism Review*, January/February 1985, pp. 21–28.

28. "EFT Bill, Consumer Privacy Act Passed," *Communications of the Association for Computing Machinery*, December 1978, p. 1093.

29. William O. Douglas, Address to the American Law Institute, 1953.

ADDITIONAL READINGS

The Nature of Privacy

Burnham, David. *The Rise of the Computer State*. New York: Random House, 1983.

Smith, Robert Ellis. *Privacy: How to Protect What's Left of It*. Garden City: Anchor/Doubleday, 1979.

Data Banks

Computer-Based National Information Systems. Technology and Public Policy Issues. U.S. Congress, Office of Technology Assessment. Washington, D.C., September 1981.

Flaherty, David H. *Privacy and Government Data Banks*. London: Mansell, 1979.

Kirchner, Jake. "Privacy: A History of Computer Matching in Federal Government." *Computerworld*, December 14, 1981.

Miller, Arthur R. *The Assault on Privacy*. Ann Arbor: University of Michigan Press, 1971.

Shattuck, John. "Computer Matching is a Serious Threat to Individual Rights," *Communications of the Association for Computing Machinery*, June 1984, pp. 538–541.

Westin, Alan F. "The Long-Term Implications of Computers for Privacy and the Protection of Public Order." In Lance J. Hoffman, ed., *Computers and Privacy in the Next Decade*. New York: Academic, 1980, pp. 167–181.

Social Security Number

Smith, Robert Ellis. "You Know my Name, Look up the Number." *Datamation*, May 15, 1985, pp. 108–111, 114.

Privacy Legislation

Rule, James, Douglas McAdam, Linda Stearns, and David Uglow. *The Politics of Privacy*. New York: Elsevier, 1980.

Turn, Rein. "Privacy Protection in Information System." In M. Rubinoff and M. C. Yovitts, eds., *Advances in Computers*. vol. 16. New York: Academic, 1977, pp. 221–335.

Future Problems

Nash, Deanna C. and David A. Bollier, "Protecting Privacy in the Age of Hometech." *Technology Review*, August/September 1981, pp. 67–75.

Westin, Alan F. "Home Information Systems: The Privacy Debate." *Datamation*, July 1982, pp. 100–101, 103–104, 106, 111–112, 114.

10

EMPLOYMENT AND UNEMPLOYMENT

A ny kind of machinery used for shortening labour—except used in a cooperative society like ours—must tend to less wages, and to deprive working men of employment, and finally, either to starve them, force them into some other employment (and then reduce wages in that also), or compel them to emigrate. Now, if the working classes would socially and peacefully unite to adopt our system, no power or party could prevent their success.

◇ *Manifesto, Cooperative Community*, Ralahine, County Clare, Ireland, 1883 (on introduction of the reaping machine.) ◇

INTRODUCTION

The most serious and complex problem associated with the impact of computers on society has to do with work. The basic and simplistic expression of this concern is the question:

Does technological change create, or destroy, jobs?

In the present context, technological change refers to innovations in computer and communications technology. Definitive answers are scarce; by way of exploration, the arguments may be briefly stated as follows. Yes, the introduction of new technology may reduce the number of jobs in the directly affected industry. On the other hand, it may actually increase the number, because increased productivity resulting from the new technology will increase demand, and more workers will be necessary to satisfy it. Even if there is a net loss of jobs in a specific industry, it is argued, new jobs will be created in support areas for the new technology, in whole new industries resulting from unpredictable technology, and in the service and white collar areas. For example, the introduction of robots will create a robot support industry to install, service, and monitor performance, to say nothing of design and manufacture. Jobs are eliminated in those industries that benefit from robots but are created in the robot support companies. The common term for this effect is *job displacement*. The question about technology and jobs can be restated in terms of the economy as a whole, to take job displacement into account.

Assuming that new jobs will be created, will there be a sufficient number to take up the slack? It is likely that in factories that manufacture robots, robots themselves will be a major factor in production. The technology associated with computers is qualitatively different from previous technologies. It brings not only ways to do things more efficiently, but also the possibility of doing many things with very few workers. The possibility that many of society's needs could be satisfied with a significantly reduced work force is of concern to many people.

What about the theory that an unending chain of inventions and discoveries will always be part of our future, creating new products and new jobs? In our time such inventions and processes as Xeroxing, Polaroid cameras, video cassette recorders, and personal computers have certainly created new industries and jobs in design, manufacturing, marketing, sales, and service. In the past 200 years, since the beginning of the Industrial Revolution in England, enough jobs have been created, it has been claimed, to accommodate growth in population, increasing urbanization and reduction of farm labor, and a rapidly accelerating chain of inventions. These observations apply only to the Western world, and not in the last few years.

Prior to the Industrial Revolution, most of the population was engaged in agriculture. With advances in farming machinery, fertilizers, and disease-resistant and weather-conditioned crops, productivity on the farm has soared. Currently, in the United States about three percent of the work force produces enough food for the entire country, as well as enormous quantities for export. Where did all the farm workers go? Most of them became blue collar workers in the rapidly growing industrial plants. Recently, the percentage of the work force in blue collar jobs has been decreasing. Most American workers are now employed in service and white collar jobs—that is, they do not produce things but work with people, paper, and information.

The expectation now is that as society moves from an industrial to an information base, the major source of new jobs will be in the office, in service areas such as restaurants, hotels, and entertainment, in the financial domain, and in government. The model of the future has a much-reduced labor force in production and an expanded number of people in the service and information areas. There is a serious problem with this view—the increasing rate of automation in the office. The introduction of computers, office networks, telecommunication systems, and facsimile machines has as its goal a major improvement in office productivity, but as a byproduct there will be fewer jobs. Of these, fewer will be the kind of low-skill jobs that have traditionally served as an entry point for many hundreds of thousands of workers.

Another major concern is with the changing nature of work. The Industrial Revolution spawned a number of responses from workers whose livelihood was threatened by the use of machines. Probably the most well-known were the Luddites, who flourished in the beginning of the eighteenth century. They are best known for having smashed newly introduced machines—in blind opposition to progress, according to the conventional view. The well-known British historian E. P. Thompson has argued as follows:

> At issue was the ''freedom'' of the capitalist to destroy the customs of the trade, whether by new machinery, by the factory-system, or by unrestricted competition, beating down wages, undercutting his rivals, and undermining the standards of craftsmanship.[1]

Since that time there has been an uneasy relationship between the worker and new technology. While welcoming the relief from drudgery and dangerous work that machines have provided, the worker has been concerned first with becoming merely an adjunct to the machine and then being replaced by it. In many cases the machines themselves were dangerous.

This fear has grown, especially in the factory, as work has become organized under such principles as scientific management (Frederick Taylor) and the assembly line (Henry Ford). The reduction of production to a series of small, repeatable actions encouraged a belief that the worker was easily replaceable, that his or her skill could be extracted, and that he or she would perform a boring, routine task efficiently for many years of working life. The computer can be seen merely as the most recent phase of technology or as a new force that gives management a powerful tool for extending its control, whether in factory or office. Computers and communications systems may reproduce the factory model in the office—at least this is the fear of many workers. The relatively open social system in the office may be replaced by a rigid, highly structured environment in which the performance of the worker at the terminal may be closely monitored.

Other associated issues are the problem of job dissatisfaction (will computers exacerbate this situation?), the attempt of labor unions in America and abroad to protect their membership from job loss, and the threats to health allegedly posed by video display terminals. Of particular interest to more than half the population is the apparently limited role that women may play in the coming information age. The bulk of data entry work is mainly seen by men as women's work. There is a trend to the decentralized office, in which women might stay at home and perform their jobs at terminals hooked up to computers over telephone lines. The term *electronic cottage* conjures up the picture of early cottage industry. Finally, what impact will automation have on the skills of workers? Work—how much, and what kind, will be a dominant issue of our time.

Most of the studies and reports cited below describe results that are frequently fragmentary, limited, and inconclusive. The impact of technology on both the nature of work and the possible loss of jobs is so immense, it is difficult to study. Attewell and Rule (1984) have stated this fact quite forcefully: ''Virtually none of the studies mounted so far have been capable of yielding a persuasive and comprehensive view of computer-induced social change.''[2] Nevertheless, available materials can suggest the kinds of problems and benefits that may emerge. The qualitative effects of computers can be articulated and discussed without definitive quantitative results.

EXPERIENCES OF WORKERS

Workers are not all alike; they have different needs, interests and motivations. Moreover, these characteristics constantly change over the career of each worker, much as the modal work values of the society as a whole shift over time.[3]

Computers will make their presence felt in several ways in both factory and office. Computers have been used to automate various decision-making processes so that workers who formerly monitored ongoing production now must watch video terminals to see what is happening. The most dramatic innnovation in the factory is the introduction of robots into the assembly line. (See Chapter 12). In both factory and office, there may be problems in integrating people and machines in an efficient, safe, and productive manner.

Workers Voice Their Concerns

The men and women who do the hard work of the world have learned from him [Ruskin] and Morris that they have a right to pleasure in their toil, and that when justice is done them they will have it. (William Dean Howells, Criticism and Fiction, *1981.)*

It is useful and important to characterize the nature of the workplace as seen through the eyes of the workers themselves. The opinions of satisfied or indifferent workers, probably a majority, are sometimes neglected in favor of the angry or frustrated one. Our interest is in real and potential problems, difficulties, and alienation, but how representative these angry voices are is a real question. It is also true that in times when unemployment rates are high, workers are less likely to complain openly.

What aspects of work are likely to be most affected by computers? In the words of a spot welder in an automobile assembly plant,

I don't understand how come more guys don't flip. Because you're nothing more than a machine when you hit this type of thing. They give better care to that machine than they will to you. They'll have more respect, give more attention to that machine. And you know *this. Somehow you get the feeling that the machine is better than you are. (Laughs.)*[4]

The theme of the machine receiving preferred treatment is likely to become more common. The machine referred to above is in fact part of traditional assembly line equipment, which differs significantly from a new generation of equipment. Robots are a form of flexible automation that can be programmed to perform a variety of tasks. The relationship of the worker to such new machines will be different. Will workers perceive themselves as mere caretakers, or as surviving only until the next generation of even more sophisticated machines? Their concern derives from a real awareness of their place in the production process.

> *You really begin to wonder. What price do they put on me? Look at the price they put on the machine. If that machine breaks down, there's somebody out there to fix it right away. If I break down, I'm just pushed over to the other side till another man takes my place. The only thing they have on their mind is to keep that line running.*[5]

Considerable stress is involved in assembly line work. One of the most publicized recent events in industrial relations was the disruption at the Lordstown plant of the General Motors Company (GM) near Warren, Ohio. A bitter strike broke out in 1972, seeming to reflect the unwillingness of young workers to put up with conditions that their elders grew up with. Supposedly, they were satisfied with job security and reasonable salaries but were concerned with the quality of work. This concern seemed to be in opposition to union goals, which have always been directed towards better salaries, pension plans, health benefits, and the shorter work week. The American Federation of Labor—Council of Industrial Organizations (AFL-CIO) argued that Lordstown was no different from previous industrial disputes and that the union was attempting to translate discontent in the workplace into negotiable issues. At the Lordstown plant, GM was attempting to modernize the assembly line with more sophisticated equipment. A younger labor force was required to cope with the demands of this new line. Apparently some of the young worker groups had arranged among themselves to rest half the group while the others worked furiously in short stretches. This informal arrangement angered management and it responded by speeding up the line. A strike resulted.

In the early 1970s there was considerable discussion about job security and decent salary versus the quality of work. Perhaps the most striking image of the frequent mindlessness of the assembly line is Charlie Chaplin in the film *Modern Times,* holding two wrenches in his hands and being transported, bodily, through a series of giant gears. Immediately following his release he chases a woman with designs on her dress that resemble the nuts he has been tightening all day. Because the Lordstown plant was built on the principle of a high-speed assembly line, the work force was younger than in other automobile plants. They could withstand the accelerated pace of the line, were less prone to illness, and would, therefore, use fewer benefits. However, there was an increased incidence of mental illness and drug use. Younger workers were much less committed to the work ethic of their elders and much more inclined to voice their complaints. The unemployment rate has risen in the 1980s, however, and the need to acquire and maintain a job has far outweighed the earlier demands for job satisfaction.

Workers have devised a variety of strategies to deal with the conditions of their jobs.

Chuck Bradley, an operator at Mountain Bell, has handled several hundred thousand long-distance calls. He reports the following way of maintaining sanity:

> *As the voices come into mind, I just freeze the information in one part of my brain and hold it there. Then I pull it out whenever I need it. This allows me to distance myself from my work and ignore the fact that callers treat me like a rock. Who I am and what I do don't meet. My identity is separate from my job.*[6]

His last sentence is certainly a fundamental statement of the disassociation of work from life. Whether or not a search for meaning in the workplace is possible, workers are concerned with many important issues such as safety, possibility of advancement, respect for their skills, and respect for their views on the production process.

Advanced automation, as it has been implemented, has apparently deprived workers of the possibility of obtaining relief from job pressures. Before robots were introduced into one plant, for example, a worker would have to pick up a part, place it correctly, fix it, wait until the machine performed its job, and then remove it. Now a robot does all these jobs and the worker must run the robot, a task which demands full concentration. "I don't have time to talk with anyone. I don't want them breaking my concentration."[7] The integration of workers with robots or information systems requires full attention by the worker who must be constantly involved in watching a screen or monitoring a robot. One might agree with the well-known saying: He who pays the piper calls the tune. The worker's role is to carry out both the spirit and the letter of his or her job requirements. A rich inner life and job satisfaction are not particular concerns of management. Perhaps. But a worker who feels an inner commitment, who feels respected by management, and whose advice is heeded will contribute to the manufacturing of a better product and will provide more conscientious service.

Some Historical Issues

The history of technological innovation and its effect on the workplace is complex. To begin with, it is almost impossible to discuss the history of work without assuming a particular political viewpoint. In its starkest form, the capitalist or free enterprise position argues that the constant pressure to increase productivity, in order to meet competition, results in increased investment in capital equipment. The worker is gradually relieved of a dangerous environment, complex decision making, and the power to disrupt the productive process. From a Marxist point of view, the basic goals of capitalist management are simply to extract skills from workers and to achieve sufficient return on investment by reducing the cost of labor. Management also wants complete control over its workers—to use them as it wishes, independently of their needs and desires as human beings.

Free enterprise spokesmen point out that industrialization has permitted workers to improve substantially their standard of living. Marxists argue that the price has been high—loss of autonomy, loss of skills, and loss of respect. Technological optimists predict that the age of computers will accelerate benefits, with more and cheaper goods available, less work necessary to maintain income levels, and improved living conditions for the Third World. A closer examination of the industrialization process reveals a rather disturbing long-term trend: Workers have been losing control, initiative, and skills.

An important examination of this process was carried out by Harry Braverman. Written from a Marxist point of view, his book has been recognized even by non-Marxist economists and sociologists as a valuable contribution to the history of labor studies.[8] In his view, the most important implication of the Industrial Revolution for the worker was loss of control. In the evolution of the craftsman working on his or her own to worker on the factory floor, the distinguishing feature is loss of control—over pace of work, the individual steps, and the quality of the product. From this loss—this sale of one's labor—many consequences follow. The worker and the work process have been endlessly studied in order to improve efficiency, reduce costs, and (in Marxist terms) squeeze out the last drop of surplus labor.

Division of Labor

The decomposition of the process of production into a series of small, relatively simple actions is a crucial step, called the division of labor. The needlemaker in Nuremberg, a guild member, performed a sequence of more than twenty steps when making a needle. In the early needle industry in England, twenty needlemakers working side-by-side, each performing only one operation of the necessary twenty, produced a single needle. By the middle of the eighteenth century, Adam Smith, the famous economist, reported that ten workers could produce 48,000 needles per day.[9] Approximately one century later, Marx wrote that a single machine could produce 145,000 needles in a working day of 11 hours. Since one person could supervise four such machines, the production rate per worker per day was approximately 600,000 needles.[10] Thus, the division of labor was a necessary precursor to the eventual mechanization of production. The advantage that accrues to the owner is the reduction in cost of the individual steps in the manufacturing process.

A task requiring a craftsman was reduced to one for which several unskilled workers were sufficient. They became replaceable, so that if cheaper labor is available, new workers are brought in. The process of deskilling work has gone hand in hand with the Industrial Revolution. Do computers increase or decrease the skills of workers? (See ''Deskilling'' below.)

Scientific Management

As enterprises grew larger the problems of organization became paramount. Near the end of the nineteenth century serious attempts were made to apply new techniques to the management of large and complex companies. Initiated by Frederick Winslow Taylor, this principled effort was called scientific management. He bluntly stated that it was management's sole responsibility and duty to control every facet of labor's activity. Although previous thought and practice had recognized this domination, Taylor set out to demonstrate in painstaking detail how management could translate its power into the closely controlled supervision of the labor process. He based all his subsequent research on the notion of ''a fair day's work''—apparently, the maximum amount of work a worker could do on a regular basis throughout his lifetime without damaging his health. In the eyes of management, when workers slow their pace, loaf or talk, they fail to fulfill their potential, and here scientific management comes into play. The worker attempts to conceal from management how fast the work can actually be done; so management is paying a salary that does not correlate with the realities of the situation. Supervision and discipline that are vague and general will not be adequate as long as the workers themselves control the labor process. From first-hand experience, and a series of experiments that took twenty-six years, Taylor derived a precise formulation by which workers could be carefully instructed in each movement of their prescribed tasks.

Taylor's contributions can be summed up in terms of three principles, as follows:[11]

1. Dissociation of the labor process from the skills of the workers. Management should organize the labor process independently of the workers' knowledge and craft.

2. Separation of conception from execution. Basically, the task of the worker is to perform a series of prescribed actions that do not involve planning or decision making. The worker must not introduce his or her ideas into the labor process because this compromises management's control.

3. The use of the monopoly over knowledge to control each step of the labor process and its mode of execution.

The implementation of these principles involves the systematic planning of each production step and the careful instruction of workers in its proper execution. Scientific management and its successor theories became a dominant force in the growth of large industrial enterprises.

The Modern Assembly Line   *Henry Ford*

At the turn of the century, the production of automobiles was essentially a craft. Individual mechanics would move around a stationary work site until the assembly of the automobile was complete. After Henry Ford introduced the Model T in 1908, the demand was so enormous that new production techniques were needed. In 1914, the first continuous assembly line was introduced at his Highland Park plant near Detroit. The improvements in productivity were astounding. Within three months an automobile could be assembled in about one-tenth the time, and ''by 1925 an organization had been created which produced almost as many cars in a single day as had been produced, early in the history of the Model T, in an entire year.''[12] The pay structure was flattened, and bonuses and incentives were done away with. They were no longer necessary to stimulate productivity, because the combination of the division of labor and the moving assembly line meant that management could precisely control the rate of production. The assembly line principle quickly spread to other industries and served as a foundation for industrial growth.

Worker reaction was decisive and negative: they left in large numbers as other work was available. In 1913, the turnover rate was 380 percent and a major unionization drive began. In response Ford increased pay to $5.00 per day, considerably above the going rate. This measure stemmed the flow of workers away and introduced another feature to the industrial scene—the use of higher wages to limit possible disruptions. This strategy has also been one of the responses appropriated by labor unions to accommodate to the potential and actual loss of jobs resulting from the introduction of computers.

The Impact on Workers

Researchers following in Taylor's footsteps have probed and studied workers in order to determine the most efficient decomposition of work into a series of small, mindless, easily reproducible steps. In some sense, the goal of the exercise is to see workers as machines so that in the future they can be replaced by machines. Taylor was interested in timing each separate step of a work process, in an unrealized hope of deriving a general way of characterizing work. He was followed by Frank B. Gilbreth, who initiated the study of motion—creating what is now called motion and time study. A notational system was developed to encompass body positions, limb movements, application of force, and eye movements. Endless studies and measurements have been performed to refine the organization of work. The psychological aspect has not been ignored either.

A series of famous experiments was conducted at Western Electric's Hawthorne plant near Chicago between 1924 and 1932. Generally, they were aimed at determining what environmental and psychological factors were important in improving worker productivity. In one set of experiments, illumination was varied to study the effect on groups of women engaged in inspection and assembly. The women apparently worked faster whether the lighting was increased or decreased. In another experiment, five women who prepared mica used for insulation were monitored at their regular work station and then moved to a special test room where they received 10-minute rest periods in the morning and afternoon. Then they were returned to their original work stations. After an initial decline following the move, performance increased by 15 percent on average, and then dropped back to its original level when they returned to their department.

On the basis of these and other experiments, it appeared that when people are selected for study, their performance may improve just because of the attention they are receiving, not because of any special property of that attention—the famous Hawthorne effect. It suggests that workers just need to know that management cares about them in order to work harder. The Hawthorne effect has enjoyed an honored position in psychological methodology, an indication of both the problems of psychological theorizing and the attitude of academics towards ordinary working men and women. Recent evaluations and reinterpretations of the Hawthorne data have shown that workers usually acted in their own self-interest—they only worked harder if they received more money. A necessary factor was that they be aware of how well they were performing. Factory workers are no different from anyone else—if they are paid according to their productivity and they know how much they are producing, their productivity will improve. For the contemporary worker in both factory and office, this long process of mechanization, measurement, study, and automation has reached a point where future jobs are threatened and present jobs are being substantially reshaped.

What does the worker want? Among possible answers are job security, good wages, safe working conditions, possibility of advancement, a sense of accomplishment, respect, a good pension and medical plan, and a congenial environment. In the early 1970s, there seemed to be a worker's rebellion, a dissatisfaction with boring and routine jobs, an unwillingness to put up with management's structuring of the workplace. Social psychologists spoke of unrealized potential, and the need for ''self-actualization''—a concept developed by the psychologist Abraham Maslow.[13] Apparently workers, especially young workers, wanted more out of life than a boring and unsatisfying job, even if it payed well. Theories were proposed, studies were carried out, and work enrichment proposals were formulated to meet these unfulfilled needs. Unfortunately, there were a number of problems with these approaches. Workers, by and large, put good wages at the top of their lists; job enrichment schemes did not really address serious issues or have any lasting value. Most importantly, as the decade wore on unemployment rates increased, and simply having a job became of paramount importance.

For many workers, their job is not a major source of satisfaction in their lives. A mere cosmetic improvement has little long-term value, and will not result in increased productivity. Perhaps some complaints will be alleviated by the introduction of new technology. Along with its arguments for increased productivity, management claims that robots will do the dirty work—painting, welding, and in general, work in unpleasant environments—thereby sparing the worker. It would be surprising if workers were not a little suspicious of management's aims. Furthermore, there are fears that the long-term process of skill reduction will reach its culmination in the fully automated plant. For the interim, one important question is how well workers will fare in close proximity to the new machines.

COMPUTERS AND EMPLOYMENT

They talk of the dignity of work. Bosh. The dignity is in leisure. (Herman Melville, Redburn.)

It is becoming clear that high technology itself is not likely to provide a sufficient number of jobs to offset those lost through its impact. The long-term trends are clear: farm labor, which constituted over 70 percent of the labor force in 1820, was reduced to less than 50 percent by 1880, less than 30 percent by 1920, and is currently running at less than 3 percent. The distribution of jobs in the nonagricultural sector is shown in Table 10-1.

Future Jobs

In May 1983 both *Time* and *Fortune* featured cover stories on the state of the economy, with special emphasis on the unemployment picture.[14] They both presented recent projections by the Bureau of Labor Statistics that showed those areas in the economy in which most jobs will be created as well as lost. Tables 10-2 and 10-3 show more recent

TABLE 10-1 Distribution of Jobs in Non-Farm Labor Force in 1920 and 1980

Non-Farm Labor Force	Percentage of Total Labor Force	
	1920	*1980*
Transportation and public utilities	13.6	6.0
Wholesale and retail trade	17.0	22.4
Finance, insurance and real estate	4.0	5.6
Services	8.6	19.6
Government and government enterprises	10.0	18.0
Manufacturing	38.8	22.4
Mining and construction	8.0	6.0

Source: Adapted from Eli Ginzberg, ''The Mechanization of Work,'' September 1982.
Reprinted by permission of *Scientific American*. Copyright © 1982 by W. H. Freeman and Company; all rights reserved.

TABLE 10-2 The Ten Job Areas with Largest Growth, 1982–95 (Based on Moderate-Trend Projections)

	Increase in Jobs (in thousands)	*Percent of Total Job Growth*	*Percent Change*
Building custodians	779	3.0	27.5
Cashiers	744	2.9	47.4
Secretaries	719	2.8	29.5
General clerks, office	696	2.7	29.6
Saleclerks	685	2.7	23.5
Nurses, registered	642	2.5	48.9
Waiters and waitresses	562	2.2	33.8
Teachers, kindergarten and elementary	511	2.0	37.4
Truckdrivers	425	1.7	26.5
Nursing aides and orderlies	423	1.7	34.8
Sales representatives, technical	386	1.5	29.3

Source: Adapted from *Employment Projections for 1995*, U.S. Department of Labor, Bureau of Labor Statistics, Bulletin 2197 (Washington, D.C., March 1984), pp. 35–47.

TABLE 10-3 The Ten Job Areas with the Largest Decrease, 1982–95 (Based on Moderate Trend Projections)

	Number of Jobs (in thousands)		Decrease in Jobs (in thousands)
	1982	*1995*	
Farmers and farmworkers	2,691	2,407	284
Private household workers	1,023	850	238
College and university faculty	744	632	112
Postal service clerks	307	252	55
Data entry operators	320	286	34
Central office telephone operators	107	87	22
Stenographers	270	250	20
Graduate assistants	140	124	16
Shoemaking machine operators	52	36	16
Postal mail carriers	234	223	11

Source: Adapted from *Employment Projections for 1995,* U.S. Department of Labor, Bureau of Labor Statistics, Bulletin 2197 (Washington, D.C., March 1984) pp. 35–47.

figures. The ten best prospects are all in the service area, not in high technology. Losses in the number of college teachers and graduate assistants indicate that higher education has ceased to be a growth area and fewer students will require fewer teachers. It is significant that manufacturing in general and high technology industries in particular do not appear in these statistics, except for the loss in data entry jobs. The figures shown in Table 10-4 indicate that manufacturing (items 5 and 6) is expected to continue decreasing in its percentage of the work force, from 24.2 to 23.7.

Clearly, the manufacturing sector will not provide the majority of new jobs in the economy and has not done so for sometime. In fact, the Bureau of Labor Statistics predicts that manufacturing will supply about 25 percent of new jobs in 1982–95.[15] In a careful analysis in 1983 of the impact of high technology on employment, *Business Week* pointed out that although high technology industries will grow almost twice as fast as other manufacturing industries, they will not provide many new jobs.[16] There are two reasons— the high technology sector is relatively small (less than 20 percent of manufacturing and construction), and its productivity is growing faster than other manufacturing sectors. The products of high technology, computers and microprocessors, will improve productivity in application area and so will have a deleterious effect on other manufacturing employment. The recession of the early 1980s resulted in the loss of some three million manufacturing jobs. By the end of 1984, only about one-third of these were restored.

TABLE 10-4 Percent Distribution of Employment by Major Occupational Group

	1982	1995[a]
Professional, technical and related workers	16.3	17.1
Managers, officials, and proprietors	9.4	9.6
Salesworkers	6.9	6.9
Clerical workers	18.8	18.9
Craft and related workers	11.4	11.6
Operatives	12.8	12.1
Service workers	16.0	16.3
Laborers, except farm	5.8	5.5
Farmers and farmworkers	2.7	1.9
Total number of jobs (in thousands):	101,510	127,110

Source: Adapted from *Employment Projections for 1995*, U.S. Department of Labor, Bureau of Labor Statistics, Bulletin 2197 (Washington, D.C., March 1984), pp. 35–47.
[a]1995 figures are based on a moderate projection.

Part of the cause of this unemployment is the increased tendency towards industrial automation as a means to improve productivity. For example, Japan—the leading country in the introduction of robots—has presented a serious challenge to other industrialized nations. The message is quite clear: Increase productivity or cease to compete on the world scene, with an accompanying loss of jobs and a lowering of the standard of living. In some sense, while Japan may be seen to be exporting unemployment, the dilemma of industrialized countries may be seen as follows:

Automate rapidly (thereby increasing unemployment, only temporarily it is hoped) in order to compete internationally and perhaps restore the immediate loss in jobs with an increase in total production.	Don't automate, in order to save jobs in the short run, but because of cheaper goods produced elsewhere domestic jobs will be in jeopardy.

A serious question arises here about the responsibility of society at large for unemployment due to technological innovation.

It seems likely that the bulk of future jobs will not be produced in manufacturing but in service. Are we heading towards a society in which a relatively small percentage of the labor force produces sufficient food and manufactured goods, while most workers are involved in white-collar activities, information processing, leisure, and other service functions?

The Computer and the Office

Office automation will enable American business to create 20 million new jobs before the end of the century.[17]

There are 20 million office workers in this country whose jobs will be put at risk in one way or another by office automation.[18]

There are at least two possibilities for the office of the future. The promising model includes an increase in productivity, more jobs, improved skills for office workers, and increased opportunities for executives. The pessimistic version suggests that the industrial model will be reproduced in the office, with rows of women at desks and terminals, automatically monitored by the computer, with a major reduction of the traditional social intercourse of the office. The clerical work force is heavily dominated by women: 62 percent in 1970, but 80 percent in 1980. Although the office and the typewriter have historically been a major source of employment for women, the next stage of technological innovation may not be so kind. In 1978 Siemens, a West German company, estimated that office automation could result in a reduction of the labor force by 25 to 30 percent. Occupations such as file clerk, bookkeeper, typist, and bank teller, which are predominantly filled by women, are the leading candidates for automation.

Interestingly enough, the term *word processing* was first introduced by IBM in the early 1960s to sell dictation equipment. In 1967, IBM also used it as part of an advertising campaign for its magnetic tape Selective typewriters. The goal for the future office is clearly stated in an encyclopedia entry for word processing: ''WP represents a further stage in modern society's application of automation, reaching beyond manufacturing and production lines into the office.''[19]

In this situation, work becomes compartmentalized and secretaries are being assigned a narrow range of repetitive activities. Typically, workers find themselves less free to move about the office. (The issue of video display terminal (VDT) safety is treated in ''Job Safety'' below). Most secretaries certainly find the use of word processors easier and more enjoyable than traditional typing. To defend, in reverence for typists' skills, the retyping of entire paragraphs or pages to correct relatively simple mistakes is to falsely romanticize an unwarranted waste of time and energy. No one should seriously object to the entry of word processing systems into the office. The difficulty arises when one attempts to evaluate the impact of the new technology on the organization of work and the number of jobs. The worry expressed by a number of women's organizations concerns management's ultimate aims, not the immediately perceived benefits of the new technology.

9 to 5, the National Association of Office Workers, which is largely made up of women, is concerned about many aspects of the future office. They are somewhat wary about favorable claims. They believe that most women will be doing such boring and repetitive tasks as data entry, that the stress level will increase as a result of long periods at a terminal and constant monitoring, that skill levels will be reduced for most workers and increased for a very few, and that the social atmosphere of the office will change for the

worse. They call for office workers to abandon their traditional hostility toward unions and organize to protect their rights.

Those who look forward to increased office automation, especially (but not exclusively) equipment manufacturers and software developers, have a much more favorable view. In the long run the routine and the ordinary will be automated, and the number of employees with higher technical skills will increase. Office work will be more satisfying as the drudgery is relegated to machines. The level of human interaction will rise among those employees who need to communicate and who have sufficient time. Besides word processing, office automation includes communication networks, electronic mail, scheduling of meetings, information retrieval, and other applications. The complete package will arrive in stages because of high capital costs as well as associated technical problems. Productivity improvements will not be spectacular and in fact may not initially appear to justify the expense and effort. Over the next few years the office will undergo a transformation that will affect work in many ways. The shape of the future is difficult to predict. A concerned and informed public can help to humanize the new technology.

The Organization of Work

His [Taylor's] "system" was simply a means for management to achieve control of
the actual mode of performance of every labor activity, from the simplest to the
most complicated.[20]

The contributions of Frederick Taylor to the organization of the productive process concerned scientific management, time studies, and the assembly line. His goal was to separate the planning process from the execution process. Management's prerogative is to decide how a product is to be manufactured and then assign workers specific tasks to perform. Because of this division of labor and the separation of thought and action, work on assembly lines has been characterized as boring, mind numbing, and alienating. The trade-off of job security and good wages for mediocre working conditions has been justified by many commentators of the labor scene. However, with the rise of Japan as a major world competitor, it became clear to many observers that the traditional means of production still dominant in the United States could not compete successfully.

Many reasons have been offered for the Japanese success story: American aid; a modern industrial plant; a special relationship among government, business, and labor; new management techniques; a premium on quality control; the use of advanced technology such as robots; and the encouragement of worker participation in industrial decision making. Much has been written about the involvement of Japanese workers in the decision-making process. Workers are organized into groups for specific tasks and are permitted to carry out these tasks as they wish as long as production goals are met. On a regular basis, workers meet with management to suggest improvements in production. This system reverses the Taylor maxim. It must be working, or management would not continue to operate under such a system. In addition, management makes a long-term commitment to its workers—to train them appropriately and find alternative work if market conditions change.

Many of the above methods actually originated in the United States and were imported to Japan, where they were enthusiastically accepted and widely used. In an interesting turn of events, the same methods are being returned to the United States. Unfortunately, the economic recession of the early 1980s has limited to a considerable degree the willingness of many companies to experiment. In fact, certain industries took advantage of high unemployment rates to renegotiate major changes in work rules with their unions. For example, in the steel, automobile, and airline industries, crews have been reduced in size and jobs enlarged with new duties. Management has gained more power to schedule work and required workers to give up relief periods in some cases. Nevertheless, some new ideas have been adopted.

Probably, the most interesting one is the quality circle, a voluntary group of workers—perhaps eight to twelve—who meet together on a regular basis to identify, discuss, and solve problems. Usually the workers all come from the same area, but this is not necessary. What is necessary is that they be listened to with interest and respect. Quality circles ''allow workers to participate, make suggestions, and solve quality problems. Most of their suggestions are implemented without much hassle.''[21] There are apparently over 10,000 quality circles in operation in over 1,000 U.S. companies. According to many reports, improvements in efficiency and savings have been dramatic. The idea is certain to spread as economic conditions improve. A recent study suggests that quality circles do have limitations.[22] There seems to be inherent instability in this type of organization that frequently leads to a difficult winding-down process. When a quality circle does terminate, possible expectations of failure may arise, making it difficult to progress to a new stage of management-worker consultations.

Finally, what direct impact will computerization have on the organization of work? Possibly no direct benefit will accrue to the worker, and claims for relief from drudgery, monotony, and danger will probably only be realized if profit margins can be maintained. It is difficult to predict whether unemployment will increase or decrease and equally difficult to determine how work and workers will be affected. A choice does exist on how workers can accommodate to the new environment. Whether or not some workers can be retrained to become programmers themselves is an important issue. For example, in the development of programs to numerically control machine tools, workers who formerly would have done the machining themselves could transfer their knowledge directly. They could monitor, make corrections, and contribute significantly to the entire process. There are choices, and human considerations must be made part of the design process.

Electronic Banking and Scanners

The office and factory are the major sites, but the computer and its related technology have had a major impact on other areas of the economy. In banking, the introduction of automatic teller machines (ATMs) at an accelerating rate has resulted in a smaller number of human tellers. Since most tellers are women, this is yet another example of women bearing the brunt of the impact. It is also an example of entry jobs for relatively unskilled labor being removed. Remaining teller jobs will be upgraded, because ATMs can handle routine transactions. In fact, banks have encouraged the use of ATMs by reducing the number of tellers on regular service and upgrading their job responsibilities. As part of this process, tellers are being renamed customer service representatives.

Scanners, which have become quite common in many supermarkets, are devices that read the standard bar code printed on most grocery products. In place of cash registers, computer terminals now determine the price corresponding to a given bar code. This price, together with a brief description of the item, is printed on the tape. One of the contentious issues associated with scanners is that prices need no longer appear on the items or the shelves. Prices can readily be changed by entering new data into the computer without the customer being informed. A small number of states—including New York, Michigan, and California—require supermarkets to keep the prices on individual items. Scanners are seen as labor-saving devices and a means for extending the supervisory function through improved inventory control.

Scanners can save labor in a variety of ways: they obviate the need for individual item pricing (if permitted by law), speed up the check-out process (thereby requiring fewer cashiers), reduce time for register balancing at the end of the day, and reduce errors in keying. There will certainly be savings in inventory control as well. As items are purchased, the system can be programmed to issue restock and reorder commands when necessary. Such commands could be sent over a communication network directly to an automated warehouse where a local computer would select the requested products in preparation for delivery.

By 1982 over 5000 supermarkets across the nation were equipped with scanners. This figure represents about one-quarter of the total, and it is predicted that before the end of this decade nearly all will have scanners. The impact on supermarket labor has been estimated by a variety of sources, with high loss figures coming from unions and low ones from the trade organizations. One study suggests that direct job losses will be minimal, but that job opportunities will be significantly reduced.[23] Many full time workers are being asked to accept reduced hours of employment. This change is important because supermarkets have traditionally served as a source of jobs for women, unskilled workers, minority groups, and part time workers. Even with an expanding food market, the number of jobs will increase more slowly because of the introduction of scanners.

THE RESPONSE OF UNIONS

With all their faults, trade unions have done more for humanity than any other organization of men that ever existed. They have done more for decency, for honesty, for education, for the betterment of the race, for the developing of character in man, than any other association of men.[24]

Labor unions are the worst thing that ever struck the earth because they take away a man's independence.[25]

Unions have their supporters and their detractors, but they are concerned about the welfare of a large segment of the work force. This segment is currently diminishing, however. Their activities represent an attempt to protect the workers they represent from threats to job security and loss of benefits. How they perceive the challenge of technology is indicative of the feelings of the workers themselves as opposed to the intentions of management.

The unions have been caught in a difficult position. Faced with the loss of jobs during the recession of the early 1980s, unions have negotiated contracts in which hard-won concessions gained over the years have been given up. They have tried to protect current jobs for a reduced work force. In this context, technological change has not been in the forefront of most unions' bargaining positions. However, for some unions the handwriting has been on the wall for quite a while. After a series of bitter strikes, the printers' union in New York settled for a contract that essentially means the end of the industry and the union. Typographers and printers have fallen victim to computerized composition and typesetting. At large newspapers reporters can enter their stories directly into the computer, where they can be edited and subsequently put together in the newspaper's layout. In a significant technological innovation, the computer-stored information can be sent across the country, and such papers as the *New York Times* and *USA Today* can be printed simultaneously in many parts of the United States.

The ability to transmit work over long distances can introduce a dramatic new factor in labor negotiations. Unions have recently been attempting to organize office workers, capitalizing in part on a growing concern among workers about the introduction of new computer technology. The Equitable Life Assurance Society's office in Syracuse, New York has been considered, by many observers, a test case of the willingness of female workers confronting automation to turn to unions to protect their rights. Unfortunately, the new technology has significantly weakened the major traditional power of unions— the right to strike. "We can't strike Equitable," said Regina Caruso, a District 925 organizer for the Serivce Employees International Union. "With this technology, they could flick a switch, and the work could be in Kansas City. This changes the whole nature of organizing."[26] Despite these fears, a contract was signed that guaranteed the 54 existing jobs until 1987. Their terms included a 15-minute afternoon break for VDT operators to relieve eye strain, the removal of attitude and attendance from pay setting, and pay increases ranging from 4 to 6 percent.[27]

In the case of the printers, in recognition of the inevitability of computers, the union decided to maintain the current jobs and benefits of its members and accept a gradually reduced work force, with positions lost through attrition. Thus, an old and honorable profession may be in its twilight time. What alternative choices do unions have in confronting technological change? Companies will always reserve the right to make whatever changes in the productive process they deem necessary. Most unions state that they welcome new technology that relieves boredom, replaces workers in dangerous and unpleasant jobs, and increases productivity. The problem is the potential and actual *loss* of jobs. The first step for unions is to develop a comprehensive definition of technological change, including not only new equipment and processes but also new methods of work organization as well. Furthermore, with the multinational nature of many large companies, unions are concerned about the loss of local jobs because of cheaper wages in Third World countries.

Some of the issues that have been addressed in union contracts are the following:[28]

Advance Notice. The union should be given advance notice of technological change and its expected repercussions.

Consultation. Prior to the introduction of new technology, the union and employer must come to an agreement.

Protection against Layoffs. There should be a clear provision to prevent any worker from being dismissed because of technological change.

Income Protection. Workers should not have their wages reduced because of management arguments that less skill is now required for the job.

Transfer Arrangements. Employees displaced by technological change should have greater opportunity to be transferred to new jobs.

Training. Workers should be trained for the new technology whenever possible instead of being displaced by outside workers.

Reduction in Hours of Work. Unions should attempt to reduce the hours of work in order to keep up employment levels.

No Monitoring of Work. Unions should attempt to remove or restrict all forms of electronic or computer surveillance.

Video Display Terminals. Working conditions related to VDTs should be negotiated (see below).

All these are issues of job security and working conditions and are consistent with the traditional concern of labor unions in North America. In Europe, unions are much more radical and are typically allied with political parties. As such, they have taken much stronger stands than their North American counterparts. For example, the British Socialist Workers Party refuses to countenance any actual or potential job losses that result from technological change. They demand ''A written guarantee from management that they will not introduce new technology without the prior agreement of the union membership.''[29] They want the workers themselves to have a say rather than the union leadership. The Swedish approach is perhaps best summed up by the following statement:

Properly applied, technological advance can lay the foundations of social progress. Technological progress is a question of power. It must not be governed by an approach implying that man is gradually becoming a more and more superfluous appendage to machines. Computerization makes many routine jobs unnecessary, but it also generates many new ones. It is trade union members who have to do these jobs and be exposed to the physical and mental stresses involved in computerization. Trade unions must therefore be able to exert profound influence on the manner in which computerization is effected in Sweden.[30]

While the concern with technological change is real, it has taken a back seat to the more immediate problem of simply holding on to jobs in the current economic climate. The threat of job loss because of the use of relatively cheap foreign labor has forced unions into unprecedented compromises. In order to save jobs at General Motors' Packard Electric Division in Warren, Ohio, the union tentatively agreed in 1983 to a contract by which all new employees "will receive only $4.50 per hour in wages and $1.50 worth of benefits . . . less than a third of the normal GM rate of $19.60."[30] Current workers would maintain their regular salaries and the entire work force would be guaranteed job security in the near future. This agreement was seen to be necessary because of low wages paid to Mexican workers and to nonunion workers in the United States. However, "union members rejected the tentative agreement, possibly endangering their job security."[32] Approximately one year later, on December 14, 1984, members ratified a renegotiated agreement by a 77 to 23 percent majority. The new terms guarantee jobs with full pay and benefits to 8,900 workers hired before January 1, 1982. New assembly workers will be hired at an hourly rate of $8.99, compared with $22 for current workers.[33]

Another kind of trade-off that must be made by unions when confronting management's intention to introduce the factory of the future occurred in negotiations associated with General Electric's new plant in Lynn, Mass. GE promised to build a new plant, called a flexible manufacturing center, if the union would agree to the following three changes in working conditions:

1. The standard shifts would be three 12-hour shifts per week followed by four the next, resulting in an average 42-hour work week. Each extra shift is to be considered overtime. Union members had no problem with this point.

2. GE wanted "day work with measurements: the company would establish reasonable and attainable measurements as to how much workers could accomplish in a shift.[34] This concession would be a breakthrough, as no previous contract had given the company this right. The impact within GE itself could be enormous as a result of such a major concession.

3. The last point, somewhat technical, involved a reduction in the number of job categories in the new factory. The result might be that workers would lose previously acquired job status.

The company threatened to build the $52 million plant elsewhere unless these terms were accepted. To sweeten the deal, GE agreed that current jobs would be guaranteed at least for one year, and that it would spend about $450 million over the next six years in the Lynn area. Under pressure from the city council and the local newspaper, and fearing loss of present and future jobs, union members voted to accept the GE offer. Union officials from other locals expressed bitterness over the terms and deplored the situation as "blackmail: 'We'll build a plant here if you give us what we want'."[35] Jonathan Schlefer, a senior editor of *Technology Review*, commented as follows:

Corporate managers will continue to be the sole designers of technology until the public, the press, the politicians realize that technologies can be designed in differ-

ent ways, and until power is more balanced between corporations and the work-force.[36]

Other labor negotiations concluded late in 1984 only reinforced the trend of union concessions being made in order to retain jobs for union members. The settlements of the United Auto Workers (UAW) with Ford and GM introduced a potentially dramatic shift in union strategy. Traditionally, unions have bargained for financial benefits and—to a lesser degree—working conditions. In the United States, management's decisions have been left to management, whereas in the European tradition union representatives often sit on the board of directors. In the new agreement with GM and Ford, the UAW agreed "to set up 'new ventures' funds with which the union and management will jointly develop and launch 'non-traditional' businesses to keep workers employed and increase profits."[37] This new role for unions, called proactive unionism by some, involves them in such management activities as new product design, production technology, new plant locations, and—most daring—employee takeovers of bankrupt companies.

JOB SAFETY: THE VDT CONTROVERSY

Our general conclusion is that eye discomfort, blurred vision and other visual dis-turbances, muscular aches and stress reported among VDT workers are probably not due to anything inherent in VDT technology.[38]

The video or visual display terminal (VDT) is the most common piece of evidence of the increasingly widespread distribution of computers in the workplace and at home. Estimates vary, but there are probably about ten million VDTs in use today and the number is expected to reach thirty million by 1986.[39] Large numbers of workers, mainly women, will be spending many hours in front of VDT screens. Over the years a number of fears have been expressed about possible threats to health from long-term interaction with VDTs. These concerns can be grouped into four main categories: visual, physical, psychological, and radiation-related. The greatest fears have been aroused because of potential genetic defects. A number of incidents have been reported of what appear to be unexpectedly high rates of miscarriages and birth defects among women working with VDTs. At a Sears Computer center in Dallas there were seven miscarriages and one premature infant death in twelve pregnancies in one year. In a two-year period, four of seven babies born to VDT operators at the *Toronto Star* had birth defects.

Subsequent investigations revealed no connection to VDTs, but these studies have been criticized by 9 to 5. The long-term effects of low-level radiation may be hazardous, as some animal experiments have shown.[40] A number of states have been considering leg-islation regulating the use of VDTs, and many unions have attempted to provide working condition rules. Some companies have agreed to transfer pregnant women from VDT stations until they return to work after the birth of their children. The trade association for equipment manufacturers in the United States has been opposed to regulation, fearing developments similar to those overseas: The Swedish and German governments have drawn up standards for the manufacture and use of VDTs. The climate of fear will only disappear when scientific research finds a way to prevent the emission of radiation. Leaded glass screens can be used, or even indirect mirror systems. However, other problems remain.

A number of visual hazards have been reported in connection with the VDT itself, the VDT environment, and the type of work being done. The VDT can cause problems because of the brightness of the screen, the flicker effect, color contrasts, and—probably most significantly—glare from background sources. Many VDT operators have complained about eye strain. The 1983 report of the National Research Council essentially absolves VDTs themselves and blames environmental factors such as poor lighting and glare. One of the panelists, however—Laurence Stark, a neuroophthalmologist at the University of California—characterized the report as a whitewash.

> All the complaints of burning, eyestrain, headache, stinging, watery eyes connected with VDT use are valid claims. Just because you cannot measure visual fatigue does not mean it does not exist.[41]

Associated with the visual problems are physical problems resulting from poor office ergonomics. The term ergonomics, quite popular recently, refers to the design of the workplace to accommodate the person and the machine. Physical problems that can arise from poor design are muscle fatigue, neck and back strain, and a variety of effects of chronic fatigue. Among these are boredom, tiredness, irritability, inattention, and eventually headaches, dizziness, loss of appetite, and insomnia. Many of these conditions can be remedied by such improvements as VDT screens that tilt and rotate, chairs with adjustable back rests and heights, and adequate rest breaks. Some VDT workers have also reported psychological stress resulting from the increased amount of data they must handle, the monitoring of their work, and the reduction of other activities that previously provided variety and interest. Manifestations of psychological stress include high blood pressure and digestive disorders. Solutions here are more difficult to implement because they require more flexible work organization and pose a direct challenge to management's perceived responsibilities.

9 to 5 has made the following recommendations:

> [that] employers design equipment to be adjustable to the worker, not vice versa; regular employer-paid eye exams be provided for all VDT operators; frequent rest breaks be given; and women who plan to become pregnant be given the choice to transfer to non-VDT work at no loss in pay.[42]

The editors of *Microwave News* have noted that "no physical or chemical agent has been shown to emanate from VDTs at levels known to damage living systems."[43] However, the question of damage from long-term exposure to low-frequency radiation remains open. Better working conditions will have a positive effect on the bodies and minds of the women who operate most the VDTs, but more research is needed. Management should demonstrate its concern for the welfare of its employees by designing a safe environment and a humane work regimen.

HOME WORK: ELECTRONIC COTTAGE INDUSTRY?

Yet this is precisely what the new mode of production makes possible: a return to cottage industry on a new, higher, electronic basis, and with it a new emphasis on the home as the center of society.[44]

The phrase "electronic cottage," apparently first used by Alvin Toffler, conjures up visions of people working at home by means of electronic devices and communication networks. It is a preindustrial vision of workers at home, performing piece work that they return upon completion to central locations and pick up new supplies. There are remnants of this mode of labor in the Western world today. In northern Scotland tweed fabrics are woven on home looms. In late 1984, the U.S. Labor Department permitted home knitters to sell their work for profit. (They are still required to observe minimum wage and child labor laws. Much of this work is done in New England and had been illegal since 1942.)[45] With computers and communication networks it is possible for some information processing tasks to be carried out at remote sites. A number of companies have chosen to encourage part of their staff to remain at home while performing their data processing activities. Unorthodox working arrangements are in fact quite common in computer-related work. Programmers have been permitted to set their own hours as long as they complete their jobs satisfactorily.

Proponents of remote office work claim that an increasing number of employees will be working at home because it makes economic sense. Commuting is eliminated, which means savings in fuel costs and time and a general reduction of the stress associated with driving. Employees have increased flexibility for arranging their working hours around their family responsibility. People will be able to choose where they live independently of the need to be close to a job. There must also be advantages for the employer, or new working arrangements will not be implemented. Productivity improvements are supposedly a major reason for physically decentralizing work. Although it is difficult to measure office productivity, one study has shown that increases of 15 percent or more occur with remote work.[46] Employees may be easier to attract if flexible work arrangements are possible. If the number of staff at a central location is reduced, the building rental costs can also be reduced—a saving somewhat offset by increased telephone charges.

The choice is not just between home and office. There are intermediary possibilities, such as satellite work centers in which a division of a company is moved from a central site to a location convenient for many of its employees. A neighborhood work center, financially supported by a number of different companies, could provide computers, facsimile equipment, and telecommunication facilities. All these arrangements represent a shift in the traditional office structure, and problems have arisen even in the early stages. For many women who want a career, there are problems about staying at home. It may appear to be convenient to work at home, but women who work there may not be taken seriously. This problem is a general one for remote workers—if they are out of sight, will they be out of mind at promotion time?

The social organization of the office provides an important social structure for the employee that may be lacking at home. Not to have coworkers available for support may lead to a decrease in enthusiasm and initiative. Team work, an important part of many jobs, will be difficult to simulate at home, although electronic mail and conferencing can help. This isolation from the support structure offered by the other workers can be used to the advantage of management. The formation of workers' organizations and unions will be difficult, if not impossible, under a system of remote work. Management faces problems of monitoring and supervision, putting a premium on selecting employees who have a high degree of self-motivation and self-discipline. In short, although hailed as a breakthrough to new forms of living and working, remote work will also mean new organizational and social structures.

ADJUSTING TO CHANGE

Superfluous workers, some experts call them, and their numbers seem likely to grow, even with an economic recovery, as the nation's economy becomes more automated, as the workplace is reorganized for efficiency, and as companies expand globally to meet foreign competition.[47]

Deskilling and Retraining

Does the introduction of new technology—computer systems, to be specific—raise or lower the overall skills of employees? The pessimistic viewpoint is that the new technology—say, office automation—will certainly raise the skills of some of the workers, but most of the office staff will have a reduced range of responsibilities. Their work will be narrowly constrained to data entry—that is, sitting at a terminal all day, rapidly typing rows and columns of numbers. Under this scenario, skills have been reduced for many of these employees, most of whom are likely to be women. As jobs are deskilled, they are also reclassified and downgraded in terms of wage scales. Thus, entry level jobs will pay less and be less secure, more routine and monotonous. Consistent with this view is the assumption that office managers are always interested in maximizing volume and speed in data processing. The only restraints are such side effects as absenteeism, high turnover, poor quality, or even sabotage. This view justifies the fears of many critics that management wishes to reproduce the factory model in the office.

Many women are concerned that the new automation will reinforce sex segregation in the office. With more women employed in routine jobs, their path for advancement will be much longer and more difficult. In fact, most women will have no opportunity for advancement because there will be no opportunity to improve their skills. On the factory floor, many workers see their future as adjuncts to powerful, computerized machines. Here also deskilling is an issue. Fewer workers will be able to exercise a broad range of skills, and most workers will be narrowly constrained. From a historical point of view, the process of separating the actions of the worker from their planning and organization will culminate in the computerized factory, where very few workers are required. An alternate scheme is to incorporate workers in the planning process in order to make use of their skills at the manufacturing level. This notion raises the whole question of training and retraining.

Even those who wholeheartedly welcome the onset of the computer age agree that there will be job dislocation, that workers will be displaced, and that new jobs will emerge. To be eligible for these new jobs, workers would have to be retrained. Past history has shown that all too frequently, displaced or young workers have been trained for the wrong jobs—wrong in the sense that the new jobs have had a very short existence. Another question is, who pays for the retraining—joint efforts among government, industry, and unions would be necessary, and past performance is not encouraging. Many workers will be too old or too set in their ways to be retrained. Despite these problems, retraining will be necessary, and planning for it should begin as soon as possible.

In the 1984 agreement between the United Auto Workers and Ford and GM, retraining was included, to the degree that the union would be involved in "the movement of workers from plant to plant and job to job. . .and will jointly administer retraining and other funds."[48] GM had previously established a New Technology Training program at its highly automated Buick and Oldsmobile assembly plant at Wentzville, Missouri. More than 400 workers—many of whom had been displaced when a nearby plant closed—have completed the basic course of 1,000 hours. The director of the program has noted as follows:

> ". . . basic training involves such things as math and physics skills, electronics, programmable controllers, robotics, data communications, and an introduction to minicomputers. . . . But we also try to make sure he has enough of a foundation to allow us to build on his education as we bring more technology into the workplace."[49]

Some critics have argued that plans by individual companies, even large ones like GM, are inadequate for the substantial number of workers requiring retraining. In 1982 Congress passed the Job Training Partnership Act (JTPA), which became operational the following year. It is concerned with the economically and culturally disadvantaged, but Title III does include provisions for retraining workers. Basically, JTPA's main purpose is to encourage the private sector to increase its involvement in retraining, by allocating block grants to states that cooperate in such programs. About 500,000 were enrolled in the first six months, and over 11,000 employers cooperated with government agencies. Critics of JTPA say it is too limited, both in money and comprehensiveness. They believe that what is necessary is a training program in the context of a national plan for dealing with the effects of large-scale automation.

One other government plan, managed by an agency called the Employment Training Panel (ETP), operates in California. It represents something of a breakthrough. Unemployment insurance (UI) funds are used to retrain people rather than provide benefits for the unemployed. ETP focusses "exclusively on experienced workers who are either un-employed or soon-to-be-displaced, rather than on training the hard core unemployed and new entrants to the labor force."[50] The EPT also tries to work with employers to help current workers deal with new technology. Because the plan does not deal with the hard-core unemployed, it is open to criticism that it is not really confronting difficult problems. Nevertheless, for some companies and employees ETP has been successful enough to inspire New York state to implement its own version.

New Jobs in Data Processing

While jobs have been lost in many areas of the economy because of computers, computer-based work throughout the economy has resulted in many new jobs. Most of these have been created for key entry operators, computer operators, programmers, and systems analysts. Between 1980 and 1990 the number of employees in all these jobs should increase by 54 percent, or about 1.7 million, to a total of 3.1 million.[51] The major growth area is expected to be in the computer operator category, largely as a result of the very rapid growth in the number of relatively small computer installations. Systems analyst positions are estimated to increase to over 500,000, and the programmer population will grow to more than 300,000. Earlier estimates were more pessimistic, but actual job figures from the 1970 and the 1980 census justify more optimism for the 1980s.

Additional information from the years 1970 and 1980 shows that the percentage of women employees has increased in all four job categories, but most significantly that of computer operators—from 29 to 59 percent. The increase has been less dramatic for programmers but is still significant: 23 to 31 percent. Finally, women are in the over-whelming majority in the low-level data-entry jobs—90 percent in 1970 and 92 percent in 1980. It is an interesting bit of computer history, that when the first electronic computer, ENIAC, was built, it was expected that programming would be such a simple and straight-forward task that women could do it. The hard part had supposedly been completed—that is, the actual building of a machine. It was soon discovered that programming was indeed a challenging and difficult exercise. At this point, women were discouraged from entering the programming profession and men were encouraged to the point that pro-gramming became essentially a male profession. The pendulum is slowly swinging back towards equality for men and women.

In the opinion of some critics, programming activities have been organized along factory lines.[52] There is a division of labor, in a hierarchical fashion, and the programmers at the bottom are only responsible for transforming small, well-defined tasks into computer programs. They are not responsible for deciding what to do, how to do it, and how to decompose a large complicated problem into a number of small easily handled ones. Most programmers, especially in large companies, can be compared to workers on a standard assembly line. Defenders of this method say that by its very nature the programming process requires an organizational structure under which complex tasks can be suitably decomposed. Even though the structure that has evolved may reflect the traditional views of management, it may be the best way discovered so far to develop large programs.

Confronting Possible
Large-Scale Unemployment

Wassily W. Leontief, Nobel laureate in economics for 1973, has long been concerned with the large-scale operation of national economies and has developed very powerful analytical tools called input-output methods. Leontief believes that recent developments in computers and robots will lead to serious unemployment, as machines replace more and more people. He has argued that the usual historical means of minimizing or at least controlling unemployment resulting from technological change, has been a reduction of the work week, except for in the recent past.[53] In 1860, the average number of hours worked per week was 67. By 1930 it had fallen to about 42, and during the years of the Depression (1933–1940), it fell to about 37. The demands of the second World War saw a rise to about 45. Since 1950 it has remained stable at about 40.

Hours per week could only be substantially reduced if take-home pay did not fall—otherwise, workers could not afford to work fewer hours. Only through parallel increases in productivity—mainly because of technological innovation—could take-home wages remain high as hours fall. Such a process of reducing hours while maintaining income levels—either through salary of increased benefits—must continue, in Leontief's opinion, and fact must be encouraged by government planning. A reduced work week raises many issues, such as how to deal with increased leisure and how to redefine the relation between dignity and work. The concern with how people will use increased leisure is probably a non-issue. It is usually the rich who are most concerned about how the poor or ill-educated will be able to enjoy newly found free time. With respect to the latter point, people will perhaps gradually learn to define themselves in ways that do not necessarily depend solely on work. Perhaps the opening question between two strangers will no longer be ''What do you do?''

FINAL COMMENTS

A major study on manufacturing automation was recently released by the Office of Technology Assessment (OTA) of the U.S. Congress. The report uses the term programmable automation (PA) to include computer-aided design, robotics and computer integrated manufacturing, and computer-aided techniques for management. The study identifies three major themes, as follows:

1. *Programmable Automation is an important and powerful set of tools, but is not a panacea for problems in manufacturing* [See Chapter 12]. . . .

2. *The changes in national employment induced by Programmable Automation will not be massive in the near term (i.e., the remainder of the 1980s). . . .*

3. *The impact of Programmable Automation on the work environment is one of the most significant, yet largely neglected issues.*[54]

Item 2, the impact on employment, is very difficult to predict: "Data available support only inferences as to the general directions of likely occupational and industry employment change."[55] After examining and evaluating a great deal of evidence, the report predicts the following long-term trends:

- *Demand for engineers and computer scientists, technicians, and mechanics, repairers, and installers on the whole will rise. . . .*
- *Demand for craftworkers (excluding mechanics), operatives, and laborers—especially the least skilled doing most of the routine work—will fall.* [*Emphasis added.*]
- *Demand for clerical personnel will fall; and*
- *Demand for upper-level managers and technical sales and service personnel will rise.*[56]

Beyond these forecasts, it is expected that blue collar workers will constitute a smaller proportion of total manufacturing employment. Another observation is very revealing: The growth of PA industries is not likely to provide an important source of employment for people displaced from traditional manufacturing jobs. Manufacturers of PA equipment are likely to use PA in their own plants and offices.

If the effect on employment is difficult to evaluate, it is no easier to determine how the work environment will be changed. The introduction of advanced industrial automation may cause management to increase its concern for the well-being of its workers. An improved work environment, together with PA, will result in a significant increase in productivity, which after all is the reason for the proposed expenditure of time and money. However, problems must be anticipated, especially with respect to such psychological effects as stress and boredom. New responsibility for monitoring complex equipment and loss of direct involvement with production can cause increased levels of stress for people. It is very important that management-labor relations be well-tuned to such real and potential workplace problems.

Another major recent report, by the United Nations' International Labour Office, has provided some insight into the possible changes in the office. Although office automation is expected to be labor-saving, so far its major effect has been reduced demand for low-level clerks rather than a reduction in overall employment. Since there has been an increase in productivity, which has led to expansion in businesses, the number of jobs has actually increased. How long such a trend will continue is not clear. In European countries, high costs of captial investment combined with sluggish economies have lowered the rate at which the new technology is being introduced. What is clear is that skill levels in the office will shift. Increased numbers of women will be employed at the data entry level, speed and accuracy of typing will no longer be valued, and the career paths of many women will be detoured.

SUMMARY

Of all the issues associated with technology, especially computers, the most important is work—how much, and what kind. The subject of jobs and computers will be with us for a very long time, and all will be affected.

The relation between technology and work is a complex one. Historically, except for periods of worldwide economic dislocation, technological innovation has not decreased the number of jobs. The open question is whether or not computers are a fundamentally different kind of technology. The contributions of Frederick Taylor and Henry Ford were key to the development of the assembly line. The separation of actual work from planning has serious consequences for workers. The process continues, with the introduction of robots into the factory and computer networks into the office. The voices of the workers themselves should be listened to. What workers really want, whether or not they are dissatisfied, and the role of computers in their lives are issues of concern to society at large.

Which jobs will be most affected by computers and how? Granted that many jobs will be lost, where will the new jobs come from? Will there be enough? Blue collar jobs are decreasing. Service and information jobs are increasing. Agricultural jobs are now only about 3 percent of the total. Fewer people are producing the products and food for society.

How does office automation affect the social organization of the office? Since women represent by far the largest number of office workers, they will be most affected. Will their jobs be more interesting, or less? Will their skills be broadened and improved, or narrowed and decreased?

Unions are dedicated to the welfare of their members. Unfortunately, in recent difficult economic times job security has overridden considerations of working conditions, wages, and other benefits. However, some unions have attempted to include technological issues in their contracts.

Questions have been raised about the physical, psychological, and long-term genetic effects of video display terminals. At the very least, a concern with glare, background lighting, and seating position is warranted.

With computers and communication networks, it may be possible for office work to be distributed. Savings in fuel costs, office rental costs, and driving times may convince both employers and employees that working at home is the wave of the future.

As a result of new computer technology, many jobs will be deskilled, and many workers may have less opportunity for advancement. Retraining programs are one attempt to address this problem. Many new jobs have been created in connection with the new technology—most of them in data processing, and most of them for women. The economist Wassily Leontief has urged that governments plan for a reduced work week in response to the serious unemployment he foresees as a result of increased automation.

NOTES

1. E. P. Thompson, *The Making of the English Working Class,* (Middlesex, England: Penguin, 1980), p. 600.

2. Paul Attewell and James Rule, ''Computing and Organizations: What We Know and What We Don't Know,'' Communications of the *Association for Computing Machinery,* December 1984, p. 1185.

3. James O'Toole, *Making America Work* (New York: Continuum, 1981), p. 5.

4. Phil Stallings, as quoted in Studs Terkel, *Working,* (New York: Avon, 1975), p. 223.

5. Ibid.

6. Chuck Bradley, as quoted in Stephen Singular, ''A Robot and Liking It, Thanks,'' *Psychology Today,* March 1983, p. 22.

7. As Quoted in Daniel Goleman, ''The Electronic Rorschach,'' *Psychology Today,* February 1983, p. 41.

8. Harry Braverman, *Labor and Monopoly Capital: The Degradation of Work in the Twentieth Century* (New York: Monthly Review Press, 1974).

9. Adam Smith, *The Wealth of Nations,* 5th ed. (London: Methuen, 1930), pp. 6–7.

10. Karl Marx, *Capital,* vol. 1 (New York: Vintage Books, 1977), p. 589.

11. Braverman, *Labor and Monopoly Capital,* pp. 112–121.

12. Ibid., p. 147.

13. Abraham H. Maslow, *Towards a Psychology of Being* (Princeton: Van Nostrand, 1962).

14. A. F. Ehrbar, ''Grasping the New Unemployment,'' *Fortune,* May 16, 1983, pp. 106–112. Charles P. Alexander, ''The New Economy,'' *Time,* May 30, 1983, pp. 60–64, 69–72.

15. *Employment Projections for 1995.* U.S. Dept. of Labor, Bureau of Labor Statistics Bulletin 2197 (Washington, D.C., March 1984), p. 23.

16. ''America Rushes to High Tech for Growth,'' *Business Week,* March 28, 1983, pp. 84–88, 90, 94–95, 98.

17. Paul Strassman, vice-president, Information Product Division of Xerox, as quoted in Englebert Kirchner, ''At the Mercy of Machines,'' *Datamation,* September 1982, p. 252.

18. Karen Nussbaum, president of 9 to 5, as quoted in Kirchner, ''At the Mercy of Machines,'' p. 252.

19. Edward W. Gore, Jr., in *McGraw-Hill Encyclopedia of Science and Technology,* vol. 14, 5th ed. (New York: McGraw-Hill, 1982), p. 708.

20. Braverman, *Labor and Monoply Capital,* p. 90.

21. Sud Ingle, *Quality Circles Master Guide* (Englewood Cliffs: Prentice-Hall, 1982), p. 17.

22. Edward E. Lawler III and Susan A. Mohrman, ''Quality Circles after the Fad,'' *Harvard Business Review,* January/February 1985, pp. 64–71.

23. Bruce Gilchrist and Arlana Shenkin, ''The Impact of Scanners on Employment in Supermarkets,'' Communications of the *Association for Computing Machinery,* July 1982, pp. 441–5.

24. Clarence Darrow, in the *Railroad Trainman,* November 1909.

25. Henry Ford (booklet distributed to Ford employees during CIO drive), as quoted in *Time*, August 20, 1945.

26. Regina Canuso, as quoted in William Serrin, ''Computers in the Office Change Labor Relations,'' *The New York Times,* May 22, 1984, p. 11.

27. Bob Arnold, ''Labor Gets a Little Toe in the Office Door,'' *Business Week,* December 3, 1984, p. 38.

28. ''Contract Language for Technological Change and Video Display Terminals,'' Canadian Union of Public Employees (Ottawa: October 1982), pp. 6–13.

29. Chris Harmon, ''How to Fight the New Technology,'' in Forester, Tom, ed., *The Microelectronics Revolution* (Cambridge, Mass.: MIT Press, 1981), p. 405.

30. 1979 Congress of the Swedish Central Organization for Salaried Employees, final report, as quoted in Dennis Chamot and Michael D. Dymmel, *Cooperation or Conflict— European Experiences with Technological Change at the Workplace* (Washington, D.C.: AFL-CIO Dept. for Professional Employees, March 1981), p. 5.

31. ''The Revolutionary Wage Deal at GM's Packard Electric,'' *Business Week,* August 29, 1983, pp. 54–55.

32. ''The 'Revolution' in Warren, Ohio'' (response to a letter), *Business Week,* September 19, 1983, p. 7.

33. John Hoerr and Dan Cook, ''A Pioneering Pact Promises Jobs for Life,'' *Business Week,* December 31, 1984, pp. 48–49.

34. Jonathan Schlefer, ''Negotiating the Factory of the Future,'' *Technology Review,* January 1985, pp. 24–27.

35. John Nickell, union official, as quoted in ''Swapping Work Rules for Jobs at GE's 'Factory of the Future','' *Business Week,* September 10, 1984, p. 46.

36. Schlefer, ''Negotiating the Factory of the Future,'' p. 27.

37. John Hoerr, ''How Unions Are Helping to Run the Business,'' *Business Week,* December 24, 1984, p. 69.

38. Edward Rinalducci, chairman, National Research Council panel on the effects of VDTs on eyesight, as quoted in ''Screen Test: Discounting VDT Hazards,'' *Time,* July 25, 1983, p. 44.

39. ''No Truce Ahead in the War over VDT Safety,'' *Business Week,* July 25, 1983, p. 85.

40. Eric Lerner, ''Experiments Show Microwaves Can Damage Chromosomes,'' *The Institute, News Supplement to IEEE Spectrum,* August 1983, pp. 1, 8.

41. Laurence Stark, as quoted in ''Screen Test: Discounting VDT Hazards,'' p. 44.

42. "The Human Factor: The Consumer Guide to Word Processors" (a 9 to 5 publication), as quoted in Willie Schatz, "Do CRTs Kill?" *Datamation,* July 1983, p. 56.

43. Louis Slesin and Martha Zybko, "Video Display Terminals: Health and Safety," *Microwave News,* 1983, p. 1.

44. Alvin Toffler, *The Third Wave* (New York: Bantam, 1981), p. 194.

45. "Home Work," *Fortune,* December 10, 1984, pp. 10–11.

46. Jack Nilles, "Teleworking: Working Closer to Home," *Technology Review,* April 1982, pp. 56–62.

47. William Serrin, "Recovery Irrelevant to Workers Left Behind," *The New York Times,* September 4, 1983, p. 1.

48. John Hoerr, "How Unions are Helping to Run the Business," p. 70.

49. Dave Evans, as quoted in Dwight B. Davis, "Workplace High Tech Spurs Retraining Efforts," *High Technology,* November 1984, p. 62.

50. Joan M. O'Connell and John Hoerr, "There Really Are Jobs after Retraining," *Business Week,* January 28, 1985, p. 76.

51. Bruce Gilchrist, Ates Dagli, and Arlana Shenkin, "The DP Population Boom," *Datamation,* September 1983, pp. 100–102, 104, 108, 110.

52. See Philip Kraft, *Programmers and Managers* (New York: Springer-Verlag, 1977).

53. Wassily W. Leontief, "The Distribution of Work and Income," *Scientific American,* September 1982, pp. 188–190, 192, 194–195, 188–189, 202–204.

54. *Computerized Manufacturing Automation: Employment, Education, and the Workplace,* U.S. Congress, Office of Technology Assessment, OTA-CIT-235 (Washington, D.C., April 1984), pp. 2–3.

55. Ibid., p. 6.

56. Ibid., p. 7.

ADDITIONAL READINGS

Introduction

Rule, James and Paul Attewell, "Computing and Organizations: What We Know and What We Don't Know." *Communications of the Association for Computing Machinery,* December 1984, pp. 1184–1192.

Experiences of Workers

Aronowitz, Stanley. *False Promises.* New York: McGraw-Hill, 1974.

Garson, Barbara. *All the Livelong Day.* Middlesex, England: Penguin, 1977.

O'Toole, James. *Work and the Quality of Life.* Cambridge, Mass.: MIT Press, 1974.

Rice, Berkeley. "The Hawthorne Effect: Persistence of a Flawed Theory." *Psychology Today,* February 1982, pp. 70, 72–4.

Computers and Employment

Briefs, Ulrich. "The Effects of Computerization on Human Work—New Directions for Computer Use in the Work-Place." In A. Mowshowitz, ed., *Human Choice and Computers 2*. Amsterdam: North-Holland, 1980.

Cougar, J. Daniel. "Circular Solutions." *Datamation,* January 1983, pp. 135–136, 138, 140, 142.

Tepperman, Jean. *Not Servants, Not Machines*. Boston: Beacon, 1976.

"The Mechanization of Work." *Scientific American* (special issue), September 1982.

"A Work Revolution in U.S. Industry." *Business Week,* May 16, 1983, pp. 100–103, 106, 108, 110.

The Response of Unions

Edid, Maralyn. "How Power Will Be Balanced on Saturn's Shop Floor." *Business Week,* August 5, 1985, pp. 65–66.

Job Safety: The VDT Controversy

King, Lorraine. "Users Are People Too." *Datamation,* April 15, 1985, pp. 104–106, 108.

Makower, Joel. *Office Hazards*. Washington, D.C.: Tilden, 1981.

Wagenaar, Willem A. "The Psychological Costs of Master Computer." *Datamation,* July 1, 1985, pp. 157, 159.

Home Work: Electronic Cottage Industry?

Olson, Margrethe H. "Remote Office Work: Changing Work Patterns in Space and Time." *Communications of the Association for Computing Machinery,* March 1983, pp. 182–187.

Vitalari, Nicholas P., Venkatesh, Alladi, and Gronhaug, Kjell. "Computing in the Home: Shifts in the Time Allocation Patterns of Households." *Communications of the Association for Computing Machinery,* May 1985, pp. 512–522.

Wiegner, Kathleen K. and Paris, Ellen. "A Job with a View." *Forbes,* September 2, 1983, pp. 143–147, 150.

Adjusting to Change

Leontief, Wassily. "The Choice of Technology." *Scientific American,* June 1985, pp. 37–45.

Werneke, Diane. *Microelectronics and Office Jobs: The Impact of the Chip on Women's Unemployment*. United Nations: International Labour Office. Geneva, 1983.

11

BUSINESS AND GOVERNMENT

*T*he business of America is business.

◇ *Calvin Coolidge, Address to the Society of American Newspaper Editors, January 17, 1925.* ◇

INTRODUCTION

In Chapter 4, a variety of applications of computers in the business world were presented and discussed. In Chapter 7, a similar exercise was carried out for the role of computers in government. The primary purpose in each of these cases was to focus on specific innovative uses within a given domain. Of course, many information processing problems do not respect arbitrary boundaries. Several issues naturally reside in the murky area between government and business.

The relationship between business and government has been long and complex. Most companies wish to pursue their activities with minimal interference from government. Government has a variety of responsibilities, among them the creation of a climate in which companies may compete openly and the protection of its citizens' welfare. To these ends, governments have to pass antitrust and consumer protection legislation. In countries where the state owns and manages all the companies, the goals of these companies and the people are taken to be indistinguishable. And even in a free enterprise system, government has found it necessary, over the years, to intervene in the marketplace in order to ensure that all companies have a fair chance to compete. The following is a list of relevant issues:

> *Antitrust Cases.* The U.S. government charged IBM with antitrust violations in a suit that lasted 13 years until it was finally dropped in January of 1982.

Regulation of the Telephone Industry. Up to fairly recently, long distance telephone lines were a monopoly run by AT&T (American Telephone and Telegraph). In January of 1982, AT&T agreed to separate itself from a number of local telephone companies under an agreement arranged by the Federal courts. The agreement took effect on January 1, 1984.

Industry Standards. The government plays an important role in helping to set standards in the computer and communication industries (and other areas as well).

Legal Protection of Software and Hardware. The government protects programs by such means as copyright and patent laws (as discussed in Chapter 8).

Protection of Privacy. Issues arising from the growth in the use of computer-based information systems have led to problems and legislation.

Electronic Funds Transfer Systems (EFTS). Future regulation of the banking and financial industries must take into account the increasing use of computer and communication systems for banking services.

Transborder Data Flows. As information becomes a major resource, governments must develop policies to control the flow of information across national borders. This process is complicated by differing national policies on privacy and freedom of information.

Technology Transfer. Individual countries are concerned with protecting their technological developments. In the United States this concern covers both economic competitors such as Japan and political ones such as the Soviet Union. In the United States open discussion of technical issues is a way of life, and restrictions will be resisted.

National Industrial Policy. Many voices have been raised proposing solutions to economic difficulties in the United States. One important proposal is that the government should formulate a plan for future industrial development.

Thus, the federal government must intrude into the marketplace from time to time. In general, its policy is to set rules for the players, monitor the resulting performance, and take specific actions only if violations occur. This is the usual procedure for competitive industries such as computers, automobiles, and household appliances. In regulated monopolies such as the telephone system and radio and television stations, the government has traditionally exerted control by the issuance of licenses, their renewals, and the setting of rates. There has been much debate about the proper role of government, which acts from a variety of motives, ranging from the accommodation of public opinion to the exercising of a particular political philosophy.

The computer industry has grown very rapidly since 1945 and no company has been more successful than International Business Machines (IBM). In fact, IBM was the leading U.S. company in terms of profits in 1984, about $6.3 billion on sales of about $46 billion. As a further indication of its dynamism and flexibility, IBM became the world leader in income from sales of personal computers in 1983, having just entered the market two years earlier. In one of the final acts of the Johnson administration, in early 1969 IBM was charged with a variety of antitrust violations. After much expense on both sides, the charges were finally dropped thirteen years later. How IBM's domination of the computer market was achieved and maintained was an important issue in the government's suit.

The other major government suit of the late 1970s and early 1980s was directed against AT&T. ''Ma Bell,'' as it was sometimes called, had been a gigantic company composed of a number of local telephone companies, a long-distance service, a manufacturing division, Western Electric, and a world-famous research facility, Bell Labs. During the 1970s, AT&T's monopoly over long-distance service was challenged, and the result was a consent agreement between the company and the federal courts that required AT&T to divest itself of its local telephone companies. AT&T currently has two major divisions: AT&T Communications and AT&T Technologies. Furthermore, it is now free to compete in the computer communications market. Thus, the two giants of the American economy, AT&T and IBM, will begin to compete along a number of fronts. The consequences could be quite staggering.

Since money plays such an important role in our lives, the new developments in banking and bill paying will have an important impact. Already, automatic teller machines (ATMs) are everywhere and are changing long-established banking habits. Additional changes taking place now include: point-of-sale terminals (POS terminals), debit cards, and regional and national banking networks. Several social issues naturally arise with the growth in electronic banking (usually called electronic funds transfer systems, EFTS)—among these are privacy, new possibilities for large scale theft and sabotage, system reliability, reduced competition, and consumer protection.

The flow of information around the world via communication networks has become an important factor in the conduct of international business. This development coincides with the growth in multinational corporations and their increasing dependence on the rapid and efficient transmission of information. Problems arise because countries have different regulations with respect to data protection. Furthermore, since the United States is the major world power in both computers and communications, there may be some resistance to its activities in this area. International agreements will be necessary to protect the interests of individual countries. The host of factors associated with the worldwide flow of information is usually referred to as trans-border data flows (TBDF).

There are at least two areas in which government initiatives are somewhat more controversial. Both can be seen as involving responses to actual or perceived threats to America's industrial superiority. The first relates to what is called technology transfer— the copying of new technology developed in the United States by both economic competitors and political enemies. To carry out international trade on a grand scale while protecting such technological developments as chip design and computer architecture is a difficult task. Recently there have even been attempts to restrict the dissemination of scientific results—especially in data encryption—for fear they will be used by political enemies. For a nation built upon principles of openness and free exchange of information, such attempts are seen by many as a serious threat to academic freedom.

The second response by the government has been called a *national industrial policy*. In response to economic challenges from abroad, many economists have urged the development of a national plan to maintain economic superiority. The centerpiece of most proposals is a national resolve to continue world leadership in computers and microelectronics. It is felt that unless a policy is enunciated, encouraged, and carried out, other countries—Japan in particular—that depend upon cooperation among government, industry, and labor will overtake the United States. Except in times of war, national mobilization has not been a hallmark of the United States system of government. Nevertheless, many important voices—including political ones—have been heard, and preliminary steps have been taken to stimulate cooperative research ventures.

While the role of government in the United States has been to aid business, new technological developments in computer and communication applications have complicated and altered this role. Should government become an active partner with business in stimulating the economy? Should the telecommunications industry, formerly the sole preserve of AT&T, be completely deregulated and changed from a monopoly to free competition? The answer to this question, as given by the actions of the Reagan administration, is yes. Should a company as dominant as IBM be permitted to become even more so? The answers are not simple, and the consequences will be far-reaching.

INDUSTRY REGULATION

> *What is good for the country is good for General Motors and what's good for General Motors is good for the country.*[1]

The U.S. government has recognized two major forms of environments in which businesses can operate. One is the typical free marketplace situation in which companies compete against one another. The other is a monopoly situation, in which the government permits a single company to operate without competition, under an agreement that its rates will be regulated. Up to fairly recently the telephone industry was the prime example of a regulated monopoly. An intermediate form is represented by the radio and television industries. Individual stations must apply for licenses, which are renewed at regular intervals if no violations occur. Governments have seen fit to try to ensure that the competition in the open marketplace is as unrestricted as possible. For example, in 1890 Congress passed the Sherman Antitrust Act in reaction to the activities of large railway and industrial trusts. In later years various companies—such as Alcoa Aluminum, American Tobacco, and Hughes Tool—were charged wtih antitrust violations. The longest antitrust case to date involved IBM.

IBM and the Computer Industry

> *Our industry is healthy and competitive, and IBM has not violated the antitrust laws.*[2]

On January 17, 1969, the last possible day it could take action, the Justice Department of the Johnson administration launched an antitrust suit against IBM. Almost thirteen

years later, on January 8, 1982, the Justice Department of the Reagan administration dropped the longest antitrust suit in history. In the interim, many millions of dollars were spent in legal fees, 66 million pages of documents were collected, and IBM was somewhat restrained in its activities. The government originally charged IBM with monopolizing the computer industry. As IBM was the dominant company in the industry with a market share ranging from 83 percent in 1961 to 70 percent in 1972, there was some reason for the charge. In 1969 the mainfame computer was dominant, and IBM was preeminent, as the percentages show.

A number of theories have been proposed to explain how IBM jumped to the lead in the early years of the computer industry and went on to extend it. It is generally recognized that IBM's success does not derive from its technological innovations. Other companies introduced commercial computers before IBM, but could not maintain their leadership. The important point seems to be that once the technological factor has been accounted for, other issues are more significant to success. Among these are marketing, sales and support staff, pricing policy, economies of manufacturing, educational discounts, and sheer size.

IBM's strength has always been its marketing ability, complemented by a conscientious and hard-working sales and service staff. For most people the name IBM is synonomous with computers. Within the industry, the reputation of IBM for reliability, service, and support is unparalleled. It may not have the most advanced line of computers, but customers have always been assured that the company is responsive to their needs, service people will be there when needed, and if competitors offer something new, IBM will not be far behind. By virtue of being the largest company, IBM sets industry standards; that is, competitors challenging IBM have had to compete within the guidelines defined by it. Whether this is a good or bad thing is debatable: on the one hand, standards do introduce an important measure of stability; on the other hand, a premature introduction of standards can stifle innovation. In any case, IBM has certainly been a stabilizing force.

Another factor contributing to IBM's success has been its use of educational discounts to encourage universities to purchase its equipment. This strategy has had a twofold effect: a generation of university students was trained on IBM equipment, and the universities carried out their research using this equipment. When they graduated, these students influenced the purchasing of computers in their companies. IBM thus achieved an important foothold in the rapidly growing computer industry. Other companies followed suit, especially Digital Equipment Corporation (DEC), but IBM reaped most of the rewards. The widespread use of IBM computers has meant that a considerable amount of research has been done on them. Both teaching and research were helped immeasurably by another IBM achievement: the development, distribution, and maintenance of the first important programming language, FORTRAN. There is no doubt that for most students and their teachers, FORTRAN and programming were synonomous. Again, other companies were forced to follow IBM's lead by encouraging the use of FORTRAN on their machines.

Since it is the undisputed leader in the industry, IBM's every move, announced or predicted, has been carefully watched and evaluated. This situation has given IBM extraordinary power in manipulating the market to suit its own needs. The government's antitrust case depended, in part, on proving that certain practices of IBM in controlling the computer industry were illegal. For example, when competitors began marketing new models that were faster and cheaper than the current IBM versions, IBM might announce a price cut or its own new models. Generally customers were forced to wait until the details of IBM's new machines were released. Making inroads into IBM's domination was not easy under the best of conditions. In order to convince an IBM customer to switch, a price reduction in equipment would not be sufficient. It was necessary to guarantee that existing programs would continue to run properly on the new computer. Nevertheless, IBM's share of the market did slowly diminish. In response to the government's charges, IBM argued that its practices were commonly accepted in other businesses, that it did not really control the market, and that in such a technically active field no single company could ever maintain control very long.

After almost 13 years, the government finally dropped the case. William F. Baxter, Assistant Attorney General in charge of the antitrust division of the Justice Department, stated: ''The government is not likely to win this case. Even if it won, there is no relief I could recommend in good conscience.''[3] During the trial some had suggested that IBM be broken up into a number of smaller independent companies. Others had argued that these new companies would still be larger than their competitors and even more aggressive than the monolithic IBM.

It had been felt that IBM had assumed a much less competitive stance during the years of the trial, to avoid the possibility of further charges. While IBM appeared to be dormant, though, there was considerable ferment below the surface. The best example of the ''new'' IBM is its stunning achievement in the personal computer market. From its introduction of the PC (Personal Computer) in 1981, IBM took the lead in dollar value of personal computers sold in 1983. In the office, IBM has almost a 50 percent share of the installed PC base, with Apple holding 13 percent (Apple's share in 1981 was 42 percent). The IBM name once again demonstrated its worth. First-time buyers found comfort in dealing with a company that had a proven track record and was not likely to go out of business. In order to survive in the personal computer market, it became necessary for IBM's competitors to market PC-compatible machines.

A whole industry has come into being that produces equipment compatible with IBM's. Companies in this market are referred to as PCM's, Plug Compatible Manufacturers. Only the existence of a relatively stable industry, guaranteed by such a major company as IBM, would encourage the growth of PCM's. Industries dominated by one or two large companies are certainly more stable but perhaps less innovative. In the personal computer market, IBM observed Apple's success and risk-taking and then made its own move. The only substantial computer market that IBM failed to recognize was minicomputers, where DEC is dominant. Otherwise its success has been remarkable. Those who favor minimal government involvement in business point to the computer industry as an example of a successful and innovative field. Even with the IBM giant, there has been room for Silicon Valley.

AT&T and the Telephone Industry

Mr. Watson, come here; I want you.[4]

The American Telephone and Telegraph Company has been referred to as the biggest company on earth, and it is not an exaggeration. On January 1, 1984, AT&T underwent a dramatic change, which will have a signficant impact on society. The combination of computers and communication systems is rapidly changing the way we live and work. The distinction between the processing of data by computers and the transmission of data by communication systems is becoming blurred. What is the role of AT&T and its competitors in this process?

Alexander Graham Bell invented the telephone in 1876. Bell Telephone Company, the predecessor of AT&T, was founded on July 8, 1877. Under the leadership of Theodore Vail, a shrewd and visionary businessman, AT&T was formed in 1885, after an early battle with Western Union. It had purchased Western Electric as its manufacturing division and forced Western Union to withdraw completely from the telephone business. The company began a period of rapid growth, stringing telephone lines across the country, fighting off competitors, and purchasing independent telephone companies. By 1910, it had even achieved control of Western Union. In 1913, under the threat of antitrust action, an understanding with the Justice Department was reached, the Kingsbury Commitment, by which AT&T pomised to sell its Western Union stock, desist from purchasing any additional competitors, and permit interconnection with independent companies. After the passage in 1921 of the Willis-Graham Act, which excluded telephone mergers from antitrust charges (if they were approved by the regulatory agencies), AT&T launched a new wave of acquisitions until by 1932 its market share had reached 79 percent.

In order to protect its position, AT&T strongly advocated regulation, arguing that where there was no serious competition public control should be in force. It prospered under the regulatory system, which after 1934 included the Federal Communications Commission (FCC). In practice, regulation precluded the entrance of competitors and protected AT&T's monopoly. In 1956, after several years of dealing with a new antitrust suit filed in 1949, AT&T and the Justice Department agreed to a Consent Decree that generally accepted AT&T's position that the basic issues of the suit should be resolved by Congress. Existing arrangements were to continue, except that AT&T was not permitted to engage in any businesses other than the furnishing of common carrier communications services. Thus, AT&T and its subsidiary, Western Electric, could only be involved in regulated services. This seemed to confirm AT&T's mandate, but the new age of computer communications was fast approaching and AT&T was excluded.

Challenges to AT&T began to appear. Besides the telephone, there are other kinds of terminal equipment: modems for connecting computers or computer terminals, key telephone sets for small businesses with several lines, and Private Branch Exchanges (PBXs— see Chapter 4) for large businesses with internal switching centers. Telephone companies only permitted their own equipment to be connected to telephone lines. In 1966 the FCC ruled that though the telephone companies could set standards, they could not prohibit devices manufactured by other companies from being attached to their networks. Both PBXs and key telephone sets entered the competitive market. This was an important development, because PBXs were soon to become the basic infrastructure of the office and its interface to the existing telephone system.

Perhaps the most significant assault on the telephone companies was launched by Microwave Communications Incorporated (MCI), which applied in 1963 for the right to build a microwave system between St. Louis and Chicago. MCI planned to offer such services as voice, data, and facsimile transmission, in direct competition with AT&T. After initial approval by the FCC in 1966 and final approval in 1969, a court challenge by AT&T was instituted and withdrawn in 1971, more than seven years after the date of the original application. The telephone companies correctly anticipated that the MCI application would have immense repercussions far beyond its modest beginnings. Other companies entered the field and MCI itself soon expanded to a nationwide network, primarily providing private-line service. Next it offered direct competition to AT&T in public, or dial-up, long-distance service. A dial-up call would use the telephone companies' lines to reach the local MCI office, then go over the MCI network to the destination city's MCI office, and finally over local telephone lines to the destination telephone. The Execunet service offered by MCI in 1975 operated in this manner. AT&T appealed to the FCC and was upheld, but eventually the case went to the courts. In May 1978 the Supreme Court supported a lower court ruling that overturned the FCC decision. Thus, after almost 100 years of operating as a monopoly, AT&T faced serious competition in the long-distance market.

The development of satellite-based communications systems also challenged AT&T's monopoly of long-distance communication, and the boundary between computer and communications technologies has continued to blur. Computer manufacturers began to compete with communications companies in the production of a range of products. The FCC permitted a policy of free market competition in the satellite communication industry in 1972. AT&T could use domestic satellites for its public long-distance monopoly service but was not allowed to compete for three years in the private satellite market. In November 1974, convinced that new technology had made the Consent Decree of 1956 outdated, the Justice Department initiated the largest antitrust suit ever against AT&T. The suit argued that AT&T should be broken up into separate companies: Western Electric for telephone equipment, Long Lines for long-distance service, and the operating companies for local service. Finally, on January 8, 1982, an agreement was reached between AT&T and the Justice Department along the lines suggested in the original suit.

> An historic agreement has been reached: AT&T agreed to a consent order divesting the company of all facilities used to provide local telephone service, and the Department of Justice dropped its antitrust case against the company.[5]

After divesting itself of its local telephone companies, AT&T is organized in two main divisions, as follow:[6]

- *AT&T Communications.* Long-distance (estimated 1984 sales: $36 billion).

• *AT&T Technologies.*   Estimated 1984 sales: $18 billion.

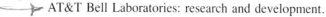   AT&T Bell Laboratories: research and development.

AT&T Network Systems: Western Electric—telephone equipment, manufacturing and sales.

AT&T Technology Systems: manufacturing and sales of components such as chips.

AT&T International: overseas marketing of equipment and services; foreign partnership.

AT&T Information Systems: computers and business systems.

On January 1, 1985, AT&T Information Systems—set up as an arms-length, deregulated subsidiary by the government—was reorganized along three lines of business: computers, large business systems, and small business systems. The remaining parts of the AT&T empire—the 22 local operating companies, about two-thirds of its assets—were reorganized into 7 independent regional companies and the Central Services Organization—a research and development division jointly owned by these companies. AT&T has begun to compete in the office automation market. Its Information Systems division is in direct competition with such companies as Wang, Xerox, and Digital. In its more central communication function, it competes with such companies as Northern Telecom and Mitel (Canada), Rolm (U.S.), L.M. Ericson, Philips, and Plessey (Europe), in the lucrative PBX market. The major confrontation, however, will be with IBM.

IBM and AT&T: When Giants Collide

The stage is set for a bout of worldwide dimensions: never before have two private corporations brought such resources and so many years of preparation into a head-on competition.[7]

During the 1970s, when the government's antitrust suit had an inhibiting effect, IBM seemed to be biding its time, reluctant to appear too aggressive. Then, in anticipation of the suit's ultimate dismissal, it took steps to preapre for the future. Probably its most dramatic action was to launch the IBM PC. One year after the suit was dropped, IBM bought a share of Intel, the large semiconductor manufacturing company, and Rolm, a manufacturer of PBXs. IBM has shown remarkable flexibility for such a large, well-established company. With the restraints imposed by possible government action removed, IBM has served notice that it will enter any sphere of computer applications it views as profitable. By virtue of its partnership in Satellite Business Systems, IBM also has a stake in the international telecommunications market.

IBM will be confronting the newly deregulated AT&T Information System along a number of fronts. Among them are the following:

Office Automation.   Work stations, PBX's, local voice and data transmissions.

Data Processing Services.

Long-Distance Networks. Interfaces to local systems, industry standards, cable operators.

Telephone Equipment. Modems, telephone switching equipment, terminals.

Office Equipment. Printers, facsimile.

Banking Equipment. Automatic Teller Machines (ATMs), Point of Sale Terminals (POSs).

Each company brings a variety of strengths and weaknesses to this growing confrontation. The relaxation of government involvement in these two gigantic corporations has had the initial effect of stimulating industrial competition and inventiveness. AT&T's strong company points are as follows:

Existing Equipment Distribution. AT&T already has equipment in every business in the country (except for that managed by independent companies, still subject to AT&T standards). This includes telephones, wiring, and PBXs.

Service Advantage. AT&T has a widespread existing service and distribution network in the United States. Every IBM communications sale will be beneficial to AT&T, but not vice versa.

Financial Strength. AT&T has the ability to raise large amounts of money through sales of stocks and bonds.

Manufacturing and Research Resources. AT&T's Western Electric division is probably the equal of its counterpart at IBM, and Bell Labs is probably superior to IBM's research facilities in innovation and creativity.

Other Assets. Teletype Corporation as a supplier of terminals. The widely-used Unix operating system for micros and minis. An in-place billing and collection system is available for new information services.

IBM's strengths are as follows:

Dominant Position. By virtue of its dominant position in the computer industry, IBM has set the de facto standards that any challenger must meet. Competitors must endure a considerable degree of vulnerability, because IBM can unilaterally change the rules of the game.

Wide Market Coverage. IBM has such a pervasive presence, there are no obvious areas for AT&T to attack. Where IBM is not present in force, Hewlett-Packard, Digital, and Japanese companies are already well in place.

Product Lines. IBM's product line is modern and comprehensive and exhibits considerable user loyalty. It is dominant in mainframes, micros, peripherals such as disk drives, and other areas as well.

Worldwide Presence. IBM is one of the world's most international companies, with manufacturing, research, service, and distribution facilities located in many countries. It is thus able to take immediate advantage of local conditions.

Manufacturing and Research Facilities. IBM produces a broad range of products, and its labs have demonstrated an ability to convert research to saleable products effectively.

Management. The past few years have demonstrated that IBM upper management is flexible, daring, and inventive. They are experienced in operating in a highly competitive, volatile market.

The struggle is just beginning. 1983 was not a particulary good year for AT&T. The first major offering of American Information Systems, formerly called American Bell Incorporated, was a data network, Net 1. Unfortunately, the name Net 1 was already being used by another company so the name was changed to Net 1000. Hailed as a great development, it did not perform as advertised. There were problems in marketing, division of responsibility, and the order entry system. 1984 was not a good year either, and earnings fell far below earlier estimates. The still-regulatd division, AT&T Communications, lost 5 percent of its long-distance market. The basic problem seems to be that AT&T has little experience in a competitive market. No doubt with its vast resources it will be a formidable adversary in the long run.

The Communications Battleground

As we have noted, AT&T's monopoly of long-distance communication has been eroding since the early 1970s. Furthermore, the January 1982 consent agreement opened up the market to increased, vigorous competition. A major player in the new game is MCI Communications, which has challenged AT&T at every step. MCI has grown rapidly. Revenues exceeded $1 billion in 1983 and some 50,000 new customers sign up every month for its intercity service. MCI and other companies have been able to undercut AT&T's rates, because AT&T's Communications division remains regulated in order to give new companies a chance to compete. However, it will become much more competitive as access charges, which local telephone companies charge to interstate carriers, are equalized. All of these changes will have a serious impact on data communications, because there will be active competition to serve the computer communication needs of both large and small businesses.

The competition is becoming particularly vigorous at the international level. It has been estimated that by 1988 the international telecommunications market will approach $90 billion.[8] The various components of this market are subscriber equipment including telephones, PBXs, telex machines and so forth, telephone company equipment—including cable, wire, exchange switches, and international transmission systems. Many major companies are attempting to obtain a share of this market. AT&T has launched joint international ventures with Philips, a Dutch-based company. The integration of computers and communication systems is necessary to serve a variety of traditional and novel needs: data communication, teleconferencing, electronic mail, facsimile transmission, and delayed voice messaging. Business is demanding such services as design, production, and marketing functions become increasingly international. The rapidly evolving information age is dependent on the growing sophistication of the telecommunications industry.

The current tendency of the U.S. government in this area seems to be toward a hands-off approach. In a period of rapidly changing technology, it is argued that government should permit the companies to fight it out before introducing guidelines. In Europe, especially in France, governments are more protective of their state-run postal, telephone, and telegraph agencies.

Over the past few years, IBM has undertaken a number of initiatives to position itself advantageously in the telecommunications market. The company's forays into telecommunications have run into a variety of problems, among them the following:

> In 1982, IBM "repatriated" its Information Network, which had been operating in Europe since the early 1970s. Set up as an Independent Business Unit (IBU) to offer network services, it failed to turn a profit between 1982 and 1984.

> Also in 1982, IBM signed an agreement with the Canadian company Mitel to develop an advanced digital public branch exchange for local networking purposes. This venture ended a year later, as IBM turned to another company, Rolm Corporation, in the United States.

> IBM has been involved since 1974 in Satellite Business Systems, in which it currently holds a 60 percent share (Aetna Life and Casualty holds 40 percent). This company, involved in the highly competative long-distance market, is a consistent money loser.

More recently, IBM has attempted to move more aggressively and with more assurance in this very crucial area. Whereas AT&T's efforts in computers have had little impact up to now, the potential for IBM in telecommunications is considerably greater. Among IBM's major actions have been the following:

> Under a $300 million contract, Motorola Corporation is developing a cellular radio system for IBM's National Service Division's field personnel.

> At the end of 1984, Rolm Corporation, a major PBX vendor, became a 100 percent owned IBM subsidiary. This acquisition will give IBM a firm footing in this important area.

> IBM has joined with Sears, Roebuck and CBS in a joint venture called Trintex, a nationwide videotex system. Although this consortium looks very promising, it will probably not be profitable until the late 1980s.

> Telecommunications Carrier Products, an Independent Business Unit, is attempting to sell to Bell operating companies as well as other telecommunications users.

In July 1985, IBM announced that it was purchasing 16 percent of MCI Communications with an option to buy up to 30 percent, thus launching a major challenge to AT&T.

IBM has stressed joint ventures and acquisitions rather than the development of in-house products in the telecommunications field.

A Status Report

IBM expects to quadruple its current sales level in ten years, an incredible rate of growth for a company its size.[9] Such a growth rate would require IBM to be virtually the world leader in almost every area where computers play a role. However, profits for the first 6 months of 1985 were down 15 percent over the same period in 1984, although sales were up 2 percent.

IBM will be competing against Apple in the schools and attempting to reestablish itself in the universities. It will expand its service facilities—in spite of increased reliability of its own products—in order to provide third party service. As software development assumes increasing importance, IBM has launched a major expansion of its resources in this area. Engaged in a major capital investment strategy to modernize its plant ($28 billion, 1979–84, and a projected $56 billion, 1985–90), IBM hopes to translate the experience gained thereby into a leading role in robotics and industrial automation. It expects to maintain its dominant position in the mainframe computer market, and to expand its market share in minicomputers and office automation. IBM gives all appearances of operating under the assumption that its manifest destiny is universal superiority.

Such projections and actions have brought renewed calls for some kind of government regulation. In separate actions, NCR Corporation and the small company BMC Software Incorporated, have launched suits against IBM that charge it with anticompetitive behavior. Stephen Jobs, formerly of Apple Computers, has charged, "A monopoly that's unregulated—that's IBM, at least in mainframes."[10] The following quotations are typical of legal opinion within and without the government:

> The Justice Dept., which continues to receive complaints about IBM, does not believe its current activities warrant the kind of antitrust suit against the company that the agency dropped three years ago.[11]

> IBM represents the essence of what the current administration wants to see in the economy. The fact that it's making life tougher for the Storage Teks of the world doesn't trouble Justice at all. They've got a very Darwinian view of things.[12]

Furthermore, IBM has been encountering growing resistance from many countries, as it threatens the survival of national companies. In 1984, the British government refused to permit IBM to cooperate with British Telecom in developing value-added networks. The European Commission, after completing a 12-year investigation of IBM's activities, has instituted a number of restrictions. The European research consortium Esprit has excluded

IBM from cooperative efforts with other companies. Mexico has turned down IBM's proposal to build a manufacturing plant because of the company's insistence on controlling ownership. These and other actions suggest that IBM may face formidable international barriers in its drive to meet its worldwide objectives. On the other hand, this foreign opposition reinforces IBM's self-proclaimed position as *the* U.S. bulwark against overseas competition, especially that posed by Japan.

AT&T has not fared as well as IBM, at least in the initial stages following its breakup. As a regulated monopoly, it lacked sufficient experience in the highly competitive markets where IBM has thrived. However, AT&T's enormous research, manufacturing, marketing, and service resources will undoubtedly help it make its presence felt in a wide range of markets. For the average telephone user, the immediate results are increased local telephone rates, a confusion in the choice of long-distance services and telephone equipment, and a lowering in overall service quality. For the business community, the benefits are apparent: lower long-distance rates and equipment and system costs because of increased competition, and a more rapid introduction of new technological innovations.

In its primary business activity as a long-distance carrier, AT&T's market share will gradually decrease in the face of increased competition, but its revenues will increase as the market grows. In computers, AT&T will not challenge IBM directly in an area such as mainframes, but in the overlapping fields of communications and computers, of which office automation is a prime example. The first phase of the post-divestiture period has required AT&T to undertake a massive reorganization of its resources. Tentative forays into the personal computer market have had only limited success, but the unrivaled past achievements of Bell Laboratories point to major technological developments in the future.

EFTS: ELECTRONIC FUNDS TRANSFER SYSTEMS

> *EFTS constitute an array of automated payment systems, in which the merger of computers and telecommunications technology is employed to improve the efficiency of our present payments system.*[13]

Financial transactions are such a common occurrence in everyday life, it is not surprising that computers have found eager acceptance in the banking community. The sheer mass of numerical computations required to record, update, and process banking records has made the industry a major purchaser of equipment and employer of data processing professionals. Early applications involved the use of keypunches to prepare financial information that was then read into the computer. Accounts were then updated and financial statements produced. As software and hardware became increasingly sophisticated, banks have updated their method of operation. Tellers could enter transaction information into a local computer via terminals at the counter. For independent banks, this information would be used directly; for branch banks, the local computer would send the information over a communication system to the central computer. The marriage of computers and communication systems seems to have been made in heaven for financial institutions. The next step was to permit the customer direct access to the electronic system.

Banking in America

The key to cutting costs, and the central challenge in retail banking . . . is "to migrate customers from the brick and mortar system to electronic delivery systems."[14]

Banks can be chartered by both the federal government and the states. The history of banking reflects the tension between the desire of rural, frontier America for local control over banks and the seeming expansionist tendencies of the national banks. This confrontation has turned on the issue of branch banking—which banks can set up branches and what constitutes a branch bank? Over 30 states restrict branch banking to some degree, and 11 prohibit it entirely.

Those who argue against unrestricted branching point to the following problems:

Serious threats against local banks, with their possible demise as a result of unfair competition.

Further growth of banking monopolies.

Concentration of deposits in large banking conglomerates will increase the cost of loans and therefore the cost of doing business.

Neglect of small businesses when large business ventures are favored.

Joint efforts between large banks and multinational companies will pose a serious threat not only to local banks but to local businesses as well.

Supporters of reduction or even removal of branching restrictions argue as follows:

Branching restrictions are no guarantee against the concentration of deposits, since state banks may become quite powerful.

The monopoly that small banks hold over local communities may not be beneficial for their customers.

Local banks may not be able to take advantage of technological innovations such as EFTS.

As a result of a 1924 Supreme Court decision, national banks became subject to state branching laws. Three years later, Congress passed the McFadden Act. Although subsequently amended, it permits national banks to establish branches in the city in which the bank was established, subject to state branching laws. There have been a number of challenges since 1927, but on the whole branches have only been permitted through changes in state regulations.

The question of branch banking is obviously crucial in the age of electronic banking by means of ATMs and POS terminals. Are such terminals branch banks? If so, those states with restrictive branching laws will prohibit the development of electronic banking.

In a 1975 case in Colorado, the federal courts ruled that by installing an ATM in a shopping center several miles away from its home office a bank had violated the state's branching laws. The growth in electronic banking has been dramatic, and there is considerable pressure in Congress to revoke the McFadden Act. In anticipation of this event, banks have been joining together in regional groups to form interstate networks over which ATMs can be used. This activity raises possible antitrust concerns, in that such networks may be seen as restraining trade for non-member banks. Furthermore, the rate of interstate bank mergers has been increasing, as a number of states have authorized acquisitions of banks in their states. In the general atmosphere of deregulation of the early 1980s, one can expect to see these trends continue.

The Dimensions of EFTS

The term EFTS covers a multitude of processes, services, and mechanisms that depend on computers and communication systems for their operation. Some components have been in existence for quite a while, others have been introduced recently, and still others are in the planning stage. The full array will certainly change the way we shop, bank, and generally carry out our financial transactions. The impact on society will be in such areas as employment, privacy, social relations and patterns of interaction, centralization of control, financial transactions, and possible major consolidation of financial institutions. An important study of EFTS, sponsored by the Organization for Economic Coopeartion and Development (OECD), appeared in 1983; it covered technical, political, economic and social issues.[15]

Preauthorizations and Automated Banking

The following were probably the first procedures that could legitimately be included in the term EFTS:

Direct deposit of regular payments: paychecks, royalties.

Direct payments of recurrent expenses: mortgages, loans.

Direct regular contributions: charity.

Payment of bills by telephone.

Once a person authorizes deposits or payments, these are made automatically without further interaction. Typically, large companies deliver tapes of employees salaries to banks for disbursement into appropriate accounts. Such tapes are of course generated by the companies' computers. Since these procedures do not require sophisticated computer techniques, they were instituted quite early in the course of electronic banking.

The use of ATMs for depositing and withdrawing money, transfers between accounts, and other services—and the authorization of credit and checks—have become a way of life for many people. More than 30,000 have been installed across the country and are heavily used because of their availability at all hours of the day and night. They have proven to be convenient, easy to use, and extremely popular. Their popularity suggests that Americans like the convenience of banking at any hour. For their part, the banks find that ATMs, which can operate 24 hours a day, save them a considerable amount of money because employees are not needed. The banks are encouraging the use of ATMs during regular banking hours as well, by reducing their staff size and reserving the remaining staff for special problems.

Another part of EFTS is the use of terminals to perform credit checks. Before authorizing a purchase, a store is able to verify electronically that a customer has sufficient funds on hand or that the balance available on a credit card is sufficiently large. This kind of checking can also be carried out by telephone, with only slightly more difficulty, but the communications networks necessary for electronic banking will discourage the use of the telephone in this context.

POS (Point-of-Sale) Operations

The common feature of POS operations is that the electronic financial transactions are made directly at the time of purchase. Thus, instead of using cash, a check, or a credit card, the customer will have a debit card that when placed in a POS terminal transfers money from the customer's bank account to the store's. The card used in ATMs is really a debit card, since its use may result in instantaneous transfers into and out of bank accounts. If the customer has insufficient funds or lacks a line of credit, the purchase will not be completed. The widespread use of the debit card will be a major step along the way to the cashless society. Another important implication is the loss of the "float period" between the time a purchase is made and the time it must be paid for. Current approximate float periods for various kinds of transactions are given below:

TYPE OF TRANSACTION	FLOAT PERIOD (DAYS)
Cash	0
Check	2–5 (depending on day of week and location of bank)
Credit card	30–45 (depending on date of purchase and billing schedule)
Debit card	0

The float period is not desirable for the banks, because it gives the customer use of the bank's money interest-free. In periods of high interest rates, substantial amounts of money are involved. With the debit card the float period is effectively eliminated and at the same time payment to the vendor is guaranteed. There is an additional reason for retailers and banks to welcome the arrival of POS terminals. Currently their costs for processing a check or a credit card transaction are more than $1 on the average, whereas POS service is being promised for about 40¢ per transaction.

Automated Clearinghouse

A major part of the cost of processing a check is the physical movement of the check itself from the merchant, to a local bank, to a central clearinghouse, to the customer's bank, and eventually back to the customer, with perhaps additional stages involved. The replacement of all this paper processing by an electronic system is well under way. Such networks have been in existence for some time to facilitate the movement of money among financial institutions. Thus, EFTS have a well-established infrastucture for servicing money flows among banks. Large networks of ATMs and POS services are being built. Banks are getting larger through mergers, acquisitions, and the formation of networks to permit customers access to banking services on a regional basis. Such growth is necessary if the costs of constructing both regional and national EFTS are to be financed.

Problem Areas

One of the byproducts of EFTS is an increase in financial information. For example, the use of a POS terminal results in a record indicating that an individual spent a particular amount of money at a particular time and place. Because these records are created electronically and stored in computer databanks, they are relatively straightforward to retrieve. EFTS operate on-line and in real time (i.e., transactions take effect instantaneously) and could be used to locate individuals whenever they initiate a transaction. Furthermore, more institutions will have access to an individual's financial records. The National Commission on EFTS was very much concerned with privacy issues. Among the recommendations of its final report, issued in 1977, were the following:[16]

> Government should minimize the extent to which it requires an institution to maintain or report records on an individual that are generated by his or her use of EFTS.
>
> EFTS should not be used for surveillance of individuals, either their physical location or patterns of behavior.
>
> Government authorities may obtain information from an EFTS only through a judicial subpoena or court order.
>
> Information necessary to complete or verify a specific EFTS transaction may be given to a participant or intermediary to the transaction.
>
> Information regarding fraud, attempted fraud, or other crime involving an EFTS tarnsaction may be disclosed to law enforcement officers by victimized institutions.

In 1978, Congress passed the Right to Financial Privacy Act, limiting the government's access to financial records. The act outlines the procedures necessary to obtain such financial records as follows:

> Customer authorization.
>
> Administrative subpoena or summons.

> Search warrant.
>
> Judicial subpoena.
>
> Formal written request, a copy of which is filed in court.

The government must notify individuals that their financial records are being requested and advise them that they may under law have the right to attempt to keep those records from the requesting agency. Records obtained by one agency cannot be provided to any other government department or agency. Such legislation represents legitimate concerns about the increasing availability of private information, in this case financial, even though the act is primarily concerned with specifying the conditions under which the government *can* have access.

The Rifkin case (discussed in Chapter 8) was an example of unauthorized access to a banking communication network that resulted in the theft of several million dollars. This case illustrates some of the problems of electronic crime associated with a far-flung communications network to which large numbers of people have access. As an increasing percentage of financial transactions are handled by EFTS, the opportunities for criminals multiply. The use of EFTS may decrease the amount of street crime and thefts as less cash is in circulation, but this benefit may be offset by an increase in crimes of potentially greater magnitude. Such crimes can take the form of theft of goods by fraudulent use of debit cards, transference of funds from one account to another, sale of secret information, and theft of computer services. The new factor introduced by EFTS is the distributed nature of the system. Access is available to large numbers of people, increasing the security problem.

Another form of crime, not directly related to the electronic aspects of EFTS, has appeared. Customers obtaining money from ATMs have occasionally been assaulted by robbers lying in wait. Other more sophisticated criminals have developed techniques to obtain the personal identification number of card holders. Such problems are being dealt with, gradually, but the ingenuity of criminals will continue to challenge security procedures. The Electronic Fund Transfer Act passed in 1978 defines a number of activities as criminal, as follows:

> *whoever knowingly . . . uses or attempts or conspires to use any counterfeit, fictitious, altered, forged, lost, stolen, or fraudulently obtained debit instrument to obtain money, goods, services or anything else of value. . . .*[17]

Because of potential threats to EFTS, security issues are a major concern. We are all familiar with blackouts in which a large power network fails. A similar possibility exists for an electronic banking system. A breakdown of such a system could create chaos. As sabotage of EFTS could pose a serious danger to national security, it is very important that adequate preventive measures be taken. The physical, personnel, and communications security of the system must be guaranteed. The increased use of EFTS will raise the stakes in cases of threats from organized crime, extreme political groups, and deranged individuals.

Will banks that do not become part of EFTS be able to survive? If not, will there be a decrease in competition in the banking industry? Such a decrease would mean fewer choices for the consumer and perhaps increased costs of banking. The general consensus is that free market forces should determine the structure of the banking industry, subject to current legislation, including antitrust proceedings when warranted. Although small banks may be threatened, the cost of such EFTS services as ATMs is becoming low enough that most banks should be able to afford them. A likely result of technological innovation is that banking mergers will increase, possibly leading to a decrease in competition. Deregulation is currently favoured by the federal government, and it is not likely to challenge this trend towards mergers.

While ATMs have proven to be quite convenient, there are potential problems for consumers. What records will be available for electronic transactions? How easy will it be to correct possible errors? What if money is stolen from an EFTS account? Will it be necessary to use EFTS? The Electronic Funds Transfer Act of 1978 requires financial institutions to (a) notify customers of the terms and conditions of EFTS services, (b) give written documentation of all EFTS transactions at the time they take place, (c) provide periodic statements at least every three months, (d) detail error limitation procedures, and (e) limit consumer liability to $500, with the burden of proof on the institution. Furthermore, no individual can be required to use EFTS.

Legal issues arising from the development of EFTS include the following:

Banking Laws.   Are terminals (POS or ATM) branches, and are merchants who permit the location of terminals on their premises subject to banking laws?

Antitrust.   These considerations relate to the necessity for banks to join together to provide EFTS services, agree to common standards, joint ownership of central switching facilities, and shared communication lines. Antitrust laws will have to be interpreted in the light of new developments.

Consumer Protection.   Many concerns have been addressed by the passage of the EFT Act. In addition, a number of states have passed legislation to protect consumers.

Privacy of Financial Records.   The Right to Financial Privacy Act does guarantee a certain protection by limiting the government's access to financial records.

The impact of EFTS on employment is not easy to predict. It does appear that many fewer tellers will be needed. Most of these positions have been held by women, and the impact will be borne mainly by unskilled women for whom such jobs have been an entry point into the labor force. Another issue is how individuals at the low end of the economic spectrum will function in a society in which electronic payments are the rule. Although the EFT Act prohibits discrimination against nonusers, some loss of choice and flexibility might be expected. In the long run, a segment of the population may be deprived of access to a variety of goods and services.

Future Developments

The credit or bank card, with its magnetic stripe on the back, has taken its place among the indispensable objects of modern life. It is used to obtain credit from a merchant and cash from an ATM. A further significant change is in progress—the development and distribution of the "smart card," which contains a microprocessor and a memory chip. Such a card can contain an enormous amount of information about an individual and his or her commercial transactions. In contrast to standard credit cards, smart cards are almost impossible to forge. The first commercial use has been in France, where a pilot project is currently in progress. The system has a built-in three day float period, because customers are familiar and comfortable with such a "grace" period. Smart cards were introduced in the United States in 1982, for use in an experimental home banking system. The Defense Department has begun using them at Fort Lee, Virginia, as a means of entry to the base facilities. In late 1985, Micro Card Technologies introduced the CPM card, based on French technology. This card incorporates an 8-bit microcomputer chip and 8,000 bits of random access memory, to store up to 250 transactions. The use of the smart card could replace all other forms of identification and records currently required by individuals. There are some problems of standardization, limited memory, and the reluctance of banks to depend on such off-line devices, but in a few years the cards will probably be widely used. "The smart card is in a sense the ultimate redistribution of processing chores, from a giant mainframe computer in a bank to millions of cards in millions of wallets."[18] The terminal that processes the card will be quite inexpensive, since it will only be required to perform input and output functions.

ATMs currently perform straightforward banking operatoins: deposits, withdrawals, and transfers between accounts—the basic, high volume transactions that are easily automated. On the horizon are more specialized functions such as the following:

> Buying or selling stocks (which would require that brokerage companies hook into the EFTS networks).
>
> Investment in term deposits.
>
> Dispensing foreign currencies at airports or border crossings.
>
> Access to line-of-credit facilities.
>
> Increased number of accounts that can be accessed.

Wherever banks can reduce their overhead by encouraging the use of automatic facilities, they will be readily introduced.

A recent advertisement, depicting a man dressed in pyjamas in front of a television set—obviously at home—announces in large print: "Chemical Would Like to Open a Branch in Your Living Room." By connecting a personal computer via a telephone to the bank's computer, all the usual functions of an ATM are available in the comfort of one's home. In addition, it will become possible to determine which checks have cleared, reconcile checkbooks, pay bills for goods and services, and send queries to the bank for later response. At-home banking permits 24-hour access and increased control over one's financial activities. Such developments will probably be part of a much larger range of services available over a two-way communications system called videotex (see Chapter 13).

Citibank of New York is offering its corporate customers in-office banking through the use of an office terminal. ''Ultimately we believe the customer should be able to access and coordinate the electronic banking services of all his banks worldwide through a single device wherever its location.''[19] In the future world of commercial banking, a bank will perform most of its functions via computers and communications systems. The branch bank will migrate to the customer's office. Computers and communication networks will replace bricks and mortar, in much of routine banking.

In 1968, the European banking community formed the Eurocheque system to coordinate banking services. By the end of 1983, more than 26 million Eurocheque cards had been distributed to provide both credit card and banking services. By the summer of 1984 these same cards also provided access to ATMs throughout Europe. In contrast to developments in the U.S., where parallel systems of credit cards (VISA, MasterCard) and bank ATM cards coexist, the Eurocheque system has successfully controlled both applications.

TRANSBORDER DATA FLOWS (TBDF)

> *Because of advances in computer communications, many experts are forecasting a global communciations revolution that will see the processing of information as the principal activity of a post-industrial society.*[20]

The increasing rate of growth of global communications has serious implications. The term transborder data flow (TBDF) refers to the communication by computer of information across national boundaries. Because the United States is the leading country of the world in large multinational corporations, computer production, and far-flung communications systems, much of the concern about controlling or regulating information flow seems to be directed toward the United States. There are two major issues involved: protection of the transmitted data and the economic implications of information processing control.

The term data protection is used in Europe to refer to privacy concerns. Since countries have different approaches to such concerns, there is apprehension that the transmission of information across borders could jeopardize desired security. Thus, most European countries have government agencies that must approve the setting up of a databank and then monitor its performance. In the United States, the basic approach has been to pass laws that define the privacy rights of individuals, who must then seek redress from the courts. When records containing information about individuals is sent across a national border, there is concern on both sides. From the U.S. point of view, Europe's preoccupation with data protection is an attempt to reduce the U.S. role in international data processing.

Ours is an age of multinational corporations that have head offices in one country and branch offices, foreign subsidiaries, plants, and research laboratories in many other countries. Such complex organizations require an intricate network of communication facilities to deal with planning, distribution, finance, personnel, research, administration, and many other business functions. A major part of this communication is now done among computers over a variety of systems: telephone lines, microwave, and satellites. Given the great importance of information, many countries have serious worries about losing control in this area and becoming second-class players. Regulation of transborder data flow is seen as a means to protect information, a new resource.

In North America, considerable amounts of information flow across the border between Canada and the United States. A former Canadian minister of state for Science and Technology, J. Hugh Faulkner, has stated that Canada is concerned about the following issues:

1. *The potential of growing dependence rather than independence*
2. *The loss of employment opportunities*
3. *An increase in balance-of-payments problems*
4. *The danger of loss of legitimate access to vital information*
5. *The danger that industrial and social development will largely be governed by the decisions of interest groups residing in another country*[21]

U.S. companies want to do their information processing at home where it is cheaper, more competitive, and (most important) under the jurisdiction of U.S. laws. France has also voiced its concern about threats to national independence resulting from unrestricted TBDF. The interests of other companies are also affected: communication carriers (such as AT&T), computer manufacturers, and service bureaus that perform data processing functions for many companies. The communication carriers would like to see more information flow. Computer manufacturers are paying increased attention to the communications interface, both in terms of hardware and software. Service bureaus within each country feel threatened when data is exported for processing and will lobby governments to protect indigenous industries. In some sense, information as a commodity will come under the same pressures as traditional goods. There will be supporters of high tariffs to protect local industries.

The OECD—composed of 24 industrial nations, including the United States—has endorsed guidelines to protect the privacy of computer records in both storage and transmission. These guidelines cover such well-established principles as accuracy, relevance, lawful disclosure, reasonable security, acknowledgment of collection and storage, accessibility by subjects for purposes of correction, and responsibility of data collectors. Adherence to such guidelines should alleviate the concerns of many countries about data protection.[22] Other legal issues associated with TBDF are explored in a recent OECD publication by Bing et al (1983). However, the economic, national, and social concerns will remain important for some time to come.

TECHNOLOGY TRANSFER

The purpose of export controls is to deny the Soviet bloc access to Western technology that contributes to the effectiveness of their defense establishment.[23]

Besides TBDF, governments are also concerned with preventing technology developed within their countries from illegally reaching their political and economic competitors. The technology includes the hardware itself (computers and peripherals), the microelectronics (microprocessors and memory chips), production processes (masks and strategies for manufacturing integrated circuits), software (operating systems and application programs), and algorithms (mathematical results in cryptography). In general, technology transfer involves much more than the computer field—for example: military electronics, specialized metallurgy, crop control, and so forth. Technology flows out of the United States by the following channels:

> *I. Legal transfers made possible by the open nature of Western society, e.g., transfers occurring through perusal of open scientific literature, academic exchanges, trade fairs, etc.*
>
> *II. Legal transfers through purchase of technologies under general license.*
>
> *III. Legal transfers through purchase of technologies under validated license.*
>
> *IV. Illegal transfers through purchase, e.g., by agents, through third countries or foreign embassies, dummy corporations, etc.*
>
> *V. Illegal transfers through industrial espionage or the theft of materials classified by the U.S. government.*[24]

Attempts to control, or limit, technology transfer have focussed on government relations with universities and academics and with business.

Controls

At no previous time in history has one nation been able to prey so deeply and systematically on the fruits of its adversary's genius and labor.[25]

The two major problems of technology transfer have to do with economic competition and military or political competition. Economic competition involves the political allies of the United States, who are mounting a serious challenge to U.S. trade dominance in such high technology areas as computers and communications. Most of this competition is carried out in the open, but periodically cases of industrial espionage are revealed. One of the most famous of these cases involved the attempts by Hitachi to obtain IBM trade secrets in 1982 (see Chapter 8). Such acts are appropriately dealt with by criminal law. Political espionage directed at industrial and military secrets is a more difficult problem.

The flow of technology is currently under the control of two bodies of regulations: The

Export Administration Regulations (EAR) are administered by the Department of Commerce and cover products that can be used for civilian or military purposes. The countries of destination are in the communist bloc. The list of affected products appears on the Commodity Control List (CCL). International Traffic in Arms Regulations (ITAR) are administered by the State Department. They cover all military items and the export or publication of data on items on the CCL or the U.S. Munitions List. There is another list, called the Military Critical Technologies List (MCTL), which is mainly concerned with the technology of processes used to manufacture the items on the other lists. When attempting to make a ruling, the Departments of State and Commerce regularly consult with the Department of Defense. An international organization—consisting of the North Atlantic Treaty Organization nations (plus Japan but minus Iceland)—called CoCom (The Coordinating Committee on Export Controls) also has a prohibited list of exports. The current system in the U.S. has become overly cumbersome; businessmen have been subjected to long waits and conflicting rulings. The Commodity Control List has grown to over 100,000 items. Equally problematic is that decision making seems subject to the existing level of tension between the United States and the Soviet Union. The most that can be said about export controls is that they have probably hindered but not substantially prevented access to Western technology.

In 1979, Congress passed the Export Administration Act to regulate east-west trade. The act recognizes the importance of trade but grants executive powers to define the special circumstances under which such trade could be abridged. Although the original intent of the act was to encourage trade, the period since its passage has witnessed a significant contraction, largely due to the executive decisions to restrict trade after the Russian invasion of Afghanistan and after the declaration of martial law in Poland.

Academic Freedom

The Defense Department blocked the presentation of about 100 technical papers just before they were to have been delivered at an international convention on optical engineering held in San Diego late last month.[26]

One of the legal and traditional means of technology transfer in the Western world is through open scientific literature. The free and open exchange of information is a basic and fundamental requirement of the pursuit of knowledge. Any restrictions on this openness would pose a threat to the practice of science. Nevertheless, in response to perceived foreign threats steps have recently been taken to control the unrestricted exchange of information. World War II was a watershed in the alteration of the longstanding freedom of university researchers to carry out their research unimpeded by government. Perceived threats of foreign domination convinced most scientists that it was necessary for military-related research to be secret and this situation has continued to the present day.

In the past few years, certain areas of computer research have been marked by the government as producing results useful to unfriendly countries. Cryptography is the development of techniques for the design of codes used to guarantee security of data storage and transmission. Both industry and government depend on codes to ensure secrecy, and the publication of results in this area might compromise this security. In 1977, the National Security Agency attempted to convince researchers to submit papers prior to publication, for a determination of whether or not they posed a security risk. Many researchers objected to this proposal. After a series of discussions, a voluntary review program was set up whose function was to suggest delays in publication, if deemed necessary. This program has worked reasonably well and may serve as a model in other areas.

The action taken by the government in San Diego (described above) came as a great surprise to many researchers. The announcement, just before the conference was to begin, was seen as ill-timed and unprecedented. Apparently, the Defense Department was concerned about the attendance of Soviet scientists. Other steps have been taken: restrictions on foreign visitors to universities, restrictions on which graduate courses foreign students can take, and requirements that research results from the Department of Defense program on very high-speed integrated circuits (VHSIC) be subject to the International Traffic in Arms Regulations. Many scientists have argued that such actions will only harm the United States and that the Soviet Union, seen as the major foreign threat, will still obtain what it needs by surreptitious means. The United States has always prospered under an open system, which benefits science, technology, and business. In fact, the lead that the United States enjoys in computers is a direct result of its basic freedom of information exchange. It is likely that in years to come, an uneasy relationship will exist between the scientific community and the government with respect to this issue, in an international atmosphere of suspicion and mistrust.

NATIONAL INDUSTRIAL POLICY

Industrial policy remains an elusive concept. It encompasses ideas, some of them contradictory, ranging from the establishment of an industrial development bank to support winning industries, to an industrial conversion agency to rehabilitate losing industries and their workers. Many proposals prescribe some type of three-way bargaining process, in which business and labor make concessions in return for Government help.[27]

Governments regulate, monitor, allocate, draw up guidelines, enforce statutes, and generally attempt to create a favorable climate for business. Periodically, the U.S. government involves itself more directly in business activities. For example, it guaranteed massive loans to the Chrysler Corporation to enable it to survive. In the early 1980s a number of voices urged the government to become a partner in future industrial development. The following reasons were among those offered:

Japan's stunning industrial success has been attributed to the long-range planning and adequate financing provided by industry and government in cooperation with labor.

High technology is so volatile and important to the economic well-being and security of the nation that government involvement is mandatory.

Other more traditional industries such as steel and automobiles—the so-called smokestack industries—are seen as supplying fewer jobs in the future, and so the government is urged to stimulate other areas of the economy.

The serious recession of the early 1980s has convinced many economists that active government participation in a national plan for growth is necessary to stabilize the economy in the future.

The government has already been so involved in piecemeal economic activities—through its funding of research, its investment credits, its antitrust prosecutions, and its import/export regulations—that a coherent, long-range strategy is quite appropriate.

Critics maintain that the United States has arrived at its current dominant position precisely because the government has not become involved in a serious way in major business activities. Many prefer the government to act as a referee, not player. They suggest that the strength of the free enterprise system is that it is self-regulating and that any interference by the government will disturb this system. They ask what special skills the government has to enable it to predict winners independent of market forces. This confrontation is not new, but current economic, social, political, and military factors have given it a new urgency.

Predictably, the two major political parties have taken opposing positions. Certain leading figures of the Democratic party, who have advocated a national industrial policy have been called Atari Democrats, in reference to the early, phenomenal success of Atari, a high-tech company, in the video game and personal computer market. Unfortunately Atari, a division of Warner Communications, suffered enormous losses in 1983 and was sold in 1984. The debate has continued. Although no national commitment has been made, the government has taken steps to encourage certain areas of the computer field.

Stimulated by well-publicized announcements from Japan about a major investment in a new generation of computers, the U.S. government has decided to increase its support of research in supercomputers and Artificial Intelligence. Supercomputers are fast computers designed to carry out the high-speed computations needed for such applications as weather forecasting, nuclear research, and economic modeling. Currently, machines in this class are built by Cray Research and Control Data Corporation, which are developing new models (see Chapter 14). An increased investment in AI is being made by the Defense Department (see Chapter 7). Such terms as smart airplanes, the automated battlefield, and intelligent missiles have been used to describe the role of AI in military equipment.

In parallel to government efforts, various companies in the computer industry have joined together to form the Microelectronics & Computer Technology Corporation (MCC), a cooperative venture headed by Bobby R. Inman, who has been deputy director of the CIA and director of the National Security Agency. Among the major companies involved are Control Data, Digital Equipment, National Semiconductor, Sperry Univac, and Honeywell (but not IBM). These companies will contribute both money and people and all will share in the results. Such close cooperation among industry leaders might be seen as restraint of trade and be subject to antitrust prosecution. However, the Justice Department has announced that it does not view the formation of MCC as an antitrust violation. Thus, this cooperative venture could be interpreted as implicit government-industry cooperation in the face of a foreign challenge. Among the areas of computer science chosen for MCC's research are database management, software, packaging, computer-aided design and manufacturing, and ergonomics. In addition, AI and parallel processing are seen as priority areas, although research staff will be difficult to find. Long-range research programs will subsequently be launched in robotics and telecommunications. Clearly, the intent of MCC is to ensure American involvement and leadership in high technology, on a world scale.

The various approaches to a national industrial policy, may be summarized as follows:[28]

> *The Accelerationists.* Try to pinpoint future major international industries and bring them along quickly from research to development.
>
> *The Adjustors.* Try to help major troubled industries modernize and slim down in order to preserve jobs and market shares.
>
> *The Targeters.* Try to stimulate overall economic growth by selecting a number of industries—such as high technology, energy, and health care—and transforming them into growth areas.
>
> *The Central Planners.* Instead of selecting certain companies or even certain industries, a larger perspective is necessary to avoid the unforeseen problems of trying to focus narrowly. Problems may arise because of the complexity of interconnections in the economic system.
>
> *The Bankers.* An industrial development bank should be created with federal support, to provide long-term high risk capital. This bank could take measures to encourage management/labor cooperation, which commercial banks are prohibited from doing.

SUMMARY

Relations between government and business in the United States have been involved, torturous, occasionally acrimonious, sometimes beneficial, usually controversial, and always unpredictable. In this chapter, we have focussed on certain industries—computers and communications—and certain problem areas—transborder data flows and technology transfer. The development and significance of electronic banking has been discussed, with special emphasis on the dimensions of EFTS and the potential problem areas. In somewhat more detail the following points have been covered:

Although committed to the free enterprise system, the U.S. government has at times found it necessary to challenge the activities of certain large companies. On January 8, 1982, the Justice Department dropped a thirteen-year antitrust suit against IBM. On the same day it also dropped an antitrust suit against AT&T, after AT&T agreed to divest itself of the local telephone companies.

IBM, freed of the antitrust suit, launched an aggressive challenge on all fronts to extend its domination of computer-related business. For example, within 3 years after the personal computer, the PC, was introduced in 1981 it held the lead in sales. AT&T's first steps after divestiture were somewhat more tentative. It was challenged in the profitable long-distance market by a number of companies and has yet to make its presence felt in the computer market.

In a major change fostered by technological innovation, the banking system is being transformed by the introduction of Electronic Funds Transfer Systems. Examples of this process are the appearance of automatic teller machines, point-of-sales terminals, and electronic banking via home computers. Concerns about EFTS include security of financial records, potential increased frequency of electronic crime, impact on competition, and impact on consumers.

Governments have become concerned about the vast amounts of information involved in transborder data flow (TBDF). Their concerns extend from privacy issues to the economic impact of loss of control over important information.

Knowledge is power and technological knowledge is considerable power. The U.S. government has become so apprehensive about other countries gaining access to new technology that exports are controlled and research results are being monitored. In the United States many politicians and economists have argued that the federal government should stimulate the growth of so-called winner or sunrise industries if the country is to ward off its many economic challengers. The Japanese model of industry, labor, and government cooperation is often held up as a worthwhile example.

NOTES

1. Charles E. Wilson, former president of General Motors, in testimony before the Senate Armed Forces Committee, 1952.

2. John Opel, president of IBM, as quoted in Bro Uttal,'' Life After Litigation at IBM and AT&T,'' *Fortune*, February 8, 1982, p. 59.

3. As quoted in Robert Pear, ''Antitrust Policies Affect Not Just Corporate Futures,'' *The New York Times*, January 10, 1982, p. E2.

4. Alexander Graham Bell, first complete sentence transmitted by telephone, March 10, 1876.

5. Charles L. Brown, chairman of AT&T, as quoted in a full-page advertisement in *The New York Times*, January 10, 1982, p. 9.

6. Jeremy Main, ''Waking up AT&T: There's Life after Culture Shock,'' *Fortune*, December 24, 1984, pp. 66–8, 70, 72, 74.

7. Frederic G. Withington, ''Sizing Each Other Up,'' *Datamation*, July 20, 1982, p. 8.

8. ''Telecommunications: The Global Battleground'' (special report), *Business Week*, October 24, 1983, p. 127.

9. Marilyn A. Harris, "IBM: More Worlds to Conquer," *Business Week,* February 18, 1985, p. 85.

10. As quoted in Harris, "IBM," p. 94.

11. Ibid., p. 94.

12. Phil Verveer, lawyer, as quoted in John W. Verity and Willie Schatz, "Fast Break in Armonk," *Datamation,* January 1, 1985 p. 70.

13. August Begnai, *The Cashless Society: EFTS at the Crossroads* (New York: Wiley, 1981), p. 27.

14. Stephen T. McLin, strategic planning chief Bank of America, as quoted in Orin Kramer, "Winning Strategies for Interstate Banking," *Fortune,* September 19, 1983, p. 118.

15. J. R. S. Revell, *Banking and Electronic Fund Transfers* (Paris: Organization for Economic Cooperation and Development, 1983).

16. *EFT in the United States,* National Commission on Electronic Fund Transfers, Final Report (Washington, D.C., October 28, 1977), pp. 1–17.

17. Electronic Funds Transfer Act (15 U.S.C. §§ 1693), §916 Criminal liability, reprinted in *Computer/Law Journal,* Winter 1980, p. 246.

18. Martin Mayer, "Here Comes the Smart Card," *Fortune,* August 8, 1983, p. 81.

19. "Electronic Banking," Electronic Banking and Cash Management Division, Citibank (New York, 1982), p. 3.

20. Michael J. L. Kirby, president, Institute for Research on Public Policy, in preface to W. E. Cundiff and Mado Reid, eds., *Issues in Canadian/U.S. Transborder Computer Data Flows* (Montreal: Institute for Research on Public Policy, 1979; distributed by Butterworth, Toronto), p. iii.

21. As quoted in Cundiff and Reid, *Issues in Transborder Data Flows,* p. 3.

22. For further exploration of legal TBDF issues, see John Bing, Peter Forsberg, and Erik Nugaard, "Legal Problems Related to Transborder Data Flows" in *An Exploration of Legal Issues in Information and Communications Technologies* (Paris: Organization for Economic Cooperation and Development, 1983).

23. William Schneider, Jr., Undersecretary of State for Security Assistance, Science and Technology, as quoted in Walter Guzzardi, Jr., "Cutting Russia's Harvest of U.S. Technology," *Fortune,* May 30, 1983, p. 108.

24. *Technology and East-West Trade: An Update,* U.S. Congress, Office of Technology Assessment (Washington, D.C.: May 1983), p. 10.

25. Richard N. Perle, Assistant Secretary of Defense for Internatioanl Security Policy, as quoted in Walter Guzzardi, Jr., "Cutting Russia's Harvest," p. 112.

26. Phillip M. Boffey, "Censorship Action Angers Scientists," *The New York Times,* September 5, 1982, p. 1.

27. Karen W. Arenson, "Debate Grows Over Adoption of National Industrial Policy," *The New York Times,* June 19, 1983, p. 1.

28. "Industrial Policy: Is It the Answer?" *Business Week,* July 4, 1983, pp. 55–6.

ADDITIONAL READINGS

Industry Regulation

"Breaking up the Phone Company" (special report). *Fortune,* June 27, 1983, pp. 60–97.

Brock, Gerald W. *The Telecommunications Industry.* Cambridge, Mass.: Harvard University Press, 1981.

"Did It Make Sense to Break up AT&T?" (special report). *Business Week,* December 3, 1984, pp. 86–89, 92–3, 96, 100, 104, 112, 116, 121, 124.

Fishman, Katherine Davis. *The Computer Establishment.* New York: McGraw-Hill, 1981.

"IBM-AT&T: The Coming Collision" (special report). *Datamation,* July 20, 1982, pp. 8–68.

Greenwald, John. "The Colossus That Works." *TIME,* July 11, 1983, pp. 36–44.

Jeffery, Brian. "Shopping for Market Share." *Datamation,* January 1, 1985, pp. 78–80, 82.

Kleinfield, Sonny. *The Biggest Company on Earth.* New York: Holt, Rinehart and Winston, 1981.

Maremont, Mark, and John Wilke, "Is the Long-Distance Deck Stacked in AT&T's Favour?" *Business Week,* February 25, 1985, pp. 101–2.

"Personal Computers and the Winner is . . . IB[M]," *Business Week,* Oct. 3, 1983, pp. 76–79, 83, 86, 90, 95.

Shooshan, Harry M., III, ed. *Disconnecting Bell: The Impact of the AT&T Divestiture.* Elmsford, NY: Pergamon, 1984.

EFTSs: Electronic Funds Tranfers Systems

Colton, Ken W., and K. L. Kraemer, eds. *Computers and Banking.* New York: Plenum, 1980.

"Electronic Banking." *Business Week,* January 18, 1982, pp. 70–4, 76, 80.

Electronic Funds Transfer (special issue). *Communications of the Association for Computing Machinery,* December 1979.

Electronics Funds Transfer (special issue). *Computer/Law Journal,* Winter 1980.

Lineback, J. Robert. "Smart Cards, in New U.S. Bid, Aim at High-Security Uses." *Electronics Week,* August 27, 1984, pp. 19–21.

Selected Electronic Funds Transfer Issues. U.S. Congress, Office of Technology Assessment Background Paper. Washington, D.C., March 1982.

TBDF: Transborder Data Flows

McGuire, Richard P. "The Information Age: An Introduction to Transborder Data Flow." *Jurimetrics,* Fall 1979, pp. 1–7.

Schiller, Herbert I. *Who Knows: Information in the Age of the Fortune 500.* Norwood, NJ: Ablex, 1981.

Technology Transfer

Gray, Paul E. "Technology Transfer at Issue: the Academic Viewpoint." *IEEE Spectrum,* May 1982, pp. 64–68.

"Technology Transfer: A Policy Nightmare." *Business Week,* April 4, 1983, pp. 94–5, 99–100, 102.

Wallich, Paul. "The Dilemma of Technology Transfer." *IEEE Spectrum,* September 1982, pp. 66–70.

National Industrial Policy

"Industrial Policy: Is It the Answer? *Business Week,* July 4, 1983, pp. 54–7, 61–2.

Rcich, Robert B. *The Next American Frontier.* New York: Times Books, 1983.

Williams, Rosalind. "Reindustrialization Past and Present." *Technology Review,* November/December 1982, pp. 48–57.

12

ROBOTICS AND INDUSTRIAL AUTOMATION

*I*t was a Luddite's nightmare come true. "Man killed by robot," was the story that first appeared in the Japanese
newspapers here and was then carried around the world.

*One major news service, apparently seeking to instill the trag-
edy with a provocative measure of machine-versus-man emo-
tionalism, prefaced its account with the headline, "Worker
Stabbed in Back by Robot, Dies."*

*In fact, a 37-year-old factory maintenance worker at Kawasaki
Heavy Industries Ltd. was crushed to death against a machine
by a robot. The accident took place last July 4 along the
plant's processing line for automobile gears, but was only
made public last week after an invesigation was completed.
The death was the first recorded fatality involving a factory
worker and a robot.*

◊ The New York Times, *December 13, 1981* ◊

INTRODUCTION

Hardly a day goes by without the media again reporting that robots are coming—to the
factory, office, mines, oceans, and even farms. Joseph Engleberger of Unimation, a major
U.S. robot manufacturer, has told of being approached by an Australian sheep rancher

who wanted to develop a robot for shearing. The expectations are high that robots will increase productivity, do the dirty and dangerous jobs for which humans are ill-equipped, be cheaper and more efficient than human labor, and make no demands on their employers for health plans, time off or better working conditions.

Although the first robot patents were issued in the United States, Japan has become the leading manufacturer and exporter of robots in the world. The Japanese have made an early and serious commitment to robotics as a way of reducing the costs of the labor component of production. The average age of their work force has been increasing, and robots are seen as a necessary substitute for human workers. Somewhat slow to respond, the United States has recognized that in order to compete worldwide its industrial plant must be modernized and made more efficient, and the United States has begun to make a concerted effort in industrial robotics. In addition, the U.S. Congress has recently published a very important study in this area.[1]

A variety of acronyms have been used to describe the various aspects of the merger between the computer and factory automation. Computer-aided design and computer-aided manufacturing (CAD/CAM) were probably the first terms to enter common usage with respect to computers in the plant. Subsequently, they were followed by computer integrated manufacturing (CIM) and flexible manufacturing systems (FMS), among others. The use of computers in every stage of the design and production process is accelerating. Companies of the future may be able to integrate planning, design, sales, marketing, and inventory control functions with automated manufacturing systems.

What are the actual details of factory automation? What are the structures and functions of contemporary robots? Industrial robots, with several current applications, are now distributed worldwide. This chapter considers the various factors associated with their use, aside from the major goal of improved efficiency as well as a number of social issues that arise from the increased use of industrial robotics.

INDUSTRIAL ROBOTICS

> . . . industrial robots are essentially programmable multijointed arms (with grippers or holders at the end) capable of moving a tool or workpiece to a prespecified sequence of points, or along a specified path within the arm's reach and transmitting precisely defined forces or torques to these points.[2]

What Is a Robot?

The major application of robots in the foreseeable future will be in the industrial environment. Automobile manufacturers are taking the lead in integrating robots into the assembly line. Automation is not a new feature on the assembly line, and it is sometimes difficult to determine what distinguishes a robot from a more traditional piece of machinery. As robots have made their appearance several definitions, including that quoted above, have been proposed. The following ''semi-official'' definition was adopted by the Robot Institute of America in 1979 and the International Society for Robots in 1981.

> *A Robot is a reprogrammable multi-functional manipulator designed to move materials, parts, tools, or other specialized devices, through variable programmed motions for the performance of a variety of tasks.*[3]

This doesn't sound very much like C3PO or R2D2, but it should be remembered that industrial robots are designed for specific tasks in the factory. Before science fact meets science fiction, considerable research and development will be required.

Brief History

It is generally agreed that George Devol is the father of the industrial robot. He has 30 patents for it, beginning with one in 1946 for a magnetic recording system that stores spatial positions for manipulators such as gripping devices. In 1954 he applied for a patent for ''Universal automation,'' or ''Unimation,'' which was granted in 1961. Eventually, Devol—together with Joseph Engelberger, a young engineer—formed a company called Unimation. It was financed by and became a division of Consolidated Diesel Electric (Condec). It manufactured its first robot in 1961, but did not turn a profit until 1975. In late 1982, Unimation was sold to Westinghouse as part of its major commitment to robotics.

Although developed in the United States, the robot has achieved widespread use in Japan. The Japanese have become the world leaders in the application and installation of robots. Japan entered the robot race in 1967, when Tokyo Machinery Trading Company began to import and market the Versatran robot made by AMF in the United States. In 1969, Kawasaki Heavy Industries began to manufacture robots under a licensing agreement with Unimation.

Over the last few years the robot market in the United States has grown quite rapidly, both in sales and in the number of manufacturers involved. In 1979 sales were approximately $60 million, with Unimation holding over 50 percent of the market. In 1980, while sales were over $100 million, Unimation's share slipped to 42 percent and Cincinnati Milicron, the other major manufacturer, held a 30 percent market share. By 1983, sales had reached approximately $200 million and Unimation's share had slipped substantially. Sales for 1984 were $332 million, up 71 percent over 1983, in figures released by the Robotics Industries Association.[4] IBM, which has been using robots in some of its assembly lines, held only 3 percent of this important market.

American companies with such familiar names as Westinghouse, IBM, General Motors, General Electric, Texas Instruments, and Bendix are among the recent entrants into the robot business. Membership in the major robotics trade association—Robotics Industries Association—grew in 1984 from 200 to about 300. There has been an astounding growth in attendance at the annual Robotic Conference, sponsored by the Society of Manufacturing Engineers. The Robots 4 conference in 1979 attracted 480, the 1980 conference had 1000, and at the Robots 6 conference in Detroit in February 1982, nearly 28,000 people attended the show and more than 100 companies displayed their products. At Robots 8, held in June 1984, about 260 builders and suppliers exhibited robots and associated equipment.

Robot Structure and Programming

Industrial robots consist basically of a large housing out of which a mechanical arm-like appendage emerges with a variety of grippers, sensors, and tools at the end. The housing is usually fixed or mounted on tracks, and the mechanical arm is able to execute a wide range of motions. Robots can be broken down structurally into the following components:

Manipulator. Base—fixed or mounted on tracks. Attached appendage—variety of forms with varying degrees of freedom.

Controller. Computers, software, teaching interface.

Drive Sources. Pneumatic, hydraulic, electrical. (Electrically powered robots—the most expensive—can handle the heaviest weights. Pneumatic power is the weakest.)

End-Effector. An auxiliary part—gripper, spray gun, welder, and so forth.

Sensor. Measurement of influences on the robot, position of the arm.

There are four basic architectures for robots: cartesian (or rectilinear), cylindrical, jointed (or rotary), and spherical, with three degrees of freedom. The first two types provide a high degree of positional accuracy, but a more limited work envelope—the maximum volume of space defined by the movement of the arm. The development of increasingly sophisticated, computer-controlled mechansisms with very flexible arm movement means that spherical and rotary architectures will dominate the market in the future.

Functionally, robots can be classified along two basic dimensions: servo and nonservo (or pick and place). The two types may be compared as follows:

SERVO (PLAYBACK)	NONSERVO (SEQUENCE)
Ability to stop at multiple points along the path.	No such ability–fixed mechanical steps limit each motion.
Ability based on (a) servomechanisms, (b) software systems.	
Intensive programming (software).	No (input) software.
Higher accuracy.	Better repeatability.
More smoothness in following irregular paths.	Path has a limited sequence of motions.
More costly ($40,000–60,000).	Less costly ($4,000–30,000).

The two kinds of servo robots, point-to-point and continuous path, have the following features:

POINT-TO-POINT	*CONTINUOUS PATH*
Path is connected in straight lines.	Capable of "rounding curves." Requires substantial memory.
Spot and linear painting, welding and drilling, some assembly, majority of sophisticated parts handling.	Used for contour applications: arc welding, spray painting.

The methods of programming depend on the kind of robot. For *non servo robots*, the steps are (a) break down the task into a series of end points, and (b) physically adjust the motor and set fixed stops to limit individual movements in a certain sequence. To program *servo robots*, the given task must first be broken down into a series of steps defined by the consecutive positions of the manipulator in space. The program, stored internally in the robot, is played back until the task is complete. The three methods of programming the robot to cycle through the positions are as follows:

Walk through. The manipulator is moved manually through all the positions required. The teaching speed is considerably slower than the actual operating speed. A thorough understanding of the task is required.

Lead through. The manipulator is remotely controlled by either a computer terminal or teach pendant. The operator positions the arm in space indirectly, and when satisfied that the position is correct, enters the position into the computer.

Plug-in. The program is set by manually inserting plugs into a plugboard or stepping drum. The robot operates on this prerecorded program without manual intervention.

The fourth, most advanced method is sometimes called *branching*—a reference to the traditional methods of programming—which allows for a variety of actions depending on different circumstances. In this system, the software can transfer control during program execution, if a signal is received from the environment. Thus, the robot may interact with a group of machines or robots. In the future, information derived from visual and/or tactile sensors may permit the robot to alter its current activity in favor of a more appropriate course. For example, if a part is misplaced on the conveyer belt a robot with a fixed program will not be able to find it, whereas one equipped with a vision system will be able to direct its arm to the object.

CURRENT USE AND DEVELOPMENT
Worldwide Distribution

To determine the number of robots at work in different countries is not an easy task. There is a problem of definition and of counting. The definitions given earlier stress the notion of programmability, and this is the crucial distinction between robots and other types of machinery associated with automation. Japan holds the lead in manufacture and installation of robots, but the size of this lead depends on what is counted as a robot. Even if a uniform and consistent definition is accepted, the count varies, and it is difficult to determine why. The highly competitive nature of the industry means that only estimates, not accurate counts, are available. The Robotics Industries Association gathers most of its data from surveys, not manufacturing reports.

Table 12-1 presents data on the distribution of several classes of robots in eleven industrialized countries as of 1982. The second part of the table, which provides infor-

TABLE 12-1 Reprogrammable Robots Installed before 1983, Including Those with Some Intelligent Capabilities

| Country | Number of Units of Reprogrammable Robots | | | | Monetary Value (millions of dollars) | Installed Robots with Some Intelligence Capabilities | | |
| | Servo Controlled | | Nonservo Controlled | | | | | |
	Point-to-Point	Continuous Path	Point-to-Point	Total		Vision	Touch	Total
Belgium	170	110	25	305	22	0	3	3
Canada	79	86	108	273	13	11	17	28
Czechoslovakia	76	18	60	154	N.A.			
France	774	219	9000[a]	9993	282.2	55	3	58
West Germany	2450	1050	800	4300	213	20	45	65
Italy	500	200	400	1100	N.A.	20	20	40
Japan	18,650		13,250	31,900	1097			2934[b]
Poland	105	165	15	285	N.A.	0	2	2
Sweden	435	175	840	1450	56	53	25	78
U.K.	283	430	264	977	53	5	12	17
U.S.	3682	1071	1548	6301	391	55	100	155
Totals				57,428	2,151			3380

Source: 1982 Robotics Industries Association Worldwide Robotics Survey, in Erik L. Keller, "Clever Robots Set to Enter Industry en Masse," *Electronics,* November 17, 1983, p. 118.

[a] variably sequenced manipulators.

[b] combined vision and tactile sensing.

mation on intelligent capabilities of robots will be discussed later in this section. Japan clearly leads the world, with its installed robot base valued at over $1 billion, compared to the total world value of $2.15 billion. Even in terms of servo-controlled robots, the most advanced form, Japan with 18,650 has a considerable lead over the United States with 4753 and West Germany with 3500. Another estimate of current and projected robots by the Organization for Economic Cooperation and Development (OECD) is given in Table 12-2. The 1981 figures are not consistent with those shown in Table 12-1; this clearly illustrates the difficulties of keeping track of where the robots are. In 1981, the international coordinators at the Eleventh International Symposium on Industrial Robots in Tokyo produced a forecast of robot growth by 1985 and 1990. These predictions were substantially less optimistic than those in Table 12-2; for Japan, they were 16,000 and 29,000; the United States, 7715 and 31,350; and West Germany, 5,000 and 12,000, for 1985 and 1990, respectively. Such a variance results in widely differing theories about the future course of events. Another estimate suggests that as of August, 1984 there were about 8000 robots in the United States.[5] Whatever the figures, it is clear that robots are definitely a growth industry, and the competition between the United States and Japan is likely to be quite vigorous.

Applications

Industrial robots are used in a wide variety of applications, as shown in Table 12-3. Spot welding is the major application of robots in the automobile industry, especially in the United States. The surprising and significant percentages in Table 12-3 are those concerned with assembly. The ability of robots to assemble parts has serious implications for long-term employment in blue collar industries. Examples of the applications are as follows:[6]

Welding. Spot welding of automobile bodies, arc welding of axles.

Painting. Spray painting of appliance components and automobile parts.

TABLE 12-2 Forecast of Robot Growth

	1981	1985	1990
Japan	9,500	36,500	111,000
United States	4,500	15,000	56,000
West Germany	2,300	8,800	27,000
United Kingdom	713	2,700	10,000
France	600	2,300	8,500

Source: Organization for Economic Cooperation and Development, advertising supplement in *Scientific American,* November 1984.

TABLE 12-3 Installed Operating Industrial Robots (U.S. Definition) by Application in the U.S. and Japan as of December 31, 1982

	Japan		United States	
	Units	Percent	Units	Percent
Welding	8,052	25.2	2,453	38.9
Painting	1,071	3.4	490	7.8
Assembly	6,099	19.1	73	1.2
Casting	557	1.7	375	13.9
Material handling	6,797	21.3	1,300	20.6
Machine loading/unloading	2,578	8.1	1,060	16.8
Others	6,746	21.1	50	0.8
Total	31,900	100.0	6,301	100.0

Source: Paul Aron, "The Robot Scene in America: An Update," Daiwa Securities America Inc., Sept 7, 1983, in *Computerized Manufacturing Automation: Employment, Education and the Workplace,* U.S. Congress, Office of Technology Assessment OTA-CIT-235 (Washington, D.C., April, 1984), p. 298.

Assembly. Assembly of aircraft parts and appliance switches.

Machining. Sanding missile wings, removing metal flash from casings.

Material Handling. Stacking automobile parts, bottle loading.

Machine Loading/Unloading. Loading of a punch press, of automobile components into test machines.

Other. Inspecting dimensions of parts, application of adhesives.

In 1972, Ford used Unimation robots to weld Maverick car bodies—the first major use of robots in the automobile industry. The company had 300–400 robots in 1981 and planned to have 4000 worldwide by 1990. General Motors has announced its intentions to install 14,000 robots by 1990. To this end it has formed a joint venture with Fanuc Ltd. of Japan—GMFANUC Robotics Corporation—to manufacture robots for a variety of applications. In Japan, about 40 percent of all robots produced were being used in the automobile industry as of March, 1980.

The range of robot applications is continually growing and diversifying. While most robots have been used in dirty and noisy factory situations, opportunities are emerging in the ultra-clean environments of semiconductor production. GMF Robotics, and IBM are offering special versions of their robots to operate in this setting.[7] Research is in progress to develop reprogrammable carts that can move around factory floors carrying parts and finished products. These carts will follow reflective tape on the floor and will also be able to avoid obstacles.[8] By equipping robots with television cameras and complex image processing algorithms, robot manufacturers can develop systems to detect defects in parts and finished products (see below).[9] Finally, "personal" robots are likely to find employment in the home, as extended home appliances and entertainment systems.[10]

Sensory Abilities

The robots developed so far might be called the first generation. They are essentially "blind" and devoid of any other sensory input, and they expect the object they are welding and painting to be at a precise location in space. Research is proceeding apace to develop the sensory abilities of robots so that they may interact with their environment. Robots need such abilities because (a) the workplace may not be standard—that is, objects may vary in their orientation, size, or shape, (b) occasional obstructions may intrude, and (c) performance may require adjustments based on unpredictable events. To increase the power, flexibility, and use of robots, designers must equip them with sensory capabilities such as force control, tactility, and vision. Variable force control is necessary for fitting operations and a tactile sense is very important for both positioning and orienting. The use of vision opens up many possibilities for tasks requiring positioning, monitoring, and inspection. The increasing use of robots in assembly operations and in quality control depends heavily on equipping them with a means for sensing their environment in a variety of ways.

The three forms of sensory functions have been characterized as "internal, remote (e.g. vision), and contact (e.g. force, pressure)."[11] The first term refers to the robot's internal monitoring of its position. In the United States, vision has been the area most researched, and systems that depend on the identification of silhouettes have been developed. At present there is no general purpose real-time vision system available, but specially designed systems do exist. Tactile sensing includes the use of pressure-sensitive detectors in the gripping device or torque sensors. Sensors can also detect temperature levels and magnetic properties of metal objects. According to Table 12-1, the production of robots, currently in operation, with sensory abilities is miniscule, excluding Japan. Even there less than 10 percent of robots have such abilities.

More than 70 companies are currently developing vision systems in the United States alone. Recent reports from West Germany announce the development of a vision system that uses radar-like methods to produce a 3-D image of objects. Such data will enable a robot to identify objects and manipulate them. Currently it takes about one second to recognize a 3-D object.[12] General Motors, the world's largest user of vision systems, has invested in four companies to work on and improve the quality of such products. The major application of such systems is in product inspection. The movement from the laboratory to the factory floor is slow, halting, and rich with problems, outrageous promises, and considerable rewards to successful companies.[13] In Japan, Hitachi is developing a mobile robot that can move around in an obstacle-cluttered environment by comparing its route to a prestored representation of its surroundings. It may be available in five years. Toshiba is working on a robot that can climb up and down steps, "see" its environment, and carry and position small objects.[14]

Table 12-4 presents data gathered from various sources in an attempt to gauge the rate

TABLE 12-4 Projections for Solutions of Key Problems in Robotics[a]

	1984	1985–86	1987–90	1991–2000	2001–
Hardware	L	C	W/A		
Lightweight, composite structures and new forms of drive mechanisms					
Hardware and software					
Force sensors	L,C		W/A		
Versatile touch sensors		L	C	W/A	
Coordinated multiple arms		L	C	W/A	
Flexible, versatile grippers			L	C,W/A	
Software					
Precise path planning, simulation and control with CAD	L		C	W/A	
3-D vision in structured environments planned to simplify the vision task	L,C		W/A		
3-D vision in unstructured complex environments not planned to simplify the vision task			L	C	W/A
Robust mobility in unstructured environments			L	C	W/A
Standards that clarify different versions of robot languages and help to ensure a common language for similar applications			L,C	W/A	

Source: Paul Aron, ''The Robot Scene in America: An Update,'' Daiwa Securities America Inc., Sept. 7, 1983, in *Computerized Manufacturing Automation: Employment, Education and the Workplace,* U.S. Congress, Office of Technology Assessments, OTA-CIT-235 (Washington, D.C.: April, 1984), p. 95.

[a] L solution in laboratories; C first commercial applications; W/A solution widely and easily available (requiring minimal custom engineering for each application).

of development of robotic abilities. (Note that skill in 3-D vision and robust mobility are not expected to be widely available until the next century.) In large measure, the successful development of intelligent robots with planning and problem-solving abilities, as well as sensory input, will depend upon research achievements in Artificial Intelligence. Many of the techniques in current use in vision systems originated in AI laboratories.

The Impact of Artificial Intelligence

Beginning in the mid-1960s and continuing through the early 1970s there was a major concern within the AI community with robotics, or what was then termed integrated AI (see Chapter 2). It was felt that many aspects of intelligent behavior such as vision, natural language, and problem solving should be treated in a uniform manner simultaneously.

One of the most important "microworlds" for research was the hand-eye system. It consisted of a mechanial arm that was able to manipulate simple objects such as children's blocks and work in concert with a television camera, which was also under computer control. Such systems were in use in the 1970s at MIT, at Stanford, and the University of Edinburgh in Scotland. It is possible to interact with such a system by typing in commands on a terminal in something close to English. In the early systems the experimenter might enter "Put the red block on top of the yellow block." A natural language program translated this request into an internal form, which provided the appropriate information for the vision and planning programs. The camera looking down at this scene provided input to the image analysis program, which identified the position of the two blocks. Finally a planning program using this information, constructed a plan—a sequence of movements, grasps, and ungrasps. After some delay, the arm would begin moving to carry out the command. In terms of elapsed time, the image processing and plan construction took much longer than the actual movements.

It was soon realized that each of the component systems represented a major research area best pursued independently. Image processing did benefit significantly from its development in the hand-eye context. Researchers started with systems that could manage simple, brightly colored blocks sitting on black velvet in a shadowless environment. Construction has now begun on systems to enable industrial robots to deal with considerably less predictable environments.

One research project stands apart from the others—a mobile robot called "Shakey" by its designers at SRI International (formerly the Stanford Research Institute). Shakey was the first and probably the only mobile intelligent robot. At some places such as shopping centers, movie theaters, and fairs, robots roll around and greet people with a "Hi, how are you doing?" or "Glad to see you here." These are all packaged devices, something like a tape recorder put inside a mannequin—a little more sophisticated, but not much more. Off to the side there is a person using a remote control device to determine the movements of the robot. In considerable contrast to this particular kind of robot, Shakey exhibited a degree of autonomous behavior. It moved about on wheels that were driven by a stepping motor under battery power. It had a television camera with a rangefinder, and was connected to its computer, first by a cable and later by a radio receiver/

transmitter. In operation it was similar to the hand-eye systems already discussed, except for a few important differences.

A task was given to Shakey in a simple command language from a terminal. At the same time, Shakey's television camera takes a picture of the world, a very simple room with the baseboard clearly distinguishing the walls from the floor. Scattered about were a large cube, block, and pyramid. The lighting was quite diffuse in order to avoid shadows. A task might be to push the block and the cube into a specified corner. On the basis of its initial "view" of the world, Shakey formulated a plan and began to execute it. It might roll over to the block first and push it into the corner, then move to the cube and push it into the corner as well. If by some chance an unexpected obstacle were in its path (perhaps placed there by a mischievous experimenter), a collision might take place. Shakey had a wire sensor (like a cat's whisker) that stopped its motor instantly if it brushed against an object that it was not expecting to push. If this happened, a new picture of the room was taken and analysed, and a revised plan was formulated. Such image processing is very time-consuming, but it is probably the most important legacy of robotics research in AI, besides the development of mechanical arms.

After a period of exploration with hand-eye systems and the integration of such components as natural language understanding, image processing, problem solving, and the control of electromechanical hardware, experimentation ceased at most institutions except for SRI International. Research continued there in a more practical form, perhaps best described as industrial automation with stress on improved visual and tactile skills.

WHY USE ROBOTS? WORK AND PRODUCTIVITY

Without robots, and the savings they will bring, American manufacturers will continue to lose ground internationally.[15]

The Case for Robots

Robots have not been introduced into the workplace as rapidly as proponents hoped or expected. Factors were reliability deficiencies in the current technology, high costs, and high interest rates. However, in reaction to the massive onslaught of "Japan Inc.," North America and Western Europe have come to view the robot as the key to restoring their economic superiority. Especially in the industry that has suffered most—the U.S. automobile industry—hopes for increased productivity have focussed more and more on a large investment in improved robots.

Robots can affect the industrial process in the following ways:

Improvement of Productivity. Increased plant operating time because of fewer shutdowns, ease of retooling, automation of small batch production.

Stability and Improvement in Product Quality. Reduced quality variation, 24-hour working days with elimination of changeover problems.

Improvement in Production Management. Reduction of manpower allocation problems, benefits of durability and accuracy of robots, overcoming of skilled manpower shortages.

Humanization of Working Life. Release of humans from dangerous, unhealthy, and monotonous work.

Resource Conservation. Saving of materials by efficient robots, saving of energy by robots working in environments with reduced lighting, air conditioning, and so forth.

Will robots be used to humanize the workplace? To convince management to use robots for this purpose, it will be necessary to demonstrate that they will reduce the costs of illness and injury resulting from a dangerous environment. It is claimed that the savings to employers in terms of reduced incidence of occupational diseases (for example exposure to noxious chemicals) and work-related injuries can be the crucial factor in the decision to install robots. The costs to be reduced are given as follows:[16]

Payments in workers' compensation, which includes both compensation of losses in wages and costs of medical care.

Reduction in productivity because of employee absences as a result of job-related injuries and illnesses.

Implementation of safety procedures and installation of related equipment. Approximately $5.2 billion was spent in 1982 in this area, an average of 1.4 percent of all capital investment.

Legal costs associated with job-related illnesses and injuries.

The substantial reduction in all these costs should serve to stimulate the introduction of robots into hazardous environments. Good business practice, not appeals to altruism, will be the determining factor.

Because robots themselves may pose a safety hazard, measures must be taken to protect their human coworkers. The Robotic Industries Association (RIA) is promoting a new industrial standard to safeguard operating personnel. Underlying this standard is a basic common sense injunction: do not venture within the robot's operating envelope while it it working. It is important to know where the emergency shutoff switches are and to have an automatic sensing system that can immediately stop the robot if anything unexpected is detected.

A study carried out by Carnegie-Mellon University surveyed robot users to determine the major reasons given for the installation of robots. The factors cited were: reduced labor costs, elimination of dangerous jobs, increased output rate, improved product quality, increased product flexibility, reduced materials waste, reduced labor turnover, and reduced capital cost.[17]

It is generally agreed that U.S. productivity rates have been steadily decreasing over the last few years. Productivity is usually defined by dividing the total output of the economy, the Gross National Product (GNP), by the number of workers (or work hours) required for its production. Productivity growth has been decreasing in the United States over the past 20 years:

> *Productivity growth slowed from an average yearly increase of 3.2 percent between 1948 and 1965 to an average of 2.4 percent between 1965 and 1973. The rate of growth then plunged to 1.1 percent between 1973 and 1978, and in 1979 American productivity began actually to decline. . . . From 1976 to 1981, Japan's productivity grew at an annual rate of 7.1 percent, France's productivity at 3.9 percent, and West Germany's productivity at 3.4 percent.*[18]

Technological improvement plays a major role in productivity. According to a report by the Brookings Institute, the following factors contribute to productivity, in percents: technology—38.1, capital—25.4, labor quality—14.3, economics of scale—12.7, and resource allocation—9.5.[19]

Capital expenditures have not been keeping pace. Thirty-four percent of U.S. machinery is over 20 years old, and 69 percent of cutting tools are over 10 years old. While the ratio of new fixed investment to GNP averaged more than 30 percent in Japan between 1960 and 1983, and between 20 and 25 percent in France and West Germany, it was only 18 percent in the United States. There is a perception among the American public that quality of work is decreasing and that worker dissatisfaction is increasing. The introduction of robots is seen as a major part of the solution to this problem.

Why Is Japan Ahead?

What has been the experience of that country most heavily involved in robot use? Robert H. Hayes, of the Harvard Business School, asserts that the Japanese have achieved their success through the use of solid management techniques along with a premium on quality control.[20] The details are as follows:

Creating a clean, orderly workplace.

Minimizing inventory.

Stability and continuity in the manufacturing process.

Preventing machine overload.

Comprehensive equipment monitoring and early warning systems.

No-crisis atmosphere.

Concepts of "zero defects" and "thinking quality in", in planning, training, feedback, and materials.

Emphasis on long-term commitments: partnership ("codestiny") and lifetime employment (actually less than one-third of workers).

Equipment independence—much of the production equipment is in-house.

According to an American manager,

> *Our whole philosophy has been to "deskill" our workforce through automation, so we end up having relatively unskilled people overseeing highly sophisticated machines. The Japanese put highly skilled people together with highly sophisticated machines and end up with something better than either.*[21]

Improving productivity does not depend primarily on such "dramatic, easily imitated or puchased solutions as quality circles, government assistance, and the use of intelligent robots."[22]

One of America's foremost management consultants, Peter F. Drucker, stresses that there is no magic in Japan's success, but rather a commitment to sound principles of managing large and complex organizations. He suggests four habits or rules for competitive success:[23]

- Take competitiveness seriously.
- Put national interest first.
- Make external relationships important ("Knowing how to sit").
- Seek no final victories.

A five-year study compared productivity at Western Electric versus five of the largest Japanese electronics manufacturers, including Hitachi, Fujitsu, and Mitsubishi.

> *"Compared with Western Electric workers, Japanese workers are not absent significantly less, and not less likely to quit, and do not work harder. The reality is that some straightforward management decisions explain the high productivity of Japanese workers."*[24]

The Japanese companies provide greater engineering support for their workers, in on-site consultation. These electronics companies attempt to hire the best workers available and depend on their intelligence and motivation. The wage structure in the Japanese companies rewards experienced employees with high wages, and new employees must start with substantially lower pay. Whereas the Japanese invest a considerable amount in equipment per employee, "this equipment is not more technologically advanced than machinery in American factories—there is simply more of it."[25] Thus, the answer to an improvement in American productivity is not necessarily more robots in the plant. No one argues that *the* contributing factor to Japan's success has been the use of robots. By general agreement the Toyota automobile complex at Toyoto City, Japan—with 35,000 employees—is considered the most efficient auto plant in the world. The Toyota approach has three major objectives: (a) keeping inventory to an absolute minimum, (b) making sure each step of the manufacturing process is done correctly the first time even though the assembly line runs slower as a result, and (c) continually reducing the amount of human labor that goes into each car. This last point refers to increased automation—not necessarily the use of robots, though they are being introduced rapidly. Most of the recent success occurred before the large-scale use of robots. From 1975 to 1981, Toyota worldwide production rose by 38 percent, from 2.3 to 3.2 million, while employment rose only 8 percent. The most striking indicator of the advantages of the Japanese system is the final price of the automobile.

> . . . major producers in Japan can manufacture and ship a small car to the United States for $1300 to $1700 less than American companies can make a similar car. Furthermore, the higher hourly wage and benefit rates paid to American auto workers—$19.65 at G.M. compared with $11 at Toyota—apparently are not the biggest part of the cost diffrence. . . . the hourly labor cost difference is probably less than $500 a car, and that is nearly offset by shipping and duty costs of bringing an auto from Japan to the United States.[26]

The Yamazaki Machinery Works has been called the factory of the future. It represents an investment of $18 million, and produces 1,400 precision components per month. Usually the labor requirements for such a plant would be 200 skilled workmen stationed at 68 different pieces of equipment. This plant operates 24 hours a day, 7 days a week, and with the use of robots only 10 to 12 workers are needed during the day, and at night just one watchman. Mr. Yamazaki has noted that the individual parts of his company's system are not new and are often made by foreign companies.[27] For example, the central computer is made by DEC. The most important feature of the Yamazaki plant is the extraordinary amount of attention that has been devoted to engineering and software development.

Labor and Technology

Robots are the wave of the future, but in isolation they will not realize their full potential or increase productivity to the degree expected. In Japan there has been a long tradition of cooperation among industry, labor, and government. This cooperation has been criticized in the United States as somehow enabling Japan to compete unfairly. In any case, Japanese industry has taken great care to consult with its workers when planning to introduce robots. Companies assure workers that the boom in integrated circuits has created more new jobs than robots have taken away. Labor and management in each company work closely together, proceed with great care, and study together the impact of robots on productivity, production costs, and working conditions. If workers must be transferred to other jobs, management sees that they are satisfied before robots are installed. Robotization takes place slowly, step by step.[28] This last point may not always be as progressive, in practice, as it sounds.

> Robots are introduced first only to part of a production line, most often to a section where the labor force is composed mostly of female workers. Since women in Japanese companies typically leave after two or three years to get married, robots can move in smoothly with no lay-offs or dislocations.[29]

In the United States, the introduction of robots, up to very recently, has taken place much more slowly than in Japan. As the pace has quickened, concerns of labor and management about the introduction of new technology have come to the fore. The economic difficulties in the United States that began in the mid-1970s have convinced many manufacturers that only by reducing the labor component of production can they compete internationally. This viewpoint has been especially well articulated by the automobile industry. General Motors recently announced a new subsidiary, called Saturn, that will produce automobiles as efficiently and cheaply as possible in order to challenge Japan's world leadership.

The Saturn concept is to integrate computers into the entire production process from the office to the factory floor. One of the goals is to reduce the labor component per car from the current level of 55 to about 20 hours. Robots will play a major role. Saturn "is going to advance significantly the state of the art in automated assembly. It will be the most robotized of any GM plant—and probably any plant in the world."[30] The plans are impressive: Robots will position sheet metal for other robots to weld as car roofs. They will install windshields and perhaps rear windows and doors, and they will attach wheels and install seats. Such applications will require the development of robots with advanced vision systems.

What is the impact of robots on the quality of work and the number of workers? Almost every commentator on these problems has stressed one point: Advanced planning and consultation with labor is necessary. It has been maintained that success often depends on paying special attention to the problems of displaced workers, gaining line management support for the change, and educating employees in the use of the equipment before installation.[31] The following comments are typical:

> *The time to notify unions is when the corporation first considers automating. That will give us ample time to meet our responsibilities—we have to plan within the community for workers to be assimilated into new jobs.*[32]

> *It should be obvious that workers who are going to work machines should be consulted. You get better results in productivity and labor relations if workers are involved in the selection of new machines and how they should be used.*[33]

A work force that is involved, is consulted, and is properly trained will be more productive and more concerned with improvements in the manufacturing process. Many companies—including Ford, Westinghouse, IBM, and General Motors—have taken pains to consult with those workers who will be most affected by robots. This responsibility must be extended, however, to include retraining and compensation. One scenario envisions displaced workers being transformed into robot technicians. The magnitude of the loss of job tasks—not worker layoffs—is difficult to predict. A recent study estimated that between one and two hundred thousand jobs will be lost by 1990, about one-quarter of them in the automobile industry.[34] However, it is not predicted that the number of workers, to actually lose their jobs will be large. Voluntary turnover rates, supposedly, will be sufficiently high to mask the jobs lost to robots. What will be lost are low-level job opportunities for unskilled labor.

Randy Hale of the National Association of Managers—which represents the managers of about 13,500 companies—has made a forthright statement: "In the short run, automation's going to hurt the unions. But in the long run, automation will increase employment because the increase in productivity and sales will translate into added jobs."[35] He claims that existing jobs will be upgraded and employees will be retained for demanding and interesting work. Many union leaders are not convinced. George Kohl, a research economist with the Communication Workers of America, has stated as follows:

> *The idea that automation creates higher-level jobs isn't quite true. There was a Boston College study of aerospace workers at a factory that was installing machine-tool automation; the researchers found that only one out of every five employees was actually trained in a high-tech area, while the remaining workers wound up in low, service-area type jobs.*[36]

Improved technology in the factory promises a future of low-cost, well-made goods. Humans will no longer have to work in unpleasant environments at jobs that are hot, dirty, and even dangerous. At the Robotics Institute of Carnegie-Mellon University, the psychological reaction of workers to the introduction of robots, and various strategies for facilitating that introduction, are being studied. Frequently, workers have less control in a job with reduced demands, and social contact in the workplace is reduced as well. Decisions formerly made by workers are now embedded in the technology. Given the long-term labor goals of management, workers on the assembly line will probably continue to be apprehensive about new technology.

INDUSTRIAL AUTOMATION

> *. . . today's industrial pioneers are hooking new technologies into electronic networks, creating "spinal cords" and "central nervous systems" for factories that can streamline operations in everything from control rooms to assembly lines to shipping docks.*[37]

A number of key terms are used to describe the various important areas of computerized manufacturing technology.[38]

Computer-Aided Design (CAD) serves as an electronic drawing board for design engineers and draftsmen, with applications in aircraft design, automobiles, and integated circuits. Included in this heading are *computer-aided drafting* and *computer-aided engineering* (CAE). CAE is concerned with interactive design and analysis.

Computer-Aided Manufacturing (CAM) includes those types of manufacturing automation used primarily on the factory floor to help produce products. Some of the important subfields are *robots, numerically controlled* (NC) machine tools, and (of increasing importance) *flexible manufacturing systems* (FMS). An FMS is a production unit capable of producing a range of discrete products with a minimum of manual intervention. It consists of production equipment work stations (machine tools or other equipment for fabrication, assembly, or treatment) linked by a materials handling system to move parts from one work station to another. It operates as an integrated system under full programmable control. Two other areas included in CAM are *automated materials handling* (AMH) and *automated storage and retrieval systems* (AS/RS).

Management Tools and Strategies include, most importantly, *computer-integrated manufacturing* (CIM) and *management information systems* (MIS) (see Chapter 4). CIM involves the integration and coordination of design, manufacturing, and management using computer-based systems. It is currently an approach to factory organization and management. Other areas are *computer-aided planning* (CAP) and *computer-aided process planning* (CAPP), which are concerned with scheduling the flow of work in an efficient manner as well as establishing the optimal sequence of production operations for a product.

CAD/CAM

Robots are only part of the manufacturing process. The factory of the future is expected to be organized around (a) computers and sophisticated graphics systems at the design stage (CAD) and (b) computers, numerically controlled machines, routing systems, and robots at the manufacturing stage (CAM). Timothy O. Gauhan, vice-president of the CAD/CAM industry service of Dataquest, a California research company, has described the boundaries of CAD/CAM as follows:

> It extends to the entire process of conceptualizing, designing, and manufacturing a
> product—any place the computer is involved. It can be said to go right down the
> line from MIS. . . . to design and simulation, redesign, material handling and
> maintenance, process control, quality control and inventory.[39]

CAD/CAM is not a well-defined production strategy, but rather a developing set of systems and strategies that are being applied to various aspects of the design and manufacturing process.

Computer Aided Manufacturing—International (CAM-I) is an important non-profit association run by a worldwide group of manufacturers. Its goal is to develop the pushbutton factory—designed, simulated, and operated by computer. CAM-I's member companies and institutes sponsor a variety of projects. A project in geometric modeling—the methods for representing three-dimensional shapes in the computer—has the goal of developing a system that can supply the data necessary for numerical controllers. The realistic presentation of solid three-dimensional objects generated by computer is obviously necessary for design purposes. For Gene Bylinsky (a frequent contributor to *Fortune*) computer graphics are the major component of computer-aided design. The real payoff will come when CAD and CAM are linked.

> *When the linkage works smoothly, the on-screen designing and testing of a product generates a bank of computer instructions for manufacturing it—or making the tools, dies, and molds used in manufacturing it. Even the tool paths, visible on the screen, can be specified. This CAD/CAM linkage greatly shortens the time between design and production. It is less costly to move to new models, make midstream design changes, customize products, set up short production runs.*[40]

New developments in graphics will have a major impact on CAD. "Today's CAD units include an expanded array of software that permits such functions as geometric modelling, simulation, engineering analysis, testing, and interfacing with manufacturing, as well as automated drafting."[41] This list of abilities actually represents a sequence of steps describing how a fully-realized system would operate. In the first stage, the shape of the desired product is formed using geometric modelling software. (This preliminary crude version will subsequently be refined.) On the basis of this geometric model, a computer model is built that characterizes both structural and dynamic relations. By simulating the model, engineers can determine whether or not the current design meets expectations and, if not, they are able to modify it. The final design can be produced on high-speed plotters to conform to standard drafting requirements. At this point, an actual prototype is constructed, tested, and evaluated. If it is found acceptable, numerically controlled machine tools can be programmed to produce the individual components. Finally, robots can be programmed to assemble these components into the finished product.

Although in some sense CAD/CAM has been superseded as a concept by more recent innovations, it remains an important technology, with such developments as "three-dimensional CAD/CAM, full factory automation, design and manufacturing integration, and distributed workstations."[42] Examples of current systems that illustrate these features are given below:

> At the Sharp Corporation in Japan, a 3-D CAD/CAM system has been developed with an interactive kinematic simulation facility and advanced graphics, featuring surface definition, shading, and texture simulation techniques.[43]

> At the Institut Géographique National and Université de Pais VII, the Geomatic system manipulates 3-D relief maps as seen from the perspective of a pilot. It can be interfaced to a geographic database to permit the simulation and display of such maps.[44]

> At Hitachi, CAD/CAM is a component of the factory automation system, which is based on distributed work stations for computer-aided engineering.[45]

CIM

Currently superseding CAD/CAM as the most talked-about computer-related manufacturing strategy is Computer Integrated Manufacturing (CIM). Its virtues are being hailed by IBM, General Electric, and many other companies. Large expenditures in the area are anticipated. ''The 1989 world marketplace for automation is variously estimated to be $65 billion to $75 billion, up from about $15 billion in 1983.''[46] Of that total market, IBM estimates that about $26 billion will be spent on CIM.

An exact definition of CIM is not possible, as most commentators characterize it as a concept or approach rather than a well-established manufacturing system. Still, it can be characterized in a variety of ways. CIM has been discussed in regard to two different organizational schemes: vertical and horizontal. Vertical integrated manufacturing, the most commonly understood reference to CIM, involves the use of CAD to design a product and a CAM system to produce it directly from the CAD instructions. The entire process, including inventory control, shipping strategies, and production schedules, and other procedures that depend on MISs and CAP systems, is controlled and regulated by CIM. The horizontal approach, on the other hand, is concerned only with systematizing the manufacturing process itself—the computer control and coordination of equipment on the factory floor. This latter approach is also subsumed under the term flexible manufacturing systems (FMS).

Another approach suggests that CIM must be viewed from three perspectives—those of the *user*, the *technology*, and the *enterprise*.[47] The user is concerned with the entire business, including financial matters, and marketing. Management techniques that have been employed include total quality control (TQC), materials requirement planning (MRP), and just in time (JIT). This last technique, popularized in Japan, is a way to reduce inventory costs by requiring suppliers to deliver components exactly when they are needed.

The technology perspective emphasizes the suppliers' contribution to CIM—computer equipment, software, database systems, and communications systems. The competition among vendors for individual segments of this large market is keen, and only such companies as IBM and DEC attempt to offer more complete product lines. A crucial factor in any integrated system is the communication network that links all the various components. The most influential approach in this area is currently General Motor's *Manufacturing Automation Protocol*. Another important area is databases, because a wide variety of information must be accessible at all points of the manufacturing process. The market for CIM will be competitive, as companies attempt to establish their presence. IBM is particularly aggressive, seeking to extend its dominating presence into every aspect of the company office and factory floor.

Finally, the enterprise view attempts to deal with issues common to two other views: ''The enterprise view of CIM contains planning and project management procedures, system and data standards, budgeting and performance controls, and organization responsibilities. . . .''[48] Standards are a pivotal factor in the entire process—a basic requirement for both the smooth growth and maximum benefit of emerging technology. Thinking about the overall picture is a prerequisite for management in its quest for improved efficiency. CIM is not an off-the-shelf product but more a philosophy or approach for utilizing developments in computer hardware, robotics, software and application programs, graphics, and information systems.

NONINDUSTRIAL APPLICATIONS

Into the foreseeable future, industry will continue to be the home for most robots, but other applications are on the horizon. A recent report by the Japanese Industrial Robot Association predicts the following applications:[49]

Nuclear Power. Handling dangerous materials related to nuclear power plants and radioactive waste processing; emergency and periodic inspection of plant operating conditions.

Medical and Social Welfare. "Nurse" robots to take care of physically handicapped people and aged patients in bed, aid in certain surgical procedures, fire-fighting, street-sweeping.

Marine Development. Work on fishing vessels. Submarine robots that can construct fish farms and build marine structures in deep water. Underwater machine processing, mining, and various other underwater operations.

Agriculture and Forestry. Insecticide spraying on farms, spreading of fertilizer, egg inspection and packing, milking, lumbering, fruit harvesting, gathering debris.

Construction. Assembling steel superstructures, painting or cleaning buildings, finishing interiors and exteriors of high-rise buildings.

Another application, mentioned above, is the home robot, perhaps autonomous or connected to the home computer. A number of companies—including Zenith Radio Corporation's Heath Company and Androbot (an offshoot of the Catalyst Technology Company, set up by Nolan Bushnell, the founder of Atari)—are currently manufacturing small robots controlled by on-board microprocessors. These have limited abilities now, but it is expected that in a few years their range of skills will be greatly expanded. Initial applications will probably be home security, maintenance, and cleaning. A central computer that controls such a device, with motor and sensor abilities, is conceivable.

SUMMARY

Although robots were first invented in the United States, Japan has taken the initiative and become the clear world leader in their production and use. Major U.S. corporations such as IBM, Westinghouse, General Electric, and General Motors have recently entered the market, in some cases in partnership with Japanese and European manufacturers. Robots can be characterized along several dimensions—including kinematics, drive sources, behavior (servo or non-servo), control (point to point or continuous path), and programmability. There is some confusion about the numbers and kinds of robots being used around the world. Japan is dominant, followed by the United States and West Germany.

Some of the major applications of robots in the factory are welding, painting, machining, assembly, materials handling, and machine loading and unloading. Robots of the current generation are severely limited in their ability to react to unplanned events. Very active research areas—deriving in part from work in AI—are vision, tactile abilities, and planning. The major arguments for introducing robots predict improvements in productivity, quality control, and production management. Human workers might be replaced in hazardous and unpleasant environments. The Japanese success in manufacturing is not based soley on robotics. It would be a mistake for U.S. companies to introduce robots unaccompanied by many good management practices. In terms of labor relations, the successful introduction of robots will depend on careful planning, consultation, monitoring, and retraining of displaced workers.

Robots are only one part of the automation picture. Such important developments as CAD/CAM and CIM are gradually changing the nature of production. CIM is probably more philosophy now than working system, but the promise is great and the stakes are high.

NOTES

1. *Computerized Manufacturing Automation: Employment, Education, and the Workplace*, U.S. Congress, Office of Technology Assessment OTA-CIT-235 (Washington, D.C., April 1984).

2. Robert U. Ayres and Steven M. Miller, *Robotics: Applications and Social Implications* (Cambridge, Mass.: Balinger, 1983), p. 29.

3. "Robot Institute of America Worldwide Robotics Survey and Directory," Robot Institute of America (Dearborn, Michigan, 1982), p. 1.

4. As reported in *Applied Artificial Intelligence Reporter*, The University of Miami, June 1985, p. 1BH. Laura Conigliaro, a robot expert for Prudential-Bache, expects 1985 sales to reach $495 million.

5. George Leopold, "Advances in Software Systems May Bring Integrated Robotics," *Electronics Week*, August 27, 1984, p. 24.

6. *Computerized Manufacturing Automation*, p. 54.

7. Wesley R. Iverson, "Robots Ready to Take Jobs in Clean-Rooms," *Electronics Week*, October 15, 1984, p. 11.

8. David M. Weber, "Smart Carts Tackle In-Plant Tasks," *Electronics Week*, August 20, 1984, pp. 37–38, 41.

9. David M. Weber, "Machine-Vision Maker Sees Industrial Inspection Rather Than Robots as its Major Market," *Electronics Week*, July 30, 1984, pp. 31–32.

10. Edith Myers, "Now It's Personal Robots," *Datamation*, August 15, 1984, pp. 57–58.

11. Ayres and Miller, *Robotics*, p. 40.

12. John Gosch, "With Radar-Like Ranging Technique, Robots Can See in Three Dimensions," *Electronics Week*, September 10, 1984, pp. 36–38.

13. John W. Dizard, ''Machines That See Look for a Market,'' *Fortune,* September 17, 1984, pp. 87–88, 92, 96, 100, 104.

14. Charles L. Cohen, ''Intelligent Robots Break New Ground,'' *Electronics Week,* January 21, 1985, pp. 46–47.

15. Richard M. Cyert (President of Carnegie-Mellon University) ''Making a Case for Unmanned Factories,'' *The New York Times,* July 15, 1984, p. F3.

16. James Cambrinos and W. G. Johnson, ''Robots to Reduce the High Cost of Illness and Injury,'' *Harvard Business Review,* May/June 1984, pp. 24, 26, 28.

17. As quoted in Stephen F. Friedman and Louise Thomas, ''Robotics: Arms for Industry,'' *The Detroiter,* February 1982, p. 22.

18. Robert B. Reich, *The Next American Frontier* (Middlesex, England: Penguin, 1984), p. 118.

19. E. Denison, Brooking Institute, as quoted in ''The Decline of Productivity and the Resultant Loss of U.S. World Economic and Political Leadership,'' Robot Institute of America (Dearborn, Michigan, March, 1981), p. 3.

20. Robert H. Hayes, ''Why Japanese Factories Work,'' *Harvard Business Review,* July/August 1981, pp. 57–66.

21. As quoted in Hayes, ''Why Japanese Factories Work,'' p. 64.

22. Ibid., p. 65.

23. Peter F. Drucker, ''Behind Japan's Success,'' *Harvard Business Review,* January/February 1981, pp. 83–90.

24. Andrew Weiss, ''Simple Truths of Japanese Manufacturing,'' *Harvard Business Review,* July/August 1984, p. 119.

25. Ibid., p. 124.

26. Steve Lohr, ''The Company that Stopped Detroit,'' *The New York Times,* March 21, 1982, p. 26F. (Figures given are from 1981).

27. ''Look, No Hands,'' *Time,* November 16, 1981, p. 89.

28. *Industrial Robots,* Japanese External Trade Organization (Tokyo, 1981), pp. 14–15.

29. Ibid., p. 15.

30. Jimmy L. Haugen, vice-president for automotive assembly systems, GMFANUC Robotics Corporation, as quoted in David Whiteside et al., ''How GM's Saturn Could Run Rings Around Old-Style Carmakers,'' *Business Week,* January 28, 1985, p. 128.

31. Fred K. Foulkes and Jeffrey L. Hirsch, ''People Make Robots Work,'' *Harvard Business Review,* January/February 1984, p. 97.

32. George Poulin, vice-president, International Association of Machinists, as quoted in Charles Bruno, ''Labor Relations in the Age of Robotics,'' *Datamation,* March 1984, p. 182.

33. William F. White, Professor at Sociology (Emeritus), Cornell University, as quoted in Peter Stone ''Humans and Robots: a Wary Alliance,'' *The New York Times,* September 25, 1983, p. F15.

34. H. Allan Hunt and Timothy L. Hunt, *Human Resource Implications of Robotics* (Kalamazoo: W. E. Upjohn Institute for Employment Research, 1983), p. x.

35. As quoted in Bruno, ''Labor Relations,'' p. 150.

36. Ibid., p. 182.

37. William J. Broad, ''U.S. Factories Reach into the Future,'' *The New York Times*, March 13, 1984, p. C1.

38. *Computerized Manufacturing Automation*, pp. 32–98. This report is an invaluable refrence on industrial automation.

39. As quoted in Kenneth Klee, ''CAD/CAM: Who's in Charge?'' *Datamation*, February 1982, p. 110.

40. Gene Bylinsky, ''A New Industrial Revolution is on the Way,'' *Fortune*, October 5, 1981, p. 107.

41. John J. Krouse, ''Automation Revolutionizes Mechanical Design,'' *High Technology*, March 1984, p. 37.

42. Tosiyasu L. Kunn, ''Practice and Progress in CAD/CAM, *Computer*, December 1984, p. 11.

43. Ken-ichi Kobori et al., ''A 3-D CAD/CAM System with Interactive Simulation Facilities,'' *Computer*, December 1984, pp. 14–21.

44. Daniel Laurent and Serge Motet, ''Geomatic: A 3-D Graphic Relief Simulation System,'' *Computer*, December 1984, pp. 25–30.

45. Norihisa Komoda, Kazuo Kera, and Takeaki Kubo, ''An Autonomous, Decentralized Control System for Factory Automation,'' *Computer*, December 1984, pp. 73–81.

46. Daniel S. Appleton, ''The State of CIM,'' *Datamation*, December 15, 1984, pp. 66.

47. Ibid., pp. 66–68.

48. Ibid., p. 68.

49. ''Japan's Robot Industry Exceeds Predictions,'' *The Futurist*, June 1982, p. 78.

ADDITIONAL READINGS

Industrial Robotics

Friedman, Stephen F., and Louise Thomas. ''Robotics: Arms for Industry.'' *The Detroiter*, February 1982, pp. 20–31.

Froehlich, Leonard. ''Robots to the Rescue.'' *Datmation*, January 1981, pp. 85–86, 88, 90, 94, 96.

Zimmerman, Marlene. ''The Robot Master.'' *Datmation*, April 1982, pp. 193–194, 196, 198.

Current Use and Development

Edson, Daniel V. ''Giving Robot Hands a Human Touch.'' *High Technology*, September 1985, pp. 31–35.

McCorduck, Pamela. *Machines Who Think*. San Francisco: Freeman, 1979.

Raphael, Bertram. *The Thinking Computer*. San Francisco: Freeman, 1976.

Why Use Robots? Work and Productivity

Argote, Linda, and Paul S. Goodman. "*Investigating the Implementation of Robotics*." Technical Report, The Robotics Institute, Carnegie-Mellon University. Pittsburgh, February 1984.

Argote, Linda, Paul S. Goodman, and David Schkade. *The Human Side of Robotics: Results from a Prototype Study on How Workers React to a Robot*. Technical Report, The Robotics Institute, Carnegie-Mellon University. Pittsburgh, May 1983.

The Decline of Productivity and the Resultant Loss of U.S. World Economic and Political Leadership. Robot Institute of America, Policy Document No. 1. Dearborn, Michigan, March 1981.

Weber, David M. "Treat 'Em With Respect, Says Robot Standard." *Electronics Week*, December 10, 1984, pp. 34–35.

Whiteside, David, et al., "How GM's Saturn Could Run Rings Around Old-Style Carmakers." *Business Week*, January 28, 1985, pp. 126, 128.

Industrial Automation

Johnson, Jan. "Pushing the State of the Art." *Datamation*, February 1982, pp. 112, 114.

Keller, Erik L. "Industry Tools up for Flexibility." *Electronics*, May 5, 1983, pp. 105, 107.

Miller, Stephen M. "Impacts of Robotic and Flexible Manufacturing Technologies on Manufacturing Costs and Employment." Technical Report, The Robotics Institute, Carnegie-Mellon University. Pittsburgh, March 1984.

13
THE INFORMATION SOCIETY

*I*n 1982, a cascade of computers beeped and blipped their
way into the American office, the American school, the
American home. The "information revolution" that futur-
ists have long predicted has arrived, bringing with it the promise of dramatic changes in the way people live and work,
perhaps even in the way they think. America will never
be the same.

◇ Time, *January 3, 1983* ◇

INTRODUCTION

Time declared the computer "Machine of the Year" for 1982. In the form of the personal
computer, it had truly arrived as a major factor in the national consciousness. On television
and in magazines a Charlie Chaplin look-alike shows how a personal computer, the IBM
PC, will save your small business. The once almost mystical mainframe has emerged
from the cloistered computing center, transformed into a terminal and television set. Other
companies are heavily engaged in trying to convince American families to purchase
computers. Such names as Apple, Commodore, Radio Shack, Digital Equipment, and
Texas Instruments have become quite familiar. The competition is fierce, and there have
been and will continue to be many casualties.

Families will continue to buy computers in great numbers to give their children a head
start, to manage the family accounts, to file recipes, and to play games. Personal computers
have another important role to play—as terminals to connect to two-way television sys-

tems, usually called videotex. The "information age" is a vision of comprehensive communication networks that link homes, businesses, and government offices. Banking, shopping, education, entertainment, and more will all be accessible from the comfort of one's home. How will such possibilities affect society? Part of the answer must be speculative, but a number of issues have already emerged.

Another aspect of the information society is the replacement of letters by electronic mail and of face-to-face meetings by teleconferencing. In the first case, information in physical form is converted to electronic form, for long-distance transmission. The transmission will be initiated and ultimately received in a variety of ways. Perhaps videotex systems play a role here as well. Teleconferencing is not a new idea, but one that has evolved somewhat more slowly than anticipated. In order to interact meaningfully, humans require a host of visual and verbal signs. The new technology must find a way to provide these efficiently and economically.

The remarkable achievements in microelectronics have meant that within a very short time computers have been drastically reduced in size, power consumption, and cost, and their power has increased. The microprocessor is now a component of almost every industrial product. Household appliances, heating and air conditioner controls, automobiles, cameras, and stereo equipment are among familiar items that now incorporate microprocessors. This equipment is lighter, more efficient, and more flexible. The use of microprocessors changes the nature of the repair process. With fewer mechanical or traditional electronic parts, the speed of production is increased, the quality of the product is improved, and to repair means to replace an integrated component.

The character of the information society is manifested in the widespread availability of computing power via personal computers, the move toward information as a prime commodity, the increasing reliance on computer communication networks at home and work, and the diffusion of microelectronics into every facet of contemporary life. In a book called *The Coming of the Post-Industrial Society,* Daniel Bell, a noted American sociologist, was reluctant to use such terms as "information society," "information age," "future shock," (and later, "the third wave") to describe what he felt was the natural next step in the evolution of western society from its current advanced industrial state.[1] He attempted to predict how institutions would respond to a decreasing dependence on production and an increasing reliance on the service area. The remarkable developments in computers and communications suggest that society will be remade in a fashion far more striking than he anticipated.

The information society does not obviate the absolute necessity of a strong, innovative, and vigorous industrial base. In early 1985, the President's Commission on Industrial Competitiveness warned that America was in danger of suffering a severe reduction in its standard of living and rate of economic growth. The foreign deficit is large and growing, and the following arguments are typically proposed to explain the situation:

> The U.S. dollar is so strong that U.S. goods cannot compete internationally.
>
> The rest of the economy is doing so well that a few trouble spots are not significant.

Since the U.S. is becoming a service economy, the manufacturing decline is not important.

With regard to the last point, the opinion of the commission is as follows:

False. . . . for two reasons. First, if America wants to go on importing foreign goods, it will eventually have to sell exports to pay for them. International trade in services is still small and is unlikely ever to be big enough for America to swap, e.g. cars for legal advice. Second, services and manufacturing go hand in hand; the first satisfies demands created by the second.[2]

Thus, whatever the postindustrial society may become, America must maintain a strong and secure industrial base. The information society will not exclude industry, it will reshape it.

THE HOME/PERSONAL COMPUTER

Though the personal computer was born less than a decade ago, it already ranks up there with soap and soft drinks in ad expenditures.[3]

What is the distinction between the terms home computer and personal computer? Although there is no clear dividing line, the home computer market is generally considered to be under $1000, usually under $500. Such computers are usually sold as a keyboard with internal memory varying from 4K to 64K. They are meant to be hooked up to a television set, which provides pictures less sharp than on a dedicated monitor. For all but the simplest of tasks, peripheral devices are necessary—such as a cassette recorder or a floppy disk drive. Printers, varying in price from $200 to $2000, are also being heavily marketed. The most successful manufacturer in this market is probably Commodore, with its Vic 20 and 64 models, and the recently announced, Amiga. Texas Instruments' 99/4A was also quite popular until the company decided in late 1983 to abandon the home computer market because of substantial losses. At the low end of the price spectrum was the Timex (or Sinclair) ZX81, which could be bought for less than $50, including an expansion 16K memory module and a built-in BASIC interpreter. It also is now discontinued.

The personal computer, usually sold for more than $2500, includes a keyboard and internal memory of at least 64K (usually 128K), a monitor, and a floppy disk drive. For more advanced uses, additional internal memory, another disk drive, perhaps a hard disk, and a printer are necessary. A large array of programs are available for financial purposes, word processing, and database management. Suitably equipped, a personal computer can be used as part of distributed computing network in both large and small businesses (see Chapter 4). They are also used quite extensively as stand-alone machines in most elementary and secondary schools in the country. The best-selling computers in this market have been produced by IBM, Apple, Radio Shack, Digital Equipment, Commodore, and Hewlett-Packard. As in other computer markets, IBM has become the dominant force;

the IBM PC is now the standard, and most personal computer manufacturers must be PC-compatible—that is, able to run PC software—to survive.

The Home

The fact that the home computer is being sold so heavily represents a triumph of American marketing ingenuity more than the fulfillment of a genuine need. As matters stand now, the home computer is a machine in search of a purpose. Consumers are assaulted by advertisements that use the following strategies:

Induce guilt. Parents will be denying their children "a piece of the future" if they do not immediately buy a computer.

Promise immediate solutions. You can save your bakery or hat factory by organizing production with a personal computer.

Urge more purchases. The computer itself is only a small part of the story. It is necessary to buy more software, a disk drive, a printer, and a modem.

Argue for the complete package. For very little you can buy the whole thing: computer, high-speed cassette recorder, and printer.

Remind the consumer of video games. Although computers are useful, a wide range of exciting video games will be sure to please the whole family.

For many families the computer that they purchased with the best of intentions is used mainly to play video games. Frequently it has been relegated to a closet because the initial excitement has worn off, and it takes too much work to do anything with it but play games. Some still use it to manage family finances, but even here there may be problems if unusual circumstances arise. Storing recipes seems like a good idea, but they must all be typed in, and additional storage may be necessary. Mr. Michael Wiener, chairman of Infinity Broadcasting, bought an inexpensive home computer to store a selection of recipes from a large collection. None of the programs available in the $20–$500 range were suitable, so Wiener's son modified a standard database program. Upon typing in his recipes, Wiener noted:

It was so tedious I soon gave up. And I realize now that leafing through the books with their pictures—and food stains—is part of what makes my hobby enjoyable.[4]

The early story of the home computer tells of more appearance than substance, but eventually it may have a happy ending. As the technology advances, the home computer will become increasingly powerful, in terms of hardware and software, until the common phrase "user-friendly" is truly realized. Apple claims that its Macintosh *is* the realization of such a home computer. The comparison between the computer and the automobile in their early stages of development offers an interesting lesson: The car would never have become so popular had the consumer been required to acquire the skills of a mechanic to use it. The computer is being sold as a powerful device, immediately useful without much knowledge of its inner workings. However, the parallel between cars and computers breaks down in a fundamental way. A car has a straightforward, but narrowly defined purpose, and knowledge of how to operate it enables the driver to use it. A computer can do so many things that a knowledge of programming gives great power to the user. In its current state, however, programming is not particularly easy, and so most users depend on others to program for them.

To computer manufacturers, selling the basic hardware is a foot in the door. The initial modest outlay buys a piece of equipment that is not very useful. It needs to be supplemented by more hardware and by a seemingly endless array of packaged programs. There are programs for all needs: educational, financial, word processing, record-keeping, and the ever-popular video games. Such progams, a necessary expenditure for most users, have spawned a highly competitive industry. The burden is on the user to become familiar with these programs and to operate within the constraints defined by them. In the future, new programming languages will be developed to encourage nonprofessionals to write their own programs. The programming process itself will probably become substantially different in the years to come. The key will be to define what is desired rather than how to achieve it. Newer programming languages that are starting to appear have a built-in problem-solving strategy. The user's task is to state the properties of an appropriate solution and characterize the nature of the problem domain.

The Office

While personal computers have been oversold in the home, they have been changing the way computing is done in the office. As the power of such computers increases, every desk has the potential to provide access to the company's database. Distributed computing (see Chapter 4) will become a reality and usher in a new period of expansion and sophistication in data processing. The combination of advanced personal computers and communication networks—both local and long-distance—will substantially alter the way business is conducted. The gathering, processing, and presentation of information in a variety of forms will occupy the time and talent of many people. Those companies able to adapt to the new technology and to control the potential chaos inherent in distributed processing will benefit from the vast power available.

For many businesses, the power of distributed processing, manifested in personal computers, has already changed operational structure. No longer are executives totally dependent on data processing professionals to supply desired information. Taking advantage of computers at their desks and homes, a new generation of executives can scan relevant data independently.

By using the company's internal computer network, employees can send messages to one another, schedule meetings, plan trips, cooperate on reports, and generally facilitate the flow of information within and without the corporation. Whatever else the term information society comes to mean, a crucial factor is the centrality of information in business operations. Information has played a significant role previously, but the new technology will redefine the importance of information processing. For some industries, information is *the* commodity—for example, local and long-distance telephone systems and banking and financial institutions. In the former case, the efficient, rapid, and inexpensive transmission of information is the main business, although these companies are moving into the computer field as well. The banking industry is undergoing a major change (see Chapter 11). Electronic banking, debit cards, and home banking are transforming banks from brick and mortar institutions into a network of computers and communication systems. Even for companies not directly involved in information as a product, operating procedures have been affected by new techniques in information handling.

The personal computer has been an important component in all of the above developments. The fact that so many people now have access to computers, that computers are no longer the carefully guarded preserve of a few, and that a concerted effort is underway to increase ease of use, can only mean that the decison-making process will be improved. One important caveat: Computers, of whatever form, are no panacea for a failure of managerial skills. New methods are needed to deal with the enormous quantities of information available. More information, in and of itself, is likely to prove an obstacle; what is needed is information that is appropriate, selective, properly presented, and available on demand.

Artificial Intelligence is expected to make an important contribution to the improvement of information access. Expert systems will enable more people to have at their disposal powerful problem-solving systems in specialized domains. Access to such systems and many others will be facilitated by the provision of natural language interfaces. Sophisticated interfaces give intelligent forms of access to many people for many different kinds of data. They should encourage interested people to make use of information that would otherwise be unavailable except by the construction of formal queries in a specialized language. The ability to interact with computers in a natural way may well be the significant step in achieving the information society. The difficulties, both theoretical and practical, associated with the achievement of feasible natural language interfaces suggest that there will be no sudden breakthroughs.

At Large

The computer has suddenly become a media star, in its ubiquitous personal form. The newsstands are becoming saturated with computer magazines—general interest ones such as *Byte, Personal Computing,* and *Popular Computing,* and others that appeal to owners of computers made by IBM, Apple, Commodore, and others. Everyone seems to be talking about home computers, either trying to decide which one to buy or justifying their purchases. Much of this activity has the feel of a typical fad, but a substantial and important residue should remain after the initial novelty has worn off. Many people have become disillusioned because of the unexpected limitations of their home computers; for many others, though, a new world has been revealed. With a computer connected via a modem to the telephone, the user has access to a growing number of databases.

For businessmen, Dow Jones provides an on-line service to the stock market, with current quotations readily available. The variety of databases is expanding rapidly in response to the increasing number of people with computers, modems, and specialized interests. Other examples are News Net, with over 200 specialized newsletters; Telerate, with information on the credit market and currency values as well as ski conditions and Japanese baseball scores; NEXIS, with access to most major magazines and newspapers; and Dialog Information Services, the largest database system, which offers access to over 200 databases. User networks have been set up that enable people with common interests to share information. The growth of such networks is a major development of the information age. The ability of people all across the country to communicate over computer networks may contribute to a kind of democratization of computer power. The more people have access to computers, communication networks, and databases, the more ideas will be exchanged and relations developed. In the view of some, the interactions facilitated by these networks are no substitute for face-to-face human relations, and in fact may retard emotional growth.

Networks have been developed for professional and research reasons. ARPANET links research facilities at universities, private institutions, and others, which carry out research funded by the Defense Advanced Research Project Agency of the Department of Defense. This network, and others like it, encourages researchers to exchange information prior to publication in journals. A network called CSNET provides a communication system for computer science researchers across the country. It actually spans several existing networks and allows geographically remote researchers to work together. Ideas can readily be exchanged and joint papers written without face-to-face interaction. One researcher prepares a draft and sends a message to a colleague, who then makes corrections or additions over the network.

A larger community of interested researchers can also share in the articulation of new ideas. One researcher writes a proposal and then sends out a message over the network to his fellow researchers encouraging them to criticize his work. In some sense, an electronic forum has been created for the free and open exchange of information. Distributed computing power, communication networks, and sophisticated software have made possible an extended, underground college. The early exchange of ideas should help advance research and accelerate the diffusion of new results in the community at large.

ELECTRONIC MAIL AND TELECONFERENCING

This book is concerned with the recent emergence of a new alternative for conducting communication among groups or networks of persons or organizations such as meetings, study groups, and teaching-learning exchanges. It uses computers and computer terminals to provide a written form of discussion or meeting among a group of people.[5]

What will be the role of the postal service in the age of microelectronics? Various challengers have appeared on the scene, and the postal service has responded with its own version of electronic mail. Teleconferencing promises to combine television and computer networks to facilitate profitable human interaction at long distance.

Electronic Mail

For some years the U.S. Postal Service has been under considerable pressure to improve its performance. Private companies have entered into competition recently with it, promising guaranteed overnight delivery to major cities. The Postal Service must serve the entire country on a regular basis and does not have the luxury of choosing only the profitable routes. In anticipation of developments in computer communication systems, and fearful of losing its role in the future, the Postal Service began to investigate the possibility of providing electronic mail several years ago. This effort culminated with a system, Electronic Computer-Originated Mail (E-COM), that began operation near the end of 1981. It combines electronic communication with traditional mail delivery and currently is available only for companies whose computers are compatible with those of the Postal Service. Using its computer, a company transmits a message to the Postal Service's computer, which then sends it via telephone lines, to computers in any one of 25 cities. At their destinations the messages are printed and automatically folded and inserted in envelopes, ready for regular mail delivery. The entire process is supposed to be accomplished within two days. In the first year of operation, a message which cost the Postal Service $5.51 to deliver was a bargain at 26 cents. By the second year, the cost to the Postal Service was reduced to $1. However, the total volume has not reached initial forecasts; 50 million pieces were expected by the second year but fewer than 18 million were delivered. Furthermore, the Postal Service is under attack from several quarters—including the Justice Department, the Federal Trade Commission, and the House of Representatives—about the possible illegality of E-COM.

Basically, the problem is that the Service is using profits from its first-class delivery to subsidize the electronic system. This action seems to violate provisions of the law under which the Postal Service was created. The Service argues that it must establish a presence in this market or face possible extinction. (On June 5, 1984, after two years of operation and losses totalling about $50 million, the Board of Governors of the Postal Service voted to discontinue E-COM.) About half of all first-class letters currently consist of bills and payments. These will eventually be handled by electronic means and their loss will be a significant one. Current trends seem to suggest that businesses will arrange for their own systems of communication with their customers, while the Postal Service will be expected to provide service for the general public. For anyone with his or her own terminal and modem, access to electronic mail is available from other sources.

MCI Communications Corporation, which successfully challenged AT&T in the long-distance telephone market, has entered the mail market in competition with the U.S. Postal Service, the new express delivery companies, and the growing activity in electronic mail. MCI seems well positioned to succeed in this new endeavor, given its substantial cross-country communications network. To customers with their own terminals MCI provides communication networks for transmitting and receiving messages. Only the senders are charged, at a rate of $1 per MCI ounce—equivalent to 7500 characters or about four pages of text. This price applies only if the recipient also has a terminal and modem. If not, the letter will be sent to one of MCI's 15 post offices and delivered a day later ($2). Overnight letters are delivered the next day by Purolator Courier ($6) or within four hours ($25). Additional "ounces" are $1 each for all categories.

When MCI began operation in September 1983, it was off to a running start with 55,000 customers and expected to have over 250,000 by the end of 1984. In fact, only 150,000 subscribers were attained, and these generated more than one million messages a month. Other features of MCI's service include no minimum number of pages and the use of laser printers, which can reproduce trademarks and logos. The competition is growing rapidly, with such companies as Tymnet, GTE (OnTym), Telenet Communications (Telemail), and General Electric Information Services (Quik-Comm), providing computer-to-computer service. Even with so many companies in the electronic mail market—over 30 at the end of 1984—no profits are being reported, and revenues are quite low. Followers of the industry believe that development will take place at a slower rate than was previously thought, with a major takeoff not occurring until the late 1980s or early 1990s. Currently, "most use of electronic mail is internal—44 percent interoffice and 31 percent intercompany." Thus, the competition in the market is for a small percentage of actual users. Many companies use an electronic mail service to gain experience prior to implementing their own in-house system, which can take advantage of competitive rates in the long-distance market.

Another form of electronic mail service makes use of something called an electronic mailbox. The different services may be compared as follows:

> A. *Direct Electronic Mail.* S at her terminal sends a message over a telephone line that R reads at his terminal as it is being sent.
>
> B. *Electronic Mail via Central Mailbox.* S sends a message to an electronic "mailbox." At some point in the future R checks the mailbox for any new messages.
>
> C. *Electronic Mail via Local Mailbox.* S uses her computer to send a message overnight because of cheaper rates. On the following day R checks his computer for any new messages.

In situation A, both parties must be connected when the message is being sent, although S may have prepared the message earlier. This situation is similar to making a long-distance telephone call. Situation B requires a centralized facility for storing the electronic mail. One such company that performs this service is called The Source. It rents mailboxes to subscribers at quite reasonable rates: $10 per month plus $.50 per 2000 characters stored, in 1983. This situation is analogous to post office mailboxes. In situation C, the mailbox is maintained on the host computer. Whenever R signs on, he is prompted to check his mail. This last use of electronic mailboxes is only viable if R's computer is on-line when the message is being sent out. A telephone answering device connected to the modem can receive the message in response to a telephone call. Appropriate communications software are necessary to receive the information and store it accordingly.

Most office automation systems have an electronic mail facility, and some companies have extended such local systems to their worldwide operations. One example is Tandem Computer, a manufacturer of mainframe computers. Every Tandem employee around the world has an electronic mailbox. This system is used for problem solving, technical information exchange, scheduling of meetings, and (interestingly enough) to transmit personal information—an important fringe benefit. The effective use of electronic mail systems within large organizations will facilitate decision making and execution. For the public at large, the growth of electronic mail systems—whether public or private—will depend on how well the perceived needs are met, and at what price. As more families purchase personal computers, there will be an increased desire to communicate with other users and to access databanks of all kinds.

Teleconferencing

Teleconferencing may be viewed as an evolution of electronic mail systems to include the simultaneous exchange of information among several conversants. Telephone teleconferencing has been used for quite a while, not altogether successfully. There are problems in conversation when participants are not able to see one another. Visual cues are very important in turn-taking, and visual feedback indicates to speakers what effect their contribution has on the other participants. It seems necessary to expand the teleconferencing mode of operation to include visual interaction via a television system. As a preliminary or even alternate step, an electronic mail system can be expanded to manage multi-user interaction. The lack of face-to-face contact will still be a problem, but other features may help.

One form of computer teleconferencing uses the computer to send messages instantaneously to all the other participants. As with electronic mail, these messages can be read as soon as they are received or stored for later access. A typical system, operating over an efficient, low-cost, packet-switched network, might operate in the following way: Once on the network, the user would be told which other members of his group were currently active, whether any messages were waiting for him, and whether there were any comments on matters currently under consideration—the conference issues. The user has a variety of options: (a) scan the messages, (b) read some or all of them, (c) scan the conference comments, (d) reply to some or all of them either directly to on-line members or others, or (e) review previous comments in the conference prior to making a new contribution. The system permits, in fact encourages, user interaction over long distances and at all times, either in real-time or by stored messages. The size of the group can grow quite large without affecting the degree of participation of the individual members. One advantage over face-to-face communication is that in some real sense, all participants can ''speak'' simultaneously and the messages are broadcast to everyone. This situation represents a real democracy in that no member of the group has precedence. Because the interaction takes place over computers, a host of services not otherwise available, are immediately accessible. Among these are editing facilities, immediate access to computer-stored data, the scheduling of face-to-face meeetings, person-to-person messages, and administration of votes. One obvious drawback is the necessity to type all information. Although typing rates are slower than speaking, typed information can usually be understood (or perhaps skimmed) more quickly than spoken languages. For the input phase, a variety of text-editing aids assist in the preparation of messages and reduce the usual difficulties of typographical error corrections. An experimental system has been developed to encourage people with minimal computer skills to feel comfortable in a teleconferencing environment. Called the Electronic Information Exchange System (EIES), it has been used to determine which features are most conducive to teleconferencing. Standard electronic mail systems were found to be too limited for long-term users. They must be able to tailor the system to their own needs by defining their own computer commands. Sophisticated word processing is mandatory for a system of communication that relies heavily on typing.

Recent developments in communications have made videoconferencing a more attractive proposition. Special computers have been designed that can effectively code television signals into digital form, compress it substantially by removing redundant information, and transmit it. The result is transmission of full-motion color pictures using a narrow band width equivalent to that of 12 phone calls. Competition among long-distance carriers has reduced the cost of transmissions. Although it is just picking up momentum, the growth in the number of fully equipped conference rooms will more than double in 1984, exceeding 200. Companies such as J.C. Penney and Boeing have found videoconferencing important, because of savings in travel and because instantaneous long-distance communications can speed up design, marketing, and advertising decisions. As with electronic mail, the industry is not growing as fast as expected—probably because of cost and also because less expensive—though less comprehensive—alternatives are available for many purposes. One of these is the private satellite video network, or one-way video, by which satellites transmit TV signals directly from in-house studios to small-dish receivers.

A network of businessmen, computer hobbyists, new computer initiates, university researchers, and the like communicate readily over computer networks. Most of the population has been largely untouched by these developments. On the horizon, however, is videotex, a new technology that may reach into many homes.

VIDEOTEX

Publishers, banks, and retailers are about to begin selling services that enable people to make purchases, check bank balances, even buy and sell stocks—all without leaving home or talking to a human.[7]

What if a two-way communications network linked the homes of the nation via regional computer centers to a large number of businesses and services? From the comfort of one's home a vast array of transactions could be carried out using a specially equipped television monitor with keyboard. Among the possibilities are the following:

Information Retrieval. Probably the most basic service, it includes electronic newspapers and specialized databases and directories including stock market, entertainment, and sports, community and health services information.

Transactions. Making reservations for entertainment, sporting events, and travel, paying bills, electronic funds transfer (EFTS), teleshopping.

Messaging. A "switchboard" to store and forward messages from one user to another, electronic mail, electronic bulletin board (one-to-many communication), computer conferencing.

Computing. The keyboard can act as a computer terminal providing access to games and financial analysis programs, as well as more sophisticated activities such as the transmission of software from the central computer facility to the home computer.

Telemonitoring. Provision of home security by the remote sensing of fire or intruders with alarms triggered at security agencies; the control of systems within the home for energy management.

Working at Home. Accelerating current trends, stockbrokers, data processing professionals, designers, draftsmen, architects, real estate agents, travel agents, secretaries, editors, and so forth can do some or all of their work at home.

Services for the Disabled. The disabled can be monitored at home and communication with them facilitated by the use of Bliss symbols, Braille printers, and voice synthesizers.

Education at Home. Extension of current television education courses can be carried out as part of regular curricula and continuing education.

Although the prospects are mind boggling, this massive transformation of the marketplace, entertainment, education, and work will not take place overnight. A massive technological investment in computers, telecommunications, videotex decoders, software, and necessary database information is required before videotex will be viable. A few systems, still experimental, are currently in operation in the United States. Other countries, especially the United Kingdom, are much more advanced in this area. The competition is heating up in North America. The Knight-Ridder newspaper chain began a major service called Viewtron in the Miami area in late 1983.

Three forms of information services may be distinguished, as follows:

- **Information retrieval via on-line databases** Large databases storing many different kinds of information can be accessed on personal computers via telephone by paying a fee for services. Examples are newspaper files, financial information, and computer hardware and software specifications. The user must access a database, formulate a query, and interrogate the database.

• **Teletext**   This system provides a continuous stream of information that is available over a television channel. The information is repeatedly broadcast in the "blanking interval" between frames on a television channel. Using a special keypad, the viewer types in a number to designate a teletext frame, and a decoder freezes the selected frame. The amount of information available and the time needed to cycle through it determine how long the user must wait.

Videotex   (The *t* is usually dropped at the end of this word). A two-way information system. Typically, telephone lines are used to connect the central computer of the system to each individual user. The home user, by means of special keypad, requests information after viewing a "menu" of possibilities. The computer retrieves information from its own databank (or others to which it has access) and transmits it. An important feature is the ability to transmit graphics as well as text.

Information retrieval has generally been used by professionals—for example, stock brokers, lawyers, and financial analysts. Computer hobbyists have been using such systems as CompuServe and The Source, more often for their electronic mail facility rather than as an information utility. Teletext is more widely used than videotex because it is considerably less expensive. In Britain there are two teletext systems, Oracle and Ceefax, and about 30 percent of new television sets are equipped with appropriate adapters. Videotex is far more flexible but much more costly to implement, and so much-acclaimed developments are proceeding somewhat more slowly than advocates had expected.

The United Kingdom: Ceefax, Oracle, and Prestel

Britain was the first country to plan and introduce a teletext and later a videotex system. Engineers at the British Broadcasting Corporation (BBC) began work in 1970 and at the end of 1976 introduced a public teletext service. By the end of 1982, four services were available: two CEEFAX services provided on two BBC networks and the two ORACLE services on commercial networks. The rate of growth has been striking—from 15,000 teletext sets in 1976 to 950,000 in 1982, with an estimate of 1.6 million in 1983.

Teletext originated with the recognition that the previously unused portion of the television signal, which could be employed for close captioning for the deaf, was available to transmit a wide range of information. Teletext is available during the entire broadcast day, some eighteen hours. Information includes newspaper headlines, sports results, weather, recipes, stock quotations, games, and seat availability on the major airlines. One of the major strengths of teletext systems is that they make use of existing technology and thus are immediately available to large numbers of people. The BBC system has about 250 pages on each of two services, where a page is equivalent to one screen-full. The access time of about 12 seconds is faster than the ORACLE system's time of 25 seconds, but ORACLE offers some 375 pages.

Two questions are important: who supplies the information, and how heavily is the system used? The material for both BBC CEEFAX systems is prepared by staff people. The main network offers hard news and results, and the other offers mostly entertainment. Because it is publicly supported, the costs of CEEFAX are paid for out of license revenues. The private network's ORACLE system obtains part of its revenue by selling advertising space (up to a limit of 15 percent of the total number of pages). The BBC estimated in 1980 that the average teletext set was used about two hours per week. Teletext is coming into competition with videotex but because it is so much cheaper it will likely remain competitive. Future developments will include improved graphics, availability of computer software, direct computer-to-computer connections for the storage of teletext pages, and—in response to regional needs—a service for local advertisers and institutions.

Prestel, introduced in September 1979 by British Telecom (formerly Post Office Telecommunications) was the world's first public videotex service (called viewdata in Britain). By mid-1982 there were almost 18,000 Prestel sets, far below the expected level. More than 230,000 pages are available, supplied by over 900 information providers (IPs). Since July 1981, overseas subscribers have been given access to Prestel.[8] It has not achieved the success predicted by the early developers. As the United States launches various forms of videotex, the history of such systems, and their problems, are relevant.

In 1970 Sam Fedida, an engineer with the British Post Office, proposed an information retrieval system that would be accessible over ordinary telephone lines (in nonpeak hours, it was hoped), with display on specially adapted television sets. After a minimal working system was developed in 1974, it was decided to introduce a commercial version, with the following guidelines:

> Reliability is of prime importance.
>
> Simplicity of operation is necessary.
>
> Access must be fast and must permit many simultaneous users.
>
> Costs must be held as low as possible.
>
> Information would be stored in duplicate on a network of computers.

To take advantage of parallel developments in teletext, the decision was made to adopt the same display standards for both systems.

How does a user locate desired information on a videotex system? Prestel is fairly typical. Its keypad has the digits 0 to 9, and the symbols * and # are used to select individual pages. The memory structure of a videotex system is in the form of a large tree, with pages of information—with access numbers, including directories or menus—at the nodes. After entering Prestel, the user is given several options such as general interest, business information, local information, or gazette. Selecting one of these by entering the appropriate number brings up a new image on the screen. If general interest is chosen, subcategories might be news and weather, sports, entertainment, travel, government information, and books. The network is thus traversed until the desired information is found. A more experienced user goes directly to a particular page by entering its number.

Some virtues of Prestel are the ease with which information can be obtained, the use of existing telephone networks, the ease of creating and updating information pages, and—more recently—the use of the system for electronic mail. There are some limitations. Since a single page can only hold about 100 words, long pieces of information must be segmented into a sequence of pages. Ease of use depends on how well the database has been constructed. Under heavy use, the system can become congested and response time will escalate. The quality of the graphics is poor, compared to Telidon, for example (see below). Prestel is designed to present relatively straightforward information; sophisticated keyword searches are not possible.

Prestel is managed by British Telecom, the telecommunications service that was formerly part of the British Post Office. Telecom works very closely with both television set manufacturers—to produce either special videotex sets or adapters—and the information providers (IPs) seeking an avenue to advertise their products and services selectively. Disturbingly, there has been a relatively high turnover of IPs—as many as two-thirds. Some of the reasons are lack of appreciation of the nature of videotex technology, difficulty in keeping up with changing standards, and the lack of a proper role as yet for videotex advertising within the context of other media. Currently, most IPs come from the publishing industries, the travel trade, the government, financial institutions, the computer industry, and the TV industry.

On the horizon are plans to offer what are called gateway services. These would allow private videotex systems to be accessed via the public Prestel system. This process will permit instantaneous response to a variety of requests, such as confirmation of travel arrangements or theatre tickets, and banking transactions. The range of available information will be significantly expanded as private systems are brought on line. Private Prestel systems have been growing along with public developments. New applications have been found. Prestel can be an in-home information system for exchange of both pictorial and text information, a way of communicating between central offices and retail outlets for parts and deliveries, and a special purpose information system for a common interest group such as stock brokers. Personal computer users can purchase adapters that permit them to communicate with Prestel and—as one of its services—to obtain programs by a process called telesoftware.

Prestel's future is not assured. The rate of growth has been slow, especially when compared with teletext systems. Participants have taken longer than expected to become familiar with this new information utility. IPs have been slow in learning to package information for the new medium so as to reach their desired audience. The most popular pages in the system are product demonstrations, games, and quizzes. The future may see an implementation of Prestel on cable television—a direction being taken in the United States. The promises for videotex have so far exceeded its achievements, but this does not mean they will not be realized. Clearly, the technology has turned out to be more complex than anticipated. Videotex seems to be a sophisticated technological accomplishment in search of a viable market.

Canada: Telidon

Canada's version of videotex was announced in 1978 after almost ten years of development. Telidon operates with menus and direct page numbers in the usual manner, and is more advanced than European systems in the quality of its graphics. The European systems—Oracle, Prestel, and Antiope, sometimes called first generation videotex—use a method of pictorial representation called *alphamosaic*. Pictures are built up from a pattern of blocks in which both color and intensity can be controlled. The resolution leaves much to be desired, as straight diagonal lines look like staircases.

Telidon is a more advanced, second generation system, employing a graphics method called *alphageometric*. A system of points, lines, arcs, and polygons are used to produce a much more sophisticated image. Underlying the picture transmission is a communication protocol, the Picture Description Instructions (PDIs). For example, using PDIs, a line is described by its endpoints. A microprocessor in the Telidon terminal decodes the description of a picture, which has been transmitted in terms of PDIs, and then displays it on the screen. The description is independent of the display characteristics, so that on a high resolution monitor, finer increments can be used and greater fidelity achieved. Telidon is well suited to the representation of detailed graphics such as architectural plans, circuit diagrams, and weather maps, and such cursive alphabets as Arabic and Chinese.

Telidon was developed under the leadership of the Department of Communication, and the total Canadian government investment has been much less than that of the United Kingdom or France. The major supplier of information has been Infomart, a subsidiary of Southam, an owner of several major newspapers. This situation suggests that newspapers view videotex as the next stage of their evolution. In the near future a Montreal company, Videoway, will be marketing Telidon over cable—a faster way to deliver the service. On the international scene, Telidon is an active competitor for a share of the American market. It was helped immeasurably when AT&T and Columbia Broadcasting System (CBS) adopted standards compatible with Telidon. Telidon trials are in progress across Canada, the United States, and elsewhere. For example, in the United States, there are Telidon trials in Bakersfield and southern California over telephone lines, and teletext experiments in Washington, D.C. and Orlando, Florida.

In early 1981 a number of objectives for 1985 were presented to the Canadian cabinet. Among them were the following:

> Operational videotex services to be made available in all major urban areas across the country.
>
> Two national teletext services, in English and French, operated by both the government-owned CBC network and the private CTV network.
>
> Readily available Telidon terminals and adapters.

A number of provincial information services based on Telidon.

A profitable export service in hardware and software.

Other Countries

In most European countries and Japan, national governments are intimately involved in developing and promoting videotex. As of January 1985 the French government, through its Direction General des Telecommunications (DGT) had installed more than 500,000 free videotex termnals in French homes at a cost of at least $280 million. Plans are in place to install additional terminals at the rate of 100,000 per month. Part of the goal is to replace telephone books with an on-line electronic system while simultaneously stimulating the development of a large market for videotex services.

In Germany, the postal communication service has spent $233 million to set up the *Bildschirmtext* videotex system. There are only 18,000 users so far. Japan's Captain system was introduced by the state-run telephone company on November 30, 1984, with an initial offering of more than 450 services, including travel information, home shopping, news, weather, and stock market quotations. Because of the high cost of videotex terminals—about $900—widespread use may be limited. The government agencies are interested in fostering videotex networks, so that they may result in an increased use of the state-run telephone system, generating increased revenues.

The United States

During much of the early development of videotex, the United States was content to wait and watch what was happening in Britain, France, and Canada. Meanwhile, commercial on-line information retrieval systems were being developed by such companies as Mead Data Central, Dow-Jones News/Retrieval, and Dialog. With the appearance of the foreign videotex systems, a number of U.S. companies began their own field trials. Perhaps the most important recent event in the brief history of U.S. videotex took place in September, 1983, when Knight-Ridder Newspapers launched its Viewtron system. The long-term aim is to sign up 150,000 subscribers in the Miami-Fort Lauderdale area. At launching time the company had spent about $26 million. It expects Viewtron to earn large profits because of the efficiency of electronic transmission—there are fewer employees and lower distribution and production costs.

The range of services to be offered by Viewtron include the following:

News, weather, and sports from such sources as Associated Press, Dow Jones, and other Knight-Ridder papers, including the *Chicago Tribune* and the *New York Daily News.*

Official air-line guide schedules.

American Encyclopedia.

> The ability to specify an interest profile for a daily selection of stories and articles from the various databases.
>
> Electronic mail facility.
>
> Home shopping from a variety of stores and catalogs.
>
> Electronic banking: bill payments and account transfers.

Customers must purchase a Sceptre terminal, manufactured by AT&T for $600 (later to rise to $900), and pay a monthly fee of $12 along with an estimated telephone bill of $14 per month. There has been some criticism of this approach because it ignores the current wide availability of home computers that with a slight modification could be used as Viewtron terminals. In response, Viewtron researchers have designed an appropriate modification for the Radio Shack TRS-80 computer. Knight-Ridder does not expect View-tron to have much of a competitive impact on current newspapers, mainly because it will not be a mass-market enterprise, at least in the short run. It is an open question whether advertisers will be attracted; the poor quality of Viewtron's graphics is a drawback. Considerable improvement will be necessary before videotex will be a serious competitor for the advertising dollar. If the Florida effort is successful, Knight-Ridder has plans for five other cities.

Other publishers have plans to introduce their own videotex systems. Among them are Field Enterprises, owner of the *Chicago Sun-Times*, and Times Mirror, publisher of the *Los Angeles Times* group, which will be offering a system called Keycom in Chicago. Unlike Viewtron, it will not require a special terminal and will offer a $50 program to enable home computers to receive video pictures and a $100 modem to send information over the telephone line. Times-Mirror will be offering its system to homes in Orange County. Subscribers will have to rent a Sceptre terminal for a monthly charge of $30. Another company, starting with a much narrower base of services, is Chemical Bank of New York with its Pronto system. For $12 per month a customer can perform banking transactions and pay bills to about 450 New York area businesses. Chemical Bank has plans to expand its services into a more complete videotex system.

A January, 1985 title in *Business Week* seems to say it all: "For Videotex, The Big Time Is Still a Long Way Off."[9] As of that date only about 500 full videotex terminals had been sold in the United States. (Such terminals offer color and graphics and are dedicated to videotex applications.) Approximately one year after launching its Viewtron service, Knight-Ridder had sold only 2800 terminals, far short of its hoped-for number of 5000.

> *Potential customers have not been willing to buy expensive terminals—or pay hefty monthly fees to lease them—because they did not see any services they particularly needed that they could not find elsewhere for less. And service providers with no ready audience have been slow to develop new offerings.*[10]

In a striking reversal of its 1983 forecast, Link Resources, a videotex market researcher, lowered its earlier estimate for 1988 from 1.9 million text-and-graphics videotex terminals to 95,000. The explanation for this sudden turnabout lies in the enormous growth in home computers. On the one hand, the owners of the approximately 17 million home computers now in use—likely candidates for videotex services—are unlikely to buy dedicated videotex terminals. On the other hand, they can avail themselves of a number of videotex services that do not require color or graphics, such as banking and information services. These services are called text-only and Link Resources expects that there will be over 4 million users by 1988. A successful future for full videotex will depend on the wide distribution of software packages that enable personal computers to perform as videotex terminals. IBM, taking advantage of its leadership in the personal computer market, has released such software for $250.

What about the source of revenues? Times-Mirror expects advertising revenue to make its venture profitable, but Knight-Ridder believes that profits will be earned by charging a commission on sales made through the system. A combination of these two sources will probably be necessary. Companies that are strictly information providers will have to pay a rental fee to the videotex operator and will recover revenues from the users of their information.

Social Issues

Customers are ultimately the most important group in the videotex story, but there are four other groups whose cooperation is necessary, as follows:[11]

Information and Service Providers. Media—Associated Press, Dow Jones, New-York Times, Reuters, CBS. Finance—Bank of America, Chemical Bank, Citibank, New York Stock Exchange. Retailing—Sears, Roebuck and Co., J.C. Penney, Grand Union.

Information Packagers. Knight-Ridder, Times-Mirror, Keycom, AT&T Comp-U-Card, Dow Jones, CBS.

Videotex Carriers. Common—AT&T. Broadcast—CBS, NBC. Cable—Times-Mirror Cable, Warner-Amex Cable, Cox Cable Communications.

Equipment Manufacturers. AT&T, Tandy, Apple, Texas Instruments, Zenith Radio.

It is immediately apparent that very large and powerful corporations will play a major role in the development and management of videotex. Some critics see videotex as a continuation of long-term trends toward diminished variety of news sources. For example, the number of cities served by a single newspaper is steadily increasing. As fewer and more powerful information providers emerge in concert with the videotex technology, there is a fear that a less informed public will result. This position is in striking contrast to the claim made for videotex—that it will usher in a new age of convenience, information accessibility, and improved communication. Aside from the concern about the large companies behind videotex, there is a feeling that the benefits will not be equally distributed. Poorer, less educated people will be unable to afford the service or perhaps unprepared to use it. The supposed universality of two-way information systems may be seen by a large segment of the population as yet another important institution from which they are excluded.

Other social concerns that accompany the growth of videotex include standards and industry regulation, possible job dislocations as a result of home shopping and electronic mail facilities, the control of content, legal liability for misuse of the system, and the protection of consumer rights. One of the most important concerns is privacy and security.

Videotex systems store enormous amounts of information for the use of their customers and maintain a record of each customer's interactions with the system. Of particular significance for privacy and security are banking records, home shopping records, types of information accessed, educational programs, entertainment choices, opinions solicited, and charitable donations. This kind of information, collected on a regular basis, can form a profile of a selected household. Particularly harmful might be the names of sexually permissive films selected on an entertainment channel, or the choice of which political, charitable, or religious causes have been supported. The operators of the system collect such information as a matter of course.

Currently there is little legislation in place that governs what operators do with the information they have collected. Parties who might like to obtain access to the information include the government and businesses that are interested in consumer buying habits and financial transactions. The operators could sell selected lists of subscribers to special interest organizations. The names of individuals with questionable credit ratings could be made available to investigating agencies. Individuals applying for loans, mortgages, or insurance might have to agree to release their profile information. Such data will also be seen as useful to government investigators in search of evidence.

To forestall government intervention in their operations, videotex system operators are formulating and adopting voluntary codes of behavior. It is still not clear how serious the threats to privacy may be because these systems are so new. Probably records should be kept for a limited time and destroyed as soon as the associated payment is made. While videotex systems are beginning to grow, debate should be encouraged among the government, the operators, and the public in order to lay the groundwork for workable legislation to protect the public interest and encourage responsible behavior by the operators.

John Tydeman and his colleagues at the Institute of the Future have studied videotex for several years. They have developed a set of contrasting pairs of scenarios to characterize possible future developments. More suggestive than predictive, they do delineate possible dimensions, as follows:[12]

> *Structure of Society.*   Will two-way information systems contribute to a return to rural areas, because people will be able to work and shop from their homes, or will they lead to increased alienation as people carry out most of their activities in isolation?
>
> *Decision-Making Processes.*   Will the systems encourage a genuine partici-

patory democracy or will they come under the control of powerful interests that will shape opinions and preferences?

New Forms of Choice. Will the consumer be faced with an incredible array of possibilities and choices? Will they make life more meaningful or merely result in confusion and waste?

Inequalities. Will increased ease of access of information and services reduce inequalities in society, or will the advantaged just improve their status?

Economic Structure. Will videotex stimulate an outpouring of new business possibilities tailored to individual needs, or will there be an actual narrowing of choice as mass producers dominate the market?

Financial Services. Will there be an accelerated move towards electronic funds transfer systems, with a corresponding decrease in the use of cash, or will the ready accessibility of financial records contribute to an Orwellian future?

THE FUTURE

If information is the wave of the future, how will society respond? Predicting the future of society has very little to do with science. Caution is frequently absent when experts and futurologists practice their trade. However, from the historical perspective of two centuries since the beginning of the Industrial Revolution, and less than forty years since the appearance of the first electronic computer, some reasonable forecasts can be attempted.

Clearly, the information age will continue to provide a stream of benefits. Productivity will increase, new goods and services will be available, information in greater quantity will be readily accessible, and—with the increasingly sophisticated use of microelectronics—dangerous and unpleasant jobs will be reduced in number. However, associated with new communications technologies are a host of free speech issues. How will hard-won freedom of expression rights operate in the electronics age?

Other impacts, on countries around the world, have been predicted as follows:[13]

Erosion of National Sovereignty. The advanced nations of the world, through their multinational corporations, will greatly expand their control over the international flow of information. As a result, much of the world may become even more heavily dependent on the Western nations and Japan.

Information Black-outs. The analogy to periodic failures of the power system is instructive. Breakdowns of large information networks whether by accident or by sabotage could have disastrous consequences.

Increased Unemployment. Simply put, the future holds reduced employment in the industrial sector because of improved productivity, and the advances in technology in the service area may reduce the rate of growth of jobs as well (see Chapter 10).

Industrial Dislocations. The current debate about the future of the so-called sunset industries—steel, for example—typifies the rocky road to the information age. Many areas of the country want to trade their smokestacks for the "clean" factories typical of Silicon Valley (although pollution caused by industrial chemicals is a problem in the Valley).

Economic Reorganization. The combination of computers and communication systems will exert an important influence on new industries, the reorganization of older ones, and the changing role of traditional enterprises.

Threats to National Cultures. The ongoing assault on national cultures will continue, fostered by direct broadcast satellites and worldwide information distribution networks. International agreements will be necessary.

The percentage of the work force engaged in information occupations is growing, at the expense of blue collar occupations. This massive shift is one of the crucial features of the information age. One can expect continued growth in those areas that support the information industries and erosion in others. Computers, electronics, and software will do well. So will financial institutions, insurance companies (fewer property claims because of fewer central office buildings), communication companies, and large retailers that are able to afford videotex promotion. Among the losers will be transportation companies and equipment manufacturers, publishers (on paper), smaller retailers, oil companies, wholesalers, and TV networks. It is expected that improved communication systems will decrease the need for physical movement. Specialized entertainment providers will challenge national television networks.

All in all, these predictions suggest a society less concentrated in large cities, with increased dependence on communication systems. Work, commercial activities, and play will be more home-centered. Perhaps society will be more fragmented. Fewer people will be required to produce the necessary goods. The gap between the technologically advanced countries and the rest of the world will widen. The image of a self-sufficient home from which most needs can be satisfied, was captured in a strikingly prophetic way by the novelist E. M. Forster, in his 1928 story "The Machine Stops."[14] It presents a terrifying image of humans isolated in their individual rooms, as the machine—which up to now has supplied their every need—begins to falter and eventually stops.

SUMMARY

The gathering, processing, storage, and transmission of ever-increasing quantities of information is becoming the major activity of economically advanced societies. The home computer, in just a few years, has become a significant consumer product. It is possible to connect from the home to a wide variety of computer networks that provide services ranging from home banking to stock market quotations. Electronic mail and teleconferencing are gradually becoming important media for communicating over long distances.

Much acclaimed but emerging at a slower pace than expected, videotex—or two-way communication networks—will provide a wide range of information services—including shopping, banking, home security, education, and so forth. In many countries government-managed telephone companies have taken an active role in stimulating the growth of videotex. There is some concern that videotex will be controlled by a few large corporations and its potential benefits will thus not be realized. The managers of videotex systems will be in possession of vast quantities of information about their customers. It will be necessary to develop regulations to protect the privacy of these people.

It is impossible to predict the future, but indications are that the information society will be home centered, that technologically advanced nations will gain in world dominance, and that commerce will be fundamentally changed. Increased fragmentation and alienation are possible.

NOTES

1. Daniel Bell, *The Coming of Post-Industrial Society* (New York: Basic, 1973).

2. "Starting at Love-Fifteen," *The Economist,* February 16, 1985, p. 30.

3. Peter D. Petre, "Mass-Marketing the Computer," *Fortune,* October 31, 1983, p. 61.

4. As quoted in "How to Tell if You Need a Computer at Home," *Business Week,* November 21, 1983, p. 139.

5. Starr Roxanne Hiltz and Murray Turoff, *The Network Nation, Human Communication via Computers* (Reading, Mass.: Addison-Wesley, 1978), p. xxvi.

6. Louis Verchot, Eastern Management Group, as quoted in Lamont Wood, "E-Mail Shootout," *Datamation,* January 15, 1985, p. 59.

7. Martin Mayer, "Coming Fast: Services Through the TV Set," *Fortune,* November 14, 1983, p. 50.

8. For an interesting and informative description of Prestel, see Eric Somers, "A User's View of Prestel," *Creative Computing,* May 1983, pp. 123–124, 126, 128, 132.

9. Catherine L. Harris, "For Videotex, the Big Time Is Still a Long Way Off," *Business Week,* January 14, 1985, pp. 128, 132–3.

10. Ibid., p. 133.

11. Jaye Scholl, "The Videotex Revolution," *Barron's,* August 2, 1982, pp. 1, 6–8, 44–46.

12. John Tydeman, "Videotex: Ushering the Electronic Household," *The Futurist,* February 1982, pp. 54–61.

13. Shirley Serafini and Michael Andrieu, *The Information Revolution and its Implications for Canada,* Canada Department of Communications, Communications Economics Branch (Ottawa, November 1980).

14. E. M. Forster, "The Machine Stops," In Arthur O. Lewis, Jr., ed., *Of Men and Machines*, (New York: G. P. Dutton, 1963), pp. 261–291.

ADDITIONAL READINGS

Introduction

Dertouzos, Michael, and Joel Moses, eds. *The Computer Age: A Twenty-Year View.* Cambridge, Mass.: MIT Press, 1980.

Forester, Tom, ed. *The Microelectronics Revolution.* Cambridge, Mass.: MIT Press, 1981.

Friedrichs, Guenter, and Adam Schaff, eds. *Microelectronics and Society.* New York: New American Library, 1983.

The Home / Personal Computer

Comer, Douglas. "The Computer Science Research Network CSNET: A History and Status Report." *Communications of the Association for Computing Machinery*, October 1983, pp. 747–753.

Seligman, Daniel. "Life Will Be Different When We're All On-Line." *Fortune*, February 4, 1985, pp. 68–72.

Toong, Hoo-Min D., and Amar Gupta. "The Computer Age Gets Personal." *Technology Review*, January 1983, pp. 26–37.

Electronic Mail and Teleconferencing

Hiltz, Starr Roxanne, and Murray Turoff. "The Evolution of User Behavior in a Computerized Conferencing System." *Communications of the ACM*, November 1981, pp. 739–751.

"MCI's Newest Strategy: Shooting for a Broader Spectrum." *Business Week*, October 10, 1983, pp. 60, 62, 64.

"Videoconferencing: No Longer a Sideshow." *Business Week*, November 12, 1984, pp. 116–118, 120.

Videotex

Brown, Herbert G., and William Sawchuk. "Telidon—A Review." *IEEE Communications Magazine*, January 1981, pp. 22–28.

Chorafas, Dimitris N. *Interactive Videotex.* New York: Petrocelli, 1981.

Fedida, Sam, and Rex Malik. *Viewdata Revolution.* London: Associated Business, 1979.

Flaherty, David H. *Protecting Privacy in Two-Way Electronic Services.* White Plains, N.Y.: Knowledge Industry Publications, 1985.

Godfrey, David, and Ernest Chang, eds. *The Telidon Books.* Victoria: Press Porcepic, 1981.

Harris, Catherine L., et al. "Overseas, Videotex is the Government's Business." *Business Week,* January 14, 1985, pp. 133, 136.

Hecht, Jeff. "Information Services Search for Identity." *High Technology,* May 1983, pp. 58–66.

Jahnke, Art. "The Medium is the Message II: Videotext." *Technology Review,* January 1983, pp. 74–76.

Mosco, Vincent. *Pushbutton Fantasies.* Norwood, N.J.: Ablex, 1982.

Sigel, Efram, et al. *The Future of Videotext.* White Plains: Knowledge Industry Publications, 1983.

Tydeman, John, et al. *Teletext and Videotex in the United States.*" New York: McGraw-Hill, 1982.

Viewdata 82, European Conference. London: Online Publications, October 1982.

Westin, Alan F. "Home Information Systems: The Privacy Debate." *Datamation,* July 1982, pp. 100–101, 103–104, 106, 111–112, 114.

"Will Knight-Ridder Make News with Videotex?" *Business Week,* August 8, 1983, pp. 59–60.

The Future

Barron, Iann, and Ray Curnow. *The Future with Microelectronics.* New York: Nichols, 1979.

Bell, Daniel. "Communications Technology—for Better or Worse." *Harvard Business Review,* May/June 1979, pp. 20–22, 26, 28, 32, 36, 40, 42.

Cornish, Edward. "The Coming of an Information Society." *The Futurist,* April 1981, pp. 14–15, 17–21.

de Sola Pool, Ithiel. *Technologies of Freedom.* Cambridge, Mass.: Harvard University Press/Belknap, 1983.

Jones, Trevor. "A New Society? The Social Impact of Microprocessor Technology." In Trevor Jones, ed. *Microelectronics and Society.* Milton Keynes, England: The Open University Press, 1980, pp. 144–170.

Poppel, Harvey L. "The Information Revolution: Winners and Losers." *Harvard Business Review,* January/February 1978, pp. 4, 16, 159.

Oettinger, Anthony. "Information Resources: Knowledge and Power in the 21st Century." *Science,* July 4, 1980, pp. 191–198.

14
FINAL REMARKS

Technology catalyzes changes not only in what we do but in how we think. It changes people's awareness of themselves, of one another, of their relationship with the world.

◇ *Sherry Turkle, 1984* ◇

INTRODUCTION

This chapter will present a number of disparate issues and tie up several loose ends. Because books in this field can only capture a slice of time in a rapidly changing scene, they should perhaps be sold in a loose-leaf binder so that the pages can be easily replaced. (They should also appear in a computer databank for ease of access and ready updating!)

Although most significant developments in hardware and software have taken place (and continue to take place) in the United States, the challengers are many and persistent. Western Europe has long been a serious rival, especially since the formation of the European Economic Community. The country whose economic threat is perceived by the average American as most dangerous is Japan. From the ruins of World War II, Japan has emerged an economic giant. Its genius has been evidenced in such industries as automobiles, shipbuilding, video cassette recorders, consumer electronics, and computers. ''Made in Japan'' once meant shoddy and unreliable; now Japanese products are renowned for quality. Japan leads the world in production of cameras, television sets, stereo equipment, and VCRs. It has become a dominant force in the world automobile industry, to the point that many Americans have called for limitations on the import of Japanese cars. Thousands of U.S. workers at General Motors, Ford, and Chrysler have lost their jobs because of the influx of cars from Toyota, Honda, Nissan, Subaru, and Mazda. In the opinion of some commentators, Japan's major export is not electronics or automobiles but unemployment.

The Japanese challenge to U.S. leadership in computer technology is being viewed with considerable alarm. A national industrial policy has been proposed, to marshal the various components of the American political and economic system in order to confront the perceived Japanese challenge (see Chapter 11). The U.S. government has made a commitment to support research in supercomputers and Artificial Intelligence. Japan is poised to challenge American leadership in computers—from personals to mainframes and supercomputers. Underlying this challenge is a secure mastery of microelectronic production technology. Japan has been criticized for jumping on technological bandwagons rather than initiating them. However, it recently launched a major research effort, called the Fifth Generation Computer Systems project, for computers in the 1990s.

This project will attempt to realize developments in AI in the next generation of computer systems. Counting computing generations is not an exact science. By one measure, the first generation is vacuum tube computers, the second is transistors, the third is integrated circuits, and the fourth is very large-scale integrated (VLSI) circuits. The fifth generation, as the Japanese see it, will not depend so much on substantially new basic building blocks but will employ new architectures, new languages, new styles of programming and problem solving, and new input-output techniques. If this very ambitious project succeeds even in part, Japan will have taken a giant step forward in making computers substantially more powerful and easier to use.

Will familiarity with computers be a requirement for economic survival in the years to come? The term computer literacy has gained considerable currency in recent years. Although the analogy with language literacy seems straightforward, there are some difficulties. Surely, the ability to read and write one's native language is obviously necessary to succeed economically. In addition, the entire written tradition—novels, plays, poetry, educational books—is inaccessible to the illiterate. Computer literacy presumably refers to knowledge about computers, programming, applications, and social issues—not necessarily in equal measure. One's career may certainly be helped by some familiarity with computers, but it is not yet a matter of economic survival, nor is its lack as devastating as the inability to read and write. Knowing more about computers will help to understand how society is changing and may improve one's job prospects. Because computer literacy is receiving increasing attention, its goals and methods should be evaluated.

From all that has been written about the current computer revolution, the opportunities seem limitless—except perhaps for women. Although the demand for programmers is growing, women have not assumed positions of responsibility in proportion to their numbers. Women have increased their representation in programming (it is now about one third) but their major presence is in data entry jobs and as computer operators (see Chapter 10). In schools computers are frequently treated as the private preserve of boys and girls are viewed as outsiders. Much of the advertising for home computers is directed towards improving the future job prospects of male children, a trend consistent with a long tradition of treating girls as if they are congenitally unable to do well in mathematics. Because skill in programming is seen as requiring mathematical ability, the exclusion of girls is taken for granted. In schools where access to computers is limited, girls are usually put at the end of the line. An enormous amount of needed talent is thus being wasted. Even those women who have managed to enter data processing have not found their career paths as straightforward as have men. Women have yet to be accepted in such positions as systems programmers and data processing managers. The urgent need for qualified people may change this situation, but increased educational opportunities at all levels must be made available to girls and women.

Finally, what are the responsibilities of the computer professional? Society expects, and indeed demands, that its professionals—doctors, lawyers, accountants, pharmacists, and engineers, among others—act ethically and responsibly. Membership in a professional organization is mandatory in such occupations. Frequently, these organizations are licensed by governments so that they may monitor their members' performance and censure them for violations. The public is supposed to place its trust in its professionals, assured that their qualifications are guaranteed and that they meet minimum standards of performance. Lapses in professional conduct are expected to be dealt with promptly and appropriately. The impression further exists that in the process of regulating its members a professional society does more: It may set rates and inhibit free competition, prevent action against incompetent members, and even limit the flow of new ideas because of built-in conservatism. How do computer professionals fit into this process? Typically, they are not self-employed but work in companies as members of teams. Shared responsibility, company loyalty, and perceived ethical standards must be reconciled. Codes of ethics have been drawn up by some professional societies, so far with little government involvement. There is debate within the computing community about the responsibility of professionals toward the potential applications of their work.

JAPAN AND HIGH TECHNOLOGY

In recent years books, television shows, and special issues of magazines have appeared, with some regularity, that purport to explain Japan to Americans. The work ethic of the Japanese is continually extolled in comparison to the well-publicized but unverified negative attitudes of the American worker. Characterizations of Japan are varied and numerous, including the following:

> The Japanese are copiers not innovators.
>
> Their success is based on unfair cooperation among government, industry, and labor.
>
> IQ tests show the Japanese to be smarter than Americans.
>
> They prevent fair competition by restricting entry to their domestic marketplace.
>
> They compete unfairly abroad by taking initial losses in order to penetrate a new market.
>
> Although they lost World War II, the Japanese obtained an advantage in the complete rebuilding of their industrial plant.

A Record of Achievement

In rebuilding their industrial might following World War II, the Japanese achieved a number of remarkable successes. The following highlights, were noted by *Newsweek* in August, 1982:[1]

1955	Sony introduces the first transistor radio for widespread use.
1964	Japan's ''bullet train'' appears—a major technological success.
1970	Nippon Steel becomes the number one steelmaker in the world.
1975	The first home video cassette recorder, the Betamax system, is introduced by Sony.
1980	For the first time Japan produces more automobiles than the United States.
1981	Japanese manufacturers assume world leadership in the production of the 64K RAM chip.

In the consumer electronics market, Japan's share of world production is significant: over 80 percent of video cassette recorders, over 70 percent of citizen band (CB) radios, more than half of the stereo systems, and about 40 percent of color television sets. (These 1982 figures are probably still representative.) In the application of new digital electronics, Japan has shown the way, and is leader in 35mm cameras, calculators, and watches. The quality of these products has totally reversed an earlier reputation for shoddy workmanship. From a devastated economy Japan has emerged as the only serious challenger to the United States' dominance in high technology. The Science and Technology agency in Japan conducted a survey during the period 1980 to 1982 to predict developments up to the year 2010. Among its highlights were the following:

1992	Use of robots in dangerous working conditions.
1993	Appearance of supercomputers based on high-speed devices.
1994	Chips with densities of 10^{10} devices.
1995	Three-dimensional memory devices with more than ten layers.
2006	Systems able to predict earthquakes up to one month in advance.

With all their accomplishments, the Japanese are seen—especially from an American perspective—as imitators, not innovators. Their forte, it is said, is to take ideas originating in other countries and to adapt and develop them in an attractive and marketable fashion. This image is not accurate. One measure of a country's success in developing new products is the percentage of foreign patents it files in the United States. As of 1950 Japan's percentage was virtually zero, compared with over 35 percent by Britain, 15 percent by France, and zero for West Germany (whose pre-World War II figure had been almost 40 percent). By 1978 Japan had achieved nearly 30 percent and Germany about 25 percent, while Britain and France had dropped to about 10 percent each. Such impressive results may be seen by some as evidence of the Japanese ability to transform fundamental results into working products more rapidly than other countries. This opinion is reinforced by Japan's record in computers.

Only in the last few years has Japan made an impact on the world computer market. The explosive growth in personal computer sales was almost missed by Japan. In a potentially significant move, Japan has now introduced the Microsoft Extended Basic (MSX) home computer into the American market. Although Japan is a world leader in semiconductor production, the complexities of computer design were thought to pose too formidable a barrier to Japanese engineers. These speculations were totally mistaken, and Japan has now begun producing computers to challenge the world leader IBM. In 1981, Japan's per capita investment in research and development almost equaled that of the United States. In light of the fact that in the United States 25 percent of this figure is spent in defense-related areas, Japan's success is more readily understood. Much of this research in Japan is carried out in industrial laboratories, further facilitating the development of new products. Other factors contributing to the success of ''Japan, Inc.'' are a stable and hard-working labor force, progressive management, effective cooperation among business, government, and labor, a concern with productivity and quality, aggressive worldwide marketing coupled with a protectionist home policy, and a focus on consumer production within the U.S. military security umbrella.

In cooperation with some U.S. computer companies, Japanese computer manufacturers are attempting to establish a foothold in the lucrative U.S. market. Major companies such as Hitachi, Fujitsu, and NEC (formerly Nippon Electric Company) have begun to market very large mainframe computers, challenging such U.S. leaders as Cray and Control Data. The race to build supercomputers is well under way, and Japan will prove a formidable competitor. Software development is an important area in which the Japanese have yet to prove themselves. However, they have launched a major effort to leap to the forefront, the Fifth-Generation research project.

The Fifth Generation Project

In October 1981, Japan held an international conference on fifth generation computers to which 86 foreigners were invited. From the Japanese point of view, the term fifth generation has two meanings, as follows:

> *Structural.* The sequence of generations is based on the basic building blocks of computers: vacuum tubes, transistors, integrated circuits, very large-scale integrated (VLSI) circuits, and ultra large-scale integrated circuits.
>
> *Functional.* Most of the publicity associated with the fifth generation project has to do with the concept of a computer able to perform a variety of tasks requiring intelligence—such as inference, natural language understanding, and image understanding.

Japan announced a ten-year project to develop the fifth generation computer and called for international cooperation. The development of such a computer will require faster hardware, new forms of computer organization, new programming languages, and breakthroughs in AI. Japan has demonstrated expertise in the hardware aspects, but its underlying purpose in pursuing this project is to challenge U.S. leadership in software. The stakes are high. Edward Feigenbaum and Pamela McCorduck issued the following call-to-arms in *The Fifth Generation:*

> *We are writing this book because we are worried. But we are also basically opti-mistic. Americans invented this technology! If only we could focus our efforts we should have little trouble dominating the second computer age as we dominated the first.*[3]

Japan plans to spend $850 million over the next ten years to produce—or at least make significant progress towards—a powerful intelligent computer. Many of the articulated goals depend heavily on developments in AI. Here, in brief, are some of the major research themes associated with Japan's fifth generation project:

Computer Architecture.   Includes parallel designs, among them dataflow systems. Distributed processing and sophisticated communications are also important and necessary ingredients.

Programming Languages.   New architectures will require programming languages based on new principles. The Japanese surprised many by choosing *Prolog* as the basic language for study.

Knowledge-Based Systems.   Sometimes called expert systems, these represent the attempt to incorporate specialized knowledge and reasoning ability in a computer program.

Natural Interaction.   To facilitate communication with computers, both natural language and image understanding will be available for input and output.

Database Management.   More sophisticated techniques will be necessary to deal with large quantities of structured data.

The basic goal is to produce a computer that is intelligent, easy to use, flexible, and adaptable. Even if a full-blown system is not achieved, it is hoped that the research will help bring about a significant improvement in the computers' usefulness. The Japanese success in achieving leadership in other industrial areas lends credence to their possible success in the fifth generation project. The vehicle of this project is The Institute for New Generation Computer Technology (ICOT), founded in April 1982. This organization has defined the terms and directions of the research and recruited the research team. The project currently has the following four areas of emphasis:

Problem Solving and Inference.   A system is intelligent to the degree that it can solve new problems in reasonable time. Instead of measuring performance by the number of additions per second, a new measure is proposed: the number of inferences per second. Computers should be viewed not as ''number crunchers'' but as inference ''engines.''

Knowledge Bases.   There is strong emphasis on the representation, storage, and retrieval of large amounts of knowledge. This knowledge is needed for all phases of the system. The acquisition and updating of knowledge is also important.

Intelligent Interfaces. The primary aim is to enable people to use computers more easily with natural language (English, Japanese) as a method of communication. Without the necessity of programming, computers will truly become a universal tool.

Intelligent Programming. For special applications programs will have to be written, but programming languages such as Prolog can facilitate this process. These languages (and those of the future) have built-in problem solving strategies, so the task of the programmer is to specify the problem precisely.

The project is ambitious and its consequences will be dramatic. The initial application areas chosen by ICOT are VLSI computer-aided design, machine translation, and consultation (or expert) systems. Furthermore, Japan has explicitly stated that the societal implications of the project are of prime importance. They envision a new age full of opportunities, but with possible dislocations if sufficient planning among government, business, and labor is not initiated. (Such a concern has not been part of the projects initiated in response to Japan's fifth generation project by Britain, Western Europe, and—most importantly—the United States.)

In November 1984, ICOT's Second International Conference on Fifth Generation Computer Systems was attended by about 700 researchers from Japan and 300 from 30 other countries. It was an opportunity to report on the three years of research of the Fifth Generation project. The formal presentation of papers and status reports revealed that some of the early projections had been scaled down and certain goals had become more focussed. Post-conference demonstrations clearly indicated that the project had achieved some significant advances in a rather short time. In terms of hardware, a high resolution computer similar to recently developed Lisp machines was shown. Called a personal sequential inference machine, it was a concrete implementation of a computer with an operating system written in an extended version of Prolog, a logic programming language. The Japanese commitment to logic programming has distinguished their approach from the North American effort and has also stimulated research in this area. Another interesting achievement is Delta, a relational database machine with large storage capabilities. Most striking is the degree to which the project has achieved, at this early stage, an integrated implementation of hardware, software, and application programs—all based on logic programming.

The Response of the West

America needs a national plan of action, a kind of space shuttle program for the knowledge systems of the future.[4]

Considerable publicity has appeared in the west about the Japanese fifth generation project and much of it verges on the hysterical. The basic message is that Japan has launched a revolutionary research program that, if successful, will catapult her to world leadership in high technology. For the current world leader, the United States, the threat seems real enough, but the appropriate response is not obvious. From the point of view of the U.S. government, a national plan—except for wars and perhaps the space project—is not the American way. In fact, part of the debate about a national industrial policy involves microelectronics and computers.

The creation of the Microelectronics & Computer Technology Corporation (MCC) can be seen as a direct response by U.S. industry. Another is the Semiconductor Research Corporation (SRC), based in Research Triangle Park, North Carolina. Its goals are to carry out advanced research in electronics and to improve the quality of graduate education. Over 30 corporations—including IBM, Control Data, Digital Equipment, and Honeywell—are members. SRC currently funds research at 35 U.S. universities and has a budget of $12 million. The competition with Japan in semiconductors is so heated that the various SRC member companies feel such an organization is necessary to compete successfully.

The Defense Advanced Research Projects Agency (DARPA) of the U.S. Department of Defense announced in 1983 a program called Strategic Computing and Survivability (see Chapter 7). It contained a proposal to spend $600 million over the next five years (and perhaps $1 billion by the end of the decade) in AI, microelectronics, and computer architecture. Given the scope of the proposed research and development and the timing, it seems clear that this program represents the U.S. government's response to Japan. It is not surprising that the U.S. response is so tightly linked to the defense establishment. Specific goals of DARPA's program include the following:

> In 10 years, a robotic tank that could navigate 80 miles from one destination to another.
>
> An automated copilot that can identify aircraft, distinguish friendly from enemy forces, and understand speech commands in a noisy environment.
>
> An advanced computer system to alert military commanders of impending problems, lay out options in battles, and monitor results. This system will be installed on the aircraft carrier *Carl Vinson.*

In a more general sense, the program's goal is to develop a new generation of computers with such abilities as vision, speech, reasoning, and planning. The mandate is remarkably similar to the stated aims of Japan's fifth generation project. One fundamental difference is that in the United States the defense establishment is in charge, and the final product must have direct military value. Consumer applications will have to depend on military spin-off. Japan intends to focus its efforts in the private sector, to improve its international trading position. A significant omission in the U.S. program is any stated concern with the impact on society of the proposed technology.

Given its third-place position in high technology, behind the United States and Japan, Europe felt particularly threatened by the fifth generation project. Governments began to formulate plans to position themselves in the exciting race to come. Britain was the first country to act. A conference of computer companies and academics held in January 1982, led to the establishment of a committee under the direction of John Alvey, director of technology at British Telecom. The Alvey committee issued a report in August, 1982 that recommended a major cooperative effort among all segments of the high technology community: government, industry, and the universities. The government accepted most of the recommendations and set up the Advanced Information Technology (AIT) Program. Funding over the next five years included over $300 million in government funds and $230 million from industry.

The main areas for research are VLSI, software engineering, man/machine interfaces, and expert systems. University research will be funded entirely by the government, while the major part of the industry research will be done in equal partnership with the government. Britain intends not to set up a focussed research center similar to ICOT but to link industry and academic research groups by a computer network. The British are confident their skill in software design will serve them well, but are less optimistic about their ability to compete in microelectronics.

At about the same time the British government announced the AIT program, the European Common Market proposed the European Strategic Programme on Research in Information Technology (Esprit). Its current phase involves an expenditure of approximately $11 million, but there is a proposal to spend some $1.5 billion over five years. The major areas for research are advanced microelectronics, software technology, advanced information processing, office automation, and computer-integrated flexible manufacturing. Esprit differs from both the Japanese effort and the MCC in the United States in that it is an international program—a partnership among companies, research laboratories, and government agencies. Esprit is intended to provide a research resource for its member countries and companies. As such, it does not intend to deliver products but rather to develop advanced technology in order to make Europe competitive. The stage is thus set for worldwide competition at the leading edge of high technology. The stakes are high, for even if the ultimate prize, the fifth generation machine, is not achieved, the advances in technology should have a major impact on society. Whether or not "thinking" machines are possible, in the near future or ever, is an open question. Certainly computers can be programmed to perform ever more complex tasks and, indeed, the development of new architectures and new programming languages will accelerate this process. Fundamental research is necessary in such areas as natural language understanding, image understanding, knowledge representation, and problem solving.

Supercomputers

As their name suggests, supercomputers are the largest and fastest of all computers. Unfortunately, some confusion has existed in the media between fifth generation computers and supercomputers. They are occasionally treated as equivalent machines. Both research projects are concerned with new architectures for computers such as parallel processing and dataflow designs. Research in supercomputers is directed towards achieving very fast machines to be used in such areas as weather forecasting, weapons design, complex simulations, digital image processing, and high energy physics. References to human abilities or artificial intelligence are not part of the research mandate, although supercomputers may make a contribution in these areas.

As in many other domains, the world leader in supercomputers, the United States—Cray, ETA Systems (90 percent owned by Control Data), and Denelcor—is being challenged by Japan— NEC, Hitachi, and Fujitsu. Because the individual architectures of computers differ so much, it is difficult to compare their performances. In general, a complex series of test problems can be run to produce average statistics. For public consumption a rather simple and occasionally misleading measure is used—the number of floating-point operations per second. A floating-point operation is a basic computational step that all computers perform very many times in any program, especially scientific ones. Currently, the supercomputers made by CDC, Cray, Hitachi, and Fujitsu operate in the 100–1,000 Mflops (million floating-point operations per second) range, with the Hitachi machine in the lead.

In comparison with these figures, the IBM 360/195 operated at about 5 Mflops in 1971. IBM has not produced computers in the supercomputer class in recent years, but there are rumors that it is preparing to enter the race. Compatibility with IBM software is an important issue, especially for the Japanese manufacturers. They want to make their machines IBM-compatible in order to compete at the top of the line. The American supercomputer companies require very special programming techniques to utilize their machines effectively; however, when agreement is achieved on a FORTRAN standard for the 1980s, FORTRAN programs will be able to run on all the different machines.

ETA Systems is looking toward 10,000 Mflops in 1986 with its ETA-10 and 60,000 Mflops in 1987. The Cray-3 projected for 1987 will operate at about 8000 Mflops. What makes the competition so important is the enormous range of applications for supercomputers, especially if their price-performance tradeoff becomes more competitive. Particularly important is the use of large-scale simulations to study problems in aerodynamics, computer-aided design using three-dimensional graphics, and particle physics. Leadership in supercomputers has been identified with both national and economic security. The physicist Kenneth Wilson has called on the government to foster the development of nationwide networks—to stimulate the dissemination of new skills required to utilize supercomputers and to develop new programming languages.

From the business point of view, supercomputers have not yet captured a significant portion of the market. About 130 machines have been sold by U.S. manufacturers since 1976. However, the market is growing, and 1985 should bring sales of about 45 systems valued at approximately $400 million, with an estimate of about $1.5 billion by 1989. One untapped market open to future sales are the universities, which have only just begun to acquire supercomputers. As of early 1985 supercomputers had been installed at eight North American universities, including Princeton, San Diego, Illinois, Cornell, Colorado State, and Calgary in Canada. Several universities have also been engaged in building computers of novel design largely based on parallel architectures. These have been made possible because of the ongoing improvements in size, speed, and cost of the basic semiconductor components. This is a very exciting time for researchers in computer architecture, software, and communications. The importance of winning the supercomputer race can hardly be overestimated.

COMPUTER LITERACY

I see computer literacy as the New Math of the 1980's.[5]

The idea that people should be knowledgable about computers in today's society hardly seems controversial. However, the details of various proposals to implement this idea have aroused some disagreement. The term commonly used to characterize a heightened awareness about computers and their role in society is computer literacy. Comparisons with the notion of general language literacy are unavoidable and frequently misleading.

Various definitions of the term have been proposed, some of which draw parallels to literacy as it refers to language skills and a minimal level of competence in some domain. Ronald Anderson and Daniel Klasson of the Minnesota Education Computing Consortium (MECC) define computer literacy as "whatever understanding, skills, and attributes one needs to function effectively within a given social role that directly or indirectly involves computers."[6] The given social role is meant to encompass general well-being as well as specific achievements.

As schools are the primary institutions of socialization, it is to be expected that considerable discussion of this issue will be centered on the appropriate role for schools. The manufacturers of home computers have been eager to warn parents about the serious problems their children will face if they do not have one. Texas Instruments, before it dropped out of the home computer market, in late 1983 launched a number of television ads for its TI-99/4A. In one of them, while a boy receives help in mathematics from a computer, a voice pronounces, "It can give your child a head start that could last a lifetime." In another advertisement, for a different manufacturer, a prospective employee is chastised for being a video-game whiz while knowing very little about programming.

In the schools, at all levels, the debate continues over the definition, importance, and relevance of computer literacy. Critics are wary of pandering to the newest, flashiest technology. In a delightful parody, Bill Lacy, the president of Cooper Union, has described the repercussions of the introduction of the pencil (later in colors and with eraser) into medieval Europe. Its introduction in schools met with the following responses:

> *"Just because they have a pencil doesn't mean they have a lot of education going on."*
>
> *"I don't know why my kid needs a pencil to learn French. We are French."*

Evaluating the claims made for computer literacy in the midst of the widespread publicity surrounding computers is not an easy task. Schools are under pressure by parents to provide their children with the best chance for a prosperous life, and that certainly includes computers.

Many universities and colleges are requiring as a condition of graduation that students take at least one course in what is sometimes called *computer appreciation*. Typically, this course includes an introduction to computer programming, a survey of computer applications, and a familiarization with the associated social issues. It is felt that every person, to be a functioning and responsible citizen, must be aware of the role of computers in contemporary society. The debate about the usefulness of computers in the curriculum turns on such issues as the intellectual content of computer literacy courses, the benefits of computer programming for the average student, the supposed transferability of computer skills, and improved job prospects. Definitive answers are not yet available, but a number of voices have been raised against the uncritical acceptance of the concept of computer literacy for everyone. Other issues arise at the primary and secondary school level, in relation to computer programming, computer-assisted instruction, and computer games.

Many commentators have argued that for most people learning to program is neither necessary nor beneficial. The long term-trend is toward sophisticated, user-friendly software as in word-processing and financial planning programs. Programming is not a skill easy to acquire or practice. It is unlikely that very many people, besides professionals and eager hobbyists, will program on their own. Thus, for every student to learn how to program skillfully should not be the major aim of the computer literacy movement.

What about the supposed beneficial side-effects of programming? Among the claims are that it teaches people to think more clearly and improves their use of English. A similar claim has previously been made for mathematics—that it improved problem-solving skills. However, the evidence is not available. Those who have the aptitude should certainly pursue programming, but for the majority it is not a direct route to an improved mind. The study of the precise rules of a programming language may contribute to an improvement in the use of a natural one, but there is no evidence for this hypothesis. The difference between a programming language like BASIC and a natural language like English is enormous. If it is beneficial to learn a new language, it should be Spanish, French, Japanese, or some other natural language. The aim of such a learning process is to make students more literate, and studying a computer language is not likely to fulfill this goal.

The primary emphasis in computer literacy should be in the historical, economic, legal, and philosophical areas. Computers must be seen in their historical context—as part of an ongoing technological process. The economic and legal implications of their use are a rich source of material for exploring many important social issues. It would be a mistake to focus on the computer itself, because treating even such a marvelous machine in isolation can only result in superficial understanding. This is a real danger, if computer literacy courses are taught by programmers with little experience in other areas. The pressure to offer such courses may result in ill-conceived projects. However, public pressure is a reality and many schools have responded with such courses, and even programs, in computer literacy.

The use of the LOGO has been widely hailed as a significant advance in the process of teaching children how to learn on their own, and in groups (see Chapter 6). Inevitably, a reaction has set in. One experimenter in New York, Roy Pea, has found that a group of children with one year's experience in LOGO were no better at solving a test problem than a comparable group of students with no programming background. Summarizing the results of other such studies, he notes, "These studies do raise serious doubts about the sweeping claims made for the cognitive benefits of learning to program."[8]

Other critics argue that it would be far more beneficial for students to acquire the ability to write a coherent English paragraph rather than vague computer application. Joseph Weizenbaum of MIT, a long-time observer of the computer scene, argues that over-emphasis on computers in the primary and secondary schools is a mistake, an attempt to apply a technological fix to some basic educational problems.[9] Technology in general and computers in particular exert a considerable fascination on the general public. This concern has been translated by the educational system into a formal structure of courses and programs. For some the unseemly haste to implement such programs is seen as a reflex response to current fashion. Others claim that it would be irresponsible not to provide the appropriate educational environment. Computers are here to stay, the latter argue, and citizens should be prepared. The debate will continue.

WOMEN AND COMPUTING

For this country to attend to the health of science, as well as provide for the common defense. . .and increase the national productivity, greater participation of women and minorities in science and technology [is necessary].[10]

The widespread use of computers has provided, and is expected to provide, many jobs for women. The impact of computers on employment is expected to affect women significantly, given their high representation in office work. Do computers represent new opportunities for women or merely a reinforcement of the old inequities? An increasing number of women have been choosing careers in computer science and engineering. Society has tended to discourage women in the sciences, and how the schools react to the challenge will be very important to girls and women.

Early indications of the situation in schools are not encouraging. Girls are being excluded, either overtly or subtly, from computer-related activities. Arguments are formulated that girls are just not suited for computers, that their minds are not logical, and that if computer time is in short supply, boys should be given priority. Whether girls think differently from boys—girls (supposedly) intuitively, boys (supposedly) logically—is neither proven nor relevant, but actions based on this assumption should be examined. In almost every area of computer use—video games, computer courses at school, computer games—boys are in the majority and in effect define the associated culture. One feature of this culture is the excitement of shared expertise. If the environment were made less competitive and less aggressive, girls could be encouraged to participate more fully.

Recent studies have shown that programming style can vary among children according to temperament. Sherry Turkle, a professor of sociology at Massachusetts Institute of Technology, has been observing young children, boys and girls, learning to program in LOGO. She has identified two basic styles exemplified by the majority of these children. The attitudes of most boys towards programming is to achieve mastery over a formal system, to cause the objective world of the computer to behave in a desired manner, to control a piece of the external world. Girls—at least those who are attracted to the computer—develop a much more subjective relationship. They tend to project themselves into the objects and events on the screen, achieving a much more intimate connection with their programs. The boys are willing to use ideas developed by the girls to improve their programs. An important lesson is that in a supportive environment, girls can enjoy programming and begin to fulfill their potential.

Encouragement of girls in their formative years will increase the proportion of women in engineering and data processing. Trends are already apparent: in 1965, 139 women received bachelor's degrees in engineering, about 0.38 percent of the total; by 1980 there were almost 6,000 women, about 10 percent; in 1983 the figure rose to 15 percent. The figures for computer science are even more revealing and hopeful. From an average of about 12 percent in the 1960s, the number of women receiving bachelor's degrees rose to almost 26 percent, or over 7,000, in 1978, and about 33 percent in 1982. For master's and doctoral degrees the figures are lower: about 19 and 10 percent, respectively, in 1978. The increased number of women graduates is reflected in recent hiring patterns. At IBM, women college graduates make up about one-third of the engineers and computer scientists hired. Starting salaries for men and women are approaching parity.

Professional women, now face an unfair struggle for career advancement and adequate recognition of advanced degrees. There seems to be an unstated reluctance to chose equally qualified women over men for management positions. The explanation frequently offered, that men simply feel more comfortable working with men, does not do justice to the depth of the problem. Men tend to patronize women, perhaps unconsciously, at a professional level. Women have only recently increased their representation in professional ranks and lack the ''old-boys'' network that has traditionally provided contacts, support, and information to successful men. This situation is changing, as several women's organizations have been formed: the Association of Women in Computing, the Society of Women Engineers, and the Aerospace Women's Committee, among others. These societies work to keep women informed of educational and professional opportunities, provide support in stressful situations, and actively promote the visibility of their members. The goals have been stated by Linda Taylor, president of the Association of Women in Computing, as follows:

> *I think our first job must be to help women gain credibility and visibility, develop*
> *their professional skills, and make real contributions to their corporations, so they*
> *can get the positions of influence. Then we can focus on more humanistic, social*
> *concerns.*[11]

There are some success stories of entrepreneurial women in the computer industry, especially the software segment.[12] Sandra L. Kurtzig is founder and chairman of ASK Computer Services, a developer of software packages for manufacturing companies, with profits of $10 million on sales of $100 million as of June 1984. Her current stock holdings are worth $46 million. Lorraine Mecca is founder, vice-chairman, and chief executive of Micro D., a wholesaler of software and computer peripherals, with profits of $1.2 million on sales of $71 million in 1983. Her shares are worth $24 million. Margaret Hamilton and Saydean Zeldin are founders of Higher Order, Inc. in Cambridge, Massachusetts.

They have raised $9.2 million in venture capital over the last seven years. The company produces software to catch mistakes in manufacturing processes before they occur. Hamilton was responsible for the onboard software in the Apollo space flights. Shirley Eis is president and chief executive officer of Software Corporation of America. In fiscal 1984 sales reached $1 million. These programs are designed to help computer-shy executives use computers.

Many professional women have children and manage to combine work and family successfully. The demands made on them, however, are clearly greater than those made on men, especially if they wish to have a family. The problems facing women who attempt to start a company are formidable: banks that do not take women entrepreneurs seriously, suspicious engineers hostile to women employers, and a limited support network. Nevertheless, many have succeeded, and their numbers are growing. On the other hand, most professional women—and men—will not form their own businesses, and their advancement must take place within a company.

Much of the discussion about women and computing has focussed on professional women, but most women who work with computers are in data entry and operator positions. For them the serious issues are working conditions and job termination, more than career possibilities. On-line monitoring by employers, the publicized dangers of video display terminals, and the possible deskilling of jobs are of concern. The increasing use of computers in the workplace has the potential to improve working conditions, but only if management takes appropriate steps.

One group of women connected to the computer industry has generally been overlooked in such discussions—Asian women who work in sweatshop conditions to produce microelectronic components. Chips manufactured in the United States are sent to Third World countries, where they are separated, their leads soldered, and then are returned for incorporation into products. The work pays little and produces considerable eye strain. Advances in technology sometimes rest on a foundation of human blood, sweat, and tears. The women in the Third World who contribute to the computer industry are not usually heralded as part of its success story.

ETHICS AND PROFESSIONALISM

> *Now the engineer's professional obligation to protect the well-being of the community, as well as to shun participation in deceptions, conflicts with another obligation: to serve as a faithful agent of his clients.*[13]

The conflicts between the responsiblity of the engineer to self versus client have long been discussed in the engineering literature. The pressure on those engaged in science and engineering is ever-increasing. To what degree should they be concerned about the possible effects of their work? What additional responsibility do they bear, beyond what is borne by all citizens in a democratic society? There is a growing urgency to answer such questions or at least to explore meaningfully the issues raised.

In its most simplistic form, ethics deals with right and wrong. Among the earliest questions considered by philosophers were: How should one know what is good? How should one act to achieve it? The task has gotten no easier over the centuries. For the doctor, lawyer and engineer, the ethical responsibilities of the ordinary citizen are compounded by professional responsibilities. The emergence of professionalism—at first through associations of individuals in the clergy, law, and medicine in eleventh-century Europe—has bestowed special privileges and special duties. In North America the movement towards professionalism seems to be a necessary step to legitimize practitioners of a given skill. Along with doctors, lawyers, dentists, engineers, and others, computer professionals have seen the need to establish standards for membership in their community.

The major distinguishing (and controversial) feature of professionalism is the self-regulatory function of professional societies. They define a separate group with membership determined by standards they set, and expulsion is determined solely by them as well. By maintaining high standards, societies hope to assure the public that all practitioners can be relied upon to serve the public responsibly and competently. For the most part the public *is* well served, and fact places considerable confidence in many of its professionals—especially doctors, dentists, and engineers. However, there is some sense that major functions of professional societies are to maintain high income levels and to close ranks around any member accused of improper action. Societies proclaim their responsibility, and try to justify their existence, by disciplining wayward members and publicizing their stringent membership requirements.

Blowing the Whistle

There can be no question of holding forth on ethics. I have seen people behave badly with great morality and I note every day that integrity has no need of rules.
(Albert Camus, The Myth of Sisyphus, *1957.)*

In 1977, Virginia Edgerton was a senior information scientist on a project of the Criminal Justice Coordinating Council (CJCC) of New York city. Since the mid-1970s, the New York Police Department has employed an on-line system called SPRINT that is used by dispatchers, to determine the nearest police car in response to emergency calls. The address of the emergency is entered into the computer, which then outputs a list of the nearest cars. Many lives have been saved because of the quick response. Edgerton's job with the CJCC was to work on another on-line system, PROMIS, to help New York city prosecutors keep track of active cases: trial dates, names and addresses of witnesses, and so forth. SPRINT was being run on two IBM 370/148 computers, one of which was backup, and Edgerton assumed that PROMIS would be run on the backup. Instead, it was run on the same computer as the SPRINT system. Edgerton became concerned that SPRINT's performance would be degraded by the additional work load, possibly resulting in slower response to emergencies and possible loss of life. She discovered that this issue had not been considered and brought it to the attention of her superior, who disagreed with her—without offering technical arguments—and ordered her not to pursue the matter. She confronted a difficult decision. Consulting with the Institute of Electrical and Electronic Engineering (IEEE) Committee on Social Implications of Technology, she was advised to prepare a memo articulating her concerns. This memo was rejected by her supervisor. A revised version was sent two weeks later to the members of CJCC, and for this action she was dismissed from her job.

The resolution of this story is not a triumph of right over wrong. Edgerton asked the IEEE Committee on Social Implications of Technology to investigate the case. A series of letters were exchanged between the committee and the City of New York. Edgerton's claim was not that the system would not work, but simply that the possibility should be carefully studied. The city's rejoinder was that the matter was under study, while according to Edgerton no qualified person had been employed by the police department. No hearing was held to air her charges, as the city had not arranged for any appeal process. Thus, when a professional employee brought up a problem that in her opinion posed a danger to the adequate operation of a system, she was dismissed without recourse. In April 1979, at the IEEE national conference, she was presented with an award for outstanding service in the public interest, which consisted of a certificate and $750. She used the money to open up a small computer service bureau.

This case brings into focus many of the issues associated with ethical and professional decision making. What guidelines are there for a computer professional confronted with an ethical problem? What should be the code of ethics and how should it be applied? At what point should an individual "blow the whistle?" The result of bringing an undesirable situation to public attention may not be satisfactory. If a person does decide to blow the whistle, what support can he or she expect to receive from professional societies, the courts, or the public at large? For the most part professional societies can help with moral, financial, and legal support, but only to a limited degree. Frequently the courts must decide the issue, in the context of an employee seeking damages for wrongful dismissal.

Codes of Ethics

An ACM member shall express his professional opinion to his employees or clients regarding any adverse consequences to the public which might result from work proposed to him.[14]

Probably the best known and oldest code governing professional behavior is the Hippocratic oath, attributed to the Greek physician Hippocrates (460?–370? B.C.) For the computing profession, scarcely 30 years old, a code of ethics may be somewhat premature, as relevant issues are still emerging. Nevertheless, there exist many concerns specifically related to computers—such as the responsibility for gathering, verifying, storing, protecting, and distributing information. Some applications of computers are so controversial that an ethics code seems to have intrinsic merit. Motivated by engineering concerns, Stephen Unger has suggested a number of features of such a code, as follows:[15]

A recognition of the responsibilities of individuals.

An attempt to create a general recognition and acceptance of ethical behavior.

The establishment of readily accessible guidelines.

Justification for actions taken in opposition to directives by superiors.

Useful in lawsuits that may follow certain actions.

A statement to the public at large that the profession is concerned about the actions of its members.

A major problem in enacting codes is how to restrict them to matters of professional concern without being influenced by political, economic, or religious opinions. For example, the U.S. Army Corps of Engineers used computer models to formulate economic policy with respect to the construction of large dam projects. The Department of Defense runs computer war simulations as a fundamental part of its planning requirements. Computer Professionals for Social Responsibilty (see Chapter 7) has focused on the role of computers and automated decision making in determining a response to stategic missiles. They act to make their colleagues aware of how their research might be used, to serve as a pressure group to influence public opinion, and to lobby the government. One's response to working on these projects certainly depends on one's political and economic beliefs. Thus, drafting a code of ethics requires extreme care, treading a line between professional responsibility and personal belief.

Codes of ethics have been adopted by the following organizations that represent computer professionals:

Association for Computing Machinery (ACM). The oldest association for computer professionals, with considerable representation among academics, it has a Code of Professional Conduct.

The Institute for Electrical and Electronic Engineers (IEEE). Although it is primarily an organization for engineers, the proportion of membership involved with computers has increased dramatically in recent years. The IEEE Board of Directors approved the Code of Ethics in 1979.

The Canadian Information Processing Society (CIPS). This organization adopted a brief Code of Ethics in 1975 and prepared a more comprehensive version in 1984.

Data Processing Management Association (DPMA). The DPMA has adopted a Code of Ethics and Standard of Conduct for Information Processing Professionals.

The ACM's Code of Professional Conduct (see Appendix A) is clearly an attempt to provide wide-ranging and specific guidelines.

Critics question the effectiveness of ethics codes and even the reasons for adopting them. Among the most prominent is Samuel Florman, engineer and author of the best-selling *Blaming Technology*.[16] His opinion is expressed forcefully as follows:

Engineers must be honorable and competent. Agreed. But engineering ethics cannot solve technical problems or resolve political conflicts. It cannot determine which tradeoffs should be made between safety or economy or between growth and envi-

ronmental protection. It cannot provide consistent guidelines for individuals who are troubled by conflicting loyalties. In sum, engineering ethics cannot cover up differences of opinion that are deep and heartfelt. . . . Engineers owe honesty and competence to society. The rest of engineering ethics is a matter of taste—which is to say, political choice.[17]

The debate on the social responsibility of engineers and computer professionals will not be settled in the near future. In the context of the enormous impact that computers are having, and will continue to have on society, the adoption of a code of ethics should be a welcome event. A code of ethics will not induce ethical behavior, but where there is doubt in the mind of a programmer the existence of such a code may provide needed support. Furthermore, if action is taken on the basis of the ethics code, a professional society can play a major role in support of the responsible individual. It can provide an open forum for investigating the situation, use its good offices to mediate, and provide legal support if necessary. The lonely individual in opposition to an organization requires—in fact demands—a network of support if responsible behavior is to be encouraged.

TECHNOLOGICAL CHANGE: A SERIOUS CHALLENGE

Views of technology as a major force in society range from the vision of a great benefactor to alarm at an independent agent sweeping civilization along in its wake. The wide array of applications of computers—perhaps the most pervasive and influential form of contemporary technology—bring with them a variety of actual and potential problems. Among these are the potential assault on privacy, the impact on work and jobs, the centralization of authority, the alienation of individuals, and the loss of control.

An uncritical tone characterizes most reporting on computing innovations. Certainly, computers and associated microelectronics and communications hardware are marvelous products of the ingenuity and genius of people. However, the important issue is how they are and will be used, and how society will be shaped. Those who are involved in teaching and research about computers have a special responsibility to both consider the implications of their work and to convey their concerns to the public at large.

Phobia and Obsession

One of the responses to technological change is fear and avoidance. A new computer system is introduced into the office. The benefits of word processing are demonstrated to the secretaries, classes are held, and the groundwork is laid for a smooth transition. Nevertheless, some of the office staff, unable to face the prospect of a strange and different environment, quit their jobs. A chief executive officer decides that a terminal on the desk of every executive and a personal computer in each of their homes will improve the efficiency of the company. A few of the executives begin to exhibit nervousness around the terminals and one or two may even take sick leave. Sanford Weinberg of St. Joseph's College has coined the term cyberphobia, to describe the anxiety produced in some people when interacting with computers. Another term is computerphobia.[18]

It is not only the initial confrontation that has led to problems. The computer, by virtue of its incredible versatility, is an overwhelming challenge to employees, who become insecure about their long-term employability. This uneasiness may persist and result in situations in which growing discomfort permeates the activities of some employees. Whether careful planning prior to the introduction of computer systems can alleviate these problems is open to question. Certainly an employer who ignores these potential difficulties may suffer morale problems along with a loss in efficiency.

The other side of the fear seems to be infatuation or even addiction. Just as there are born musicians and athletes, there are born computer programmers. Such people tend to establish a relationship with the computer that is so all-consuming, it may lead to self-imposed alienation from friends and fellow workers. The term computer widow has entered the common lexicon to describe the woman whose husband has chosen to spend most of his spare time in front of a video terminal. This effect is an unanticipated by-product of home computers, although it should be noted that sales have been largely directed towards men. The extreme fascination with computers presumably fills a need not otherwise satisfied. It is not a major problem yet, but an increasing number of women are approaching psychologists with reports of husbands who, upon arriving home, retreat immediately to the computer until the early hours of the morning. The computer seems to be filling a role previously held by the television, the workshop, the bar, or the poker game.

Another group of people exhibiting extreme devotion to the computer are the hackers or, as Joseph Weizenbaum has called them, compulsive programmers:

> . . .*bright young men of dishevelled appearance, often with sunken, glowing eyes, can be seen sitting at computer consoles, their arms tensed waiting to fire their fingers, already poised to strike, at the buttons and keys on which their attention seems to be riveted as a gambler's on the rolling dice.*[19]

What would such people have done had the computer not been invented? In 1980, *Psychology Today* published a purported transcript of an exchange of computer messages by a few Stanford students. One student code-named G. Gandalf initiated the electronic discussion by broadcasting a message on hacking, in which he describes his narrow escape from a very restricted life style.

> . . .*in creating a subculture and isolating it, we are destroying the chances that computers might be used wisely as an integral part of our society. We are precluding the human values so necessary for the wise application of this technological achievement.*[20]

In a cry full of pathos, Gandalf bemoans the loss of interest in other academic studies, the abdication of normal living patterns, the restriction of social patterns to include only other hackers, and finally, an adjustment in the hacker's personality to accommodate to his life style. The other messages are varied, including supporting as well as opposing opinions. A. Anonymous argued that it requires considerable time and effort to become proficient at programming and compared his devotion to that of a musician. He pointed out that, in developing his talent, a musician must sacrifice human relationships for awhile, but is not criticized for this. This "conversation" about alienation has itself taken place via the computer.

The Social Costs of Technology

We live in an age of serious contradictions. Technological development is accelerating, and without doubt the benefits to society have been massive and persuasive. To list some of them is to stand in awe of human ingenuity: electrical power, airplanes, space exploration, television, communication networks, microelectronics, genetic engineering, and computers. Surely the improvements in health, food supply, longevity, living standards, safety, working conditions, and so forth are real and largely attributable to discoveries in science and technology. This fact applies to the industrialized countries of the world. Many other countries, to a greater or lesser degree, are facing such basic issues of survival that the relevance of technology as a major force has not yet been established.

Most attempts to describe and analyze the impact of technology on society inevitably give a list of good effects, a shorter list of bad effects, and an assurance that we can ultimately control how the actual technology will be used. Perhaps the choice is ours, but in certain areas control seems elusive at best. Nuclear power is an example, in its domestic and international contexts. Compared to the potential holocaust of nuclear war or serious power-plants accidents, all other issues fade into insignificance. The use of the technology of nuclear weapons could result in the absolute desolation of our planet. Control rests on a delicate balance of mutual threats and assured destruction.

Having created nuclear and thermonuclear weapons, humanity survives under a shadow that affects every person's life. Here is an example of a technology that seems to control us. A study of the history of the atomic bomb reveals that many of the scientists involved in its original development assumed they would subsequently be consulted about its uses. Such was not the case. Decision making was assumed by the executive branch of the government and the bomb became an instrument of national policy. It is a fact that technological innovators rarely continue to exercise authority over their invention or discovery after it leaves the laboratory. If technology can be controlled for the benefit of society, we must ask: controlled how and by whom?

Even the peaceful uses of nuclear energy have not met the initial optimistic expectations of very low-cost safe power. Plant costs have escalated, and the environmental protection movement has rallied public support to limit the growth of the nuclear industry. Anxiety about the safety of nuclear reactors for power generation has been translated, in North America, into a marked reduction of plant construction. The impact of aroused public opinion has been effective in this area and demonstrates the possibility of an aware populace exercising its political power. Other concerns currently reaching public awareness are acid rain, genetic engineering, and antibiotic supplements for animals. In each of these cases,

growing political activity may result in the enactment of controls to protect health and safety.

Meeting the Challenge

It is a formidable undertaking to evaluate the effect of technological change on social, political, and economic institutions. A study of the past is informative and necessary, but predictions of the future have not been particularly accurate, notwithstanding the emergence of a forecasting industry and such powerful tools as large computers and refined simulation techniques.

In a recent book on computers and culture, J. David Bolter makes the following forceful statement:

> Until recently, however, our technical skills were so feeble in comparison with the natural forces of climate and chemistry that we could not seriously affect our environment for good or ill, except over the millenia. High technology promises to give us a new power over nature, both our own nature and that of our planet, so that the very future of civilization depends upon our intelligent use of high technology.[21]

He further notes that the crucial element in high technology is the computer. Clearly, the attempt to locate the computer in the history of technology, to survey its applications, to probe associated benefits and problems, and to assess the future impact is a worthwhile and in fact necessary exercise.

As with most technological innovations, the choice of when and how to proceed is not usually left up to the individual members of society. Governments and companies, both large and small, multinational and local, have the power and resources to make the important decisions. As ordinary citizens, we live in a world that for the most part is not of our making. Nevertheless, an informed and sufficiently aroused public can make a difference. In discussing the nature of a liberal democracy, the Canadian political scientist C. B. MacPherson analyzed the opinions of John Dewey as follows:

> He had few illusions about the actual democratic system, or about the democratic quality of a society dominated by motives of individual and corporate gain. The root difficulty lay not in any defects in the machinery of government but in the fact that the democratic public was "still largely inchoate and unorganized," and unable to see what forces of economic and technological organization it was up against. There was no tinkering with the political machinery: the prior problem was "that of discovering the means by which a scattered, mobile, and manifold public may so recognize itself as to define and express its interests." The public's present incompetence to do this was traced to its failure to understand the technological and scientific forces which had made it so helpless.[22]

SUMMARY

Japan has emerged as the main challenger to U.S. world leadership in computer and communications technology. The Japan success story is amazing: world leadership in television, video cassette recorders, robots, and automobiles. In 1981, Japan launched its Fifth Generation Project in an attempt to start a new age of intelligent computers. The United States and Europe responded with similar projects of their own. In the area of supercomputers—the largest and fastest of all computers—current U.S. leadership is also being challenged by Japan.

It is very fashionable to be concerned with computer literacy, although this term is not well defined. Familiarity with computers has been equated with language literacy, a connection criticized by many.

How computers will affect the work of women both directly and indirectly is an important issue. Women are increasing their representation in the data processing industry, but still encounter resistance in their career paths.

What responsibility do computer professionals have to their clients and to their work? The issues of ethics and professionalism are of increased importance as the impact of computers on society becomes more evident. A number of professional organizations have drawn up codes of ethics. How well these serve the general public is debatable, but similar codes have been proposed for data processing professionals.

Technological change is not without its price—for example, the problems associated with pesticides, consumption of antibiotics by cattle, genetic engineering, and nuclear power plants. It should not be surprising, therefore, that the increasing use of computers is accompanied by its own set of problems and benefits.

NOTES

1. Douglas Ramsey et al., "Japan's High-Tech Challenge" (special report), *Newsweek,* August 9, 1982, pp. 50–51.

2. "Technology Development Forecast up to 2010 in Japan." *Science & Technology in Japan,* April/June 1983, p. 24.

3. Edward A. Feigenbaum and Pamela McGorduck, *The Fifth Generation* (Reading, Mass.: Addison-Wesley, 1983), p. 3.

4. Ibid.

5. Daniel McCracken, as quoted in Joseph A. Menosky, "Computer Worship," *Science 84,* May 1984, p. 40.

6. Ronald E. Anderson and Daniel L. Klassen, "A Conceptual Framework for Developing Computing Literacy Instruction," Minnesota Educational Computing Consortium (St. Paul, November 5, 1980), p. 7.

7. Bill N.Lacy, "The Pencil Revolution," *Newsweek,* March 19, 1984, p. 17.

8. As quoted in Menosky, "Computer Worship," p. 46.

9. Stephen L.Chorover, "Cautions on Computers in Educaiton," *Byte,* June 1984, p. 225.

10. Shirley Macom (Head of the Office of Opportunities in Science of The American Association for the Advancement of Science), as quoted in Carol Truxal, "The Woman Engineer," *IEEE Spectrum,* April 1983, p. 58.

11. As quoted in Truxal, "The Woman Engineer,"p. 62.

12. "A Friendly Frontier for Female Pioneers," *Fortune,* June 25, 1984, pp. 78–85.

13. Stephen H. Unger, *Controlling Technology: Ethics and the Responsible Engineer* (New York: Holt, Rinehart & Winston, 1982), p. 1.

14. Disciplinary Rule DR 5.21 of the Association for Computing Machinery Code of Professional Conduct, *Communications of the ACM,* March 1982, p. 183.

15. Unger, *Controlling Technology,* pp. 32–55.

16. Samuel C. Florman, *Blaming Technology* (New York: St. Martin's, 1981).

17. Samuel C. Florman, "A Skeptic Views Ethics in Engineering," *IEEE Spectrum,* August 1982, p. 57.

18. Rachael Wrege, "High (Tech) Anxiety," *Popular Computing,* January 1982, p. 46.

19. Joseph Weizenbaum, *Computer Power and Human Reason* (San Francisco: Freeman, 1976), p. 116.

20. "The Hacker Papers," *Psychology Today,* August 1980, p. 63.

21. J. David Bolter, *Turing's Man, Western Culture in the Computer Age* (Chapel Hill: University of North Carolina Press, 1984), pp. 3–4.

22. C. B. MacPherson, *The Life and Times of Liberal Democracy,* (Oxford: Oxford University Press, 1980), p. 73.

ADDITIONAL READINGS

Introduction

Turkle, Sherry. *The Second Self: Computers and the Human Spirit.* New York: Simon and Schuster, 1984.

Japan and High Technology

Alexander, Tom. "Reinventing the Computer." *Fortune,* March 5, 1984, pp. 86–90, 94, 98.

Christopher, Robert C. *The Japanese Mind.* New York: Simon & Schuster/Linden Press, 1983.

Davis, Dwight. "Supercomputers: A Strategic Imperative." *High Technology,* May 1984, pp. 44–53.

Fuchi, Kazuhiro. "The Direction the FGCS Project Will Take." *New Generation Computing,* vol. 1, no. 1, 1983, pp. 3–9.

Gallagher, Robert T. "Europe's Esprit Finally Sets Sail." *Electronics Week,* February 4, 1985, pp. 17–18.

"Japan, A Nation in Search of Itself." *TIME,* August 1, 1983 (special issue).

Japan's Strategy for the 80's. *Business Week,* December 14, 1981, pp. 39–120. (special issue).

"Japan's Technology Agenda." *High Technology,* August 1985, (special issue), pp. 21–67.

Johnson, Jan. "America Answers Back." *Datamation,* May 15, 1984, pp. 40, 43, 46, 51, 54, 57.

Johnson, Jan. "Cray and CDC Meet the Japanese." *Datamation,* April 1, 1984, pp. 32–34, 38, 42.

Manuel, Tom. "Cautiously Optimistic Tone Set For 5th Generation." *Electronics Week,* December 3, 1984, pp. 57–63.

Marbach, William D., et al. "The Race to Build a Supercomputer." *Newsweek,* July 4, 1983, pp. 58–64.

Ouchi, William G. *Theory Z.* Reading, Mass.: Addison-Wesley, 1981.

Peltu, Malcolm. "U.K. Eyes 5th Generation." *Datamation,* July, 1983, pp. 67–68, 72.

"Supercomputers Are Breaking Out of a Once-Tiny Market" *Business Week,* November 19, 1984, pp. 164D, 164H.

"A Survey of Japanese Technology." *The Economist,* June 9, 1982.

"Tomorrow's Computers." *EEE Spectrum,* November 1983 (special issue).

Uttal, Bro. "Japan Inc.'s Entry in Home Computers." *Fortune,* January 21, 1985, pp. 72–73.

Weizenbaum, Joseph. "The Computer in Your Future." *The New York Review of Books,* October 27, 1983, p. 58ff.

Wilson, Kenneth G. "Science, Industry, and the New Japanese Challenge." *Proceedings of the Institute of Electrical and Electronics Engineers,* January 1984, pp. 6–18.

Yasaki, Edward K. "Tokyo Looks to the '90s." *Datamation,* January 1982, pp. 110, 112–115.

Computer Literacy

McCracken, Daniel D. "A Skeptical View of Computer Literacy. In *Fifteenth SIGCSE Technical Symposium on Computer Service Education,* Feb. 16–17, 1984. Philadelphia: *Association for Computing Machinery.*

Menosky, Joseph A. "Computer Workshop." *Science 84,* May 1984, pp. 40–46.

Seidal, Robert J., Ronald E. Anderson, and Beverly Hunter, eds. *Computer Literacy: Issues and Directions for 1985.* New York: Academic, 1982.

Women and Computing

Kesler, Sara, Lee Sproull, and Jacquelynne S. Eccles. "Second-Class Citizens?" *Psychology Today,* March 1983, pp. 40–43, 46–48.

Kolata, Gina. "Equal Time For Women." *Discover,* January 1984, pp. 24–27.

Simons, G. L. *Women in Computing.* Manchester, England: NCC Publications, 1981.

Turkle, Sherry. "The Intimate Machine." *Science 84,* April 1984, pp. 40–46.

Ethics and Professionalism

Mulvey, John M. "Computer Modeling for State Use: Implications for Professional Responsibility." *IEEE Technology and Society Magazine,* June 1983, pp. 3–8, 29.

Myers, Edith. "Because It Was New York." *Datamation,* September 1979, pp. 96, 98, 101.

Parker, Donn B. *Ethical Conflicts in Computer Science and Technology.* New York: American Federation of Information Processing Societies Press, 1981.

Weiss, Eric A., ed. "Self-Assessment Procedure IX." *Communications of the Association for Computing Machinery* March 1982, pp. 181–195.

APPENDIX A

ACM Code of Professional Conduct[1]

PREAMBLE

Recognition of professional status by the public depends not only on skill and dedication but also on adherence to a recognized code of Professional Conduct. The following Code sets forth the general principles (Canons), professional ideals (Ethical Considerations), and mandatory rules (Disciplinary Rules) applicable to each ACM member.

The verbs ''shall'' (imperative) and ''should'' (encouragement) are used purposefully in the Code. The Canons and Ethical Considerations are not, however, binding rules. Each Disciplinary Rule is binding on each individual Member of ACM. Failure to observe the Disciplinary Rules subjects the Member to admonition, suspension, or expulsion from the Association as provided for by the Procedures for the Enforcement of the ACM Code of Professional Conduct, which are specified in the ACM Policy and Procedures Guidelines. The term ''member(s)'' is used in this Code. The Disciplinary Rules of the Code apply, however, only to the classes of membership specified in ARTICLE 3, Section 4, of the Constitution of the ACM.[2]

CANON 1

An ACM member shall act at all times with integrity.

Ethical Considerations

EC1.1. An ACM member shall properly qualify himself when expressing an opinion outside his areas of competence. A member is encouraged to express his opinion on subjects within his area of competence.

---

[1]Reprinted by permission of the Association of Computing Machinery. Part II of ''Self-Assessment Procedure IX'' edited by Eric A. Weiss, March 1982. Copyright © 1982 by the Association of Computing Machinery; all rights reserved.

[2]Editor's Note: The Constitution of the ACM was last published in Communications, July 1980, pp. 420–426. Although the section referenced doesn't specify classes of membership, the intent of the Code is that the rules apply only to individual members and not to corporate members.

EC1.2. An ACM member shall preface any partisan statements about information processing by indicating clearly on whose behalf they are made.

EC1.3. An ACM member shall act faithfully on behalf of his employers or clients.

Disciplinary Rules

DR1.1.1. An ACM member shall not intentionally misrepresent his qualifications or credentials to present or prospective employers or clients.

DR1.1.2. An ACM member shall not make deliberately false or deceptive statements as to the present or expected state of affairs in any aspect of the capability, delivery, or use of information processing systems.

DR1.2.1. An ACM member shall not intentionally conceal or misrepresent on whose behalf any partisan statements are made.

DR1.3.1. An ACM member acting or employed as a consultant shall, prior to accepting information from a prospective client, inform the client of all factors of which the member is aware which may affect the proper performance of the task.

DR1.3.2. An ACM member shall disclose any interest of which he is aware which does or may conflict with his duty to a present or prospective employer or client.

DR1.3.3. An ACM member shall not use any confidential information from any employer or client, past or present, without prior permission.

CANON 2

An ACM member should strive to increase his competence and the prestige of the profession.

Ethical Considerations

EC2.1. An ACM member is encouraged to extend public knowledge, understanding, and appreciation of information processing, and to oppose any false or deceptive statements relating to information processing of which he is aware.

EC2.2. An ACM member shall not use his professional credentials to misrepresent his competence.

EC2.3. An ACM member shall undertake only those professional assignments and commitments for which he is qualified.

EC2.4. An ACM member shall strive to design and develop systems that adequately perform the intended functions and that satisfy his employer's or client's operational needs.

EC2.5. An ACM member should maintain and increase his competence through a program of continuing education encompassing the techniques, technical standards, and practices in his fields of professional activity.

EC2.6. An ACM member should provide opportunity and encouragement for professional development and advancement of both professionals and those aspiring to become professionals.

Disciplinary Rules

DR2.2.1. An ACM member shall not use his professional credentials to misrepresent his competence.

DR2.3.1. An ACM member shall not undertake professional assignments without adequate preparation in the circumstances.

DR2.3.2. An ACM member shall not undertake professional assignments for which he knows or should know he is not competent or cannot become adequately competent without acquiring the assistance of a professional who is competent to perform the assignment.

DR2.4.1. An ACM member shall not represent that a product of his work will perform its function adequately and will meet the receiver's operational needs when he knows or should know that the product is deficient.

CANON 3

An ACM member shall accept responsibility for his work.

Ethical Considerations

EC3.1. An ACM member shall accept only those assignments for which there is reasonable expectancy of meeting requirements or specifications, and shall perform his assignments in a professional manner.

Disciplinary Rules

DR3.1.1. An ACM member shall not neglect any professional assignment which has been accepted.

DR3.1.2. An ACM member shall keep his employer or client properly informed on the progress of his assignments.

DR3.1.3. An ACM member shall not attempt to exonerate himself from, or to limit his liability to clients for his personal malpractice.

DR3.1.4. An ACM member shall indicate to his employer or client the consequences to be expected if his professional judgement is overruled.

CANON 4

An ACM member shall act with professional responsibility.

Ethical Considerations

EC4.1. An ACM member shall not use his membership in ACM improperly for professional advantage or to misrepresent the authority of his statements.

EC4.2. An ACM member shall conduct professional activities on a high plane.

EC4.3. An ACM member is encouraged to uphold and improve the professional standards of the Association through participation in their formulation, establishment, and enforcement.

Disciplinary Rules

DR4.1.1. An ACM member shall not speak on behalf of the Association or any of its subgroups without prior authority.

DR4.1.2. An ACM member shall not knowingly misrepresent the policies and views of the Association or any of its subgroups.

DR4.1.3. An ACM member shall preface partisan statements about information processing by indicating clearly on whose behalf they are made.

DR4.2.1. An ACM member shall not maliciously injure the professional reputation of any other person.

DR4.2.2. An ACM member shall not use the services of or his membership in the Association to gain unfair advantage.

DR4.2.3. An ACM member shall take care that credit for work is given to whom credit is properly due.

CANON 5

An ACM member should use his special knowledge and skills for the advancement of human welfare.

Ethical Considerations

EC5.1. An ACM member should consider the health, privacy, and general welfare of the public in the performance of his work.

EC5.2. An ACM member, whenever dealing with data concerning individuals, shall always consider the principle of the individual's privacy and seek the following:

- To minimize the data collected.
- To limit authorized access to the data.
- To provide proper security for the data.
- To determine the required retention period of the data.
- To ensure proper disposal of the data.

Disciplinary Rules

DR5.2.1. An ACM member shall express his professional opinion to his employers or clients regarding any adverse consequences to the public which might result from work proposed to him.

APPENDIX B
Magazines, Journals, and Associations

The number of popular magazines devoted to computers is large and growing. Most of these appeal to users of specific home computers such as the IBM PC, the Apple IIc or Macintosh, and the Commodore 64. This list includes only magazines of more general interest.

POPULAR MAGAZINES
Computer

Byte	For computer professionals and home users. Reviews of new products and occasional articles on social issues.
Computers & Electronics	The leading computer magazine in sales. For computer professionals and business users.
Computerworld	Tabloid format. For business users. Reviews of major trends, government policies, and occasionally social issues.
Datamation	Sold primarily by subscription. For business professionals. Wide coverage of the industry. Informed articles by data processing professionals and academics. Renowned for its annual list of the top 100 data processing companies.
Personal Computing	Very large circulation, for business users. Regular reviews of new equipment and software.

Technology

Discover	A Time-Life publication with a wide coverage of scientific and technological developments, including a section on computers.
Electronics Week	Excellent survey of developments in electronics with both national and international coverage. Somewhat more technical than a typical newsstand magazine. Regular analyses of production, sales, and applications of electronic components.
High Technology	Probably the best popular magazine for detailed descriptions of new technologies, especially computer-related ones. Excellent graphics, references, and associated business opportunities.
New Scientist	A British publication with wide coverage of scientific and technological innovations. Somewhat oriented to British issues.
Science 85	Published by the American Association for the Advancement of Science (AAAS). In depth studies of scientific issues. Excellent regular columnists.
Scientific American	The most prestigious popular science magazine in the United States. The articles are written by prominent scientists, with excellent graphics. Computers and related technology are treated infrequently but very well.
Technology Review	Published by the Massachusetts Institute of Technology. Well-written and interesting articles on a variety of issues. High level of social concern.

Education

Psychology Today	Excellent treatment of computers in education and AI, and the psychological overtones of computer use.

Financial and Business

Business Week	Regular, extensive coverage of technological developments and associated business, labor,

and economic issues. Frequent in-depth studies of videotex, electronic funds transfer systems, and the computer industry, especially IBM.

Fortune

Well known for the FORTUNE 500 list of leading U.S. companies. Excellent coverage of technology. Good record of spotting trends and anticipating problems.

General

Time, Newsweek

Regular, limited coverage of developments in computers.

The New York Times

Excellent treatment of scientific issues in the Tuesday "Science Times" section. Extensive coverage of business and social problems, especially privacy and labor issues.

Technical Journals

Computer

A publication of the Institute of Electrical and Electronics Engineers. Covers technical issues in papers written by academics. Special issues on such topics as security and CAD/CAM.

Communications of the ACM

A publication of the Association of Computing Machinery. Includes state-of-the-art articles by leading figures in computer science. In depth analysis of many social issues. Overall, a high proportion of theoretical papers.

Science

A publication of the American Association for the Advancement of Science. Most of the articles deal with advanced research topics in biology, chemistry, physics, and so forth. Periodic, serious coverage of technological advances and their social impact.

IEEE Spectrum

Important technical journal that treats important topics at a nonspecialist level. Special issues on social impact of technology, the Fifth Generation, and education. Highly recommended.

Harvard Business Review	Coverage of important issues associated with computers in business. Regular treatment of management information systems, impact on labor, and Japanese management practices.

ASSOCIATIONS AND SOCIETIES

ACM Special Interest Group on Computers and Society (SIGCAS)

SIGCAS publishes a quarterly newsletter that deals with many issues such as privacy, copyright laws, crime, work, and so forth. It is edited by Richard S. Rosenberg, Department of Mathematics, Statistics, and Computing Science, Dalhousie University, Halifax, Nova Scotia, Canada B3J 3J5.

IEEE Society on Social Implications of Technology (SSIT)

SSIT publishes a magazine with papers on a wide range of technological issues. It also sponsors conferences and workshops. For more information contact Professor S. H. Unger, Department of Computer Science, Columbia University, New York, NY 10027.

Computer Professionals for Social Responsibility (CPSR)

This organization has chapters in Berkeley, Los Angeles, Palo Alto, San Jose, Santa Cruz, Boston, New York, Washington, Madison, and Seattle. It is concerned with more radical issues than the above two organizations. Its newsletter has carried articles on military applications of computers, American computer professionals helping in Nicaragua, and the role of computers in nuclear weapons planning. The CPSR newsletter is published quarterly by Computer Professionals for Social Responsibility, Mark Hall and Daniel Ingalls, eds., P.O. Box 717, Palo Alto, CA 94301.

There are numerous organizations for computer professionals in such areas as the following:

Data Processing	Data Processing Management Association 505 Busse Highway Park Ridge, ILL. 60068
	Canadian Information Processing Society (L'Association Canadienne de l'Informatique) 243 College Street, 5th floor Toronto, Ontario, Canada M5T 2Y1
Information science	The American Society for Information Science 1010 Sixteenth Street, N.W. Second Floor Washington, D.C. 20036

Academic issues	The Association for Computing Machinery 1133 Avenue of the Americas New York, N.Y. 10036
	The Institute of Electrical and Electronics Engineers Computer Society 1109 Spring Street Suite 202 Silver Springs, Md. 20910
Artificial intelligence	The American Association for Artificial Intelligence 445 Burgess Drive Menlo Park, Calif. 94025
	The ACM Special Interest Group on Artificial Intelligence (See ACM address).
Information retrieval	The ACM Special Interest Group on Information Retrieval (See ACM address).

INDEX